KJE
6964
.M67
1993

Mosteshar, Said.

European Community
  telecommunications
  regulation.

$125.00

DATE DUE

European Community
Telecommunications Regulation

Time present and time past
Are both perhaps present in time future
And time future contained in time past.

T.S. Eliot

To Mother, Mahmonir Mosteshar

European Business Law & Practice Series

European Community Telecommunications Regulation

Sa'id Mosteshar

BSc, MSc (Econ.), DPhil, FCA, Attorney (Cal.), Barrister

Graham & Trotman / Martinus Nijhoff
Members of the Kluwer Academic Publishers Group
LONDON/DORDRECHT/BOSTON

Graham & Trotman Limited
Sterling House
66 Wilton Road
London SW1V 1DE
UK

Kluwer Academic Publishers Group
101 Philip Drive
Assinippi Park
Norwell, MA 02061
USA

British Library Cataloguing in Publication Data
Mosteshar, S. Alexander
    European Community Telecommunications
    Regulation. – (European Business Law &
    Practice Series)
    I. Title   II. Series
    341.7577

    ISBN: 1-85333-756-0
    Series ISBN: 1 85333 714 5

Library of Congress Cataloging-in-Publication Data
Mosteshar, Said..
    European Community telecommunications regulation / Sa'id
Mosteshar.
        p.   cm. – (European business law & practice series)
    Includes index.
    ISBN 1-85333-756-0
    1. Telecommunication – Law and legislation – European Economic
Community countries. I. Title.   II. Series: European law library.
European business law & practice series.
KJE6964.M67   1993
343.409'94–dc20
[344.03994]   93-10460
                                                     CIP

Computer typeset in 10/11 Garamond by Acorn Bookwork Ltd, Salisbury, Wiltshire
Printed and bound in Great Britain by Hartnolls Ltd, Bodmin, Cornwall

Contents

Preface

The aim of this book is to provide to those engaged in the conduct of telecommunications in the European Community an understanding of Community regulation affecting the sector. Although the various regulatory instruments collected here are published by the Commission, there has not until now been a collected set of relevant documents to assist industry participants and practitioners in the field. By bringing together the source material and examining the relationship between them, the book provides a coherent view of European Community telecommunications policy.

The book is divided into two main parts. The latter part comprises the documents, arranged in chronological order. The first part is a narrative consideration of the source material, and is divided into 12 chapters. Chapter 1 sets out the historical background to the development of the Community policy in telecommunications and the influences in the process of liberalization of telecommunications markets. The Guidelines on the application of competiton rules to telecommunications activities is also examined. Chapter 2 covers the issues and documents relating to competition in the terminal equipment market. Chapter 3 deals with the procurement requirements as they apply to telecommunications. The important issue of standards and the role and workings of the European Standards Institute are covered in Chapters 4 and 5. Competition in telecommunication services is one of the central, as well as the most controversial, areas for the attention of the Commission. These are treated in Chapter 6. Chapter 7 is on competition in telecommunications infrastructure, including Open Network Provision requirements and mutual recognition of licences. Chapter 8 covers matters relating to tariffs. Spectrum management is the subject of Chapter 9. Issues of privacy and data protection are dealt with in Chapter 10. Chapter 11 is on the various Commission initiatives aimed at promoting telecommunications in the Community. Chapter 12 covers the 1992 Review of telecommunications and the future direction of telecommunication policy within the Community.

The book covers the position as at 1 October 1992, although some later material has been included. It was expected to include an Appendix indicating the extent to which Member States have implemented the measures covered in this book. However, despite the tenacity of my many colleagues who have attempted to collate such information, it is not available in relation to many Member States. It is hoped that such a table can be included in a subsequent edition.

The idea for this book was first conceived in 1990. Since that time I have received advice, help and encouragement from many people: too numerous to mention them all by name. I would, however, like to recognise particularly the valuable contributions of Mr. Frede Ask, Mr. Vassili Cassapoglou, Mr. Paul Lippens de Cerf and Dr. Klaus-Jürgen Kraatz. Thanks are also due to the Bodleian Law Library and its staff for their assistance with the material.

I very much appreciate the patience and hard work of Miss Janet Robinson in typing the manuscript, of Miss Jean Kay in efficiently shielding me from distractions, and the ingenuity and good humour of Mr. Eliot, Rudy and Chandler for providing timely diversions. Miss Candy Kuhl's enthusiasm, encouragement and helpful hints have been invaluable in writing the book. I am much in her debt.

Finally, I would acknowledge with gratitude the support and patience of my Publishers and Mr. Fergal Martin during the preparation of the manuscript, and the speed with which they have brought the book to print.

Underwood   S M-G

CHAPTER 1
Historical Background

GENERAL COMPETITION LAW AND BASES OF EXCLUSION OF TELECOMMUNICATIONS FROM ITS APPLICATION

It is accepted today that with very few exceptions the rigour of the competition rules of the European Community apply to the telecommunications sector. This is the case in relation both to telecommunications equipment and to services. At times it is hard to remember that only a decade ago any idea of competition in the telecommunications market was considered revolutionary.

Viewed from a European perspective, three main reasons may be identified for the creation and preservation of monopolies in telecommunications networks and services. First, telecommunications were regarded as an instrument of social policy with an influence on economic activity. Today telecommunications are seen primarily as a significant economic activity with some impact on social policy. Second, the need to provide universal service was regarded as a primary objective, the achievement of which required the maximum possible economies of scale and of scope. Such economies were considered to be jeopardised by the introduction of competition. Neither the market nor the technologies for the provision of value-added services were available on any significant scale. This made it more difficult to introduce competition, even in services other than the provision of voice telephony or telex services. Third, although these arguments are still used to exclude from the application of the competition rules, both the monopoly provision of the universal network and voice telephony service,[1] the developments in technology and demand for data and value-added services, have created the incentive and the scope for extensive application of the competition rules to the telecommunications sector.

The opening of the telecommunications market to competition did not only entail the abolition of exclusive rights of provision. The barriers to competition, both domestic and international, were much more complex. In addition to their operational activities, the

---

[1] See Services Directive, 90/388/EEC, recital 18.

TOs[2] were also entrusted with administrative and quasi-regulatory functions. Both because of their technical expertise in the field and the fact that any equipment would either have to be connected to their networks or form a part of their network, they were the natural body to define standards and certify terminal equipment for conformity. They were also entrusted with the management of the frequency spectrum and licensing telecommunications systems to the extent that any were permitted to be run by other entities. Such systems were normally confined to those run by entities for their own use.

Although the International Telecommunications Union[3] regulates certain aspects of international telecommunications and provides for interface between national systems, it does not require any uniformity of national systems. The diversity of technology and standards of the networks operated by Member States reinforced the barriers to competition.

The TOs also relied on ITU Regulations and Recommendations to justify certain anti-competitive measures.[4] In particular, the CCITT[5] Recommendations on international call charges[6] resulted in disproportionately high tariffs for international calls. This, in turn, affected the tariffs for domestic services which were in some instances subsidised from profits on international calls.

Therefore, another element which needed to be considered by the Commission on the introduction of competition was the need to rebalance tariffs so as to avoid a distortion of the market.

FACTORS INFLUENCING THE COMMISSION'S APPROACH TO TELECOMMUNICATIONS

Telecommunications has from the outset been a business activity. The objects and manner of its conduct have changed over the years. But it is important not to lose sight of the fact that even in countries where it continues to be a government monopoly, factors affecting commercial enterprises influence also the telecommunications sector.

What has changed in a number of countries is the extent to which the government directly participates in the conduct of telecommunications and the level of competition which is permitted in the telecommunications sector. This in turn is influenced and dictated by a number of factors, of which the following are perhaps the most relevant:

1. economic considerations;
2. political influences;
3. technological developments;
4. regulatory and legal requirements.

Governments and other national interests can and have used these factors either to encourage competition in specific telecommunications activities or to establish barriers

---

[2] In all Member States telecommunications activities were conducted by a state-owned monopoly. This is still the case in many, and the same organisations continue to dominate the telecommunications sector in Member States. They have varying degrees of exclusive or special rights not enjoyed by other entities. In this work any such telecommunications organisation, whether state-owned or privately owned, which enjoys special or exclusive rights is referred to as a Telecommunications Organisation, or TO. The context will make clear the particular nature of the relevant organisation and the extent of the relevant rights.

[3] ITU.

[4] See p. 20 et seq.

[5] International Telegraph and Telephone Consultative Committee of the ITU.

[6] Recommendation D150 which provides for the manner in which settlements are made between TOs for international call charges.

to such competition. An obvious example is the use of technical standards for terminal equipment. These can be such that other manufacturers can produce equipment that can be easily operated within a system or to exclude the use of any competitive equipment.

The tendency within Europe is to encourage competition and in the European Community to abolish barriers to competition, with the result that no telecommunications activity can be regarded as safe from competition and the sacred preserve of the existing operators.

As with all other economic activities, the competition rules of the Community have always had application to telecommunications. What was different about telecommunications, as with other utilities and transport, was that it could more readily be argued to fall within the legal provisions[7] permitting exceptions from the full application of the competition rules.[8]

With the convergence of computer technology and telecommunications, it became possible to provide many services and facilities independently of the telecommunications network. Furthermore, many new services, not traditionally provided by the TOs, became economically feasible. It therefore became increasingly difficult to sustain the argument that the provision of these new services and the application of competition rules to the sector would 'obstruct the performance, in law or in fact, of the particular tasks assigned to [the TOs]'.[9] Added to the technological factor, the increasing economic importance of information and exchange of information provided the Commission with a strong motive for liberalisation. The Commission had to take action to ensure that the sources of information, representing major assets in the new economic age, as well as the routes by which the flow of information took place, were both efficient and provided competitively throughout the Community.

The equipment supply market is an important part of the telecommunications sector and has undergone significant changes both in the European Community[10] and elsewhere. However, I will concentrate here on the telecommunication services with reference to the equipment market as it affects services.

The Commission also could not ignore the international developments taking place, notably in the United States and Japan.

Historic perspective

Before the break-up of AT&T, telecommunications in every country was a monopoly, in most cases belonging to the government.[11] The United States was the first to introduce wider competition in the telecommunications market, by abolishing the domestic monopoly of AT&T. The Regional Bell Operating Companies were split from AT&T and established as separate entities to provide local telecommunications services. AT&T was confined to providing long-distance telecommunications services, in competition with Sprint, GTE and MCI.

The liberalisation in the US was due to a number of factors. The Federal Communications Commission and the State Department wished to encourage greater activity and

---

[7] Rome Treaty, Art. 90(2). Determination of this question rests with the Commission, Eirpage Case Board Telecom Eireanne (BTE) and Motorola Ireland, OJ L 306/22, 7 November 1991.

[8] Rome Treaty, Arts 59, 85 and 86.

[9] Rome Treaty, Art. 90(2).

[10] One of the early measures introduced by the Commission was to end, by Dir. 88/301/EEC, the monopoly of the TO in the supply of terminal equipment.

[11] AT&T was always a private monopoly protected by legislation, but without government ownership.

growth in the equipment supply market and end the abuse by AT&T of its monopoly. It would be wrong to assume that AT&T was totally unhappy about the change. AT&T wished to be freed from the restriction on its participation in the then rapidly growing computer market.

Next in time came the United Kingdom. In 1984 a new regime was introduced for both political and economic reasons. The government was politically committed to turning to private ownership many previously nationalised industries. Telecommunications as a candidate for privatisation also served the need to raise large sums to finance reductions in taxation and to attract foreign investment into the United Kingdom. Consequently, a majority interest in British Telecom was sold to the public and foreign investors. At the same time Cable & Wireless was licensed to construct and run telecommunications network in competition with BT. This duopoly was informally guaranteed until 1991, with vaguely defined exceptions.

Japan then followed by privatising NTT,[12] but without splitting it into different companies or permitting free competition over a broad range of services. New rules were introduced to allow other carriers may compete with NTT under certain conditions. However, international communications has been separated from domestic communications and is conducted by the privately owned KDD.[13]

These initiatives have been followed with plans by many other countries to liberalise their own telecommunications markets to varying degrees. This trend is another aspect of the ever changing global environment in which telecommunications companies must operate.

The European context

There are many factors underlying the motivation for and causes of the trend to liberalisation. Many attribute this to the desire of governments to secure better and cheaper communication services for the customer. But there are more fundamental and complex forces at work. All that can be said with any degree of certainty is that the various factors outlined above are at work and interact to bring about the current situation.

As those forces change in relative importance and emphasis, so does the overall communications environment. Viewed from the perspective of the European Commission, a dominant force is the achievement of the single European market.

Following the objectives identified in the 1987 Green Paper,[14] in 1990 the Commission issued its Services Directive.[15] This sets the current scene for telecommunication services within the Community. The Services Directive requires the achievement by Member States of the following main objectives:

1. withdrawal of all special or exclusive rights for the supply of telecom services, other than voice telephony;[16]
2. authorising simple resale services from 1993;

---

[12] Nippon Telegraph and Telephone.

[13] Kokusai Denshin Denwa Co.

[14] Towards a Dynamic Economy Green Paper on the Development of the Common Market for Telecommunications Services and Equipment, COM (87) 290.

[15] Commission Dir. of 28 June 1990 on Competition in the Markets for Telecommunication Services, 90/388/EEC; see p. 50 et seq.

[16] These measures were required to be completed and notified to the Commission by the end of 1990. For the validity of Commission measures to curtail 'special rights' see p. 13.

3. licensing procedures for data services to be determined and notified to the Commission by 30 June 1992;
4. establishment of objective and non-discriminatory access to networks;
5. conditions of use and charges for use of the public network to be non-discriminatory;
6. the regulatory function, including equipment type approval and allocation of frequencies, to be separated from the telecommunications organisations.

The scope of these measures are more far reaching than may at first appear. The freedom to maintain exclusive rights to provide and operate the physical network infrastructure is subject to the exception of satellite communication systems not connected to the public network.[17]

Even the reservation of voice telephony is quite limited. The Services Directive defines voice telephony in terms of *real time speech carried within the public switched network*. This leaves scope for many services such as voice messaging, involving store and forward, and other voice services over leased circuits.

An essential ingredient of creating a single market in telecom services is the adoption of Open Network Provision, addressed in the ONP Framework Directive. An important feature of the Directive is the proposal for mutual recognition of licences, whereby each Member State will permit a Licensee to provide in its territory certain services licensed by another Member State.

Other aspects of opening the market to cross-border competition involve Community-wide standards and harmonised tariff structures. These are also receiving attention from the Commission.

In 1992 the Commission made an overall assessment of the telecommunications sector in relation to the aims of the Directive.[18] The assessment is wide-ranging and also takes account of the development of the market outside the Community. It is likely that the review of the approach to reserved services could result in introducing more competition into the voice telephony market and network infrastructure provision.

The international context

For the first time in its current Uruguay Round the General Agreement on Trade and Tariffs is also addressing a General Agreement on Trade in Services,[19] including telecommunication services. The GNS paves the way for access to the networks of other telecommunications operators and the harmonisation of regulation and tariffs and implementation of international standards.[20]

Even without the GNS and an international framework for access to other telecommunications markets, there are many instances of bilateral agreements which promote cross-border competition in telecommunications services. For example, the United Kingdom has arrangements relating to international value added services with Japan, the United States, Canada and a number of other countries. There is also a movement for the mutual recognition of licences between members of CEPT.[21]

---

[17] See the Green Paper on a Common Approach in the Field of Satellite Communications in the European Community, COM(90) 490 final.
[18] See p. 126 et seq.
[19] GNS.
[20] Draft Telecommunications Annex to GNS, paras 10 et seq.
[21] European Conference of Postal and Telecommunications Administrations founded on 26 June 1959.

On the international front, countries will generally only extend the full scope of their liberal regime to foreign companies if the foreign country is prepare to do the same in the case of a company from the host country. This has been illustrated by the refusal of the United Kingdom to license certain US companies on the unspoken grounds that the United States restricts to 25 per cent the involvement of a foreign investor in a US telecommunications company.

It must be said that the mutual recognition of licences internationally is an ideal which is fraught with problems. Experience of the agreement between the US and the UK has shown that even among regulators speaking roughly the same language there are great difficulties in understanding the licences granted by the other. A necessary first step must be to harmonise the regulatory language and to simplify licences.

THE IMPACT OF THE ENVIRONMENT ON TELECOMMUNICATIONS BUSINESS

To illustrate the impact of the factors at play in the telecommunications environment on the day-to-day decisions that face companies in the sector, it is useful to take examples from the United Kingdom.

The United Kingdom, regarded as the forerunner in telecommunications liberalisation within the Community, could not persist in protecting the voice market of BT and Mercury. It had to amend its regulations in June 1991 to permit certain voice services in order to comply with the requirements of the Services Directive.

Fixed services

In 1984 Mercury was licensed to compete with BT across the full range of services including network provision. It was expected that it would build an extensive network for local telephony. Soon after the grant of the Licence to Mercury, the Government, for mixed political and economic reasons, abolished full tax relief for capital expenditure in the year it was made. This increased the capital funding cost of the Mercury network.

A part of the Government strategy was also to licence a number of cable television companies who would build local networks. Telecommunications services, including telephony, could be offered by the cable companies only under an agreement with BT or Mercury. Mercury might have been expected to be the more likely beneficiary of this opportunity, as BT already had an extensive local network of its own. There were two main reasons why this did not occur. First, with the loss of generous capital allowances the return from cable operations was not sufficiently attractive to investors. Second, under the procedures established, BT was able to delay interconnection agreement between cable operators and Mercury or itself. At the same time, Mercury was too busy building a national network to expend money or time on local services to relatively small numbers of customers in different parts of the country.

BT which was not permitted to provide cable television services on its own network started to obtain licences for many of the cable franchises. Initially it was one of very few operators with the necessary background and the funds to do so. There has been a notable failure by United Kingdom cable companies to attract investors from the Community, with few notable exceptions such as Companie Général des Eau. It is worth noting that cable companies were soon seen as unlikely competitors in the market because their regulation limits non-Community participation to 20 per cent. This regulatory barrier has not been removed and initially kept out US and Canadian cable operators from the market. But, today the major players in the United Kingdom cable market are Canadian cable companies and US RBOCs. This has been achieved by a technique which gives those operators full ownership and de facto control while conforming to the letter of the law.[22]

Mobile

Later there was PCN.[23] Whether the economics of establishing the necessary network will allow for sufficiently low tariffs to compete with BT local network remains to be seen. What is clear is that the three operators have different approaches to the market. Also, the potential competition from the existing operators is now considered to be greater than at first appeared. They are upgrading their service and may soon be able to offer many of the services available on PCN. A serious blow to the PCN operators could also have resulted from the proposal by Oftel[24] to allow BT to charge larger amounts for interconnection to its network. After strong arguments put to Oftel an exemption from such additional charges was secured. But this may change in the future and leaves a level of uncertainty which is not encouraging for newcomers to the market. The position is worse for operators of fixed services who will have to pay the additional charges at an earlier date.

US influences

The arrival into the United Kingdom of US telecommunications companies changed dramatically the market and the environment in which the domestic companies operate. With investment in cable operations the US companies increased both their presence and understanding of the United Kingdom market and of the European market. Their experience in the US makes their approach to regulatory and political issues more proactive than their European counterparts. They have been more readily prepared to challenge behaviour of their competitors and the Conventions applied by the regulators.

The recent application by Sprint[25] for a licence to provide a network and services, including international telephony, in competition with BT and Mercury is putting to the test the extent of liberalisation in the UK. Following the duopoly review the government invited applications for such licences. Under the new rules there is no restriction on the grant of a licence to a US company. But in practice the United Kingdom has refused to license foreign companies if the regulation of the relevant country restricts operation by United Kingdom companies in its market. This has been the case with the US in the past, but the FCC has recently proposed changes in this respect.

Potential entry by Sprint into the United Kingdom market is a good illustration of how the environment for telecommunications services can change as a result of actions of a

---

[22] The technique is to create a Jersey discretionary trust which owns the majority voting rights in the company without any right to capital or dividends. The remainder of the shares are held by the foreign investor, carrying all the rights to the capital and dividends. The foreign investor also has a Management Agreement with the company for the running of the system. The Directors are the trustees and nominees of the investor, the trustees having a majority.

[23] Personal Communication Networks.

[24] Office of Telecommunications, responsible for overseeing telecommunications activities in the United Kingdom.

[25] Financial Times, Tues., 7 Jan. 1992.

foreign agency with no apparent influence on the relevant domestic market. If the GNS is eventually finalised and ratified the scope for such events will be increased.

Of course, the other side of such changes is that the size of the international competitive market is enlarged, offering additional opportunities for exploiting new markets.

Satellite services

Satellite service operators in the United Kingdom have experienced some of the most serious changes to their market. Initially six operators were granted licences to provide *one-way domestic* services. They argued vigorously for two-way international service. The Government eventually made a limited concession by allowing *one-way European* services, confined to member countries of EFTA. By November 1990 some of these operators had developed limited businesses on that basis, under the handicap of Germany allowing *two-way international* satellite services. However, as a part of the Duopoly Review, the Government issued a class licence permitting *two-way international* services.

One of the advantages enjoyed by the existing operators over their new competitors is the close links they have established with Eutelsat. However, they still have to involve BT as the Signatory to apply for and finalise allocation of capacity for their services. They have pressed the Government and the European Commission to establish rules for direct access to Eutelsat and Intelsat by private operators. The Satellite Green Paper proposes the establishment of such rules. Their success eroded some of their competitive advantage.

Increased privatisation

It is well known that since its privatisation BT has been one of the most profitable companies in the world. This is partly because the price controls imposed by Oftel did not apply to international services which is a major contributor to the BT profits. The domestic price controls also overestimated the impact of competition on call charges and the erosion of BT's market. There is also a strong feeling among many in the industry that the BT profits were allowed to rise because the Government wished to maintain and increase the value of its remaining shares in BT. With the sale of those shares in 1992, there is a likelihood that the proposed review in February will result in greater controls on BT prices and profits.

Again the environment would change. With lower prices BT could become more competitive. This will put pressure on the other operators to lower prices, while the charges for interconnection to the BT network could rise.[26] A change in the Government could result in a similar alteration in the balance in the market. The Labour Party would be inclined to impose greater controls over the profitability of BT. A Labour government is also less likely to encourage competition in provision of public networks. Its freedom to reduce competition in other services is, of course, severely limited by the requirements of EC Directives.

---

[26] The interconnection charge is partly based on the difference between the cost of connecting a customer to the network and the amount BT can charge the customer for that connection. Currently BT is the only significant operator able to connect customers to the public networks. Therefore, if the BT price control limits the charge to the customer, other operators whose customers are connected to the network by BT will have to make a greater contribution to BT's costs.

Community and international influence

Member States of the Community have limited scope for interfering with the development of a competitive market. Even in controlling prices they have to have regard to the harmonisation of tariffs on a cost related basis. If prices are to be lowered, there can always be a challenge by competitors on grounds of abuse of dominant position. The dominant operator can generally not be forced to lower prices below a reasonable level without leaving itself open to such a challenge. The United Kingdom regime for price capping requires the agreement of the operator, which makes such cap legally voluntary. In fact BT has agreed to every price control introduced by Oftel.

The changing international scene has enlarged the market for competition in telecommunications. If GNS is implemented a growing number of foreign operators will enter almost every domestic market. More particularly, there will be an erosion of the monopoly profits earned on international communications, as there will be a choice of operators offering service.

On international calls, the CCITT Recommendations are already undergoing revision and the accounting rate system for international calls is being disbanded. As long as a monopoly continues in a country it may be possible to reach agreement with overseas operators to keep the accounting rate for international calls high. But once competition is allowed, this will be more difficult.

Even without competition on provision of international circuits, there is more at stake than merely maintaining profits from international calls. As well as the link between economic success of countries and international call traffic, pressure to enter into international joint ventures will increase. The other joint venturers will want to reach agreement on international calls generally, including accounting rates between them.

Most multi-national companies prefer to deal with one entity for the whole of their international communication needs. This, added to the necessity of telecommunications operators to form international alliances and develop other markets, in the face of increasing competition at home, has added a new dimension to the telecommunications market. Joint ventures are being formed to provide global circuits and Global Virtual Private Networks.[27] Availability of such facilities and services are a major incentive for international corporation in locating their operations. Most governments will want to ensure that such facilities can be offered to attract foreign businesses.

There is growing pressure on telecommunications operators to take part in such ventures. With the changes in technology and increasing role of software in switches, technical compatibility is much easier to achieve. Therefore, it would be wrong to assume that competition from such joint ventures will be delayed because of inconsistent standards.

Within the Community, joint ventures of the type likely to be made between telecommunications companies are caught by the competition laws.[28] However, in its Guideline on the Application of Competition Rules in the Telecommunications Sector,[29] the Commission recognises the spread of many joint venture and co-operation agreements. The Guidelines state:

> The Commission welcomes and fully supports the necessity of co-operation particularly in order to promote the development of trans-European services and strengthen the competitiveness of the EEC industry throughout the Community and in the world markets . . .

---

[27] GVPN.

[28] Joint ventures are subject to the provisions of Arts 85 and 86 of the Rome Treaty.

[29] OJ 91/C 233/02, 6 June 1991; Guidelines.

Regulation No 17 provides well-defined clearing procedures for such co-operation agreements.

Under the Regulation even if a particular agreement is caught by the competition rules:[30]

an exemption can be granted by the Commission under Article 85(3) . . . when the agreement brings about economic benefits . . . which outweigh its restriction on competition.

There have already been agreements formed between BT, AT&T and France Telecom. The fact that agreements may relate to activities outside the Community does not mean that the Commission will not intervene.[31]

APPLICATION OF COMPETITION RULES

From the earlier discussion,[32] it is clear that the tasks facing the Commission, ranging from the separation of operational and other functions of the TOs to formulating rules for access to and inter-connection with the networks operated by them, were highly complex and political.

The Commission initially set out its policy approach to the telecommunications sector in its 1984 Action Programme,[33] followed by its more extensive proposals in its subsequent Green Paper[34] on the development of the common market for telecommunications services and equipment. The confirmation of the Commission's motivation can be found in the opening statement[35] of the Green Paper:

Information, exchanges of knowledge and communications are of vital importance in economic activity and in the balance of power in the world today. Policy makers are therefore concentrating on ways of acquiring, processing, storing and transmitting information. Telecommunications is the most critical area for influencing the 'nervous system' of modern society. To flourish, it has to have optimum environmental conditions. In this respect, the convergence of telecommunications, computing and applications of electronics in general has now made possible the introduction of a wider variety of new services. The traditional form of organisation of the sector does not allow critical development of the potential of these new services. In order to create an open and a dynamic market in this area it therefore seems necessary to introduce regulatory changes to improve the sector's environment. These changes should allow the full development of the supply of services and equipment, thus making it possible for industry to take full advantage of this potential. In particular, national frontiers should not be allowed to hamper the development of a consistent communications system within the European Community.

The Commission recognised from the outset the enormity of the task it had undertaken and acknowledged the need for a gradual and progressive approach, taking into account the views of all parties concerned. It stated in the Green Paper:[36]

---

[30] Art. 85.

[31] The proposal for the merger of Haviland of Canada and Westland Aircraft in the United Kingdom was prevented by the Commission on the grounds that it would substantially reduce competition in the world market, affecting trade between Member States; Re the Concentration between Aerospatiale SNI and Alenia-Aeritalia e Selenia SpA and de Havilland, 91/619/EEC, OJ L 334/42, 5 December 1991; Woodpulp Case, [1988] 4 CMLR 901; A Åhlström Osakeyhtiö and Others v The Commission 88/C 281/09, OJ C 281/16, 4 November 1988.

[32] See p. 1 et seq.

[33] COM (84) 277.

[34] Towards a Dynamic Economy – Green Paper on the Development of the Common Market for Telecommunications Services and Equipment COM (87) 290 final, 30 June 1987.

[35] COM (87) 290 final, presentation of the Green Paper on telecommunications, p. 1.

[36] COM (87) 290, p. 12. The Commission's proposals were subsequently outlined in its long awaited Green Paper on the subject.

Given their importance and wide ramifications, regulatory changes in telecommunications can only be introduced progressively. Time must be allowed for present structures, which have grown up historically over a long period to adjust to a new environment.[37]

The Commission, therefore, embarked on an iterative implementation of its policy of progressive introduction of competition based on its growing experience of the telecommunications and telematic sectors. In doing so the Commission has closely adhered to its 'Proposed Positions'[38] set out in the Green Paper. In view of the importance of these 'Proposed Positions', which have since more aptly become known as the 'Ten Commandments', they may usefully be repeated here in full.

Proposed Positions

The general objective of the positions set out is the development in the Community of a strong telecommunications infrastructure and of efficient services: providing the European user with a broad variety of telecommunications services on the most favourable terms, ensuring coherence of development between Member States, and creating an open competitive environment, taking full account of the dynamic technological developments underway.

A. Acceptance of continued exclusive provision or special rights for the Telecommunications Administrations regarding provision and operation of the network infrastructure. Where a Member State chooses a more liberal regime, either for the whole or parts of the network, the short and long term integrity of the general network infrastructure should be safeguarded.

Closely monitored competitive offering of two-way satellite communications systems will need further analysis. It should be allowed on a case-to-case basis, where this is necessary to develop European-wide services and where impact on the financial viability of the main provider(s) is not substantial.

Common understanding and definition regarding infrastructure provision should be worked out under E below.

B. Acceptance of continued exclusive provision or special rights for the Telecommunications Administrations regarding provision of a limited number of basic services, where exclusive provision is considered essential at this stage for safeguarding public service goals.

Exclusive provision must be narrowly construed and be subject to review within given time intervals, taking account of technological development and particularly the evolution towards a digital infrastructure. 'Reserved services' may not be defined so as to extend a Telecommunications Administration service monopoly in a way inconsistent with the Treaty. Currently, given general understanding in the Community, voice telephone service seems to be the only obvious candidate.

C. Free (unrestricted) provision of all other services ('competitive services' including in particular 'value-added services') within Member States and between Member States (in competition with the Telecommunications Administrations) for own use, shared use, or provision to third parties, subject to the conditions for use of the network infrastructure to be defined under E).

---

[37] This approach was reiterated in the subsequent White Paper, COM (88) 48, 9 Feb. 1988: Towards a Competitive Community-Wide Telecommunications Market in 1992: Implementing the Green Paper on the Development of the Common Market for Telecommunications Services and Equipment.

[38] COM (87) 290, p. 184 et seq.

'Competitive services' would comprise all services except basic services explicitly reserved for the Telecommunications Administrations (see B).

D. Strict requirements regarding standards for the network infrastructure and services provided by the Telecommunications Administrations or service providers of comparable importance, in order to maintain or create Community-wide interoperability. These requirements must build in particular on Directives 83/189/ EEC and 86/361/EEC, Decision 87/95/EEC and Recommendation 86/659/EEC.
Member States and the Community should ensure and promote provision by the Telecommunications Administrations of efficient European-wide and worldwide communications, in particular regarding those services (be they reserved or competitive) recommended for Community-wide provision, such as according to Recommendation 86/659/EEC.

E. Clear definition by Community Directive of general requirements imposed by Telecommunications Administrations on providers of competitive services for use of the network, including definitions regarding network infrastructure provision.
This must include clear interconnect and access obligations by Telecommunications Administrations for trans-frontier service providers in order to prevent Treaty infringements.
Consensus must be achieved on standards, frequencies, and tariff principles, in order to agree on the general conditions imposed for service provision on the competitive sector. Details of this Directive on Open Network Provision (ONP) should be prepared in consultation with the Member States, the Telecommunications Administrations and the other parties concerned, in the framework of the Senior Officials Group on telecommunications (SOG-T).

F. Free (unrestricted) provision of terminal equipment within Member States and between Member States (in competition with Telecommunications Administrations), subject to type approval as compatible with Treaty obligations and existing Directives. Provision of the first (Conventional) telephone set could be excluded from unrestricted provision on a temporary basis.
Receive Only Earth States (ROES) for satellite down-links should be assimilated with terminal equipment and be subject to type approval only.

G. Separation of regulatory and operational activities of Telecommunications Administrations. Regulatory activities concern in particular licensing, control of type approval and interface specifications, allocations of frequencies and general surveillance of network usage conditions.

H. Strict continuous review of operational (commercial) activities of Telecommunications Administrations according to Articles 85, 86 and 90, EEC Treaty. This applies in particular to practices of cross-subsidisation of activities in the competitive services sector and of activities in manufacturing.

I. Strict continuous review of all private providers in the newly opened sectors according to Articles 85 and 86, in order to avoid the abuse of dominant positions.

J. Full application of the Community's common commercial policy to telecommunications. Notification by Telecommunications Administrations under Regulation 17/62 of all arrangements between them or with Third Countries which may affect competition within the Community. Provision of information to the extent required for the Community, in order to build up a consistent Community position for GATT negotiations and relations with Third Countries.

It will be noted that although certain provisional exclusive or special rights were initially accepted, the Commission has given clear indication that these are not for an indefinite period and will be subject to continuous monitoring and review.[39]

Encouraged by the level of consensus and support for its proposals with regard to terminal equipment, the Commission used its powers to address Directives directly to Member States for the first time in this area.[40] This Directive met substantial resistance from Member States who challenged the legal basis for the Commission's action. The contents of the Directive were not themselves controversial and most Member States had either opened the terminal market to competition or had definite plans for doing so within the time frame envisaged by the Directive.

Perhaps particularly objectionable to the Member States was the fact that the Commission founded its Directive on the grounds that the TOs in Member States abused their dominant position in the market for terminal equipment in relation to which they had special or exclusive rights to import and market.[41] The Directive refers to the restrictions on user choice in the linking of the use of the network to acceptance of additional services and the limitations put on technical progress by the unnecessarily limited range of equipment offered by the TOs.

The Member States, led by France,[42] complained that the action of the Commission in issuing the Directive did not take account of the provisions of the Treaty[43] requiring that the TOs not be obstructed in performing their tasks.

In its decision on the complaint[44] the Court of Justice held that:

1. Article 90 of the Treaty empowers the Commission to use its powers to abolish special or exclusive rights.
2. The exercise of exclusive rights in the telecommunications sector could restrict or distort Community trade. It was therefore appropriate for the Commission to require their abolition.
3. The equipment Directive was not sufficiently specific and particular on what constituted 'special rights'. Therefore, all references to special rights in the Directive are ineffective.

Following the substantial victory on that occasion, the Commission also founded its Services Directive[45] on the basis of its powers to issue Directives under the Treaty.[46] By contrast with the equipment Directive,[47] the Services Directive directly addresses the provisions permitting derogation[48] from the competition provisions in this context.[49] Furthermore, it specifically defines the term *'special or exclusive rights'*.[50] Therefore, the Commission was of the view that the Services Directive is the more effective exercise of

---

[39] The Proposed Positions are confirmed in the White Paper, COM (88) 48, at fig. 1.
[40] 88/301/EEC.
[41] Ibid., recital 13.
[42] France v Commission, Case 202/88, 91/C 96/04, OJ C 96/6, 19 March 1991 – Italy, Belgium, Germany and Greece intervening. See also the Eirpage Case, Board Telecom Eireanne (BTE) and Motorola Ireland, 18 October 1991, OJ L 306/22, 7 November 1991.
[43] Art. 90(2).
[44] Decision given March 1991.
[45] Commission Dir. of 28 June 1990 on competition in the markets for telecommunications services, 90/388/EEC, OJ L 192/10, 24 July 1990.
[46] Art. 90(3).
[47] 88/301/EEC.
[48] Rome Treaty, Art. 90(2).
[49] See in particular 90/388/EEC, recitals 18 and 19.
[50] 90/388/EEC, Art. 1(1).

the Commission's powers in abolishing restrictive practices and providing for the freedom to provide services throughout the Community.

However, the Commission's exercise of its Treaty powers to issue the Services Directive was also challenged by Belgium, France, Italy and Spain. In the event the matter came before the European Court of Justice at the suit of Spain, Belgium and Italy.[51] They argued that the Treaty only gives the Commission the right to oversee existing rules under the Treaty, not take a pro-active role to dismantle monopolies. The aim of the complainants was to ensure that the Commission could only intervene under the authority of the Council of Ministers.[52]

The Court rejected the complaints[53] that the Commission had abused its powers under the Treaty. The Court ruled that the Commission's powers should not be limited to surveillance of rules already in existence but that it has a general right to implement new measures such as those under attack. The fact that the Directive should have been implemented by the Council of Ministers did not affect the competence of the Commission to act.

The Court held that the measures in the Services Directive were lawful and that *exclusive* rights of establishment and exploitation of telecommunications services given to the TOs could be abolished. However, again[54] the Court held the abolition of *special* rights was defective in that the Commission failed to define them precisely. The right to terminate long-term contracts was also unlawful on the ground that other Treaty provisions should have been used.

GUIDELINES ON THE APPLICATION OF COMPETITION RULES

The full application of competition rules is central to the Commission's overall approach to telecommunications. It is therefore important for all participants in the telecommunications sector to have a clear view of how these rules may apply to the sector and, in particular, to their own activities. This will assist the participants to shape their plans and arrangements in a manner which is consistent with the competition rules. In view of the Commission's commitment to review and continuously monitor developments in the sector, participants must also be aware of the possibility that the Commission's approach to the application of competition rules in this area remain subject to adaptation.

In view of the significance of the competition rules to market participants, the Commission has issued Guidelines[55] on the application of these rules in the telecommunications sector. One strength of the Guidelines is that they deal with the competition rules in the specific context of the telecommunications sector and take account of the overall Community telecommunications policy.[56] In considering the Guidelines a clear distinction must be drawn between those competition rules which are directly applicable to telecommunications entities[57] and those which are applicable to and concern the laws

---

[51] Cases C-271/90, 281/90 and 289/90.
[52] See Rome Treaty, Art. 100.
[53] Spain, Belgium and Italy v Commission, Joined Cases C-271/90, 281/90 and 289/90, ECJ FC, 17 Nov. 1992, Financial Times, 18 Nov. 1992, p. 2, and 24 Nov. 1992, p. 18.
[54] See ECJ decision on Terminal Dir., p. 13.
[55] Guidelines on the application of EEC competition rules in the telecommunications sector, 91/C 233/02, OJ C 233/2, 6 Sept. 1991.
[56] Guidelines, 91/C 233/02, preface, para. 1.
[57] Rome Treaty, Arts 85 and 86.

or regulations of Member States.[58] The Guidelines address the autonomous behaviour of TOs which are the result of their own free choice.[59] If the behaviour inconsistent with competition rules is one required by the rules and regulations of a Member State, the Commission will have recourse against the Member State[60] and not the TO involved.

Anti-competitive behaviour of TOs

In circumstances where the rules and regulations of a Member State do not require the anti-competitive behaviour of an entity, but nevertheless the Member State endorses or encourages the entity in taking such a course of its own free will, then both the Member State[61] and the TO[62] will be subject to action by the Commission.[63]

The Guidelines make clear that the Open Network Provision[64] does not constitute a part of the competition rules for the sector, but is a distinct and complementary set of rules.[65] The function of ONP is to enable network users throughout the Community to have harmonised access conditions to Community-wide inter-connected public networks. The ONP rules, while aimed at developing a common market for telecommunications services and equipment, are not and cannot be regarded as implementation of Community competition rules.[66] Therefore, although the ONP rules must be consistent with the competition rules, the competition rules will continue to apply even after ONP has been fully implemented.[67]

In order to ensure that competition rules are coherently applied, it is recognised that TOs may justify behaviour that derogates[68] from the competition rules, on grounds that would have been available to the Member State if it had imposed restrictions consistent with such behaviour. In particular, Member States are permitted to introduce restrictions on the grounds of 'essential requirements'[69] when implementing the Services Directive. Therefore, at least theoretically, where a Member State has not imposed any restrictions,

---

[58] Rome Treaty, Art. 5 in conjunction with Arts 85, 86 and 90.

[59] 90/C 233/02, para. 12.

[60] Under Rome Treaty, Arts 5 and 90 in conjunction with Arts 85 and 86. In Pabst and Richarz KG v The Bureau National Interprofessionnel de l'Armagnac (BNIA) [1976] CMLR D63, the Court held that the body set-up under national law to regulate the quality of armagnac was an association of undertakings, and that the controls were aimed at restriction of supply for commercial reasons, contrary to Article 85(1). In the Télé-Marketing Case, Centre Belge d'Études de Marché-Télé-Marketing SA v Luxembourgoise de Télédiffusion SA, 85/C 281/04, OJ C 281/4, 2 November 1985, the Court held that Article 85 applies to an entity holding a dominant position, not as a result of any activity by the entity, but as a result of legal powers exercised by the Member State.

[61] Under the terms of Directives issued pursuant to Art. 90.

[62] Under the terms of the Treaty, Arts 85 and 86.

[63] 91/C 233/02, paras 12 ‹88› 14.

[64] ONP; see p. 71.

[65] 91/C 233/02, para. 17.

[66] 91/C 233/02, paras 15 and 16.

[67] 91/C 233/02, paras 17 and 18.

[68] Under Rome Treaty, Art. 90(2).

[69] See Services Directive 90/388/EEC, Art. 3. In International Air Couriers Case, Bull. EC 1-1985, point 2.1.10, the Commission stated that it "regards the Member States' postal and telecommunications authorities as commercial undertakings, since they supply goods and services for payment and that any extension by one or more of these undertakings of their dominant position may constitute an abuse under Article 86 of the EEC Treaty". See also the German Cordless Telephone Case, Bull. EC 3-1985, point 2.1.43, and the Modem Case, cited in the Telecommunications Green Paper, page 125, where the intervention of the Commission in both cases persuaded the German government not to extend the exclusive rights of the Bundespost to cordless telephones and to modems respectively.

it is nevertheless open to the TO to argue that its restrictive behaviour is justified on grounds of 'essential requirements'.[70] However, in practice, it will be difficult for a TO to succeed on such an argument and claim that its behaviour may be justified on grounds of 'essential requirements', where the Member State has itself not deemed such a restriction necessary.

Co-operation between TOs

The application of competition rules, in particular those relating to agreements and the decisions and the abuse of dominant position in the market,[71] require the definition of the relevant market. Different markets will be relevant in the context of specific cases; they may be a product or service market or a geographic market.[72] With rapidly changing and developing technology, 'market definition is dynamic and variable'.[73] The Guidelines provide general indications and criteria for the determination of a product market and of a geographic market.[74]

One of the major policy goals of the Community[75] is:

> Stimulating European co-operation at all levels, as far as compatible with Community competition rules and particularly in the field of research and development, in order to secure a strong European presence in the telecommunications market and to ensure the full participation of all Member States.

The achievement of Europe-wide services and networks will generally require a large measure of co-operation and collaboration between TOs. The Commission not only recognises this, but also in some specific instances[76] the Commission supports and calls for co-operation to promote trans-European services and to strengthen competitiveness of Community industry in world markets.[77]

There is clearly a risk that co-operation in these areas and in other activities could lead to agreements and decisions that would be inconsistent with the Community competition rules. Those engaging in such co-operative activities can take advantage of the block

---

[70] 91/C 233/02, paras 21–4.

[71] Rome Treaty, Arts 85 and 86; See also Merger Policy in Telecommunications, Regulation 4064/89, OJ L 257/13, 1990.

[72] 91/C 233/02, para. 25.

[73] 91/C 233/02, paragraph 25. In Eirpage Case, OJ L 306/22, 7 November 1991, the Commission considered paging to be a separate market from mobile communications generally, partly on the basis of the size of the equipment and that paging provided a one way service, as well as the lower costs involved. All these factors are subject to change.

[74] 91/C 233/02, paras 26–35; the geographic market will in most cases not extend beyond the territory of a Member State, until greater Community integration is achieved, when it may extend to the whole Community; Eirpage Case, OJ L 306/22, 7 November 1991. See also Re the Concentration between AT&T and NCR, Case IV/M.050, 91/C 16/15, OJ C 16/20, 24 January 1991, in which the merger was cleared and the notified operation held to be within Council Regulation 4064/89, the Commission examined product market share, geographic market, vertical and horizontal integration issues.

[75] Council resolution of 30 June 1988 on the development of the Common Market for telecommunications services and equipment up to 1992, 88/C 257/01, para. 7; see p. 115.

[76] For example, in the case of ISDN, Council Recommendation 86/659/EEC; and in the case of cellular digital land-based mobile communications, Council Recommendation 87/371/EEC.

[77] 91/C 233/02. para. 36.

exemptions[78] or Commission Notices[79] in certain circumstances. There are also clearance procedures[80] under which TOs may apply for clearance of co-operation agreements.[81]

The Guidelines examine the circumstances in which co-operation agreements and arrangements can give rise to competition issues and the general approaches that the Commission will adopt.[82] The Guidelines draw a distinction between *reserved* and *non-reserved services*.[83] Co-operation in relation both to reserved and non-reserved services can give rise to establishing or strengthening a dominant position and these issues are addressed in the Guidelines.

In applying the competition rules to co-operation between TOs the Commission is faced with striking a balance between the benefits of co-operation in developing and strengthening the telecommunications sector within the Community and the world market, and the anti-competitive effects of such co-operation. These issues are well-illustrated in the approach of the Commission to Managed Data Network Services.[84] These are based on 'one-stop shopping' arrangements between TOs, consisting of a broad package of services which include providing facilities, value-added services and management of those services. In 1989 twenty-two TOs entered into a joint venture to provide a Europe-wide MDNS.[85] In considering whether to grant clearance for the venture, the Commission had to balance the benefits from the project against its risks to competition. The benefits included:

1. economic benefits of one-stop shopping, offering users access to Europe-wide service through a single operator;
2. accelerated European standardisation;
3. increased quality of services;
4. development and offer of new services; and
5. reduction of costs.

The risks to competition included the restriction of competition between the venturers and increased barriers to entry by other service suppliers. These could particularly have

---

[78] The Commission has issued block exemption Regulations under the provisions of the Rome Treaty, Art. 85 (3), giving automatic exemption for agreements conforming to the Regulations; Examples are, Notice on Cooperation Agreements, OJ C 75/3, 27 July 1968; Block Exemption for Research and Development Agreements, 418/85, OJ L 53/5, 1985; Specification Agreements Regulations 417/85, OJ L 53/1, 1985.

[79] The Commission from time to time issues Notices and Agreements which in its view do not appreciably restrict competition and trade between Member States and do not justify Commission action; and see Competition Law in the European Communities, Vol. I, published by the Commission.

[80] Regulation No. 17.

[81] 91/C 233/02, paras 36 and 37. In the context of airline tariffs, the Court has ruled that bilateral and multilateral tariff agreements are automatically void under Article 85(2), and may constitute an abuse of a dominant position; Ahmed Saeed Flugreisen and Silver Line Reisbüro GmbH v Zentrale zur Bekämpfung inlauteren Wettbewerbs eV, 11 April 1989, 89/C 122/05, OJ C 122/4, 17 May 1989.

[82] 91/C 233/02, paras 39 ‹88› 77.

[83] Broadly, reserve services are the provision of network infrastructure and voice telephony; for further discussion see p. 60 et seq.

[84] MDNS. In RE ECR 900, 90/446/EEC, OJ L 283/31, 22 August 1990, the Commission approved a cooperation agreement between NEG AG of Germany, Alcatel NV of the Netherlands and Oy Nokia AB of Finland, for the development of the Groupe Spéciale Mobile system, GSM, on the basis of the benefit to the Community and that the companies would not individually have the required resources to develop the system; Compare RE the Joint Venture between ING C Olivetti and C Spa and Canon Inc, OJ L 52/51, 26 February 1988, which was approved for a limited period. See also Plessey Co plc v. General Electric Co plc and Siemens AG, 1 September 1989, 90/C 239/02, OJ C 239/2, 25 September 1990, clearing the merger of the telecommunications activities, partly on the basis of the size of the international competition.

[85] The project was abandoned for commercial reasons after it was considered by the Commission.

arisen from discrimination against private service operators and cross-subsidisation. The Commission had indicated to the TOs involved that it would require from them certain guarantees of non-discrimination and against cross-subsidisation.[86]

Abuses of dominant position

Dominant positions may arise or be strengthened not only as the result of agreements such as those considered already, but also independently of them. The Guidelines examine some circumstances in which a dominant position might exist and those in which a dominant position might be considered to have been abused.[87] The Guidelines particularly highlight abuses of dominant position arising from TOs restricting access to circuits[88] or discriminating[89] between users or the type of use.[90]

An example of this kind of abuse arose in relation to conditions under which the Belgian RTT[91]leased circuits to private providers of value-added services. On a complaint from the users and following intervention by the Commission, RTT permitted the use of leased circuits by the value-added service provider, subject only to the restriction that the circuits not be used for simple transport of data without any other value.[92] RTT further undertook to apply the same conditions to all its leased circuits.[93]

Abuse of dominant position need not be a result of any direct activity by the dominant entity. It may arise as a consequence of the exercise of legal powers by a Member State which restrict competition on the market. It would also be an abuse of dominant position for a dominant entity to reserve to itself or a member of its group ancillary activities on a neighbouring but separate market, with the possibility of eliminating competition from such entity.[93a]

IMPACT OF EEC COMPETITION LAW ON INTERNATIONAL ORGANISATIONS AND RULES

The International Telecommunications Union

The major purpose and focus of the International Telecommunications Union[94] is the promotion of international co-operation to maintain and improve the rational use of

---

[86] 91/C 233/02, para. 63; The Spanish Direccion General de Corrios y Telegrafos (DGCT) refused to give Mercury interconnection for telex, the Commission intervened on 19 November 1991, applying the terms of the Guidelines. In RE Infonet Services Corporation, 11 January 1992, 92/C 7/03, OJ C 7/3, 11 January 1992, the Commission required a number of undertakings aimed at safeguarding against discrimination and cross-subsidization by the Consortium of TOs of five Member States and of six other European countries.
[87] 91/C 233/02, paras 78 ,88, 121.
[88] Contrary to Rome Treaty. Art. 86(b).
[89] Contrary to Rome Treaty. Art. 86(c).
[90] 91/C 233/02, para. 90.
[91] Régie des Télégraphes et Téléphones.
[92] Commonly known as 'simple resale'; see p. 63.
[93] 91/C 233/02, para. 93; Commission Press Release IP (90) 67 of 29 Jan. 1990.
[93a] Télé-Marketing Case, 85/C 281/04, OJ C 281/4, 2 November 1985.
[94] ITU.

telecommunications on an international level.[95] The attainment of these objectives involves the ITU in the management of the frequency spectrum, definition of technical standards and harmonisation of means of settlement between TOs in relation to international traffic.[96] Because the technology and the needs of international telecommunications undergo frequent and rapid changes, the ITU Regulations[97] address largely general provisions.[98] Matters of detail, which are nevertheless essential to efficient operation of international communications, are the subject of Recommendations by CCITT[99] and CCIR.[100]

As already indicated, the CCITT and CCIR Recommendations[101] address:

1. international standardisation;
2. frequency allocation;
3. accounting practices and principles for settlement between TOs.

These clearly have an impact on the conduct of telecommunications within the Community and implications for competition. In addition, World Administrative Telegraph and Telephone Conference[102] and World Administrative Radio Conference[103] Regulations address specific matters, such as specialised networks for value-added services, which also have implications for Community regulation.

The position of the Commission with regard to these Recommendations and Regulations is set out in the Guidelines.[104] This raises the issue of supremacy of the Rome Treaty and of international Conventions entered into by Member States.

The relevant provision of the Rome Treaty[105] provides:

> The rights and obligations arising from agreements concluded before the entry into force of this Treaty between one or more *Member States* on the one hand *and* one or more *Third Countries* on the other, shall not be affected by the provisions of this Treaty. To the extent that such agreements are not compatible with this Treaty, the Member State or States concerned shall take all appropriate steps to eliminate the incompatibilities established.[106]

The Commission argues that the Treaty is intended to protect the interests of Third Countries and does not affect relations between Member States. Therefore, within the Community, the WATTC and WARC Regulations must be applied in such a way as to

---

[95] The International Telecommunications Convention, Art. 4(1) provides:
The purposes of the Union are:
(a) To maintain and extend international co-operation between all Members of the Union for the improvement and rational use of telecommunications of all kinds, as well as to promote and to offer technical assistance to developing countries in the field of telecommunications;
(b) To promote the development of technical facilities and their most efficient operation with a view to improving the efficiency of telecommunication services, increasing their usefulness and making them, so far as possible, generally available to the public;
(c) To harmonise the actions of nations in the attainment of those ends.
[96] International Telecommunications Convention, Art. 4(2).
[97] These comprise the Telegraph Regulations, Telephone Regulations and Radio Regulations.
[98] It should be noted that the Radio Regulations contain substantial detailed provisions as compared to the Telegraph and the Telephone Regulations.
[99] The International Telephone and Telegraph Consultative Committee.
[100] The International Radio Consultative Committee.
[101] The work of the Committees is done through Study Groups, who draw up recommendations which are then submitted to the ITU Plenary Assembly for approval and publication.
[102] WATTC.
[103] WARC.
[104] 91/C 233/02, paras 139 ‹88› 44.
[105] Art. 234.
[106] Emphasis added.

eliminate incompatibilities with Community competition rules. In any event, on each occasion when the ITU Convention or the Regulations are modified, the Commission asserts that the ITU members recover their freedom of action, the implication being that they need not continue with their ITU obligations and therefore the Convention and the Regulations do not pre-date the Rome Treaty.[107]

The British Telecom Case

The CCITT and CCIR Recommendations pose a slightly different problem and have an added dimension in view of their impact on international call charges.[108] The Commission takes the view that the CCITT Recommendations are not legally binding.[109] This view was shared by the European Court of Justice in the *British Telecom Case*.[110]

The case arose from a prohibition introduced in 1978 by British Telecom preventing message forwarding agencies from taking advantage of the lower telex rate between the United States and the United Kingdom rather than those between other Member States and the United States. The agencies were engaged in relaying traffic between third countries and the United Kingdom. The prohibition, contained in a letter from British Telecom, prevented communication bureaux operators from providing international services, where:

1. messages in data-form were sent or received internationally by telephone and converted into messages to be received in telex, facsimile-written or other visual form;
2. telex messages were forwarded in transit between places outside the United Kingdom; and
3. telex messages were sent or received via other message-forwarding agencies.

British Telecom introduced this prohibition on the basis that the activities of agencies in the United Kingdom through which other countries sent their telex messages undermined 'the arrangements we have been able to negotiate with other countries and so endanger the low tariffs we at present charge to our own customers in the United Kingdom'.[111]

The Commission treated these Recommendations as issues of fact and not of law, since they are not binding on ITU members. The Commission ruled that British Telecom, by limiting the activities of United Kingdom telephone and telex subscribers who were message forwarding agencies, to the detriment of nationals of other EEC countries, had abused its dominant position.[112]

---

[107] 91/C 233/02, para. 140. Although this may be strictly true from a legal perspective, it is a highly artificial interpretation of either the relative power of the Member States within the ITU or of their freedom to conduct international telecommunications activities outside the ITU regime.

[108] See Green Paper, COM (87) 290, app. 4, para. 3.3, p. 122 et seq.

[109] 91/C 233/02, para. 144.

[110] Telespeed Services Limited v United Kingdom Post Office, Commission Decision, 10 December 1982, 82/861/EEC, OJ L 360/36, 21 Dec. 1982; confirmed in Judgement of 20 Mar. 1985, Case 41/83, Italian Republic v Commission [1985] ECR 873 'British Telecom Case'.

[111] The British Telecom prohibition was in implementation of CCITT Recommendation F60 on Telex Operating Methods which provides:

administrations and recognised private operating agencies should refuse to take the telex service available to a telegraph forwarding agency which is known to be organised for the purpose of sending or receiving telegrams for retransmission by telegraphy with the view to evading the full charges due for the complete route. Administrations shall refuse to provide international telex service to a customer whose activity would be regarded as an infringement of the functions of an administration in providing a public telecommunications service. CCITT Recommendation F60, s 3.5.

Although British Telecom did not appeal against the Commission's decision, the matter was taken up by the Italian Government. Before the European Court of Justice, they argued that the Commission had failed to take into account:

1. that pre-existing rules of international law override EEC law;[113] and
2. that British Telecom was an undertaking entrusted with operations of services of general economic interest.[114]

The Commission had rejected the first argument on the basis that, by virtue of the revision and re-adoption of the ITU rules in 1973, they were not pre-existing obligations of the United Kingdom. The Court did not rule on that question, but decided the first issue against the Italian Government on the ground that British Telecom was under no obligation of international law to adopt this Recommendation. It interpreted the Recommendation as 'aimed solely to oppose the activities of message forwarding agencies which were "set up" or "known to be organised" with a view to evading the full charges due for the complete route'. The measures envisaged by those provisions could, therefore, affect only agencies which 'employed improper methods in an attempt to allow certain messages to escape the full charges due'.

The provisions relating to undertakings entrusted with the operation of services of general economic interest exempt certain undertakings from the application of the competition rules, if the application of the rules would otherwise act against the interests of the public.[115] The Court ruled that, although British Telecom was at the time an undertaking of the kind to which the provisions could apply, nevertheless,

> the legal form adopted by British telecommunications in order to prevent the retransmission of international telecommunications through the forwarding agencies poses no barrier to the applicability of Article 86 . . . The power confirmed on British Telecom to introduce schemes was strictly limited to those provisions which were designed to lay down a tariff and other conditions under which it performed services for users. That being so, the schemes referred to by the disputed decision must be regarded as an integral part of British Telecom's business activities.

A related issue is whether the application of competition rules would prevent British Telecom from performing the tasks which were assigned to it. In the case of British Telecom, the Commission found that the application of the competition rules 'does not obstruct the performance of its duties in an efficient and economic way. For British Telecom to be exempted, it is not sufficient that such compliance would make performance of its duties more complicated'. The Court upheld the Commission on this point also.

The Commission argues that the CCITT Recommendations are not legally binding and alternatively that TOs, and not the Member States, are themselves members of CCITT and therefore adherence to its Recommendations amounts to agreements between them.[116] Both these assertions are open to question. First, both the Telegraph[117] and the Telephone[118] Regulations specifically require that:

---

[112] Rome Treaty, Art. 86.
[113] Rome Treaty, Art. 234.
[114] Rome Treaty, Art. 90.
[115] Rome Treaty, Art 90; It is a matter for the Commission to decide when an exception to Article 90(2) applies, Eirpage Case, OJ L 306/22, 7 November 1991.
[116] 91/C 233/02, para. 143.
[117] Telegraph Regulations, Art. 1(1)(2).
[118] Ibid.

In implementing the principles of the Regulations, [TOs] should comply with the CCITT Recommendations, including any Instructions forming part of those Recommendations on any matter not covered by the Regulations.

Therefore, it can be argued that the CCITT Recommendations form part of the relevant Regulations and adherence to them is mandatory. The use of the word 'should' is not helpful, but not entirely detrimental to this argument.

Furthermore, CCITT Recommendations gain their force and validity through the ITU Convention and only gain validity and may be enforced through the States that are the members of the ITU. It should also be noted that Recognised Private Operating Agencies[119] have no automatic right to membership of CCITT and may only participate with the approval of the relevant ITU member.[120] Nevertheless, implementation of any Recommendations of the CCITT which are not compatible with the Community competition rules can be challenged by the Commission on the basis of state implementation[121] or as constituting acts of an 'Association of Undertakings'.[122]

International satellite organisations

All the international satellite agreements[123] were made long after the Rome Treaty and are, therefore, not subject to any exemption with regard to the competition rules, even as between Member States and Third Countries.[124] Many of the arrangements under the satellite Conventions, particularly those relating to co-ordination and access to the space segment are caught by the competition rules.[125] The international satellite organisations were created by arrangements between a number of governments but their operations are fully governed by the operating agreements made between the various TOs. Therefore, there is a stronger case for the direct application of the competition rules to the TOs by the Commission than might be the case with the CCITT Recommendations.

The Guidelines[126] set out the Commission's general approach in the field of satellites.[127] The Commission has issued a Green Paper on Satellite Communications[128] but a Directive is yet to come. Once it has issued a Directive on this area the position will become clearer. However, certain issues, such as direct access to space segment, covered in the satellite Green Paper, are being addressed by the ISOs[129] in discussion with the Commission.

---

[119] RPOA.
[120] ITU Convention, Art. 11(2)(b).
[121] Under Rome Treaty, Art. 90(1).
[122] 91/C 233/02, paras 143 and 144.
[123] Intelsat Convention, Eutelsat Agreement and Inmarsat Convention. Intelsat, Eutelsat and Inmarsat are together referred to as the International Satellite Organisations, 'ISOs'.
[124] Rome Treaty, Art. 234; 91/C 233/02, para. 140.
[125] Rome Treaty, Arts 85 and 86.
[126] 91/C 233/02, paras 122–8, 144.
[127] For further discussion see p. 65.
[128] Satellite Green Paper: Towards Europe-wide Systems and Services: Green Paper on a Common Approach in the Field of Satellite Communications in the European Community, COM (90) 490.
[129] For a discussion of these issues, see p. 67.

Standards organisations

It is clearly in the interest of Community competition that any standards adopted within the Community are as widely accepted as possible. Therefore, the Commission encourages standard setting activities for the Community which are based on other recognised international standards.[130] This is particularly true of the activities of CEPT.[131] The Community has entered into a Memorandum of Understanding establishing a framework for co-operation between the Community and the CEPT.[132] Under the MoU, in its annual working programme CEPT takes account of the requirements of the Commission, in consultation with the Senior Officials Group on Telecommunications.[133]

CEPT, following the MoU, established the Technical Recommendations Applications Committee[134] to determine a list of standards requested by the Commission, known as NETs.[135] In particular, NETs do not contain any clauses which may restrict competition.[136] CEPT has since established the European Telecommunications Standards Institute[137] in collaboration with and encouragement of the Commission.[138]

The level of influence of the Commission in the activities of CEPT was well illustrated by the alteration of a CEPT Recommendation. The relevant Recommendation[139] concerned principles for the leased international telecommunications circuits and the establishment of private international networks. One of the Recommendations was that a 30 per cent surcharge be made in relation to any Third Party traffic carried over such leased circuits.[140] The Commission took the view that the Recommendation amounted to a price agreement contrary to the competition rules,[141] substantially restricting competition within the Community. It therefore intervened with CEPT, which then decided to abolish the Recommendation.

---

[130] See p. 38.
[131] European Conference of Postal and Telecommunications Administrations founded on 26 June 1959.
[132] Signed in July 1984.
[133] SOG-T.
[134] TRAC.
[135] Normes Européennes des Télécommunications.
[136] CEPT has also reached agreement with CEN and CENELEC to avoid overlap between the work carried out by each.
[137] ETSI.
[138] See p. 39.
[139] PGT/10.
[140] See 91/C 233/02, para. 46.
[141] Rome Treaty, Art. 85.

CHAPTER 2
Competition in Terminal Equipment

HISTORIC BACKGROUND

Throughout the Community the TOs had a monopoly in the supply of terminal equipment as well as in the provision of networks and services.[1] As a result of this monopoly the terminal equipment market was in the gift of the TO which either manufactured such equipment itself or acquired it from a limited number of suppliers. CEPT was the appropriate framework for bringing about harmonisation of networks. Harmonisation would have lead to common definition of standards for connections, interface and equipment. But CEPT had been slow to act.[2] This monopoly was perpetuated in most countries by type approval procedures which were discriminatory and protectionist and they were invariably protracted and complex.[3] Another major obstacle to manufacturers wishing to market throughout Europe was that approval in one country was seldom considered valid in another.

As a first step towards achieving a common market in terminal equipment, the Commission proposed a structure for mutual recognition of type approval between Member States.

Type approval and mutual recognition

The proposal for the Council Directive on mutual recognition of type approval for terminal equipment was made together with the proposal for the Council Directive on standardisation in the field of information technology and telecommunications.[4] These proposals were made against the background of the Commission's communication on

---

[1] Commission's Communication to the Council of 18 May 1984 on telecommunications.
[2] The opinion of the European Parliament of 7 May 1981, OJ C 144/71, 15 June 1981, para. 3.
[3] The opinion of the European Parliament of 7 May 1981, OJ C 144/71, 15 June 1981, para. 22.
[4] OJ C 232, 19 Sept. 1985, pp. 9 and 3 respectively.

telecommunications,[5] which set out the thinking and initial proposals for an action programme in telecommunications. The action programme had three objectives:

1. to provide the users of telecommunications networks with the requisite equipment and services as soon as possible and at the lowest cost;
2. to stimulate the production of telecommunications equipment and services in the Community;
3. to enable carriers to expand their networks under optimum conditions and with minimum risk.

These objectives were to be achieved by:

1. breaking down the barriers between small-scale national markets;
2. dispelling carriers' and manufacturers' uncertainties with regard to development strategies in the other countries;
3. promoting basic technologies;
4. giving less favoured regions a boost.[6]

The special or exclusive rights relating to terminal equipment enjoyed by the TOs was exercised in such a way as, in practice, to disadvantage equipment from other Member States, notably by preventing users from freely choosing the equipment that best suited their needs in terms of price and quality, regardless of its origin. The exercise of such rights was clearly in contravention of the Treaty of Rome.[7]

The TOs also retained the monopoly in the installation and maintenance of equipment, which the Commission recognised as a key factor in purchasing and rental of terminal equipment.[8]

As providers of the national telecommunications network, the TOs held a dominant position and a substantial part of the market within the meaning of Article 86 of the Rome Treaty. Not surprisingly, the Commission was of the view that the effect of the special or exclusive rights granted to such dominant players in the market to import and market terminal equipment was to:

> restrict users to renting such equipment, when it would often be cheaper for them . . . to purchase this equipment. This effectively made contracts for the use of the network subject to acceptance by the user of additional services which had no connection with the subject of the contracts,
> limit outlets and impede technical progress since the range of equipment offered by the TOs was necessarily limited and would not be the best available to meet the requirements of a significant proportion of the users.[9]

This conduct of the TOs significantly affected trade between Member States and was clearly prohibited by the competition provisions of the Treaty.[10]

---

[5] See above.
[6] Opinion of the Economic and Social Committee, OJ C 303/2, 25 November 1985. The decision of the Court in the Télé-Marketing Case, 85/C 281/04, OJ C 281/4, 2 November 1985, significantly strengthened the band of the Commission by confirming the legal basis for liberalizing the terminal and the value added service markets.
[7] Art. 37, Commission Dir. 88/301/EEC, OJ L 131/73, 27 May 1988, para. 5.
[8] Commission Dir. 88/301/EEC, OJ L 131/73, 27 May 1988, para. 6.
[9] Commission Dir. 88/301/EEC, OJ L 131/73, 27 May 1988, Art. 13.
[10] Arts 86(b) and (d).

Harmonisation of standards

Clearly mutual recognition of type approvals would have little or no impact on the terminal equipment market within the Community, without at the same time ensuring that the Member States applied the same technical standards to such equipment. Therefore it was essential that the harmonisation of standards go hand in hand with any mutual recognition requirements. Therefore, the Commission combined its initial proposal for a Directive on mutual type approval with the proposal for a Directive on common standards in the field of information technology and telecommunications.[11] The Economic and Social Committee gave its full support to these initial proposals, although it did not believe that they went far enough to permanently dismantle the barriers between national markets within the Community.[12] The committee expressed the view that the Community's policy on telecommunications standardisation, as proposed by the Commission and set out in the proposed Directives, would remain a dead letter if the Member States did not act firmly to create the uniform technical standards which are a precondition of its implementation. It also recognised that mutual recognition of type approval of terminal equipment and their use throughout the Community was not possible without standardisation of the technical specifications for the national networks and without uniform standards.[13]

The creation of Community standards faced two difficulties. First, with the keen international competition in information technology, it was vital for Member States to develop Community-wide technology to create a large European market and put the industry in the favourable position to compete on the world market. It was also necessary to ensure that any standards would be as widely accepted as possible so as not to hinder the European industry in gaining access to the world market.[14]

To achieve these ends and in the absence of a Community Standards Institute the Commission made arrangements with CEPT and CEN/CENELEC.[15]

The Commission entered into a Memorandum of Understanding with the European Conference of Postal and Telecommunications Administrations[16] and has agreed general outlines with the European Committee for Standardisation[17] and the European Committee for Electrotechnical Standardisation[18] enabling the Commission to entrust to those bodies the specialised technical harmonisation where necessary.[19] Under the mechanism introduced,[20] there are formal adoption procedures for the implementation within the Community of certain CEPT Recommendations which are then designated as NETS.[21]

Another feature of the background to the Directive on mutual recognition of type approval was that a general standardisation programme was being implemented in the field of information technology in compliance with the Standards Code of the General

---

[11] Commission Standards Dir., 85/C 303/02, OJ C 232, 19 Sept. 1985, pp. 3 and 9.
[12] 85/C 303/02, par. 1.5. The committee also highlighted the connection between the proposed policies and public procurement contracts; see para. 1.5. This aspect will be considered further in Chap. 4.
[13] 85/C 303/02, paras 1.6, 2.1.
[14] 85/C 303/02, paras 2.2, 3.1.
[15] 85/C 232/04, p. 10.
[16] CEPT.
[17] CEN.
[18] CENELEC.
[19] 85/232/04, p. 10.
[20] Agreement drawn up at Copenhagen on 15 Nov. 1985.
[21] Normes de Télécommunications; C 86/361/EEC, OJ L 217/21, 5 Aug. 1986.

Agreement on Tariffs and Trade.[22] Also, an earlier Council Directive[23] which laid down a procedure for the provision of information in the field of technical standards and regulations is applicable to telecommunications and information technology.[24]

Initial Directive on type approval

One of the perceived advantages of mutual recognition and common standards was to make it possible for users to apply the best systems solutions to their telecommunications requirements. This would mean that users did not have to obtain all elements of the system from one supplier, bringing benefits of increased competition, optimised solutions and limiting the risk of the initial purchasing decision which in turn can stimulate the market.[25]

The Council Directive on mutual recognition of type approval,[26] in recognition of the different environment and technical and administrative constraints in Member States, was only the initial stage of the mutual recognition of type approval for terminal equipment.

The Directive sets out detailed rules which are applicable to mass produced telecommunications terminal equipment.[27] It requires Member States to implement mutual recognition of the results of tests of conformity with common conformity specifications.[28] The scope of the Directive in terms of equipment to which it applies is sufficiently broad to apply to a wide range of equipment. 'Terminal equipment' is defined as:

equipment directly or indirectly connected to the termination of a public telecommunications network to send, process or receive information.[29]

The Directive does not define 'public telecommunications network' which could lead to differing interpretations by Member States.[30] However, in practice this has not lead to any disparities in the Member States and there is slight assistance in the interpretation of the term contained in the definition of 'telecommunications administrations'.[31]

The Commission established the Working Party of Senior Officials on Telecommunications Committee[32] to assist the Commission to perform its functions under the Direc-

---

[22] GATT.

[23] 83/189/EEC, OJ L 109, 26 Apr. 1983, p. 8. See p. 59.

[24] 86/361/EEC, p. 21.

[25] 85/C 303/02, para. 1.7.

[26] Council Dir. of 24 July 1986 on the initial stage of the mutual recognition of type approval for telecommunications terminal equipment, 86/361/EEC, OJ L 217/21, 5 Aug. 1986.

[27] Art. 1.

[28] Art. 2(13); Common Conformity Specification means a conformity specification used in all the Community Member States by the authority competent for testing the conformity of terminal equipment, including requirements made necessary in a given Member State by historical network peculiarities or established national provisions concerning the use of radio frequencies. Art. 2(11) defines Conformity Specification as a document giving a precise and full description of the technical characteristics of the relevant terminal equipment . . . together with a precise definition of the tests and test methods enabling the conformity of the terminal equipment with the prescribed technical characteristics to be verified.

[29] Art. 2(2).

[30] A definition is provided in the later Directive of 29 Apr. 1991 on the approximation of the laws of the Member States concerning telecommunications terminal equipment, including the mutual recognition of their conformity, 91/263/EEC, OJ L 28/1, 23 May 1991, Art. 1(2).

[31] Art. 2(1), telecommunications administrations means the administrations or private operating agencies recognised in the Community in providing public telecommunications services.

[32] Art. 5.

tive.[33] The Commission, after consulting the Committee, each year draws up a list of international standards and technical specifications and a list of terminal equipment for which common conformity specifications need to be drawn up according to a timetable.[34] The Commission then requests CEPT to draw up such specifications in the form of NETs which are regarded as the equivalent of the common conformity specifications.[35]

Member States are required to use the common conformity specifications for any verification demanded for type approval purposes of the relevant terminal equipment with some minor exceptions.[36] Member States are also required to ensure that telecommunications administrations use common conformity specifications when purchasing terminal equipment for which the specifications apply, subject to specified exceptions.[37]

Therefore, the thrust of this initial stage towards liberalising the terminal equipment market was to obviate the need for multiple approvals to be obtained by manufacturers within the Community for terminal equipment which conformed to a NET. It was neither designed to nor achieved the abolition of the monopoly enjoyed by TOs in the provision of terminal equipment to end users. At the time of the publication of the Commission's Green Paper on telecommunications services and equipment[38] in ten of the twelve Member States the supply of the first telephone set was a monopoly of the network operator.[39] The only exceptions to this were France and the United Kingdom where a competitive market existed for the first telephone set.

The main task of the Commission with regard to terminal equipment has been one of co-ordinating, directing and encouraging the already established trend towards the full opening of the terminal market to competition. The technological evolution towards multi-function computer-based terminal equipment, including ISDN[40] terminals, further encouraged this trend. Nevertheless, the monopoly of the TO and the supply of terminal equipment, particularly the first telephone set, required particular attention from the Commission.[41]

The Commission proceeded with synchronising the existing move towards full competition in the terminal sector on the basis of the established legal framework. This consisted of the provisions of the Rome Treaty on the free movement of goods, the decisions taken on common standards and mutual recognition of type approval and on the opening of public procurement.

The elements making up this framework are:

1. the general surveillance and control function imposed by the Rome Treaty regarding the free movement of goods and the adjustment of state monopolies of a commercial character; in particular the Commission made clear that it would apply Articles 37 and 86 of the Treaty directly, as well as Article 90 in conjunction with Article 86 and use the means at its disposal under Article 90 (3) in support of increasing competition in the terminal equipment market;

---

[33] Art. 4(1).
[34] Ibid.
[35] Arts 4(2) and 6(1).
[36] Art. 6(3).
[37] Art. 7(4).
[38] COM (87) 290 final, 30 June 1987, Towards a Dynamic European Economy: Green Paper on the Development of the Common Market for Telecommunications Services and Equipment.
[39] Green Paper on telecommunications services and equipment, COM (87) 290 final, p. 61, para. 3. It should be noted that the provisions of the 1986 Directive on mutual recognition of type approval required compliance by Member States within a period of one year from its adoption which, by June 1987, had not yet expired; Art. 11, 86/361/EEC, OJ L 217/21 at 25.
[40] Integrated Services Digital Network.
[41] Green Paper on telecommunications services and equipment, COM (87) 290 final, p. 61 et seq.

2. this application of the Council Directives on the first phase of establishing mutual recognition of type approval for terminal equipment[42] and on standardisation in the field of information technology and telecommunications;[43]
3. the Community-wide definition of technical interfaces of the network with the subscriber terminal equipment, namely the Network Termination Points;[44]
4. application of Council Recommendation on opening bidding for a proportion of the supply contracts awarded by TOs to suppliers in other Member States.[45]

The Commission identified three specific measures to achieve the transition towards a Community-wide competitive terminal equipment market. These measures were:

1. clear definition of NTPs to assist in fixing the conditions under which the network infrastructure is provided by the TOs to users and to competitive service providers;[46]
2. extension of the Directive on mutual recognition of type approval[47] to full recognition of type approval;
3. broadening the Recommendation on procurement by TOs[48] to a binding Directive on terminal equipment to establish full transparency and Community-wide opening of procurement by TOs in the terminal market.

These proposals, although further advancing competition in the terminal equipment market, did nothing to expand the market to end users. In other words, Member States continued to preserve the monopoly of the TOs in the supply of certain terminal equipment, particularly the first telephone. An essential element of extension of the market to end users was the right of the user to have access to NTPs.

Having established the groundwork and prepared Member States and their TOs for further and fuller opening of the terminal equipment market, the Commission made further proposals in this regard in 1988.[49] The Commission based its proposals on the overriding aim of achieving the Internal Market before the end of 1992 and the obligation fully to apply the provisions of the Treaty of Rome to the telecommunications sector. It proposed a number of measures for rapid full opening of the terminal equipment market to competition.[50]

The proposals for achieving this objective were:

---

[42] 86/361/EEC, adopted by the Council on 9 June 1986, OJ L 217/21, 5 Aug. 1986.

[43] 87/95/EEC, adopted by the Council on 22 Dec. 1986, OJ L 36/31, 7 Feb. 1987.

[44] NTP. It will be noted that NTPs were not defined in Dir. 86/361/EEC, but there are guidelines on this point in Council Recommendation 86/659/EEC on the co-ordinated introduction of ISDN, OJ L 382/36, 31 Dec. 1986.

[45] 84/550/EEC, OJ L 298/51, 16 Nov. 1984. The Recommendation provides for an experimental period during which network operators will give unrestricted access to the calls for all new terminals and for 10% by value of their total annual orders of Conventional terminal equipment.

[46] This formed the basis for the introduction of the Open Network Provision ('ONP'), which is discussed in Chap. 7.

[47] 86/361/EEC, OJ L 217/21, 5 Aug. 1986.

[48] 84/550/EEC, OJ L 298/51, 16 Nov. 1984.

[49] Towards a Competitive Community-wide Telecommunications Market in 1992 – Implementing the Green Paper on the Development of the Common Market for Telecommunications Services and Equipment, COM (88) 48 final, 9 February 1988. Another significant step of general application by the Commission relates to the requirement of transparency of relations between Member States and their public undertakings. This requirement is a theme that runs through the telecommunications policy of information gathering and was established in The Commission v Italian Republic, Case 118/85, 87/C 118/07, OJ C 118/5, 9 July 1987, where the Italian government's refusal to provide information about Amministrazionne Autonoma dei Monopoli di Stato was held to contravene Article 5(2).

[50] COM (88) 48 final, p. 16.

to ensure unrestricted provision of terminal equipment within Member States and between Member States and in competition with the TOs, subject only to type approval. The timetable for this was targeted for the end of 1990 at the latest, which would allow a sufficient transition period for all equipment, including the first telephone set. The Commission proposed to issue a Directive under Article 90 (3) before the end of March 1988.[51]

It was intended that the Commission would, in parallel, propose a Directive on full mutual recognition of type approvals before the end of 1988, extending the progressive introduction of NETs.[52] To achieve a competitive market in terminal equipment it is not sufficient to have mutual recognition of type approval and fair approval procedures.[53] It is also necessary to enable manufacturers to provide suitable connectors for connection of the equipment to network termination points. Therefore, the Commission imposed compulsory supply of a suitable NTP to TO customers on request. Additionally the physical characteristics of the NTPs would need to be published for the benefit of manufacturers.[54]

COMPETITION IN THE MARKETS IN TELECOMMUNICATIONS TERMINAL EQUIPMENT

The Directive[55] on competition in the markets in telecommunications terminal equipment was issued by the Commission on 16 May 1988 in exercise of its powers under Article 90 (3) of the Rome Treaty.[56] This Directive established a timetable[57] for the withdrawal of special or exclusive rights granted to an entity for the importation, marketing, connection, bringing into service or maintenance of telecommunications terminal equipment.[58] Other than the dates specified for the withdrawal of such rights, the Directive envisages a period of two and a half years[59] and establishes a means of monitoring progress in this regard.[60]

---

[51] The challenge to the Commission's use of Art. 90(3) for this purpose is discussed in Chap. 1.
[52] The proposal for rapid extension of Dir. 86/361/EEC to include full mutual recognition of type approval was said by the Commission to have found universal backing; COM (88) 48 final, p. 20. In the event Council Directive 91/263/EEC on mutual recognition of conformity was adopted on 29 Apr. 1991; OJ L 128/1, 23 May 1991.
[53] The Commission required that fair approval procedures involve complication of such procedures and appropriate cost and time required for completion of the procedures.
[54] This is a requirement under Dir. 88/301/EEC, Art. 4.
[55] Commission Dir. on Competition in the Markets in Telecommunications Terminal Equipment, 88/301/EEC of 16 May 1988, OJ L 131/73, 27 May 1988.
[56] 88/301/EEC, OJ L 131/73, 27 May 1988, para. 1 at 73 and Art. 11 at 76. For the challenge to the exercise of Art. 90 powers by the Commission in the circumstances see Chap. 00. Art. 90 of the Treaty provides:
  1. In the case of public undertakings and undertakings to which Member States grant special or exclusive rights, Member States shall neither enact nor maintain in force any measure contrary to the rules contained in this Treaty, in particular to those rules provided for in Art. 7 and Arts 85–94.
  2. Undertakings entrusted with the operation of services of general economic interest having the character of a revenue-producing monopoly shall be subject to the rules contained in this Treaty, in particular to the rules on competition, in so far as the application of such rules does not obstruct the performance, in law or in fact, of the particular tasks assigned to them. The development of trade must not be affected to such an extent as would be contrary to the interests of the Community.
  3. The Commission shall ensure the application of the provisions of this Art. and shall, where necessary, address appropriate Directives or Decisions to Member States.
[57] Art. 2.
[58] Art. 1. For the validity of the Commission's measures to curtail 'special rights' see France v Commission, Case 202/88 and p. 13.
[59] OJ L 131 at 75, para. 16.
[60] Art. 9.

The requirement to withdraw special or exclusive rights to service or maintain equipment is motivated both by breaking the link between installation and maintenance services and the marketing of terminal equipment, which is seen as an important factor,[61] as well as removing the monopoly in the provision of such services themselves.[62] Another important feature of the Directive is to enable customers to terminate long-term contracts for maintenance services which may have been imposed by the monopoly provider.[63]

Member States were also required to ensure that from 1 July 1989 type approval and the drawing up of specifications for terminal equipment was entrusted to a body independent of undertakings which offered telecommunications goods or services.[64] A timetable was established for drawing up of specifications and publication of type approval procedures for terminal equipment, including the first telephone set.[65]

The Directive requires that users are given access to any public network termination points and that the characteristics of these NTPs are published.[66]

The Directive gives a broad definition of 'terminal equipment'.[67] This extends to computers and other terminals which are directly connected to the NTP or where the connection is indirect, for example through a modem. The Directive also covers receive-only satellite earth stations which are not *reconnected* to the public network. This inclusion means a receive only satellite earth station may be connected to the public telecommunications network if it receives signals from a satellite dish that forms a part of the public network.[68] Otherwise a reconnection would be made.

HARMONISATION AND MUTUAL RECOGNITION OF CONFORMITY OF TELECOMMUNICATIONS TERMINAL EQUIPMENT

The establishment of a competitive Community market in terminal equipment is, clearly, dependent on extensive mutual recognition of type approval between Member States.[69] The Council in its Resolution on development of the common market for telecommunications services and equipment up to 1992[70]identified as a major policy goal in telecommunications policy 'developing further an open, Community-wide market for terminal equipment; for this purpose reaching agreement quickly on full mutual recognition of type-approval for terminal equipment, on the basis of the rapid development of common European conformity specifications'.[71] The intention of the Council is that the harmonising conditions for placing on the market of telecommunications terminal equipment will create the conditions for an open and unified market and envisages bilateral talks between the Community and other countries and that multilateral negotiations within GATT will contribute to access to third country markets by Community manufacturers.

[61] OJ L 131 at 73, para. 6.

[62] Such restrictions on the freedom to provide services are contrary to Art. 59 of the Rome Treaty; see OJ L 131 at 74, para. 7.

[63] Para. 18 and Art. 7.

[64] Art. 6.

[65] Arts 5 and 8 and Annex I. In other case of first telephone sets this had to be achieved by 30 June 1990.

[66] Para. 14 and Art. 4.

[67] Art. 1.

[68] A connection may be made electromagnetically, as well as by wire or optical fibre; Art. 1.

[69] Dir. 88/301/EEC, Arts 5 and 8, established a regime for type approval. However, it does not address the issue of mutual recognition, which is required to speed up the marketing of any new equipment throughout the Community.

[70] 88/C 257/01 of 30 June 1988, OJ C 257/1, 4 October 1988.

[71] 88/C 257/01, para. 4. This Directive follows on from Dir. 86/361/EEC, OJ L 217/21, 5 Aug. 1986, and supersedes that Directive from 6 Nov. 1992 (Art. 16).

To allow for technical development of products the 1991 Council Directive[72] gives a more general definition of *'terminal equipment'*.[73] In particular, instead of referring to *indirect connection* to the termination of a public telecommunications network, there is a reference to *'interwork with a public telecommunications network being connected directly or indirectly to the termination of a public telecommunications network'*.[74] As envisaged in the earlier Directive,[75] this Directive expands on the *'essential requirements'*. These are the common conformity specifications of such importance that necessitate compliance as a matter of legal obligation for the implementation of the mutual recognition of results and conformity tests on terminal equipment as an integral part of the type approval procedure.[76]

The European Parliament took the view that the safeguard clause for the Member States provided in the proposed Directive[77] on mutual recognition of type approval, could weaken or nullify entirely the effect of the Directive and that such a clause would create uncertainty in industry about the status of common specifications.[78] On this basis and in view of the fact that the safety of users was already covered by the 1973 Directive on low voltage equipment[79] and the ability of Member States to ensure safety and inter-operability through participation in the senior officials committee for telecommunications, Parliament decided to delete the proposed provision.[80]

---

[72] Council Directive on the approximation of the laws of the Member States concerning Telecommunications Terminal Equipment, including the Mutual Recognition of their Conformity, 91/263/EEC of 29 Apr. 1991, OJ l 128/1, 23 May 1991.
[73] Art. 1(2).
[74] Ibid.; compare with 86/361/EEC, Art. 2(2).
[75] 86/361/EEC, Art. 2(17).
[76] 91/263/EEC, Art. 4.
[77] Art. 7.
[78] 91/263/EEC, Art. 7, Opinion of the economic and social committee, 85/C 303/02, OJ C 303/2, 25 Nov. 1985, paras 13 and 16.
[79] 73/23/EEC.
[80] Opinion of the economic and social committee, 85/C 303/02, OJ C 303/2, 25 Nov. 1985, paras 14, 15 and 17.

CHAPTER 3
Competitive Procurement Requirements

HISTORICAL BACKGROUND

The early procurement requirements[1] in the Community did not extend to the telecommunications sector.[2] The main reason for this was that it was considered necessary to avoid subjecting the production, distribution and transmission, and telecommunications services contract to different supply systems, depending on whether they came under the State, regional or local authorities, or other legal persons governed by public law, or whether they had separate legal personalities. Therefore, these sectors were excluded from the application of the general procurement Directive until a final solution could be adopted in the light of experience. It was not until 1990 that the competitive procurement procedures were fully applied to the telecommunications sector.[3]

Application of procurement rules

The solution arrived at to ensure the real opening of the market and achieving of balance in the application of procurement rules to the telecommunications, and the other sectors mentioned, was to identify the relevant entities on a basis other than by reference to their legal status.[4] The solution arrived at was to apply the rules to entities which conducted certain activities,[5] which included the provision for operation of public telecommunications networks or the provision of public telecommunications services.[6] This, however, excludes television and radio broadcasting entities.[7]

---

[1] See 90/531/EEC, recitals 6 and 7.
[2] See in particular Dir. 77/62/EEC, Art. 2.
[3] Council Dir. of 17 Sept. 1990 on the procurement procedures of entities operating in the water, energy, transport and telecommunications sectors, 90/531/EEC, OJ L 297/1, 29 Oct. 1990.
[4] 90/531/EEC, recital 9.
[5] 90/531/EEC, Art. 2(1)(b).
[6] 90/531/EEC, Art. 2(2)(d).
[7] 90/531/EEC, Art. 1(14).

The procurement procedures broadly requires that in awarding contracts there is no discrimination between suppliers or contractors.[8] Telecommunications entities frequently enter into framework agreements with their suppliers and contractors setting out the terms, including prices, likely quantities and other terms[9] under which specific contracts are awarded to the supplier or contractor. Where the framework agreement conforms to the requirements of the procurement procedures,[10] the contracts awarded under the framework agreement need not themselves conform to the procurement requirements.[11]

There are detailed procedures dealing with the award of contracts,[12] including time limits for providing contract documents and information,[13] selection of contractor or supplier and the award of contracts.[14] There are arrangements for telecommunications entities to specify and publicise technical specifications and standards used by them in contracts.[15] In the interests of fair competition, all negotiations with specific candidates or tenderers that are likely to distort competition are prohibited.[16]

The procurement Directive also includes numerous provisions for the communication of information to the Commission in order that progress and compliance with the Directive may be monitored.

Scope

The requirements of the Directive also do not apply to contracts awarded for the purposes of resale or hire to third parties, as long as the telecommunications entity does not enjoy special or exclusive rights in relation to the resale or hire.[17] Nor do they apply where the services in relation to which the procurement is made are open to competition,[18] or which are made pursuant to certain international agreements or arrangements.[19]

The procurement procedures and requirements apply only to contracts above specified values.[20] There are specific rules for determining the value of contract so as to prevent evasion by spreading supplies over a number of contracts.[21]

Enforcement

Although the procurement Directives[22] establishes procurement procedures aimed at ensuring fair competition in supplies and contracts in the telecommunications sector, there are no adequate enforcement procedures to ensure its effective application. Conse-

---

[8]   90/531/EEC, Art. 4.
[9]   Such agreements are referred to in the Directive as 'framework agreements', 90/531/EEC, Art. 1(4).
[10]   90/531/EEC, Art. 5(2).
[11]   90/531/EEC, Art. 5(2),(3) and 15(2)(i).
[12]   90/531/EEC, Arts 15–23.
[13]   90/531/EEC, Art. 21.
[14]   90/531/EEC, Arts 24–9.
[15]   90/531/EEC, Arts 13 and 14.
[16]   Statement concerning Art. 15 of Dir. 90/531/EEC, OJ L 297/48, 29 Oct. 1990.
[17]   90/531/EEC, Art. 7.
[18]   90/531/EEC, Art. 8.
[19]   90/531/EEC, Art. 11.
[20]   90/531/EEC, Art. 12.
[21]   Ibid.
[22]   90/521/EEC.

quently, Council introduced measures[23] to ensure that the procurement rules were effectively applied by Member States. In its opinion on the Directive[24] co-ordinating the laws, regulations and administrative provisions relating to the application of procurement procedures to the award of public supply and public works contracts, the Economic and Social Committee[25] pointed out the need for means to ensure implementation of such procedures.

In particular, the ESC highlighted the need for an enforcement Directive which would provide for:[26]

1. co-operation between the Commission and Member States on establishing uniform provisions regarding time limits, penalty payments and administrative procedures;
2. Commission powers to impose sanctions as of those to be given to the national authorities under the enforcement of the Directive; and
3. some form of arbitration machinery set up at Community level to avoid systematic recourse to the highly cumbersome procedure of the Court of Justice.

Implementation Directive

The implementation Directive[27] largely achieves these objectives. The implementation Directive introduces a degree of Community-wide harmonisation[28] in the currently widely differing remedies available in Member States. These concern rules of access to remedies by persons having[29] an interest in obtaining a particular contract who have been[30] harmed by alleged infringement. In particular, Member States are required to ensure that fundamental guarantees offered by different national systems are equivalent in effect,[31] while allowing Member States sufficient latitude in the practical implementation of the requirements to accord with their administrative and judicial systems.[32]

The implementation Directive provides alternative enforcement provisions for:[33]

1. a speedy hearing of urgent cases in the shape of interim measures to halt alleged infringements; and
2. setting aside unlawful decisions and removing discriminatory technical and economic specifications in the invitation to tender.

There are provisions for the award of damages and the Member States are free, in cases where a contract has already been concluded following an unlawful award, to confine remedies to damages only.[34] This has the merit of removing uncertainty where a late

---

[23] Council Dir. of 25 Feb. 1992 co-ordinating the laws, regulations and administrative provisions relating to the application of Community rules on the procurement procedures of entities operating in the water, energy, transport and telecommunications sectors, 92/13/EEC, OJ L 76/14, 23 Mar. 1992.

[24] 89/669/EEC.

[25] ESC.

[26] See opinion of the ESC on the proposal for a Council Directive co-ordinating the laws, regulations and administrative provision relating to the application of Community rules of the procurement procedures of entities operating in the water, energy, transport and telecommunications sectors, 91/C 60/06, OJ C 60/16, 8 Mar. 1991.

[27] 92/13/EEC.

[28] Ibid., Art. 1.

[29] Or having had.

[30] Or risk being.

[31] 92/13/EEC, Art. 1(2) and (3).

[32] 91/C 60/06, para. 4.

[33] 92/13/EEC, Art. 2(1).

[34] 92/13/EEC, Art. 1(6).

claim of infringement is made. Where claims for damages relating to the cost of preparing a bid are made, the claimant only need show that the infringement had vastly affected his chances of being awarded the contract and not that he would have been awarded the contract in the absence of the infringement.[35]

A form of prior approval, referred to as attestation,[36] should be made available, whereby Member States give contracting entities the opportunity of having their procurement procedures investigated and approved periodically.

The Directive[37] provides for a corrective mechanism whereby the Commission is entitled to intervene and enforce compliance with Community procurement procedures during a contract award process.

The conciliation procedure[38] is open to any person who has[39] an interest in obtaining a particular contract within the scope of the Directive and who has been[40] harmed by alleged infringements.[41] The conciliation procedure is voluntary[42] and the parties must agree to submit to a conciliator appointed in consultation with the Advisory Committee of Telecommunications Procurement.[43]

Member States are required to comply with the implementation Directive by 1 January 1993.[44] However, Spain, Greece and Portugal have been given extensions for compliance.[45]

---

[35] 92/13/EEC, Art. 2(7).
[36] 92/13/EEC, Arts 3–7.
[37] 92/13/EEC, Art. 8.
[38] 92/13/EEC, Arts 9–11.
[39] Or has had.
[40] Or risks being.
[41] 92/13/EEC, Art. 9.
[42] 92/13/EEC, Art. 10(1).
[43] 92/13/EEC, Art. 13.
[44] Spain, 30 June 1995; Greece and Portugal, 30 June 1997.

CHAPTER 4
European Telecommunications Standards

HISTORICAL BACKGROUND

Although on an international level technical standards are an essential ingredient of inter-operability of telecommunications systems, they assume an even greater significance in the context of the European Community. The impact of Community-wide standards on terminal equipment has already been discussed.[1] Uniform technical specifications are central to the operation of mutual type approval between Member States and to the development of a single European market to provide a strong domestic base for European manufacturers. Community-wide standards are also central to the operation of competitive procurement policies[2] in the infrastructure equipment market. In addition, for a truly competitive market to develop in telecommunication services, the infrastructure and terminal equipment in Member States need to operate to the same specified technical standards.

The Commission, in its proposal for a Directive on standardisation,[3] underlined in particular the impact of standardisation on mutual recognition of type approval and public sector procurement. The proposal for the standardisation Directive was made at the same time and coupled with the proposal for the Directive on mutual recognition of type approvals for terminal equipment.[4] The two draft Directives form a part of a comprehensive Community policy aimed at the gradual creation of a harmonised internal

---

[1] Chap. 3. See also generally The Commission v International Business Machines Corporation (IBM) and the resulting IBM undertaking relating to System/370 and to Systems Network Architecture, SNA, accepted by the Commission on 1 August 1984, Bull. EC 10-1984, point 3.4.1, [1984] 3 CMLR 147. The IBM Case is also important for the fact that the Commission made clear that it would review the conduct of private enterprises with the same vigour as administrations of Member States, to prevent abuse of dominant positions.

[2] See para. p. 34.

[3] COM (85) 230 final, 85/C 232/03, OJ C 232/3, 12 Sept. 1985, proposal for a Council Directive on standardisation in the field of information technology and telecommunications, submitted by the Commission to the Council on 30 May 1985.

[4] 85/C 232/09, OJ C 232/9, 19 Sept. 1985.

market in information technology products and the linking up of national telecommunications networks. The proposed Directive on mutual recognition of type approval was an important addition to the proposed Directive on standardisation in connection with public networks, and the standards which relate to that activity. Therefore, the two draft Directives cannot be seen in isolation.[5]

In the Economic and Social Committee's view the telecommunications policies of the Community and the Member States, and the Commission's proposals for telecommunications and of the standardisation of mutual recognition Directives, are interdependent. For the policy on telecommunications standardisation to work, Member States were called on to act firmly to create the uniform technical standards which are a precondition of its implementation.[6] The Committee was keen to see Member States take improvement measures, by developing technology on a Community scale to create a large market, to ensure that European industry is competitive on the world market. To this end and to create a single market the creation of uniform standards was seen as vital. In particular the Committee endorsed the Commission's remark that standards have to be laid down at an international level with worldwide recognition if possible, to prevent the Community's being isolated from world markets.[7]

The Committee also expressed its view that the ground must be prepared immediately for the strategic decisions which will pave the way for further advances and lead to the establishment of optical-fibre-based broadband ISDNs.[8]

The European Parliament welcomed the proposal for a Directive on standardisation and approved the pragmatic approach adopted in the proposal, making use of existing technical institutions,[9] CEN, CENELEC and CEPT, to formulate European standards on the basis of international standards, and where known international standards exist to formulate European standards which would be valid throughout the Community.[10]

The European Parliament considered it an absolute minimum requirement that the European standards for information technology and common specifications for telecommunications formulated on the basis of the proposal in the Directive be used as a reference for public procurement contracts originated by the Community institutions and the Member States.[11]

While proceeding with standardisation in general the Council was also making Recommendations on the adoption of standards for ISDN.[12]

Council Directive for the provision of information in the field of technical standards and regulations

The harmonisation of standards within the Community is clearly a continuing task. It is, therefore, impossible for the Commission ever to reach a position where there is no room for Member States to introduce divergent technical standards in relation to goods or services. The impact of divergent standards on the movement of goods and provision of

---

[5] Opinion of the economic and social committee, 85/C 303/02, OJ C 303/2, 25 Nov. 1985, para. 1.1.
[6] Opinion of the economic and social committee, 85/C 303/02, OJ C 303/2, 25 Nov. 1985, para. 1.6.
[7] 85/C 303/02, OJ C 303/2, 25 Nov. 1985, paras 2.2 and 3.1.
[8] 85/C 303/02, OJ C 303/2, 25 Nov. 1985, paras 3.6; Integrated Services Digital Network ('ISDN').
[9] The formation and work of ETSI is discussed in Chap. 5.
[10] Resolution of 14 Jan. 1986. Document A 2-176/85, OJ C 36/55, 17 Feb. 1986.
[11] Opinion of the economic and social committee, 85/C 303/02, OJ C 303/2, 25 Nov. 1985, para. 3.
[12] Council Recommendation 86/659/EEC, OJ L 382/36, 31 Dec. 1986.

services within the Community is self-evident and has already been discussed.[13] In order that the Commission may prevent the creation of such barriers as well as keeping itself informed of the areas in which technical standards need to be defined and harmonised, a framework[14] has been established for the exchange of information on standards within the Community.

Under the Directive for the provision of information on technical standards and regulations,[15] standards organisations within Member States are obliged to inform the Commission and other Member States standards bodies,[16] as well as CEN and CEN-ELEC, of their programmes relating to standards[17] and of any new draft standards.[18]

Where a Member State proposes the introduction of new standards, the Commission and other Member States have the opportunity to comment on those standards and request a European standard to be established.[19] Pending the establishment of such standard, the national standard body is prevented from introducing a new standard[20] with some exceptions relating to urgent matters[21] and where a European standard is not established within certain time limits.[22] These rules correspond to similar provisions of the ETSI Procedures.[23]

COUNCIL DECISION ON STANDARDISATION

The Commission's proposal for the Council Directive on standardisation[24] was in the event issued as a Council Decision of 22 December 1986.[25] The Decision establishes terms of reference for work on standardisation to be undertaken at an early stage by CEPT, CEN and CENELEC.[26] The Decision seeks to establish necessary procedures before the creation and adoption of the necessary standards and introduces the provisions needed for the implementation of Community policy on standardisation in the fields of information technology and telecommunications.[27] The Decision establishes a new advisory committee to assist the Commission in pursuing and managing the objectives and activities laid down by the Decision, the Senior Officials Group on Standardisation of Information Technology consisting of representatives appointed by the Member States

---

[13] See p. 37.

[14] Council Directive of 29 March 1983 laying down a Procedure for the Provision of Information in the Field of Technical Standards and Regulations, 83/189/EEC, OJ L 109/8, 26 Apr. 1983.

[15] 83/189/EEC.

[16] These bodies are identified in an Annex to Dir. 83/189/EEC, last amended in May 1990 by Commission Decision, 90/230/EEC, OJ L 128/15, 18 May 1990.

[17] 83/189/EEC, Art. 2.

[18] 83/189/EEC, Art. 4.

[19] 83/189/EEC, Art. 6.

[20] 83/189/EEC, Art. 7.

[21] 83/189/EEC, Art. 9.

[22] 83/189/EEC, Art. 7.

[23] See p. 45 et seq.

[24] COM (85) 230 final, 85/C 232/03, OJ C 232/C, 12 Sept. 1985.

[25] Council Decision of 22 Dec. 1986 on standardisation in the field of information technology and telecommunications, 87/95/EEC, OJ L 36/31, 7 Feb. 1987.

[26] This work is undertaken by CEPT under the Memorandum of Understanding with the Commission, and by CEN/CENELEC in the context of approved general guidelines; see 87/95/EEC, OJ L 36/31, 7 Feb. 1987 at 31.

[27] The standardisation Dir. 83/189/EEC, OJ L 109/8, 26 April 1983, does not contain all such provisions; see 87/95/EEC, OJ L 36/31, 7 February 1987, preamble at 31.

and entrusts the same function for telecommunication issues to the Senior Officials Group for Telecommunications.[28]

The specific objectives of the Decision are set out under the Decision itself.[29] They are broadly the integration of the Community market and improving international competitiveness of Community manufacturers. They include facilitating the exchange of information within the Community by promoting compatible and precise standards[30] and ensuring that users' requirements are taken into account.[31]

The Decision came into application on 7 February 1988[32] and covers:

1. European standards, European pre-standards, international standards accepted in the relevant Member State[33] and, in certain cases,[34] draft international standards[35] in the field of information technology; and
2. functional specifications[36] for services offered over public telecommunications networks specifically for exchange of information and data between information technology systems.[37]

The Decision does not cover technical specifications for terminal equipment connected to the public telecommunications network,[38] nor specifications for new equipment forming any part of the telecommunications networks.[39]

The circumstances in which these standards are applied are:

1. in public procurement orders;[40] and
2. in cases where exchange of information and data is made between information technology systems which use the standards referred to,[41] through public telecommunication networks. For such services specifically intended functional specifications must be used for the means of access.[42]

In certain circumstances departures from the requirements of the Decision are permitted,[43] such as contracts of a value lower than 100,000 ecu,[44] as long as the equipment purchased under such contracts does not prevent the use of the specified standards in contracts of greater value.[45] The ONP requirements also help ensure inter-operability.[46]

---

[28] Art. 7; the Senior Officials Group for Telecommunications (SOG-T) is established under Art. 5 of Directive 86/361/EEC. SOG-T was set up by the Council on 4 Nov. 1983.
[29] 87/95/EEC, OJ L 36/31, 7 Feb. 1987, Annex, para. 1.
[30] 87/95/EEC, Art. 3, Annex 1(c).
[31] 87/95/EEC, Annex (d).
[32] 87/95/EEC, Art. 10.
[33] For the purposes of information technology the relevant Member State is one whose contracting authority is making a public procurement order to which Art. 5 applies.
[34] Member States have an option of referring to draft international standards which would be suitable as the basis for the exchange of information and data for systems' inter-operability; 87/95/EEC, Art. 5(4).
[35] 87/95/EEC, Arts 3(2) and 5(1).
[36] For the definitions of European standard, European pre-standards, international standard, draft international standard and functional specification and other definitions, see 87/95/EEC, Art. 1.
[37] 87/95/EEC, Art. 3(2).
[38] These are covered by Dir. 86/361/EEC.
[39] 87/95/EEC, Art. 3(3).
[40] 87/95/EEC, Art. 5(1).
[41] See p. 38 above.
[42] 87/95/EEC, Art. 5(2).
[43] See 87/95/EEC, Art. 5(3).
[44] This threshold will be reviewed in 1992; 87/95/EEC, Art. 5(7).
[45] Notice 87/95/EEC, Art. 5(7).
[46] See p. 71 et seq.

In order to prepare and apply the standards there is a procedure laid out in the Decision, including the regular determination of priorities for standardisation requirements.[47]

The definition of standards for the telecommunications infrastructure itself form a part of the open network provision requirements[48] which was the subject of a subsequent Directive introduced in June 1990.[49]

MOBILE RADIO COMMUNICATIONS

Under its policy, to bring about both a Community market in telecommunications services and to utilise telecommunication networks for the economic development of the Community, the Commission has made a number of Recommendations. In October 1990 it recommended the co-ordinated introduction of pan-European land-based public radio paging.[50] At that time ETSI had been developing specifications for an advanced public radio paging system known as ERMES[51] which the Council wished to see used to establish a pan-European paging service.[52] The Recommendation envisages the service to commence at the end of 1992 and extend in coverage to at least 80 per cent of the population in each Member State by January 1997.[53] However, there are no specific standards specified in the Recommendation save for the frequency band range to be used.[54] The Recommendation specifies the requirement as to efficient use of the spectrum,[55] access to the system and outlines for the receiver specifications, radio subsystem, system implementation and the service and facilities which should be supported by the system.[56] The Recommendation also addresses tariff considerations.[57]

In 1987 the Council[58] effectively recommended the adoption of the GSM[59] for the public pan-European cellular digital land-based mobile communication systems,[60] defining the frequency bands[61] within which the systems should operate.[62] The Recommendation set a timetable for specification of different features of the systems, although at that stage choice of transmission system was already agreed by Member States to be based on

---

[47] 87/95/EEC, Art. 2.

[48] See Chapter 7, p. 71 et seq.

[49] The introduction of ONP was one of the proposed positions in the White Paper towards a competitive Community-wide telecommunications market in 1992, COM (88) February 1988, Figure 1 and pp. 12, 18 and 19.

[50] Council Recommendation on the coordinated introduction of pan-European land-based public radio paging in the Community, 90/543/EEC, OJ L 310/23, 9 November 1990.

[51] European Radio Messaging System.

[52] As defined in para. 1 of the Recommendation 90/543/EEC at 26.

[53] 90/543/EEC, Annex, para. 7 at 27.

[54] It is recommended that the system be suitable for operation over the frequency band range 169.4 MHz to 169.8 MHz with 25 KHz radio channels; 90/543/EEC, Annex, para. 1 at 26.

[55] Spectrum usage and grade of service should be comparable to systems based on CCIR radio paging code number 1 (Pocsag).

[56] 90/543/EEC, Annex, paras 1–5.

[57] 90/543/EEC, Annex, para. 6.

[58] Council of the European Communities.

[59] Group Speciale Mobile.

[60] Council Recommendation of 25 June 1987 on the co-ordinated introduction of public pan-European cellular digital land-based mobile communications in the Community, 87/371/EEC, OJ L 196/81, 17 July 1987.

[61] 890–915 MHz and 935–960 MHz.

[62] 87/371/EEC, Annex, para. 1 at 83.

GSM.[63] The timetable for the introduction of the systems was set for 1991 at the latest, with coverage of major urban areas by 1993 and establishment of links between these areas by 1995 at the latest.[64] The Recommendation also addressed tariff considerations.[65]

Closely allied with the GSM standard, ETSI was concurrently developing the European Telecommunications Standard[66] for Digital European Cordless Telecommunications,[67] greatly enhancing the possibilities of cordless telecommunications.[68] Therefore, the Council issued the Recommendation[69] on the co-ordinated introduction of DECT. The Council recommended that the Commission should encourage the completion of the specifications and introduction and exploitation of DECT technology and prepare a long-term strategy for the evolution of digital systems in an environment which was developing towards universal personal communications systems.[70]

As with other Recommendations in this area, the DECT Recommendations identify the frequency band which should be available for DECT[71] as well as other general characteristics of the standard, including tariff considerations.[72] However, the timetable for the introduction of DECT technology is only generally defined, requiring progressive availability of technology from the end of 1992.[73]

UNIFORM NUMBERING SYSTEMS

As the Community draws together, and relocations as well as business and private travel between Member States increase, it is clearly desirable to harmonise certain telecommunications features. Perhaps motivated more by social considerations than economic and market-related factors, the Commission wishes to minimise numbering differences in certain services provided by the telecommunications system. Notably, the Commission has taken steps to harmonise the international access code as well as emergency call numbers within Member States.[74]

EMERGENCY CALL NUMBER

A single emergency call number has long been advocated by CEPT.[75] The Council adopted number 112 recommended by CEPT, as the single European emergency call number.[76] The Council Decision does not call for the adoption of 112 as the only emergency number and Member States may continue to use their current national

---

[63] Agreement made in May 1987; 87/731/EEC, Annex, para. 2 at 83.

[64] 87/731/EEC, Annex, para. 8 at 84.

[65] 87/731/EEC, Annex, para. 7.

[66] ETS.

[67] DECT.

[68] 91/288/EEC, OJ L 144/47, 8 June 1991.

[69] Council Recommendation of 3 June 1991 on the co-ordinated introduction of digital European cordless telecommunications (DECT) into the Community, 91/288/EEC, OJ L 144/47, 8 June 1991.

[70] 91/288/EEC, OJ L 144/47, 8 June 1991, paras 3 and 4.

[71] 1880–1900 MHz in conformity with Dir. 91/287/EEC.

[72] 91/288/EEC, OJ L 144/47, 8 June 1991, Annex, paras 1–6.

[73] Annex, para. 7.

[74] See p. 43.

[75] CEPT Recommendation T/SF1 of 1976.

[76] Council Decision of 29 July 1991 on the introduction of a single European emergency call number, 91/396/EEC, OJ L 217/31, 6 Aug. 1991. This Decision was adopted under the Treaty powers of Art. 235.

emergency numbers but must also provide the service with call number 112.[77] The Council Decision calls for the introduction of the single European emergency call number by 31 December 1992 save where particular difficulties exist, in which event a Member State may be permitted an extended period for its introduction which must not be later than 31 December 1996.[78]

INTERNATIONAL TELEPHONE ACCESS CODE

For broadly the same reasons as those for the adoption of a single European emergency call number, the Council decided to call for the introduction of a standard international telephone access code.[79] Again, the code selected is one recommended by CEPT,[80] namely '00'. Some Member States already use '00' as the international telephone access code. In some cases, there are special arrangements between Member States for calls between adjacent locations across borders. These arrangements may continue and need not be affected by the adoption of the standard international telephone access code.[81]

The Council Decision calls for the adoption of the standard code by 31 December 1992, save in cases where Member States experience particular technical, financial or organisational difficulties in introducing the code. In those cases a new date for the introduction of the standard international telephone access code may be notified to the Commission as long as it is not later than 31 December 1998.[82]

ELECTRO-MAGNETIC COMPATIBILITY

One of the essential requirements which has to be met in order that terminal equipment qualifies for mutual recognition of type approval is the protection of public telecommunications networks from harm.[83] Member States also have responsibility for providing adequate protection for radio communications[84] against the degradation caused by electro-magnetic disturbances, and for ensuring that electric energy distribution networks are protected from electro-magnetic disturbance.[85] Although most Member States controlled permissible electro-magnetic disturbance levels, there were disparities between those provisions, which hindered trade within the Community. To eliminate these disparities the Council issued a harmonising Directive.[86] The Directive defines protection requirements relating to electro-magnetic compatibility which, once complied with, are proof of compliance with the protection requirements. The setting of harmonised

---

[77] 91/396/EEC, Art. 1(2).

[78] 91/396/EEC, Arts 2 and 3.

[79] Council Decision of 11 May 1992 on the introduction of a standard international telephone access code in the Community, 92/264/EEC, OJ L 137/21, 20 May 1992.

[80] CEPT Recommendation T/SF1 of 1976.

[81] 92/264/EEC, Art. 4.

[82] 92/264/EEC, Arts 2 and 3.

[83] Council Dir. 86/361/EEC, OJ L 217/21, 5 Aug. 1986, Art. 2(17).

[84] And the devices, apparatus or systems whose performance may be degraded by electro-magnetic disturbance produced by electrical and electronic apparatus.

[85] Council Dir. 89/336/EEC, OJ L 139/19, 23 May 1989.

[86] Council Dir. of 3 May 1989 on the approximation of the law to the Member States relating to electro-magnetic compatibility, 89/336/EEC, OJ L 139/19, 23 May 1989; amended by Council Directive 92/31/EEC OJ L 126/11 12 May 1992.

standards are entrusted to CENELEC and CEN and are adopted in accordance with the general guidelines for co-operation between these bodies and the Commission which was signed on 13 November 1984. For these purposes a '*harmonised standard*' is the technical specification[87] adopted by CENELEC on a remit from the Commission.[88]

The harmonisation Directive applies to all electric and electronic appliances and equipment and installations containing electrical or electronic components which may cause degradation of performance of other equipment or systems.[89] Certain apparatus fall outside the requirements of the Directive, including equipment used by radio amateurs,[90] which is not commercially available.

The requirements of the Directives ensure that the apparatus covered has a certain level of immunity from external electro-magnetic disturbance and does not prevent other apparatus from operating normally.[91] The Directive establishes a means of assessing and evaluating standards and provides for modifications where appropriate.[92] It also provides for standard forms of certifying and marking apparatus which conform to the appropriate standards.[93] The requirements of the Directive came into operation on 1 January 1992.[94]

---

[87] European standard harmonisation document.
[88] The remit was made under Dir. 83/189/EEC, OJ L 109/8, 26 Apr. 1983; this was last amended by Directive.
[89] 89/336/EEC, Art. 1(1),(2) and Art. 2(1).
[90] 89/336/EEC, Art. 2(2),(3).
[91] 89/336/EEC, Art. 4 and Annex III.
[92] 89/336/EEC, Art. 9.
[93] 89/336/EEC, Art. 10 and Annex I.
[94] 89/336/EEC, Art. 12.

CHAPTER 5

The European Telecommunications Standards Institute

ETSI: THE EUROPEAN TELECOMMUNICATIONS STANDARDS INSTITUTE

In September 1987 the CEPT took the basic[1] decision to establish a European Tele-communications Standards Institute by April 1988. The Commission was keen that the establishment of European Telecommunications Standards Institute should build on and complement the Community's policy on telecommunications and information technology standards and promote open international standardisation. The Commission also expressed the view that ETSI could best assist in promoting an open competitive market if it were open both to those in telecommunications and to those involved in information technology and allowed for active participation of industry and users.[2]

By resolution of 27 April 1989[3] the Council invited Member States, ETSI and CEN-CENELEC and the Commission to take a number of steps aimed at providing the infrastructure for ETSI to carry out its standard setting functions.

Standard setting procedures

Standards approved by ETSI are known as European Telecommunications Standards (ETS).[4] In some circumstances[5] ETSI can approve temporary standards known as Interim European Telecommunications Standard (I-ETS).[6] The Work Programme lead-

---

[1] ETSI.

[2] COM (88) 48 final, para. v.3, p. 19.

[3] 89/C 117/01, OJ C 117/1, 11 May 1989, Council resolution on standardisation in the field of information technology and telecommunications.

[4] Rules of Procedure of the European Telecommunications Standards Institute, 3 Apr. 1992, (ETSI Procedures), Art. 14.1.

[5] The Technical Assembly may in a particular case decide that a draft standard has a limited period of application because it is immature or a more complete standard will follow; ETSI Procedures, Art. 14.5.

[6] ETSI Procedures, Art. 14.1.

ing to the elaboration of ETS or I-ETS is determined by the Technical Assembly,[7] which also decides the priority to be given to each item within the Work Programme and whether or not to include work proposed by sources other than members. Any work proposed by the European Commission, which is not a member but is granted Counsellor status within ETSI,[8] falls within this category.

Items within the Work Programme are divided by the Technical Assembly into those which are of general interest and fall within the Costed Annual Programme and those which are of less immediate general interest and included in the Special Voluntary Programme.[9] Those parts of the programme which form part of the Costed Annual Programme are met out of the general ordinary budget of ETSI[10] and those within the Voluntary Programme are met by the parties interested on a voluntary basis.[11]

To avoid unnecessary duplication and prejudice to ETS which is under preparation by ETSI, the National Standards Organisations[12] and ETSI members can be required to refrain from any national standardisation activity that could prejudice the preparation of an ETS which is subject or a work item accepted by the Technical Assembly, with a precise scope and target date.[13] There are certain limited exceptions to this rule, including the adoption by an NSO, after notification to the Technical Assembly, of a national standard conforming to published CCITT or CCIR Recommendation.[14]

Before an ETS is approved by ETSI the NSOs will carry out a public inquiry and any comments on the ETS will be considered by ETSI.[15] More internationally based public inquiries[16] have to be carried out where a draft ETS is a candidate for NETs and for draft candidate CTRs.[17]

A draft ETS is approved[18] by weighted voting[19] in the Technical Assembly[20] or by correspondence.[21] An ETS may be established for EC Member States[22] if they have voted for approval, even though the standard is not otherwise approved.[23] The standard will then become an ETS for EC Member States and other countries that have voted in favour.[24]

Once an ETS has been approved, all conflicting national standards have to be withdrawn.[25]

---

[7] ETSI Procedures, Art. 6.4.2.
[8] ETSI Procedures, Art. 1.2.4.
[9] ETSI Procedures, Art. 6.4.3.
[10] ETSI Procedures, Arts 11.2.1 and 11.3.1.
[11] ETSI Procedures, Arts 11.2.2 and 11.3.2.
[12] NSO.
[13] ETSI Procedures, Art. 14.3.1.
[14] ETSI Procedures, Art. 14.3.2(b).
[15] ETSI Procedures, Art. 14.4.
[16] GATT provides arrangements for world-wide public enquiries.
[17] ETSI Procedure, Arts 14.4 and 15.1 set out the procedure for such enquiries and their consideration by ETSI. CTR denotes Conformance Testing Report.
[18] ETSI Procedure, Art. 14.5.
[19] Under the procedures of ETSI Procedure, Art. 12.2.
[20] Under rules provided in ETSI Procedure, Art. 14.2.
[21] ETSI Procedure, Art. 14.5.
[22] The Member State votes are counted in accordance with Art. 148 of the Rome Treaty.
[23] ETSI Procedures, Art. 14.5.
[24] ETSI Procedures, Art. 14.5 bis.
[25] Art. 14.6.

The relationship between ETSI and the European Commission

While recognising the importance of standards in the achievement of its objective to create a single European telecommunications market, the Commission has not itself been directly involved in defining standards.[26] It has always relied on competent standard setting bodies, in particular CEPT and CEN and CENELEC to define and approve standards in specific areas. By 1987 the Commission had reached the view[27] that the resources permanently engaged in standards and specifications were not sufficient to deal with the rapid development in telecommunications and information technology.

This view was shared by CEPT, which had also decided[28] to establish by April 1988 a European Telecommunication Standards Institute, based on the existing co-operation of the TOs with CEPT and CEN and CENELEC, but also drawing on the substantial expertise of manufacturers and users.[29] The Commission envisaged that the Institute would 'be in a position efficiently to draft the specifications with the status of standards, with the participation of all interested parties, *in full alignment with the Community principles applicable to technical harmonisation*[30] and with adequate links with existing European standardisation bodies'.[31]

Since its establishment ETSI has fulfilled these expectations. With both the human and financial resources made available to it, ETSI has been able to define many of the standards relevant to the harmonisation process undertaken by the Commission. In its turn, the Commission as Counsellor[32] to ETSI, has been able to influence some of the work undertaken by ETSI. Furthermore, the procedures of ETSI[33] facilitate approval of standards applicable within the Community.

Intellectual property rights (IPR) in ETSI standards

By their nature, all technical standards can be the subject of intellectual property rights[34] which may be owned by those developing the standard or by other parties. Once incorporated in the standard, unless non-infringing solutions can be devised by manufacturers, equipment conforming to the standard cannot be produced without a licence from the IPR owner. Without a regime established by the standards organisation to ensure the availability of licences on reasonable terms, the IPR owner is put in a strong negotiating position in relation to those requiring a licence.

The International Standards Organisation[35] deals with this difficulty by asking IPR owners whether they are willing to grant a licence to other manufacturers on fair, reasonable and non-discriminatory terms in relation to any standards set by the ISO. If the IPR owner is not willing to do so, the ISO standard is withdrawn or modified so that no infringement of the IPR occurs. However, in its basic form the ISO policy is not entirely suitable for adoption by ETSI. A number of factors are at play in the telecom-

---

[26] See p. 38.
[27] Green Paper, COM (87) 290 final, p. 133.
[28] Decision of Sept. 1987.
[29] White Paper, COM (88) 48, p. 19.
[30] Emphasis added.
[31] White Paper, COM (88) 48, p. 20.
[32] See p. 46.
[33] See p. 45; ETSI Procedures, Art. 14.5.
[34] IPR.
[35] ISO.

munications sector which do not arise in many other areas of standardisation. In brief, these factors are as follows.

1. The rapid rate of technological development in telecommunications does not always allow those contributing to standards to become immediately aware of IPR which may be infringed.
2. The need for a large number of standard interfaces involved in a telecommunications system make it almost inevitable that some IPR will be involved and that non-infringing solutions cannot easily be found.
3. The requirement for inter-operability of systems further diminishes the range of solutions available.
4. The rapidity of technological advance necessitates manufacturers to track ETSI standards and base their research and development efforts accordingly.
5. There are vast resources devoted to development of standards by ETSI and enormous investment made by telecommunications organisations in implementing ETSI standards, making any subsequent change inordinately expensive and unrealistic.[36]

In the context of the European Community, once the Commission has specified an ETSI standard and legally enforced it within the Community, these factors take on an even greater significance, putting the IPR owner in an almost unassailable position. Accordingly, the IPR committee of ETSI concluded that the ISO policy needed amplification and modification to provide a realistic solution for problems that may be encountered in relation to IPR in defining ETSI standards. Given its limited membership, ETSI cannot unilaterally devise a solution which would apply equally to IPR owned by its members and those owned by non-members. However, the adopted policy does facilitate the obtaining of licences from members by non-members. Broadly, there are two instruments under which access to IPR may be obtained. Entities within the Standards Application Area[37] can sign the ETSI IPR Undertaking. Entities outside the Standards Application Area may obtain IPR licences under the Code of Conduct.[38]

The ETSI IPR policy preserves the essential ingredients of the ISO policy on IPR by leaving open the option for ETSI to withdraw a standard if satisfactory solution on IPR cannot be reached. However, it minimises the risk of this occurring by requiring its members that own a relevant IPR to notify ETSI immediately prior to an item entering the ETSI work programme whether they propose to withhold licences in respect of the IPR. Unless a member makes a timely declaration to this effect, it will be obliged to provide licences to all other entities that have signed the Undertaking, on terms which are fair, reasonable and non-discriminatory. In the event that a dispute arises as to the terms on which the IPR owner is prepared to grant a licence there are provisions for the resolution of the dispute by arbitration.

---

[36] ETSI devoted 300 man years to the standardisation work on GSM before discovering 20 patents affecting the standard.

[37] The Standards Application Area is that in which a specific ETSI standard is being effectively applied. The terms of any Undertaking entered into with a non-member will apply only for that area and in relation to the specific standard.

[38] The Code of Conduct is entirely voluntary and an ETSI member will state in relation to each standard and prior to its adoption whether the member will follow the Code of Conduct. Once a member agrees to follow the Code of Conduct it is thereafter obliged to do so. The Code of Conduct is in part devised to fulfil the obligations of the European Community to extend no less favourable terms to enterprises importing into the European Community than those established within the Community; GATT, Arts 2 and 43.

Non-members of ETSI within the European Community have a choice as to whether to sign an Undertaking or obtain licences under the Code of Conduct. The signing of an Undertaking provides the safeguard to members with regard to future IPRs. Signatories to the Undertaking are obliged to extend reciprocal advantages to the IPR owner in respect of future standards.

Although the ETSI policy considerably reduces the risks associated with IPR in standards, by its nature and scope ETSI cannot eliminate such risks. However, the extension of the Standards Application Area and closer co-operation between ETSI and other telecommunications standards bodies[39] will increase the benefits of the ETSI policy. Furthermore, the current IPR policy is seen by ETSI as an interim solution and it is proposed that a more definitive policy will be devised once ETSI has had the opportunity to evaluate the working of the interim policy.[40]

---

[39] These include the USA T1 Committee and the Japanese TTC.
[40] See generally European Telecommunications Standards Institute: Explanatory Note on the Intellectual Property Rights Framework, 20 Aug. 1992.

CHAPTER 6
Competition and Services

GENERAL POLICY BACKGROUND

The most comprehensive review of telecommunications in the Community was made in the Green Paper on telecommunications services and equipment.[1] As already discussed,[2] both the Green Paper and the Commission's implementation proposals,[3] highlighted specific areas for action[4] for the liberalisation of services as well as the equipment market within the Community. The proposed positions most directly related to the provision of services are summarised below.[5]

1. Exclusive provision or special rights for the Telecommunications Administrations to provide a limited number of basic services, where exclusive provision is considered essential . . . for safeguarding public service goals.[6]

   These services are to be *narrowly* construed and be subject to regular review within given time intervals, taking account of technological development, particularly the evolution towards a digital infrastructure.[7] 'Reserved services'[8] may not be defined a service so as to extend a Telecommunications Administration service monopoly in

---

[1] Towards a dynamic European economy: Green Paper on the development of the Common Market for telecommunications services and equipment, COM (87) final, 30 June 1987.

[2] See Chap. 1.

[3] Towards a competitive Community-wide telecommunications market in 1992 – implementing the Green Paper on the development of the Common Market for telecommunications services and equipment, COM (88) 48, 9 February 1988.

[4] Referred to as 'proposed positions'.

[5] For the full text see Green Paper, COM (87) 290 final, p. 16, fig. 3; White Paper, COM (88) 48 final, p. 11, fig. 1; and see p. 11.

[6] It is argued that in order to safeguard the TO's ability to maintain networks with full coverage of the population they should enjoy exclusive or special rights to provide high revenue earning services, notably voice telephony.

[7] A cental element of the Commission's policy is to encourage and create the conditions for the development of Community-wide integrated services digital networks. The progressive move to digitalisation will make the distinction and differentiation between different services and traffic over networks increasingly difficult.

[8] Reserved services are those in relation to which the TOs may enjoy exclusive or special rights.

a way inconsistent with the Treaty.[9] Currently, given general understanding in the Community, voice telephony service seems to be the only obvious candidate.[10]

2. There must be free competitive provision[11] of all other services ('competitive services'[12]), within[13] Member States and between Member States for own use, shared use, or provision to third parties, subject to the conditions[14] for use of the network infrastructure.[15]

3. Regulatory and operational activities of telecommunications administrations[16] must be separated. Regulatory activities concern in particular licensing, control of type approval and interface specifications,[17] allocations of frequencies[18] and general surveillance of network usage conditions.[19]

4. Competitive offering of two-way satellite communications systems[20] . . . should be allowed on a case-to-case basis, where this is necessary to develop European-wide services[21] and the impact on the financial viability of the main providers is not substantial.[22]

These proposals must, of course, be viewed in the context of the Commission's overall policy in the liberalisation of telecommunications generally. In the case of telecommunications services, these proposals are not alone sufficient for a Community-wide competitive services market. In particular, access to the network infrastructure by providers of services and a free market in terminals are, among other factors, essential to the development of free provision of services within and between Member States. Nevertheless, although interdependent with other policy elements of the Commission, the factors identified here may usefully be separately examined.

SEPARATION OF REGULATORY AND OPERATING FUNCTIONS OF TOs

In all Member States the TO traditionally acted as the regulator of telecommunications, in some cases under delegated powers.[23] These regulatory functions could extend to the

---

[9] It has to be assumed that a 'monopoly' can only be consistent with the Treaty if it falls within the exceptions provided by the Treaty, Art. 90(2).

[10] Proposed Position B.

[11] Clearly, TOs can participate in competitive provision of services.

[12] Competitive services would comprise all services such as value-added services, except basic services explicitly reserved for the telecommunications administrations; see para. 1.

[13] Emphasis added.

[14] These conditions have been partially defined and will continue to be further defined under the ONP provisions; see p. 73 et seq.

[15] Proposed Position C.

[16] Proposed Position G.

[17] See Chaps 5 and 7.

[18] For certain services such as land-based radio communications (see p. 104), the Commission has taken steps to allocate specified frequency bands. However, even in those circumstances it falls to the regulatory authorities within the Member States to assign specific frequency bands within the allocated band to particular operators. It is at the assignment level where the power of TOs to exercise regulatory power can be most effectively abused to restrict competition.

[19] This issue has been addressed in the ONP Directive, 90/387/EEC; see p. 84.

[20] Emphasis added.

[21] Emphasis added.

[22] Proposed Position A. This proposal is made in the context of accepting TO monopolies on the provision of network infrastructure.

[23] In most Member States the government ministry responsible for telecommunications is distinct from the TO.

whole range of telecommunications activity, including licensing, type approval of terminal and other equipment as well as the definition of mandatory specifications, the allocation and assignment of frequencies and surveillance of conditions for the use of the telecommunications network.

The separation of reserve services and competitive services under the Community telecommunications policy created an environment in which the TO then became one of the competitors in the non-reserved services.[24]

In such an environment, the TO could not continue to be both a regulator and a market participant. Therefore, the separation of regulatory and operational activities is one of the important pre-requisites for the effective application of competition rules to the providers of telecommunications services.[25]

This proposal merely reflected the inevitable. By the time the White Paper[26] was issued, Member States had fully endorsed the principle of the separation of regulatory and operational responsibilities of the TOs.[27] This was further endorsed by the European Parliament in its resolutions on the White Paper.[28] The Council had also identified clear separation of regulatory and operational duties as a major policy goal.[29]

The Services Directive[30] identifies the specific regulatory functions of the TOs which, combined with their commercial function, have the most direct impact on entities offering telecommunications services in competition with the TO.[31] The functions identified are licensing, control of type-approval and mandatory interface specifications, frequency allocation and monitoring of conditions of use. Attention is particularly drawn to cases where the TO is given discretion within general principles defined by legislation, leaving it to the TOs to determine the specific operating conditions for licensed services.

Clearly, the combination of the two functions enables the TO to influence substantially the supply of services offered by its competitors. Given the dominant position of the TO in operating the network, its power to regulate access to the market for telecommunications services strengthens that dominant position. The Directive particularly identifies the impact this will have on restricting competitors' access to the markets in telecommunications services, the limitation of users' freedom of choice, and the possibility of limiting outlets for equipment, resulting in the inhibition of technological progress in the field.[32]

Therefore, the Directive[33] requires Member States to entrust to a body independent of the TO[34] the specific regulatory functions mentioned above.

---

[24] It is Community policy that the TOs compete in the market with other service providers.

[25] Green Paper, COM (87) 290 final, 30 June 1987, p. 73, para. 4.3.2(3).

[26] COM (88) 48 final, 9 Feb. 1988.

[27] COM (88) 48 final, p. 12.

[28] Resolutions of the European Parliament, document A 2-0259/88, 11 Nov. 1988, p. 7.

[29] Council resolution of 30 June 1988 on the development of the Common Market for telecommunications services and equipment up to 1992, 88/C 259/01, OJ C 257/1, 4 Oct. 1988, para. 5.

[30] Commission Dir. of 28 June 1990 on competition in the Markets for telecommunications services, 90/388/EEC, OJ L 192/10, 24 July 1990.

[31] 90/388/EEC, Recitals 28 and 29.

[32] 90/388/EEC, Recital 29. The strengthening of the TOs dominant position by the combination of these activities is regarded by the Commission as constituting an abuse of the dominant position under Art. 86 and, given that they generally result from state measures, there is also usually a breach of Art. 90(1).

[33] 90/388/EEC, Art. 7.

[34] Member States were required to inform the Commission of the measures taken or proposed to this end not later than 31 Dec. 1990 and to implement them by 1 July 1991.

SEPARATION OF PROVISION OF INFRASTRUCTURE AND SERVICES

The convergence of telecommunications and information technology coupled with technological development in both areas has had a profound impact on the provision of telecommunications services. This has led to a position where an increasing number of services can be operated independently of the operation of the network infrastructure, making telecommunications services tradable in their own right. Furthermore, the provision of services, unlike the provision of telecommunications network infrastructures, does not require the physical presence of the provider in the geographical area where the services are provided. In the context of the Community, the possibility of providing services between Member States is a significant element in the creation of a common market in such services.

This separation of the two activities encouraged Member States, as well as the Commission, to view and treat the provision of the network infrastructure distinctly from the provision of telecommunications services. In considering the special or exclusive right of TOs to provide the network infrastructure the following factors have been of major significance.

1. TOs must continue to fulfil their public (universal) service mandate.
2. The current and future integrity of the basic network infrastructure must be maintained or created.
3. The necessary level of investment be maintained to build up new generations of telecommunications infrastructure.
4. The financial viability of the TOs must be maintained to ensure the above.

Continued exclusive or special rights granted to the TOs in relation to the provision of the network infrastructure does not involve a departure from the provisions of the Rome Treaty or the competition rules of the Community. The provisions of the Treaty[35] implicitly recognise the right of Member States to grant exclusive or special rights to undertakings. Therefore, although undertakings such as TOs are subject to the provisions of the Treaty and its competition rules, there may be circumstances in which the full application of such provisions would be suspended. The limited circumstances in which exception from the application of the provisions of the Treaty may be made are circumstances where undertakings are entrusted with the operation of services of general economic interest and the application of the provisions of the Treaty, in particular the rules on competition, would obstruct the performance of the tasks assigned to them.[36]

The provision of the network infrastructure coupled with public service obligations of the TOs can legitimately be regarded as being of 'general economic interest'[37] and thus qualify for the exception provided under the Treaty. There is inevitably a balance to be

---

[35] Art. 90(1), which provides:
In the case of public undertakings and undertakings to which Member States grant special or exclusive rights, Member States shall neither enact nor maintain in force any measure contrary to the rules contained in this Treaty, in particular to those rules provided for in Art. 7 and Arts 85 to 94.

[36] Art. 90(2), which provides:
Undertakings entrusted with the operation of services of general economic interest or having the character of a revenue-producing monopoly shall be subject to the rules contained in this Treaty, in particular to the rules on competition, in so far as the application of such rules does not obstruct the performance, in law or in fact, of the particular tasks assigned to them. The development of trade must not be affected to such an extent as would be contrary to the interests of the Community.

[37] Rome Treaty Art. 90(2).

struck between the economies of scale and the trade-off between the flexibility resulting from competition on the one hand and higher transaction costs resulting from parallel networks on the other. The trend within the Community has been for Member States to opt for maintenance of exclusive provision of network infrastructure by a single or a small number of TOs.[38] Nevertheless, permissible exclusive network infrastructure provision is narrowly defined[39] and a different treatment is afforded to satellite communications, mobile radio and cable television networks.[40]

Although these proposals of the Commission[41] were endorsed by resolution of the Council,[42] the European Parliament drew attention to some difficulties that would arise and was critical of the network monopoly provisions.[43]

In an Explanatory Statement, Parliament observes:[44]

Network Monopoly: The Commission assumes that all Member States have granted their telecommunications administrations exclusive rights to provide and operate telecommunications networks.[45] Network monopolies in the US, however, were abolished under a divestiture agreement in 1982; at least three large providers operate there. In the United Kingdom, two competing enterprises operate two mutually independent networks;[46] provided statutory requirements were met, further network operators could be licensed.

A message service independent of the telecommunications network ('Radio Messagerie') is already operating in France, while a Bill is being drafted to enable private network operators to be licensed where the public network is unable to provide an adequate service.

Unlike the United Kingdom Government, which regards network expansion and enhancement (e.g. conversion to fibre-optic cabling) as a purely commercial concern for telecommunications businesses, the Commission takes the view that the Member States should be responsible for providing an integrated and efficient network infrastructure, in both the short and long terms, as the basis for optimised Community and world-wide communications services. This principle is endorsed by the overwhelming majority of Member States; the trend is towards maintaining exclusive powers for a single telecommunications administration or a limited number of non-competing regional administrations.

The Commission insists, however, that this exclusive right be narrowly defined and not in the new technologies in adjacent areas (satellite communications, mobile communications and cable television), arguing that, given the size of the European telecommunications market, an efficient network infrastructure can only be provided at reasonable cost by a single operator. Network operators already compete with each other in one Member State, however, which raises the problem of what approach to take to the private British operator (Mercury) if it proposed to extend its network to other Member States. Mercury would be unable to justify this by invoking the principle of freedom to provide services under the EEC Treaty,[47] though it would indeed be more than problematic to reconcile confining operations to the territory of one Member State with a single internal market. We should therefore advise the Commission

---

[38] The United Kingdom continues to be an exception to this trend, where the duopoly of BT and Mercury Communications was terminated in 1991 and a growing number of network providers are being licensed.

[39] See p. 61.

[40] See p. 64 et seq.

[41] COM (87) 290 final; COM (88) 48 final.

[42] 88/C 257/01 of 30 June 1988, OJ C 257/1, 4 Oct. 1988.

[43] Report drawn up on behalf of the Committee on Transport on Posts and Telecommunications, document A 2-0259/88, 11 Nov. 1988.

[44] Document A 2-0259/88, Explanatory Statement, para. 8.

[45] This is not entirely correct. Even in the Green Paper, (Com) 87 290 Final, p. 70, to which this Statement refers, clearly indicates that the Commission has in mind the duopoly then existing in the United Kingdom.

[46] This statement is also not entirely correct. In practice, from a competitive point of view, Mercury still depends heavily on its interconnection with the BT network.

[47] See the opinion of the Legal Service of the European Parliament.

to countenance Government network monopolies for the time being: as soon as modernisation (digitalisation, fibre-optic cabling) and arrangements to provide access for peripheral and disadvantaged regions have been funded and completed, thought should be given to licensing more and more network operators throughout the Community.

In formulating the Services Directive[48] the Commission continues at least to accept monopoly provision of networks within Member States. The Commission argues that the provision of the network constitutes a distinct separate market, as it is not interchangeable with other services.[49] The Commission appears further to argue that the task of providing and exploiting a universal network, that is, one having general geographical coverage and being provided to any service provider or user on request within a reasonable period of time, constitutes the performance of a particular task assigned to the TOs which qualify for the exception permitted under the Treaty[50] to the application of the competition provisions[51] of the Treaty.[52]

The Commission goes further than this in justifying continued exclusive rights in relation to voice telephony.[53] Although the concern of the European Parliament is with difficulties that might arise should Mercury wish to extend its network to other Member States, it is not a problem that presents itself only in that or similar circumstances. The same considerations would apply if any entity from any Member State was to establish a network in any other. However, criticism of the Commission on the basis that it has assumed all Member States have granted special or exclusive rights to their telecommunications administrations may be met by the definitions used in the Services Directive.[54] In particular, the Services Directive refers to *telecommunications organisations*[55] which may be *public* or *private* bodies with *special* or *exclusive* rights to provide a public *telecommunications network*. The Services Directive distinguishes between *telecommunications organisations*, which are entities with special or exclusive rights in relation to the network infrastructure (although they may also enjoy such rights for the provision of telecommunications services), and *economic operators, operators or service providers*[56] which may have special or exclusive rights for the provision of telecommunications services by virtue of licensing or other requirements of the Member State.[57]

The maintenance of exclusive or special rights to provide the network infrastructure is therefore restricted to those which fall within the definition of 'public telecommunications networks'.[58] The maintenance of such rights is also conditional on the Member States ensuring that conditions for access to the networks are objective and non-discriminatory and are published.[59] Given the importance of leased lines in the liberalisation of the telecommunications services market, their provision is made subject of particular focus in the Services Directive.[60]

---

[48] 90/388/EEC.
[49] 90/388/EEC, Art. 13.
[50] Art. 90(2).
[51] Rome Treaty, Arts 59 and 86.
[52] 90/388/EEC, Recital 18.
[53] See pp. 60 and 61.
[54] Art. 1(1).
[55] Art. 1(1), first indent.
[56] See Arts 3, 4 and 6.
[57] Art. 1(1) Second indent.
[58] As defined in Art. 1(1).
[59] 90/388/EEC, Art. 4. And these requirements are also embodied in greater detail in the ONP Dir. 90/387/EEC; see p. 74.
[60] 90/388/EEC, Art. 4.

Leased lines must be provided to operators requesting them within a reasonable time and there can be no restrictions on their use, save restriction or prohibition of provision of voice telephony[61] or as may be justified on the basis of *essential requirements*.[62]

For the purposes of the Services Directive, *essential requirements*[63] are a number of non-economic reasons in the general interest justified on the basis of security of network operations, maintenance of network integrity, inter-operability of services and data protection.[64]

Integrated services and digital networks (ISDNs)[65]

In its Recommendations on telecommunications[66] the Commission suggested that the planning phase for ISDN be utilised to create a Community 'umbrella' for the adaptation measures which had then been initiated by TOs. The economic and social committee commenting on the Commission Recommendation[67] agreed with those Recommendations of the Commission[68] and expressed the opinion that:

> application of new technologies in telecommunications . . . will offer significant future prospects for the Member States. Telecommunications users can expect a considerably enhanced range of communications facilities, and operators and manufacturers can expect opportunities for rapid growth.[69]

The European Parliament, in its resolution[70] [71] in particular expressed the opinion that:

> these new technologies have, or could have, a vital role to play in the growth of industry and services, increased productivity and competitiveness, energy conservation, the reduction of regional disparities, the balance of the European foreign trade, the shaping of a new form of growth and in the changes they will bring about in living conditions and social and administrative structures.[72]

At the time the Community was falling seriously behind the United States, Japan and Canada in the relatively new field of ISDN.[73] There was, therefore, concern that the Commission should play an active role in bringing about urgent measures by the Council

---

[61] 90/388/EEC, Art. 2.
[62] 90/388/EEC, Art. 4.
[63] Art. 1(1).
[64] 90/388/EEC, Recital 9 provides the interpretation of these expressions for the purposes of the Directive.
Security of network operations means ensuring the availability of the public network in case of emergency.
Technical integrity of the public network means ensuring its normal operation and the interconnection of public networks in the Community on the basis of common technical specifications.
Inter-operability of services means complying with such technical specifications introduced to increase the provision of services and the choice available to users.
Data protection means measures taken to warrant the confidentiality of communications and the protection of personal data.
[65] ISDN.
[66] COM (80) 422 final.
[67] Opinion of the economic and social committee, 25 Feb. 1981, OJ C 138/26, 9 June 1981.
[68] Para. 3.4.
[69] Para. 3.1.
[70] Resolution of 7 May 1981, OJ C, 15 June 1981.
[71] COM (80) 422 final; embodying Parliament's opinion on the Commission's recommendation to the Council on telecommunications through the general objectives of the Commission to create an efficient telecommunication infrastructure for the new information technologies.
[72] Resolution 1.
[73] Opinion of European Parliament, OJ C 1.4/72, 15 June 1981.

to establish such networks throughout the Community. In particular, Parliament expressed its support for the Commission's project to achieve the greatest possible degree of harmonisation in ISDN.[74] The Commission has been especially keen to ensure that the introduction of ISDN by Member States is harmonised from the outset throughout the Community.[75]

Against this background the Council issued a Recommendation[76] aimed at harmonised introduction of ISDN. One of the main objectives of the Commission was to create a range of harmonised telematic[77] services, offering users throughout the Community the chance to communicate efficiently and economically.[78] The introduction of ISDN, as well as the new broadband communications services, offered a prime opportunity for harmonisation considered essential to achieve these objectives.[79]

The Council, therefore, recommended that TOs should:

1. consult one another, before introducing any new services, particularly between Member States, so that new developments take place under conditions which are compatible with harmonisation;
2. ensure that from 1985 onwards all new services are introduced on a common harmonised approach;[80] and
3. from 1986 onwards, when ordering digital transmission switching systems designed for progressive integration of services, take full account of recognised standards in the Community.[81]

In relation to the Commission's public communications policy, ISDN presents a slightly special case. The running of the network constituting ISDN falls clearly within the infrastructure exception to the liberalisation policy of the Commission.[82] The Council Recommendation on ISDN[83] recognises this fact[84] and envisages a degree of Community financial assistance for the development of infrastructures where appropriate.[85] However, the availability of infrastructure capacity is in theory no different from capacity for other services which may be provided competitively. But, the services element of ISDN will frequently include an element of voice telephony, also reserved to the TOs.[86] Therefore, until such time as voice telephony ceases to be a reserved service, certain ISDN services will remain within the monopoly of the TOs.

---

[74] Resolution 8.

[75] Among the Commission's Recommendations, which were supported by Parliament, was that 'no new telematic services should be created without prior consultation, that no digital transmission and switching system should be ordered unless the equipment has previously been standardised or made compatible'; Resolution 8.

[76] Council Recommendation of 12 Nov. 1984 concerning the implementation of harmonisation in the field of telecommunications, 84/549/EEC, OJ L 298/49, 16 Nov. 1984.

[77] The word 'telematic' as used by the Commission applies to all those services, systems, apparatus and products which are based on the combined use of electronic techniques of information, that is, digital processing and transmission; 84/549/EEC, fnote 3.

[78] 84/549/EEC, Recital 2.

[79] 84/549/EEC, Recital 3.

[80] In this connection TOs were urged to take account of standardisation work by CEPT, CEN/CENELEC, CCITT and ISO (the International Standards Organisation); 84/549/EEC, para. 2.

[81] See 84/549/EEC.

[82] Services Directive 90/388/EEC, see p. 63.

[83] Council Recommendation of 22 Dec. 1986 on the co-ordinated introduction of the Integrated Services Digital Network (ISDN) in the European Community, 86/659/EEC, OJ L 382/36, 31 Dec. 1986.

[84] 86/659/EEC, para. 4, Annex, para. 1.2.

[85] 86/659/EEC, Recital 8, para. 5.

[86] Services Dir. 90/388/EEC, see p. 60 et seq.

The Council Recommendation of 1986[87] invited TOs to implement a detailed set of Recommendations[88] aimed at directing the investment taking place in digital switching and digital transmission equipment to the development of ISDN. This entails providing harmonised and compatible services throughout the Community[89] which would also make it possible to establish a European market in telephone and data processing terminals enabling the European industry to maintain and increase its share of the world market.[90] The Commission received favourable opinions from GAP as well as from CEPT.[91]

The Recommendation, set out the framework of the specification of the technical aspects of ISDN, and provided a broad timetable for the specification of services.[92] The detailed Recommendations concern both the public network and common standards for private networks, including PABXs[93] and terminals connected behind them.[94]

The Recommendation addresses the definition of interface between the public and private network,[95] recommending a standard physical interface between ISDN terminals and the public network. The Recommendations on the interface carry the implication that the missing access at the first point of termination will be provided by the public network operator.

A number of services are recommended to be specified by the end of 1987, if possible with implementation in the period 1988–93, where other services could be specified by the end of 1990, with no indication as to possible implementation.[96] The Recommendation set a target of penetration at 80 per cent of customers by the end of 1993.[97]

The Recommendation rightly recognises the importance of tariff levels to the expansion of ISDN.[98] It makes a number of suggestions, including that tariffs for services should be less dependent on distance than was then the case and in comparison with telephone services.

MOBILE SERVICES

The provision of mobile telecommunications services shares with ISDN the feature that the provision of the service is closely linked with the re-establishment and running of a specialised network infrastructure. However, unlike ISDN, mobile radio telephony is specifically excluded from the ambit of the Services Directive.[99] Furthermore, the development of the market has been such that Member States have developed a competitive market in mobile communications, often licensing two or more.[100]

---

[87] 86/659/EEC.
[88] 86/659/EEC, para. 1.
[87] 86/659/EEC, Recitals 3 and 4.
[88] 86/659/EEC, Recital 5.
[89] 86/659/EEC, Recitals 11 and 12.
[90] 86/659/EEC, Annex.
[91] Private Automatic Branch Exchange.
[92] 86/659/EEC, Annex, para. 1.1.
[93] 86/659/EEC, Annex, para. 1.2.
[94] 86/659/EEC, Annex, paras 3 and 4. It is worth noting that the network capacity envisaged, largely at 64 KBit per second, is probably in excess of what would be required with a modern transmission system and updated compression techniques.
[95] 86/659/EEC, Annex, para. 8.
[96] 86/659/EEC, Annex, para. 6.
[97] 90/388/EEC, Art. 1(2).
[98] This generally includes the TO (operators offering competitor mobile communications services).
[99] 87/371/EEC, Recitals 3 and 4.
[100] 87/371/EEC, Recitals 8 and 9.

One of the primary aims of the Commission in relation to mobile communications systems was to facilitate the access to a compatible mobile communications system by users living within the Community.[101] To achieve a mobile communications system throughout the Community which would permit users to use mobile services while moving through the Community, two matters had to be addressed. The first, a basic set of standards needed to be established to harmonise both the networks and the mobile terminals in order that a conforming terminal could access basic services on the network throughout the Community. This aspect was also important in establishing a European market in mobile and portable terminals, giving Community entities a strong presence in world markets.[102]

The other feature of central importance is the allocation and availability of suitable frequencies on a Community-wide basis.[103] Therefore, both these features had to be addressed concurrently.[104] Nevertheless, it is logical that the Commission wished first to ensure the availability of relevant frequency bands. The Commission, therefore, proposed a Directive to be adopted by the Council[105] [106] which was approved by Parliament[107] and subsequently issued.[108] [109]

This Directive was issued at the same time as the Council Recommendation on the co-ordinated introduction of mobile communications.[110] Both were timed to take advantage of the changeover taking place to the second generation digital mobile communication systems, based on the GSM standard[111] to further its policies of establishing pan-European mobile communications[112] and facilitating the development of a European market in mobile and portable terminals.[113] The Recommendation was issued at a time when systems in use within the Community were largely incompatible and could not altogether provide a European-wide service. The harmonisation Recommendations in this area are also designed to bring about systems for voice and data services based on digital techniques and compatible with ISDN[114] developing within the Community.[115]

---

[101] 87/372/EEC, Recital 4.

[102] Frequencies allocated for mobile communications systems also had an impact on the definition of standards for the network and mobile terminal.

[103] Proposal for a Council Directive on the frequency bands to be made available for the co-ordinated introduction of public pan-European digital mobile communications in the Community, submitted to the Council on 9 Feb. 1987.

[104] Com (87) 35 Final OJ C 69/9, 17 Mar. 1987.

[105] Opinion of the European Parliament of 10 Apr. 1987, OJ C 125/159, 11 May 1987.

[106] Council Directive of 25 June 1987 on the frequency bands to be reserved for the co-ordinated introduction of public pan-European cellular digital land-based mobile communications in the Community.

[107] 87/372/EEC, OJ L 196/85, 17 July 1987.

[108] Council Recommendation of 25 June 1987 on the co-ordinated introduction of public pan-European cellular digital land-based mobile communications in the Community, 87/371/EEC, OJ L 196/81, 17 July 1987.
87/372/EEC, Art. 3. A public pan-European cellular digital land-based mobile communications service means a public cellular radio service provided in each of the Member States to a common specification, which includes the feature that all voice signals are encoded into binary digits prior to radio transmission, and where users provided with a service in one Member State can also gain access to the service in any other Member State. Provision for the establishment of the Common specification is contained in a Council Recommendation 87/371/EEC.

[109] GSM refers to the Working Group set up by Sept, known as Groupe Speciale Mobile, to plan all system aspects of the second generation cellular mobile radio infrastructure.

[110] 87/371/EEC, Recital 5; 87/372/EEC, Recital 6.

[111] 87/371/EEC, Recital 8.

[112] Introduced on a harmonised basis according to the Recommendations of 86/659/EEC; C.

[113] 87/371/EEC, Recital 7.

[114] 87/372/EEC.

[115] 87/372/EEC, Art. 1(2).

The frequency band Directive[116] requires that frequency bands 890–915 and 935–960 MHz are made available to public pan-European cellular digital mobile communications services[117] as soon as there is commercial demand for these bands, and in any event to reserve exclusively[118] 9 MHz in each of those bands[119] for the service by 1 January 1991.[120]

The detailed provisions of the Council Recommendation[121] set out the general requirements of the system[122] as well as a timetable for the definition of specifications,[123] choice of transmission systems and network architecture,[124] signalling, tariff considerations and geographical coverage.[125] Throughout there is an emphasis on the compatibility of the systems with ISDN.[126] In keeping with the general policy of the Commission on tariffing, it is recommended that tariffs for mobile communications move towards becoming less distance-dependent, while making allowance for the scarcity of frequency resources and the duration of radio channel use.[127]

The coverage requirements are left rather flexible. It is recommended that the systems be introduced by 1991. However, coverage is defined in terms of 'major urban areas' which are to be covered by 1993 and the main links between such areas by 1995.[128] The needs of travellers on roads and by air are particularly highlighted in the call for TOs to study their needs in particular.[129]

Member State governments are required to advise the Commission annually on the measures taken and the problems they have encountered in implementing the Recommendation. There is a provision for such information to be examined by the Commission in collaboration with the SOG-T.[130]

VOICE TELEPHONY

The central aim of the Services Directive and of the Green Paper on services and equipment[131] was to open the telecommunications network infrastructure[132] to service providers who would compete with the TOs in providing services over that network. However, disappointingly, although not surprisingly, the Commission from the outset

---

[116] With the exception of the use of these frequencies for point- to-point connections existing when the Directive came into force provided that they do not interfere with, or in any way impede, the development of the public pan-European cellular digital mobile communications service. This Directive came into force in Member States at the latest by 26 Jan. 1989, 87/372/EEC, Art. 4(1).

[117] The Directive indicates a preference for the bands 905–914 and 950–959 MHz frequency bands.

[118] Art. 1(1)

[119] 87/371/EEC.

[120] 87/371/EEC, Annex, para. 1.

[121] 87/371/EEC, Annex, paras 4 and 5.

[122] 87/371/EEC, Annex, paras 2 and 3.

[123] 87/371/EEC, Annex, paras 6, 7 and 8.

[124] 87/371/EEC, Annex, paras 1, 5 and 6.

[125] 87/371/EEC, Annex, para. 7.

[126] 87/371/EEC, Annex, para. 8.

[127] Ibid.

[128] 87/371/EEC, para. 8.

[129] COM (87) 290 final.

[130] In conjunction with the ONP Directive.

[131] At the time of the publication of the Green Paper voice telephony accounted for at least 85% of the telecommunications revenue within the Community.

[132] COM (87) 290, p. 57.

accepted the continuation of TO monopolies over the provision of voice telephony.[133] The Commission justified the continued special or exclusive rights of the TOs to provide voice telephony services to the need to safeguard the financial viability in order to ensure the build-up of the new generations of telecommunications infrastructure and the necessary level of investment.

This was partly dictated by the Commission's view of the role of the TOs as the entities which would guarantee efficient national, Community-wide and worldwide communications which would secure future economic and social development and satisfy emergency and security needs.[134]

Although the Green Paper identified a number of 'new basic services',[135] the Commission formed the view that[136] to justify any continued exclusive provision of basic services must be weighed carefully against the restrictions it would impose on users' applications for their own use, shared use or provision of services to third parties, thus leading it to the conclusion that exclusive provision of services must be narrowly construed and made subject[137] to periodic review.[138] It should, however, be noted that competitive service providers must be allowed to provide voice telephony, and data communication services, to any limited number of customers. The exceptions,[139] permitting exclusive or special rights for their services, related only to provision to the general public. This follows from the definitions[140] of '*voice telephony*' and '*packet- and circuit-switched data services*'. Therefore, provision of these services to all banks, or to groups of companies, is open to competition.

Although the Commission proposals would entitle Member States to maintain TO monopoly over voice telephony, in the opinion of the Economic and Social Committee[141] this did not go far enough and should extend to telegraph, telex, digital and data transmission as well as all two-way transmission systems.[142]

Nevertheless, in its White Paper[143] the Commission took account of the general support for exclusive provision of voice telephony, as long as it was defined as switched voice telephony intended for the general public and as long as it was subject to review.[144] It therefore proposed[145] continued exclusive provision or special rights for the TOs regarding voice telephone service and the opening to competition of all other services

---

[133] These are services made possible through technological developments and which are accepted only in some Member States as basic services. Examples include: packet switched data networks; circuit switched data networks; teletex; electronic mail; videotex.

[134] COM (87) 290 final, p. 34.

[135] The view of the Commission was based on the requirements of the Rome Treaty, Art. 90(2) providing that any functions entrusted to undertakings by Member States must not affect the development of trade to such an extent as would be contrary to the interests of the Community; and the explicit recognition by the European Court of Justice of the right of network users to benefit fully from new opportunities offered by technological progress; British Telecom Case 41/83, Commission v Italy, 20 March 1985; see p. 20.

[136] This is on the basis of ongoing integration of services brought about by technological development and trends, although developments in the market and the commercial and regulatory trends within Member States are at least equally important.

[137] COM (87) 290 final, p. 65.

[138] 90/388/EEC, Arts 2 and 3. For the validity of the Commission's abolition of "special rights" see the decision of the Court in Spain, Belgium and Italy v Commission, Joined Cases C-271/90, 281/90 and 289/90, invalidating the relevant provisions of the Services Directive; See also p. 13.

[139] 90/388/EEC, Art. 1(1); both definitions refer to 'commercial provision for the public . . .'.

[140] Opinion on the Green Paper, 87/C 356/12, OJ C 356/46, 31 December 1987.

[141] Para. 5.5.

[142] COM (88) 48.

[143] COM (88) 48, p. 13.

[144] COM (88) 48 final, p. 17.

[145] Council Resolution of 13 June 1988, 88/C /257/01, OJ C 257/1, 4 Oct. 1988.

by 31 December 1989. However, it proposed special consideration for telex services and packet- and circuit-switch data services intended for general public use in order to allow sufficient time for the elaboration of schemes to ensure future service provision for the general public for this type of service. These proposals received broad approval from the Council.[146]

The European Parliament[147] was again somewhat critical of the proposed monopoly. It observed:[148]

> Basic Service Monopoly: The Green Paper draws a distinction between basic and value-added telecommunications services. Value-added services would be open to competition, on the whole, while Member States would be able to continue to grant their telecommunications administrations exclusive rights, at least for a transitional period to provide basic services. This would not be entirely straightforward, particularly in view of the fact that, according to Court of Justice case law,[149] the maintenance of such Government monopolies in utilities is permissible only if justified in the public interest.
>
> Distinguishing between basic and value-added services is also problematic, given that there are no generally binding definitions whatsoever; in the final analysis, classification is virtually ad hoc. The Commission tends to the view that only telephony should be regarded as a basic service, arguing that telecommunications administrations require a monopoly in telephone services in order to be able to finance the high level of investment for network modernisation and expansion. This position is consistent with the Commission's ruling that ensuring network integrity and inter-operability is a public duty, but implies, in practice, a considerable scaling down of the area open to competition: income from telephone services currently accounts for some 85–90% of telecommunications enterprises' total revenue. Consequently, exclusive and special rights to provide basic services will have to be accepted *for the time being*,[150] though, where monopoly privileges in respect of telephone services are granted, there is a convincing case to be made for Member States to be able to ban certain 'cream-skimming' practices, e.g. the resale of voice capacity on leased telephone lines.

In the Services Directive[151] the Commission acknowledges the risks of granting to TOs special or exclusive rights both over networks and telecommunications services. In particular, the power it would give to TOs to prevent or restrict access to the market for telecommunications services by their competitors and to link the provision of network to the use of certain services which have no connection with network provision. As the Services Directive states[152] '[to institute] a system ensuring that competition in the Common Market is not distorted, and [requiring] a fortiori that competition [is] not eliminated Member States have an obligation[153] to abstain from any measure which could jeopardise the attainment of [these] objectives'.

The Directive also acknowledges that the combination of exclusive rights to provide telecommunications services and to provide networks are incompatible with the provi-

---

[146] Report drawn up on behalf of the Commission on transport on posts and telecommunications, document A 2-0259/88, 11 Nov. 1988.

[147] Document A 2-0259/88, explanatory statement, para. 9.

[148] See the opinion of the Legal Services of the European Parliament.

[149] Emphasis added.

[150] 90/388/EEC, Recital 16.

[151] Recitals 16 and 17: Each of these types of conduct represents a specific abuse a dominant position which is likely to have an appreciable effect on trade between Member States, as all the services in question could in principle be supplied by providers from other Member States. The structure of competition within the Common Market is substantially changed by them. At all events, the special or exclusive rights for the services give rise to a situation which is contrary to the objectives of the Rome Treaty, Art. 3(f).

[152] Rome Treaty, Art. 5.

[153] 90/388/EEC, Recital 17; Rome Treaty, Art. 90(1) in conjunction with Art. 86.

sions of the Rome Treaty.[154] However, it relies on the derogation permitted,[155] where the strict application of the competition rules would obstruct the performance of the particular tasks assigned to the TOs. The task identified in the Directive is the provision and exploitation of a universal network.[156]

The Services Directive states:[157]

> The financial resources for the development of the network still derive mainly from the operation of the telephone service. Consequently, the opening-up of voice telephony to competition could threaten the financial stability of the telecommunications organisations.[158] The voice telephony service, whether provided from the present telephone network or *forming part of the ISDN service*,[159] is currently also the most important means of notifying and calling up emergency services in charge of public safety.

By excluding the application of the Services Directive, and therefore the more liberal competitive regime to voice telephony,[160] the Commission has left open to Member States the opportunity to restrict the development[161] not only of competitive voice telephony services, but also ISDN services with a significant voice telephony element.

However, the Services Directive envisages reappraisal of the position by the end of 1992,[162] when greater relaxation of voice telephony may well be brought about. There is also the safeguard against linking the provision of network to the supply of services[163] by the requirements of objectivity and non-discrimination in the provision of public telecommunications networks.

SIMPLE RESALE

The continued acceptance of TO monopoly in the provision of voice telephony is substantially justified by the Commission on the basis of the requirement for financial viability of TOs to provide their universal service.[164] The financial viability of the TOs could come under threat if competitor service providers could offer their leased lines for the *pure* resale of voice capacity.[165] The factors which could bring about a loss of revenue to the TOs in the circumstances include:

1. The competitor service providers would be entitled to lease circuits from the TO[166] on routes that generate high profits. These leased lines would be provided by the TO at tariffs which are independent of the nature of the traffic carried over them.[167]
2. The competitive service providers would divert traffic away from the public switched network through leased lines by offering lower tariffs than the TO.[168]

---

[154] 90/388/EEC, Recital 18; Rome Treaty, Art. 90(2) allowing derogation from the application of Arts 59 and 86.
[155] See p. 3.
[156] 90/388/EEC, Recital 18.
[157] This has not been borne out by the experience in the UK.
[158] Emphasis added.
[159] 90/388/EEC, Art. 2.
[160] The Review by the Commission has now taken place. For a discussion of the Review see p. 126 et seq.
[161] 90/388/EEC, Art. 10.
[162] 90/388/EEC, Art. 4, and Recital 16.
[163] See p. 71 et seq.
[164] For present purposes this would be resale of capacity with limited or zero value added by the service provider.
[165] See p. 61.
[166] See p. 83.
[167] This concept is frequently referred to as 'cream-skimming'.
[168] Green Paper, COM (87) 290, p. 74.

3. The TO would not be able to compete with the tariffs offered by the competitive service providers without simultaneously lowering its rates on low profit and low traffic routes, because of its obligation to provide basic service at comparable prices throughout its national territory.[169]

The options open to the Commission for the prevention of cream-skimming were to permit Member States either to ban simple resale or to impose different tariff requirements in relation to simple resale, which would discourage such activity. In the event, the Commission opted for the former.[170] Because it continues to be open to Member States to prohibit or restrict the provision of voice telephony service,[171] the Services Directive needed only to address simple resale for the transmission of data. The Services Directive,[172] therefore, permits Member States until 31 December 1992[173] to prohibit competitor service providers from offering leased line capacity for simple resale[174] of packet-switched or circuit-switched data services[175] to the public.

The opportunity for cream-skimming would clearly not arise if the TO charges for the use of data transmission service on the switched network were comparable to those for the use of leased lines. In order not to jeopardise the tasks assigned to the TOs by Member States[176] which the Commission thought could have resulted from an immediate requirement for the TOs to balance tariffs, the Services Directive provided the transition period to 31 December 1992.[177] By the end of the transition period Member States are required to ensure that equilibrium in other relevant charges is achieved.[178]

VALUE-ADDED SERVICES

The continuing erosion of the boundary between what the Green Paper referred to as *basic services*[179] and *value-added services*[180] dissuaded the Commission from using such concepts in formulating its telecommunications services policy. The services Green Paper drew a distinction between *reserved services*[181] and *competitive services*, comprising all other services not so reserved.[182]

However, the Commission soon concluded that it was possible to identify specific

---

[169] 90/388/EEC, Recital 19.
[170] See below.
[171] Art. 3.
[172] Subject to proper licensing procedures identified in Art. 2.
[173] Art. 1(1) defines 'simple resale of capacity' as the commercial provision on leased lines for the public of data transmission as a separate service, including only such switching, processing, data storage or protocol conversion as is necessary for transmission in real time to and from the public switched network.
[174] Art. 1(1) defines 'packet- and circuit-switched data services' as the commercial provision for the public of a direct transport of data between public switched network termination points, enabling any user to use equipment connected to such a network termination point in order to communicate with another termination point.
[175] These are tasks of general interest which fall within Article 90(2) of the Rome Treaty; see Recital 18 of the Services Directive, 90/388/EEC.
[176] 90/388/EEC, Art. 3.
[177] 90/388/EEC, Recital 19; see also Art. 3 for the measures that need to have been put in place by 30 June 1992.
[178] Green Paper, COM (87) 290 final, p. 34, paras 3.1 and 3.2.
[179] Services Green Paper, 90/388/EEC, p. 35, para. 3.4.
[180] Which comprise services for which exclusive provision by the TOs would continue.
[181] Services Green Paper, 90/388/EEC, p. 65, para. 4.1.3.
[182] COM (88) 48, p. 17.

services for which special reservation might be justified and permitted.[183] The services accepted as candidates for exclusive provision were voice telephony and telex.[184]

Therefore, the concept of *value-added services* which was a feature of early regulation in many Member States[185] is not a feature of Community regulation of telecommunications.

BROADCASTING AND PROGRAMME SERVICES

The Services Directive does not address or apply to 'mass communication services such as radio or television'.[186] Such services present distinct and different problems,[187] such as intellectual property rights and advertising issues, not commonly present in other telecommunications services.[188]

However, a distinction must be drawn between mass communication services, which essentially comprise broadcasting and other programme services, and the networks over which they are provided. With rapid technological development there has been and continues to be a rapid convergence between telecommunications and the audio visual sector. Particularly, as networks become digitised and improved in efficiency, the possibility of providing mass communication services over public telecommunications networks will become both possible and attractive.

Currently Member States prohibit the provision by TOs of programming services over their networks. But, with the increasing competition in their more traditional services there is growing pressure from the TOs to utilise their modern networks for provision of television and other mass communication services. Should a Member State proceed to permit this,[189] the Services Directive does not provide the framework for ensuring competition in mass communication services over the public network.

SATELLITE SERVICES

Satellite communications are specifically excluded from the application of the Services Directive[190] although it was addressed at some length in the Green Paper.[191] This was in part due to the perceived unique characteristics of satellite communications and systems compared with terrestrial systems, including the wide geographic coverage by such systems, and the different economic structure of the services they provide.[192]

The satellite Green Paper proposes an end to this structure. It proposes to liberalise the space segment market by permitting space segment providers to market their services

---

[183] See Services Directive, 90/388/EEC, Art. 2 and Recital 21. Note in particular that although Member States are permitted to deal with telex on an individual basis, the decision in the British Telecom Case 41/83, clearly establishes the right of telex agencies to receive telexes on the telex network and retransmit them on the more efficient voice telephony network.

[184] See for example the UK value added data services licence (VADS Licence).

[185] Services Directive, 90/388/EEC, Recital 1.

[186] See Green Paper Television Without Frontiers, COM (84) 300 final, 14 June 1984.

[187] Such issues and concerns are not always absent in telecommunications activity and a growing area of concern currently being addressed by the Commission is that of access to and extraction of data from databases, usually by means of telecommunications networks; see proposal for a Council Directive on the legal protection of databases, COM (92) 24 final, 13 May 1992.

[189] The UK may revise its policy on this issue in 1998; see White Paper Competition and Choice: Telecommunications Policy for the 1990s, Cm 1461, March 1991, paras 5.7 and 5.19.

[190] 90/388/EEC, Art. 1(2).

[191] COM (87) 290, pp. 37–39, 83–88.

[192] COM (87) 290, p. 38.

directly to end users. It also proposes unrestricted access to space segment capacity by permitting direct access to space segment capacity by users, without the intervention of the ISO Signatories.[193]

Although satellite communications is a sector of the communications market in which there is great potential for new services, liberalisation of the market has been slow and little progress has been made in implementing the satellite Green Paper. This is so even to the extent that the proposals for mutual recognition of licences[194] do not apply to satellite services.[195] This was despite the declared objective of Commission officials to establish a framework for single Community satellite licensing.[196]

Scope of satellite Green Paper

The satellite Green Paper[197] made proposals for the extension of the application of generally agreed principles of Community telecommunications policy to satellite communications. The satellite Green Paper proposes four major changes:[198]

1. Full liberalisation of the earth segment, including both receive-only and transmit/receive terminals;[199]
2. Unrestricted access to space segment capacity on an equitable, non-discriminatory and cost-oriented basis;[200]
3. Full commercial freedom for space segment providers, including direct marketing of satellite capacity to service providers and to users;[201]
4. Harmonisation measures as far as required to facilitate the provision of Europe-wide services, including mutual recognition of licensing and type approval procedures and frequency co-ordination.

The satellite Green Paper advocates that regulation of satellite communications and in particular the granting of any special or exclusive rights should conform[202] to the principles set out in the Services Directive.[203] However, it adds that any future regulatory conditions for satellite communications should not introduce any restrictions beyond those appropriate to the specific conditions of satellite communications and any licensing schemes should be based on objective facts, proportionate to the requirements they fulfil, be transparent and non-discriminatory.[204]

---

[193] COM (90) 490 final, paras 18, 21–3.
[194] Draft Proposal for a Council Directive on the Mutual Recognition of Licences and Other National Authorisations to Operate Telecommunications Services, Including the Establishment of a Single Community Telecommunications Licence, ONP-COM 91/79, 12 Dec. 1991, internal working document.
[195] ONP-COM 91/79, para. 16.
[196] Satellite communications in the European Community, T. Howell and P. Verhoef, CEC, DG XIII D4, s. 4A.
[197] Towards Europe-wide Systems and Services: Green Paper on a Common Approach in the Field of Satellite Communications in the European Community, COM (90) 490 final, 20 Nov. 1990; this Green Paper had been expected to be published considerably earlier and the many missed deadlines for its publication are an indication of the difficulties encountered in reaching an acceptable level of consensus within the Community.
[198] COM (90) 490 final, p. 3.
[199] This would be subject to type approval and licensing procedures that may be justified to implement necessary regulatory safeguards, such as those covered by 'essential requirements'; see p. 73.
[200] Access can be made subject to licensing, to safeguard exclusive or special rights and regulatory provisions in the Member States which conform to Community law and telecommunications policy.
[201] These may also be made subject to licensing procedures as above, conforming to Community law and competition rules.
[202] COM (90) 490 final, p. 123.
[203] 90/388/EEC.
[204] COM (90) 490 final, p. 123, para. 8.

Terminals and satellite connection to PSN

Under the Green Paper proposals, satellite communication systems can be made subject to regulation regarding electro-magnetic interference.[205] Satellite communications systems which are not connected to the public switched network can only be subject to licensing requirements which are intended to ensure avoidance of harmful interference,[206] data protection, including protection of privacy, and harmonisation of standards.[207] Receive-only terminals are treated in the same way as TV receive-only satellite antennas[208] and should only be required to comply with electro-magnetic interference standards no stricter than those applying to other radio receivers and should not be subject to any licensing.[209] Transmit/receive stations may, however, be subject to type approval and licensing requirements applicable to other terminal equipment.[210]

It is proposed that the reservation of exclusive or special rights only be maintained by Member State for satellite communications systems as far as these may be considered equivalent to two-way public service networks or services.[211] The satellite Green Paper asserts that large-scale two-way satellite communication systems, such as extensive VSAT[212] systems, should only be considered as public if they are connected to the public switched terrestrial network infrastructure. However, Member State are left with the opportunity to argue that a given system which is not connected to the public switched network can nevertheless be subject to special or exclusive rights.[213] This would be on the basis that such a network would compete with the TO to such an extent as to obstruct the TO in providing public telecommunication services.[214]

Mobile communications

The satellite Green Paper envisages no greater constraints on mobile satellite services than those applicable to fixed satellite services.[215] In the view of the Commission, such services will be focused on specific user segments which will be relatively small in size and comparable to other one- or two-way point-to-multipoint applications.

ISOs

One of the major factors distorting competition in satellite communications is the absence of a direct relationship between the international satellite organisations, Intelsat and Inmarsat, and the European Telecommunications Satellite Organisation, Eutelsat, and end users. Under the provisions of their operating agreements, the ISOs[216] can only

---

[205] This must be in accordance with the Council Directive on electro-magnetic compatibility (89/336/EEC; see p. 43).

[206] In this context harmful interference has the meaning given in the ITU Radio Regulations, Art. 1: 'Interference which endangers the functioning of a radio-navigation service or of other safety services or seriously degrades, obstructs or repeatedly interrupts a radiocommunication service operating in accordance with these Regulations.

[207] COM (90) 490 final, pp. 124 and 125, paras 9 and 13.

[208] Commission Directive 88/301/EEC.

[209] COM (90) 490 final, p. 127, para. 19.

[210] Council Directive 91/263/EEC, OJ L 128/1, 23 May 1991.

[211] Telecommunications Council consensus of 7 Dec. 1989; COM (90) 490 final, p. 123, para. 7.

[212] Very Small Aperture Terminal.

[213] COM (90) 490 final, p. 125, para. 12.

[214] This argument would have to conform to the requirements of the Services Directive, 90/388/EEC.

[215] COM (90) 490 final, p. 126, para. 17.

[216] International Satellite Organisations.

make available their space segment capacity to their Signatories, which in most Member States are the TOs. Conversely, users cannot obtain space segment capacity from the ISOs, but must do so through the Signatory.

CHAPTER 7

Competition in Infrastructure

HISTORICAL REVIEW

Traditionally in Europe, as in the rest of the world, the provision of the telecommunication infrastructure was the monopoly of the TOs.[1] In Europe the position pertained not only in running the infrastructure network but also in its provision. The construction and running of an alternative network requires significant investment operating as an added barrier to the regulatory barriers against entry of competitors to the market. TOs also guarded against resale of network capacity by competitors. In protecting and further establishing their monopolies over infrastructure, the TOs introduced exclusive rights into ITU[2] Regulations and Recommendations.[3]

This monopoly over infrastructure continued to survive without serious challenge from the Commission.[4] Furthermore, in its Recommendation on the introduction of ISDN[5] and in the Recommendation on the introduction of cellular digital mobile communications[6] the Council does not advocate competition in the provision of network infrastructures. The Recommendations implicitly recognise and accept continued monopoly by TOs. In its ISDN Recommendation the Council expresses the view that co-ordinated introduction of the ISDN:

> will lead to closer co-operation, at Community level, between the telecommunications industry and the administrations and the recognised private operating agencies offering telecommunications services[7]

---

[1] Although in the US the TO, AT&T, was not owned by the government, unlike its counterparts in Europe, it nevertheless constituted a monopoly, albeit privately owned.

[2] International Telecommunications Union.

[3] See for example CCITT Recommendation D series, in particular D6.

[4] The decision in the British Telecommunications Case did not give rise to changes in the monopoly relating to provision and use of infrastructure; see Commission Decision 82/861/EEC, OJ L 360/36, 21 Dec. 1982; and p. 20.

[5] 86/659/EEC, OJ L 383/36, 31 Dec. 1986.

[6] 87/371/EEC, OJ L 196/81, 17 July 1987.

[7] In their Recommendation the administrations and recognised private operating agencies are referred to as 'telecommunications administrations'.

69

and recommends

that the *telecommunications administr*ations[8] implement the detailed Recommendations concerning the co-ordinated introduction of the integrated services digital network (ISDN) in the
Community.[9]

The cellular digital mobile communications Recommendation contains parallel terms with
appropriate changes.[10]

The Commission continues to permit monopoly over the network infrastructure. In its
White Paper on the development of the common market for telecommunications services
and equipment,[11] in addressing the progressive opening of the telecommunications
services market through competition, it states:[12]

Continued exclusive provision or special rights for the Telecommunications Administrations
regarding provision and operation of the network infrastructure, and at this stage of voice
telephone service, is accepted.

This position was to be reviewed by 1 January 1992.[13]

The Economic and Social Committee was critical even of the opening through competition of non-voice services. In its opinion[14] on the White Paper the Committee states:[15]

The Committee regrets the decision to confine the exclusive or special rights of telecommunications administrations to voice telephony. This may prejudice the original role of the
public service.

It goes on to state:[16]

The Committee hopes that the final decision will reflect the point of view expressed in its
[November 1987] Opinion,[17] to the effect that all two-way communications systems should
be regarded as forming an integral part of the network and should therefore be covered by the
exclusive or special rights of the telecommunications administrations.

The Commission has not followed this course in certain circumstances, such as in the case
of satellite networks not connected to the public telecommunications network.[18]

---

[8] Emphasis added.
[9] 86/659/EEC, para. 1.
[10] 87/371/EEC, preamble and para. 1.
[11] Towards a competitive Community-wide telecommunication market in 1992: implementing the Green Paper on
the development of the common market for telecommunications services and equipment, COM (88) 48 final, 9
Feb. 1988.
[12] COM (88) 48 final, para. IV(ii), p. 17.
[13] Ibid.
[14] 88/C 175/13, OJ C 175/36, 4 July 1988.
[15] 88/C 175/13, para. 2.2.
[16] 88/C 175/13, para. 3.1.
[17] Committee opinion on the Green Paper, 87/C 356/12, OJ C 356/46, 31 Dec. 1987. The opinion referred to is
contained in para. 5.1 which states: 'Firstly, we approve entirely the maintenance (or creation) of the current and
future integrity of the basic network infrastructure, which should include the cable and satellite T.V. networks,
used for two-way communications, as recommended in the Green Paper. Similarly we support the continued
exclusive or special rights of the telecommunication administrations to provide and operate the network infrastructure and to provide certain basic services; the aim being primarily to safeguard the public service role.
[18] Satellite Green Paper, Towards Europe-wide Systems and Services: Green Paper on a Common Approach in the
Field of Satellite Communications in the European Community, COM (90) 490 final, 20 Nov. 1990.

OPEN NETWORK PROVISION REQUIREMENTS

Against the background of monopoly providers of the network infrastructure, it has been recognised as central to the future functioning of the competitive market that the use of the network by providers of competitive services be subjected to clear Community-wide definition or general requirements imposed by telecommunications administrations.[19] Such Community-wide definition has been called Open Network Provision (ONP).

Even where Member States do not grant monopoly rights for the provision of network infrastructure, it is still vital to the creation of the competitive market that the operators conform to Open Network Provisions.

By February 1988 the SOG-T's[20] sub-group GAP[21] had started to define the general approach to the ONP concept. The background to the introduction of ONP was set out by the Commission in its communication, *Towards a Competitive Community-wide Telecommunications Market in 1992: Implementing the Green Paper on the Development of the Common Market for Telecommunications Services and Equipment*,[22] in which it stated:[23]

> In order to allow timely input to the Community-wide definition of fair access and usage conditions, it is suggested to concentrate on those issues most critical to providers of competitive services and a competitive market environment and to work according to a stringent time schedule:
>> analysis of conditions of open provision of leased lines to be completed by mid 1988;
>> analysis of conditions of open provision of the general public data networks to be completed by end 1988;
>> analysis of conditions of open provision of the future integrated services digital network (ISDN) to be completed by mid 1989.
> In a subsequent study period, the conditions of access to frequencies may be a suitable subject.
> Analysis should cover technical interfaces, tariff principles, and conditions of use. It should include the clear definition of network termination points where appropriate.

In its opinion[24] on the Green Paper which it later confirmed[25] the Economic and Social Committee implicitly approved the proposals for the development of ONP.[26] The Committee therefore agreed with the Commission that participation of both the TOs and other suppliers in the new market opportunities implies the implementation of harmonised access conditions to the networks and services operated by the TOs – the concept defined in the Green Paper as Open Network Provision – ONP.[27]

ONP should lead to an open, efficient and harmonised environment for the development of non-reserved services[28] in the Community, in particular the value-added services. The development of conditions for ONP is a progressive and participative process

---

[19] COM (88) 48 final, 9 Feb. 1988, p. 18, para. v.2.

[20] The Senior Officials Group on Telecommunications established under Art. 5 of Directive 86/361/EEC. SOG-T was set up by the Council on 4 Nov. 1983.

[21] Group for Analysis and Forecasting.

[22] COM (88) 48 final, 9 Feb. 1988.

[23] COM (88) 48, para. v.2, p. 18.

[24] 87/C 356/12, OJ C 356/46, 31 Dec. 1987.

[25] 88/C 175/13, OJ C 175/36, 4 July 1988.

[26] The Committee approved the Commission proposal 'to develop the conditions for the market to provide European users with a greater variety of telecommunications services . . . ' while advocating continued monopoly by TOs in the provision of the network infrastructure; 87/C 356/12, paras 4.2 and 5.1.

[27] Telecommunications: Progress on the Definition of Open Network Provision (ONP): Short Status Report, COM (88) 718 final, 13 Dec. 1988, p. 3.

[28] These are services which are not reserved to the TOs by special or exclusive rights; see p. 68 et seq.

requiring clear definition by Community Directives of general requirements imposed by TOs on proprietors of competitors' services for use on the network, including definitions regarding network infrastructure provision. This must include clear inter-connect and access obligation by TOs for trans-frontier service providers in order to prevent Treaty infringements. It also entails consensus on harmonised standards, frequencies and tariff principles, in order to agree on the general principles imposed for service provision in the competitive sector. The Commission envisaged the details of this Directive on ONP being prepared in consultation with the Member States, the TOs and the other parties concerned, in the framework of the SOG-T.[29]

The work of GAP started in 1987 and produced a report which was adopted by SOG-T in early 1988.[30] This established the reference framework for ONP, based on a number of principles. These principles were:

- harmonised ONP conditions must be based on objective criteria; be transparent and published in an appropriate manner; must not discriminate between nationals of Member States; and must guarantee equality of access;
- the development and implementation of ONP conditions should be progressive, emphasising development of harmonised offerings specifically suited for value-added service providers but available to all users;
- the importance of the development of open network standards should be emphasised in the framework of the overall Community approach to European standardisation.

This lead to defining three main areas of the development of harmonised ONP conditions:

1. Definition of harmonised technical interfaces and service features. These should be existing technical interfaces wherever possible. ETSI should be requested to develop new technical standards which may be required for ONP offerings.
2. Definition of harmonised usage conditions. Common usage conditions which should apply for ONP offerings include provision time, contractual period, quality of service, conditions for shared use, third party use, resale of capacity and network interconnection.
3. Definition of harmonised tariff principles. These should include the principle that tariffs be cost oriented, be properly published and apply to all users on a non-discriminatory basis.[31]

Council Directive on ONP

Following the GAP report and based on its proposals, the Commission made a proposal for a Directive on ONP[32] which aimed to establish a stable framework for the progressive creation of harmonised conditions for open access to, and open use of the public telecommunications network infrastructure and public telecommunications services.[33] The proposed procedures which are now contained in the Council Directive on

---

[29] COM (88) 718 final, p. 4.
[30] The Report by the Analysis and Forecasting Group (GAP) on Open Network Provision in the Community, 20 Jan. 1988, adopted by SOG-T on 13 Apr. 1988.
[31] The matters dealt with in the GAP Report, including those set out here, are referred to in COM (88) 718 final.
[32] COM (88) 825 final: SYN 187, 9 Jan. 1989.
[33] The establishment of such a framework was emphasised by the Council in its resolution of 30 June 1988, 88/C 257/01, as central to the achievement of an effective Community market for telecommunications services.

ONP[34] formed the basis on which specific Directives will be submitted by the Commission to the Council for each particular area of telecommunications.[35] The areas for which ONP conditions are to be drawn up under the framework established by the ONP Directive[36] are divided into eight categories.[37] The areas particularly identified are:[38]

1. leased lines;
2. packet- and circuit-switched data services;
3. ISDN;
4. voice telephony service;
5. telex service;
6. mobile services.

The Directive[39] establishes a work scheduled to 31 December 1992, starting with leased lines and voice telephony, and moving to harmonise technical interfaces and service features for packet-switched data services and ISDN by 1 January 1991. It also directs the European Commission to present to the Council for its adoption by 1 July 1991 Recommendations on technical interfaces, conditions of usage and tariff principles regarding packed-switched data services. The Commission's Recommendation would in particular call on each Member State to provide at least one data service in compliance with proposed or finalised ONP terms and conditions. Some specific Directives have already been drawn up and are considered further.[40]

Overview of ONP Directive

The ONP Directive[41] aims to bring about harmonised ONP conditions in each Member State and throughout the Community. The regulatory and legislative means by which it seeks to achieve this are contained in the Directive. The means employed by the Directive to achieve harmonised open access to, and use of, the public telecommunications network infrastructure and public telecommunications services are substantive rules concerning the *basic principles* and *essential requirements* with which the ONP conditions within and between Member States[42] must comply. The rules according to which specific Council Directives will be prepared are procedural and organisational rules.

The Directive establishes the scope and application of ONP conditions,[43] defines the *basic principles* with which ONP conditions must comply and the essential requirements on which they must be based;[44] provides the procedures for the definition of ONP conditions in stages;[45] concerns the future progressive process for the mutual recognition of authorisation procedures in the Community[46] and provides for a review of progress on

---

[34] Council Directive of 28 June 1990 on the Establishment of the Internal Market for Telecommunications Services through the Implementation of Open Network Provision, 90/387/EEC, OJ L 192/1, 24 July 1990.
[35] COM (88) 825 final, p. 3.
[36] 90/387/EEC.
[37] Art. 4 and Annex I.
[38] Annex I.
[39] 90/387/EEC, Annex III.
[40] See p. 83 et seq.
[41] 90/387/EEC.
[42] Art. 1(2).
[43] 90/387/EEC, Art. 1 together with the definitions, Art. 2.
[44] 90/387/EEC, Art. 3.
[45] 90/387/EEC, Arts 4–6.
[46] 90/387/EEC, Art. 7.

harmonisation and the progress of ONP during 1992.[47] It establishes the principle of consultation with those concerned in implementation of the ONP Directive and particularly with the advisory committee which in practice is SOG-T[48] and sets out the procedures for ensuring inter-operability of services and the data protection.[49]

Criteria for ONP

The substantive criteria for ONP are embodied in the *basic principles* and the *essential requirements*.[50] The basic principles:[51] objectivity, transparency, non-discrimination and equality of access, were particularly emphasised by the GAP report.[52] The *basic principles* established the principles aimed at achieving harmonised liberalisation of the provision of telecommunications networks and services by the monopoly operators. However, certain limitations may be placed on access to public telecommunications networks or public telecommunications services but, with some exceptions,[53] as long as they are all reasons based on *essential requirements*[54] which are of a non-economic nature and are for general public interest.[55] In addition, ONP conditions can include restrictions 'derived from the exercise of special or exclusive rights granted by Member States and which are compatible with Community law'.[56]

To achieve the objective of full inter-operability between all public networks in the Community two factors are of importance to the Commission. These are standards for the network infrastructure and services[57] and the protection of individuals relating to the automatic processing of personal data.[58]

Although regarded as an important element, the Directive effectively transfers to the Member States the responsibility for the level of protection afforded the data. The Directive[59] includes as an *essential requirement*, which can form the basis of restriction on access to public telecommunications networks or public telecommunications services, such protection of data as is *'appropriate'*. Furthermore, while including data protection within the definition of 'essential requirements', this need not but *'may* include protection of personal data . . . as well as the protection of privacy'.[60]

---

[47] 90/387/EEC, Art. 8.

[48] 90/387/EEC, Art. 9.

[49] Arts 11 and 12 relate to the bringing into force of the Directive.

[50] See p. 73 above; 90/387/EEC, Arts 3(1) and (2).

[51] 90/387/EEC, Art. 3(1).

[52] Report by the analysis and forecasting group (GAP) on open network provision (ONP) in the Community, 20 Jan. 1988; see p. 72.

[53] 90/387/EEC, Art. 3(3).

[54] 90/387/EEC, Art. 2(2); these are security of network operation, maintenance of network integrity, in justified cases, inter-operability of services and protection of data and the essential requirements in general applicable to the connection of terminal equipment to the network (see Dir. 86/361/EEC).

[55] The Green Paper COM (87) 290 final sets out the key role of these requirements.

[56] 90/387/EEC, Art. 3(3).

[57] These are dealt with more fully by Arts 4–6; see p. 76 et seq.

[58] The importance of protection of personal data was emphasised by the Council in its resolution of 30 June 1988, 88/C 257/01, 4 Oct. 1988; see also Recommendation 81/679/EEC concerning the ratification of the Council of Europe Convention for the protection of individuals with regard to automatic processing of personal data; see also p. 110 on the proposed Council Directive concerning the protection of personal data and privacy in the context of public digital telecommunications networks, 5 June 1990. Convention for the protection of individuals with regard to automatic processing of personal data, done at Strasburg 28 January 1981, European Treaty series No. 108.

[59] 90/376/EEC, Art. 3(2).

[60] 90/376/EEC, Art. 2(6), emphasis added.

Scope of application of the Directive

The Directive requires that Member States adopt harmonised ONP conditions for open access to and use of public telecommunications networks and appropriate public telecommunications services.[61] Although the present Directive does not extend to the totality of public telecommunications networks and services,[62] the Commission has the power to enlarge the scope of a Directive.[63]

There is a slight difference between the scope of application of ONP conditions with regard to networks and to services. When the Directive was originally proposed[64] the draft Directive specified that

ONP conditions will apply to access or use of those public telecommunications networks and public telecommunications services for which the telecommunications organisations[65] . . . are in law or in fact the sole or main providers either singly or jointly.[66]

This in effect would have confined the application of the ONP conditions to TOs providing networks or services. However, the Directive defines 'open network provision conditions'[67] in terms only of public telecommunications networks and public telecommunications services. Of these only public telecommunications services are defined by reference to public telecommunications organisations with special or exclusive rights.[68] However, in practice this will make little difference as throughout the Community the running of public telecommunications networks are subject to special or exclusive rights granted by the Member States.

In order to achieve the Commission's objective of creating a harmonised Community-wide telecommunications network and services market, the ONP conditions established under the Directive must be applied 'to facilitate the provision of services using public telecommunications networks and/or public telecommunications services, *within*' Member States as well as between them.[69]

The scope of the Directive will become progressively clearer as subsequent Directives lead to more detailed definitions of terms, for example such as the meaning of 'network termination point'.[70] The Directive is not intended to 'address the problems of mass media, meaning problems linked to broadcasting and distribution of television programmes via telecommunications means, in particular cable television networks, which need special consideration',[71] nor questions of communication by satellite.[72] The Directive specifically excludes application to radio broadcasting and television services.[73]

---

[61] 90/376/EEC, Art. 1(1), and 4th Recital.

[62] 90/376/EEC, Annex I.

[63] 90/376/EEC, Art. 4(2).

[64] Proposal for a Council Directive on the establishment of an internal market for telecommunications services through the implementation of open network provision, COM (88) 825 final, 9 Jan. 1989.

[65] Art. 2(1) of the draft Directive defined 'telecommunications organisations' as 'the administrations or private operating agencies recognised in the Community, providing public telecommunications networks and/or public telecommunications services'.

[66] Art. 2(4) of the draft Directive.

[67] 90/387/EEC, Art. 2(10).

[68] 90/387/EEC, Arts 2(1) and (4).

[69] 90/387/EEC, Art. 1(2).

[70] 90/387/EEC, Art. 2(5).

[71] 90/387/EEC, 22nd Recital.

[72] 90/387/EEC, 23rd Recital.

[73] 90/387/EEC, Art. 2(4), definition of 'telecommunications services'.

Procedural rules

This Directive, as already noted,[74] establishes the framework for the application of open network provision conditions to specific areas of telecommunications by means of Directives.[75] The Directive establishes a procedure for this progressive introduction of open network provision. This procedure involves the Commission, the Council, the ONP committee and standardisation organisations, including ETSI, as well as telecommunications organisations, users, customers, manufacturers and service providers.[76] There are broadly eight distinct steps to be gone through eventually leading to the adoption of a Directive on ONP in a specific area. These steps are set out below.

1. Selection of the area to which ONP conditions relate.
   These areas are set out in the Directive,[77] as noted above.[78] The list of relevant areas is subject to modification by the Council, as necessary.[79]
2. Selection of area for immediate action.
   From the areas designated by the Council and those referred to above, the Commission will select areas which form the subject of the work programme for each year.[80] This is a flexible procedure and in attaching priorities for action in its work programme the Commission consults the ONP committee which in turn will consult representatives from industry, consumers and service providers.[81]
3. Analysis and reports on work programme.
   The Commission, in consultation with the ONP committee, will initiate detailed analysis of the proposed work programme and draw up reports.[82] The procedure for the analysis and reports corresponds to established procedures of the Commission involving SOG-T and its sub-group GAP, but with increased participation by industry, user organisers and other interested parties.[83]
4. Invitation and consideration of public comment.
   This procedure again underlines the Commission's view of the importance of participation in the definition of ONP conditions by user organisations, industry, trade unions and consumer groups.
5. Commission request to ETSI to draw up European standards as a basis for harmonised technical interfaces and service features, where required.[84]
   In these circumstances ETSI is expected to take account of international standards and co-ordinate its activities with the European Standards Institution CEN/CENELEC. This procedure accords with the Commission's policy to delegate the elaboration of Community-wide standards to ETSI, rather than get involved in defining standards by lengthy law-making procedures.
6. Publication by the Commission of its request to ETSI for the drawing up of standards in the official journal.

---

[74] See p. 73.
[75] 90/387/EEC, Art. 4(1).
[76] 90/387/EEC, Arts 4–6 and 9.
[77] 90/387/EEC, Annex I.
[78] See p. 73.
[79] 90/387/EEC, Art. 4(2).
[80] 90/387/EEC, Art. 4(3).
[81] 90/387/EEC, Art. 9(1).
[82] 90/387/EEC, Art. 4(4)(a).
[83] The increased participation by outside groups was urged by the Commission in its Progress on the Definition of Open Network Provision: Short Status Report, COM (88) 701.
[84] 90/387/EEC, Art. 4(4)(c).

This publication gives notice to all concerned of the prospect that a European standard will be defined, which carries with it the presumptions associated with the standard under the Directive.[85] There is also a procedure for a Member State or the Commission to consult the ONP committee if the harmonised standards is considered inadequate for fulfilling the objectives of the Directive.[86]

7. The Council adopts the specific Directives.

On adoption of the relevant Directives[87] the Council also sets out a time schedule for their implementation.

8. The Member States implement the Directives according to their terms.

Removal of barriers to inter-operability of services

There are circumstances in which access to a public telecommunications network or to public telecommunications services in a Member State may be restricted without any breach of the terms of the ONP Directive. First, a Member State may apply its essential requirements[88] in such a way as to limit access to the public telecommunications network or services.

In that event the Commission will determine rules for uniform application of the essential requirements so that the needs of inter-operability and data protection as well as the other essential requirements are met.[89] The Commission will make its determination in consultation with the ONP committee under the procedures specially defined for this purpose.[90]

The second circumstance in which inter-operability of services could be jeopardised under the Directive relates to the implementation of European standards. If the implementation of the European standards provided for in the Directive[91] does not ensure inter-operability of *trans-frontier*[92] services in one or more Member States, the Commission may make reference to European standards compulsory.[93] The procedures to be followed by the Commission are the same as those relating to the essential requirements.[94]

Such compulsory reference can only be made by the Commission to the extent that it is '*strictly*[95] necessary to ensure . . . inter-operability and to improve freedom of choice for users'.[96]

The Directive makes clear that the procedures of the Directive for ensuring implementation of European standards to secure inter-operability is not a substitute for nor prevents the separate application of the competition rules[97] of the Treaty.[98]

---

[85] 90/387/EEC, Art. 5(1),(2). The presumptions are that by complying with standard (a) a serious provider fulfils the 'essential requirements' and (b) a telecommunications organisation fulfils the requirements.
[86] 90/387/EEC, Art. 5(4).
[87] 90/387/EEC, Art. 6.
[88] See p. 74 and 90/387/EEC, Art. 3(2) for a definition of 'essential requirements'.
[89] 90/387/EEC, Art. 3(5).
[90] 90/387/EEC, Art. 10.
[91] 90/387/EEC, Art. 5(2).
[92] Emphasis added.
[93] 90/387/EEC, Art. 5(3).
[94] 90/387/EEC, Art. 10.
[95] Emphasis added.
[96] 90/387/EEC, Art. 5(3).
[97] Rome Treaty, Arts 85 and 86.
[98] 90/387/EEC, Art. 5(3).

Mutual recognition of licensing procedures

The progressive harmonisation of ONP conditions is recognised by the Commission as only achieving a part of its objective of creating a single and uniform market for the provision of services over public telecommunications networks throughout the Community.[99] Another major factor in realising the Commission's objective is the 'mutual recognition of declaration and licensing[100] procedures'.[101] The natural progression following on from such mutual recognition is that service providers that have fulfilled the declaration and licensing requirements in one Member State will then be entitled to provide the services throughout the Community without being subjected to any further procedures.[102]

The ONP Directive provides the mechanism for the initial steps towards this process.[103] It provides for the Council to take measures to harmonise the declaration and licensing procedures where these are required by Member States for the provision of services by public telecommunications networks. The Directive identifies the aim of such harmonisation to be the establishment of conditions for mutual recognition. As with all harmonising processes, the Directive permits the special circumstances of particular Member States to be taken into account depending on their economic circumstances which result in differences in the development of the services subject to the harmonising process.[104]

MUTUAL RECOGNITION OF LICENCES

Expanding on the basis provided for the mutual recognition of licences in the ONP Directive,[105] the Commission has issued its proposals for a Council Directive[106] for a Single Community Telecommunications Licence.[107] In introducing the Draft Community Licence Directive, the Commission states its aim as 'establishing a balanced and efficient procedure for the mutual recognition of licences or other authorisations for the provision of *telecommunications services*[108] issued by Member States'.[109] The statement makes clear that the Proposed Directive covers only situations where Member States grant licences or authorisations[110] for the provision of services *on* telecommunications

---

[99] COM (88) 825 final, p. 15.

[100] Practises in Member States vary as to the method by which telecommunications services are permitted. In some Member States there is a requirement for registration rather than declaration, similarly in some Member States authorisations, rather than licenses, are granted.

[101] 90/387/EEC, ONP Dir., Art. 7.

[102] Mutual recognition of licenses raises fundamental issues which are addressed in relation to services at p. 82.

[103] 90/387/EEC, Art. 7.

[104] Rome Treaty, Art. 8c.

[105] 90/387/EEC, Art. 7.

[106] Proposal for a Council Directive on the Mutual Recognition of Licences and other National Authorisations to Operate Telecommunications Services, including the establishment of a Single Community Telecommunications Licence and the setting up of a Community Telecommunications Committee (CTC), COM (92) 254 final, 15 July 1992.

[107] Draft Community Licence Directive.

[108] Emphasis added.

[109] COM (92) 254, Summary, P. 2.

[110] Such licences must, of course, comply with community law as specified by Dir. 90/388/EEC on Telecommunications Services whereby Member States can subject telecommunications services to licensing of declaration procedures which are warranted by essential requirements or where they may grant special or exclusive rights; see COM (92) 254, Explanatory Memorandum, para. 1.

networks[111] and not to licences for the provision of network infrastructure which may, and in some Member States continues to be, subject to monopoly provision. The provision of mobile radio services and satellite services are also excluded from the scope of the Proposed Directive.[112]

The application of the Directive to mobile and satellite communications has been excluded on the basis that there is no sufficient harmonisation in the use of frequencies within the Community. Thus, until the allocation and co-ordination of frequencies has been harmonised, these services are not intended to be covered. However, in its most recent work, the Commission[113] is considering the establishment of procedures for mutual recognition of licences to provide satellite communications services.

Once implemented, the mutual recognition of licences throughout the Community will enable service providers to avoid the need for time-consuming parallel applications for licences before they can operate services in two or more Member States. Currently, the need for such applications can act as a significant barrier to the 'provision of Community-wide telecommunications services and keep the Community telecommunications services market divided in twelve national markets'.[114]

The impact of mutual recognition

The Community Licence Directive establishes the principles and a mechanism for giving effect to the principle that 'any service provider authorised and supervised by the competent authorities of any Member State may operate the services covered by the authorisation in all other Member States without the need to wait for complete harmonisation of the licensing conditions'.[115] The Proposed Directive does not dispense with or replace the need to proceed with harmonisation of licences and includes certain harmonisation provisions for specific service categories.[116]

The mutual licence procedures apply also in cases where a Member State does not impose any licensing or declaration requirements for the provision of certain telecommunication services.[117] Extension of procedures to such a Member State is achieved in the Proposed Directive through the definition of 'national authorisations'.[118]

One underlying reason for the need for the Proposed Community Licence Directive is that 'essential requirements', on the basis of which Member States may impose restrictive conditions on the provision of services, have not yet been fully harmonised at Community level.[119] This is particularly the case with regard to voice telephony; nor is there sufficient harmonisation with regard to data protection. Another continuing difference between Member States, for which there is yet no harmonisation, is the scope of the services which are subject to special or exclusive rights, in conformity with Community law.

Therefore, the mutual recognition procedure establishes the means for attaching additional requirements to any national authorisation before such national authorisation

---

[111] COM (92) 254, Proposed Community Licence Directive, Art. 1.
[112] Proposed Community Licence Directive, Art. 3.
[113] There are proposals for mutual recognition of licences in respect of satellite communications from DG XIII.
[114] COM (92) 254, Explanatory Memorandum, para. 1.
[115] COM (92) 254, Explanatory Memorandum, para. 2.
[116] Proposed Community Licence Directive, Arts 14 and 15.
[117] Most Member States permit the provision of value added services without any former requirement for a licence or declaration.
[118] See Proposed Community Licence Directive, Art. 2(2).
[119] A measure of harmonisation has been achieved through the Directive applied ONP to leased lines.

is given the benefits of mutual recognition.[120] In the circumstances, mutual recognition will be given to the national authorisation together with any additional conditions affixed to those of the authorisation.

Committees involved in the mutual recognition process

One of the major difficulties involved in the recognition and implementation of a telecommunications licence granted by the regulatory authority in one country, by the regulatory authority of another, is the differences in language and the concepts that exist between jurisdictions. This problem is often encountered in negotiation and formulation of bilateral arrangements in this area.[121] For example, store and forward services may be regarded as value added services in one jurisdiction and not another.

The Proposed Directive in part overcomes this difficulty through the establishment of the Community Telecommunications Committee,[122] comprising representatives of national regulatory authorities of Member States and chaired by a Commission representative.[123] The CTC would assist the Commission and advise on the implementation of the requirements of the Directive.[124]

The Proposed Directive also envisages the possibility of extending the provision of services in relation to which mutual recognition is being sought, to countries outside the community which are members of CEPT.[125] In those circumstances the procedure involves consultation with the European Committee for Telecommunications Regulatory Affairs.[126] ECTRA is a committee set up by CEPT.

Although the CTC and ECTRA have been specifically identified as having an active role in the mutual recognition of authorisations process, the Commission will clearly also rely on the expertise developed within the ONP Committee, the ECTRA Committee as well as SOGT and the Joint Committee on Telecommunications. There will also be co-ordination with ETSI, CEN-CENELEC as well as ITU bodies such as CCITT and CCIR.[127]

The nature of mutual recognition

The Proposed Community Licence Directive establishes two routes by which national authorisations can be given recognition throughout the Community and in country members of CEPT.

1. *Individual services*
   One approach is to grant recognition to individual and specific national authorisations in the form of a Single Community Telecommunications Licence.[128] The Single Community Telecommunications Licence is not an additional Licence, but a certificate of recognition that a national authorisation can be used to operate the authorised service in all other Member States. Through consultation with ECTRA,

---

[120] Proposed Community Licence Directive, Art. 12(6).
[121] See, for example, the arrangements between the US and the UK for the provision of valued added services.
[122] CTC.
[123] Proposed Community Licence Directive, Art. 20.
[124] Proposed Community Licence Directive, Art. 21.
[125] See Community Licence Directive, Art. 8.
[126] ECTRA.
[127] COM (92) 254, Explanatory Memorandum, para. 5.
[128] Proposed Community Licence Directive, Arts 4 and 5.

the Commission also provides the prospect of extending the provision of services to CEPT countries outside the Community.[129]

In processing applications for the Single Community Telecommunications Licence, the Commission invites the national regulatory authorities of all other Member States to submit any objections to the grant of the Community Licence.[130] Any objections by national regulatory authorities must, of course, be on grounds compatible with Community law.[131]

In granting a Single Community Telecommunications Licence, the Commission will take account of any objections and may, under the Single Community Licence, impose conditions additional to those contained in the national authorisation.[132] If, however, there are no objections raised by other Member States, a Single Community Telecommunications Licence will be granted after the expiry of time allowed for objections.[133]

In arriving at any additional conditions to be imposed in the Single Community Telecommunications Licence, the Commission seeks first to obtain the consent of all parties concerned.[134] However, if agreement is not reached, the Commission can still proceed with the grant of a Single Community Telecommunications Licence, taking account of the opinion of the CTC and, where appropriate, of ECTRA.[135] There are, naturally, requirements for national regulatory authorities to facilitate those granted national authorisations to apply for a Community Licence[136] and to grant national authorisations in a form that will facilitate their recognition through a Single Community Telecommunications Licence.[137] The applicant need not make his applications through the national regulatory authority that provided the national authorisation. It may do so through the national regulatory authority of any Member State.[138] There are also provisions for direct submission by operators of applications for a Community Licence directly to the Commission.[139]

As already stated, the need to grant Single Community Telecommunication Licences arises out of the absence of complete harmonisation of telecommunications licences in the Community.

2. *Category of services*

The Proposed Community Licence Directive codifies the basis and procedure for harmonised licensing conditions for certain telecommunications services.[140] This provides a second approach to Community-wide authorisation. Where harmonisation of any category of service is realised, there will be no requirement for a service provider to obtain a Single Community Telecommunications Licence to provide that category of service.[141] It is also open to the Commission to decide that in the case of some categories of service there is no requirement for either harmonisation

[129] Proposed Community Licence Directive, Art. 8.
[130] Proposed Community Licence Directive, Art. 7.
[131] Proposed Community Licence Directive, Art. 10.
[132] Proposed Community Licence Directive, Art. 12.
[133] Proposed Community Licence Directive, Art. 9.
[134] Proposed Community Licence Directive, Art. 12.
[135] Proposed Community Licence Directive, Art. 13.
[136] Proposed Community Licence Directive, Arts 6 and 7.
[137] Proposed Community Licence Directive, Art. 4.
[138] Proposed Community Licence Directive, Art. 17.
[139] Proposed Community Licence Directive, Art. 18.
[140] Proposed Community Licence Directive, Art. 14.
[141] Proposed Community Licence Directive, Art. 14(4).

or individual application for a Single Community Telecommunications Licence.[142] Such services may also be provided as if a Single Community Telecommunications Licence had been granted in respect of them.[143]

In keeping with its policy of avoiding duplicate work on procedures, the Commission will rely on ECTRA to develop harmonised conditions where appropriate. Therefore, the Commission can request ECTRA to determine harmonised licensing conditions for specified categories of services.[144]

The limitations of mutual recognition

The process for the granting of a Single Community Telecommunications Licence ensures that the licence will be subject to conditions that are acceptable to all Member States.[145] The additional conditions that may be appended to the national authorisation in granting the Single Community Licence appear to be applicable within all other Member States, even though only one of them may have objected to the national authorisation and secured the additional conditions.[146] The practical impact of this procedure will be that the Single Community Licence will contain conditions that are consistent with those prevailing in the least liberal Member State. Although this will not make the service provider subject to conditions any more stringent than would be acceptable under Community law, they may, nevertheless, be far less liberal than those of other Member States who have liberalised their telecommunications services market beyond the level required by Community rules.

The Proposed Community Licence Directive does not envisage circumstances in which a service provider may voluntarily exclude the extension of his service to a particular Member State. This is consistent with the policy of the Community to create the environment and encourage Community-wide services. However, there are two consequences for the service operator. First, the service provider cannot choose to exclude the less liberal Member States and thus maintain the ability to provide a more extensive service. Second, even where the service provider has no intention of extending its service to a particular Member State, it will nevertheless have to deal with any objections raised by the regulatory authority of that Member State to its application for a Single Community Licence.

In practice it becomes a question of balance as to whether to apply for a Single Community Licence or to make multiple applications to the regulatory authorities of the Member States in which the service is intended to be provided.

Perhaps the most unsatisfactory aspect of the Proposed procedures is that relating to later modification or withdrawal of a Single Community Telecommunications Licence.[147] Once having recognised a Licence under which services are to be provided, it creates an unnecessary degree of uncertainty to permit subsequent modifications. The service provider will undoubtedly rely on the terms of the Single Community Licence in providing its services within Member States. Although the procedure envisages consultation and conciliation, it nevertheless keeps open the possibility of additional conditions or withdrawal of the Single Community Licence. There is no clear indication in the Proposed

---

[142] Proposed Community Licence Directive, Art. 14(3).
[143] Proposed Community Licence Directive, Art. 15(4).
[144] Proposed Community Licence Directive, Art. 14(1).
[145] See p. 79.
[146] Proposed Community Licence Directive, Art. 12(6); see p. 80.
[147] Proposed Community Licence Directive, Art. 19(3),(4).

Community Licence Directive on the duration of any Single Community Telecommunications Licence and whether this is to be the same as the national authorisation in relation to which the Single Community Licence is granted. It would be preferable for a fixed term to be determined rather than to leave open to Member States, having already had the opportunity to object to the grant of a Single Community Licence, later to initiate variation or withdrawal of that Licence.

Application of ONP to leased lines

The first of the specific Directives implementing ONP relates to leased lines.[148] The Directive covers the offer of transparent transmission capacity between network termination points[149] as a separate service, excluding switching.[150] In implementing the requirements of the ONP Directive, this Directive is closely linked to the Services Directive[151] since a major objective of ONP is to facilitate the provision of competitive services within the Community. The Directive does not apply to international leased lines[152] not between Member States.[153]

The Directive seeks to harmonise the specifications to be published and the form of such publications, considered best designed to further the objectives of the Services Directive[154] as well as giving effect to the principle of non-discrimination.[155]

The principle of non-discrimination requires that leased lines be offered and provided on request, without discrimination, to all the users.[156] This principle includes the availability of technical access, tariffs, quality of service, delivery period, fair distribution of capacity in case of scarcity, repair time, availability of network information and protection of customer proprietary information (subject to regulatory provisions on data protection).[157] The restrictions that the Directive aims to remove include technical restrictions which Member States have been applying to the interconnection of leased lines to other leased lines or to public telecommunications networks. In the rare cases where these restrictions may be necessary, they can be replaced by less restrictive

---

[148] Council Directive of 5 June 1992 on the application of open network provision to leased lines, 92/44/EEC, OJ L 165/26, 19 June 1992.

[149] Network termination points are physical connections and their technical access specifications which form part of the public telecommunications network which are necessary for access to the public network; ONP Dir. 90/387/EEC, Art. 2(5); leased line Dir. 92/44/EEC, Art. 2(1).

[150] 92/44/EEC, preamble 2 and Art. 2(2).

[151] Commission Dir. of 28 June 1990 on competition in the markets for telecommunications, 90/388/EEC, OJ L 192/10, 24 July 1990.

[152] Recital 24.

[152] The work leading to the leased line Directive was commenced in April 1988 by GAP under its mandate from SOG-T. From an early stage consensus emerged on a number of features which are included in the leased line Directive. These include:

1. harmonised ONP arrangements should extend to both intra-Community and national leased lines;
2. there should be a mandatory set of analogue and digital leased lines conforming to ONP conditions;
3. common administrative and maintenance procedures for ONP leased lines should be aimed for;
4. ONP leased line tariff should be cost oriented based on a set of common principles.

In parallel to this work on the leased lines Directive GAP has been engaged, since early 1989, in working on ONP for public packet-switched data networks and on ONP for ISDN. See generally Telecommunications: Progress on the Definition of Open Network Provision: a Short Status Report, COM (88) 718 final, 13 Dec. 1988.

[153] Services Dir. 90/388/EEC, Art. 4.

[154] 92/44/EEC, Recitals 3 and 4.

[155] 92/44/EEC, Recital 4.

[156] See 92/44/EEC, Arts 1, 3, 4, 6, 7, 8 and 10 and Annex II.

[157] As defined in 92/44/EEC, Art. 6(3).

regulatory measures. Furthermore, any restrictions in access to and use of leased lines can only be sustained on grounds of justified essential requirements[158] and must follow the principle of proportionality and not be excessive in relation to the aim pursued.[159]

Access and usage conditions

Conditions for access to and use of leased lines must be such as to facilitate the provision of competitive services using leased lines both within and between Member States. To achieve this they must be objective and non-discriminatory.[160] More particularly, any restrictions on access to and use of leased lines must be based on essential requirements which can be objectively justified and must be proportional and not excessive to the essential requirements on which they are based.[161]

Implementing these principles, the Directive requires that any such restrictions be imposed by the national regulatory authorities[162] through regulatory means.[163] Furthermore, no technical restrictions are allowed to be imposed on the interconnection of leased lines and the remainder of the public telecommunications networks.[164] Terminal equipment connected to the leased lines will be regarded as fulfilling any access conditions if the equipment complies with the terminal equipment Directive.[165]

The manner in which essential requirements can be applied to leased lines is amplified in the Directive,[166] and Member States are required to identify the particular essential requirement on the basis of which access to leased lines is restricted.[167]

Clearly, harmonisation of conditions for access to and use of leased lines will not alone ensure the growth of a competitive market in telecommunications services based on these lines. It is also necessary to ensure that Member States require that their telecommunications organisations, primarily the TOs, provide a minimum number of leased lines conforming to harmonised specifications. The leased lines to be made available will, in accordance with the requirements of free access and use conditions, be available for single or shared use or for the provision of services to third parties and facilitate communications both within and between Member States.[168]

Therefore, Member States are required to ensure that their telecommunications organisations, between them, provide a specified minimum set of leased lines that conform to defined technical characteristics.[169] Member States must ensure the availability of such

---

[158] 92/44/EEC, Recital 6 and 7.

[159] 92/44/EEC, Recital 3.

[160] 92/44/EEC, Recital 7.

[161] In pursuance of the objective of separating the regulatory and operational activities within Member States, as set out in the Green Paper on the development of the common market for telecommunication services and equipment, COM (87) 290, 30 June 1987, p. 17, the leased line Dir. 92/44/EEC, defines national regulatory authority as: 'The body or bodies in each Member State, legally distinct and functionally independent of the telecommunications organisations, entrusted by that Member State inter alia with the regulatory functions addressed in this Directive.' 92/44/EEC, Art. 2(2).

[162] 92/44/EEC, Arts 6(1).

[163] 92/44/EEC, Art. 6(1).

[164] 91/263/EEC; leased line Dir. 92/44/EEC, Art. 6(4).

[165] 92/44/EEC, Art. 6(3).

[166] 92/44/EEC, Art. 6(2).

[167] 92/44/EEC, Recital 12.

[168] 92/44/EEC, Art. 7(1) and Annex II. The types of lines and their characteristics which are set out in Annex II may be changed by the Commission in response to changes in market demand and new technical developments; Art. 7(3).

[169] 92/44/EEC, Arts 7(2) and 15.

leased lines on the date when they conform to the requirements of the Directive, which cannot be later than 4 June 1993.[170] There may be other leased lines provided by Member States in addition to the minimum set required. Such additional leased lines must also conform to the requirements of the Directive and their provision must not interfere with the provision of the minimum set of leased lines.[171]

Where TOs use leased lines to offer services which are not reserved and are competitive, they are required to provide the same type of leased lines to other users under equal conditions to those which they enjoy.[172]

Tariff principles

The principles set out in the ONP Directive[173] on tariffs is followed in this Directive.[174] In particular, tariffs must be cost oriented, while some latitude is permitted for rebalancing[175] tariffs. The Commission also favours flat rate periodic rentals, save in cases where other types of tariff may be justified by costs.[176] The tariff policy of the Directive also aims to promote fair sharing in the global cost of the resources used as well as allowing for a reasonable level of return on investment which is needed by the TOs for the development of their telecommunications infrastructures.[177] There is an underlying requirement that tariffs 'be sufficiently unbundled in accordance with the competition rules of the Treaty'.[178]

These principles are put into effect by the requirement of the Directive that tariffs for leased lines should normally separate the initial connection charge and include a periodic rental charge comprising a flat rate element and must be independent of the type of use made of the leased line by the users.[179] Tariffs will usually be for the whole of the leased line between the network termination points at which the user can access the leased line. However, where two or more telecommunications organisations provide the total circuit, it is permissible to have half circuit tariffs which will apply between one network termination point to a hypothetical mid-circuit point.[180] On this wording it would appear that even if three network providers are involved in making available the whole circuit, only half circuit tariffs can be stipulated and any adjustments must be made between the operators involved.

There are detailed arrangements for linking tariffs to costs,[181] with the possibility of using different cross-accounting systems, subject to notification to the Commission.[182]

---

[170] 92/44/EEC, Recital 13, Art. 7(4). A Member State which can prove that the state of development of its public telecommunications network or the conditions of demand on that network are such that providing a minimum set of leased lines by the required date would impose an excessive burden on the telecommunications organisation can make arrangements to defer the date of compliance, Art. 13(1), (2), (4) and (5). However, a Member State cannot rely on this right of deferment if the reason why it cannot comply is the activities of the telecommunications organisations in competitive areas and not in the services reserved to them, Art. 13(6).

[171] Art. 8(2).

[172] 90/387/EEC, Annex II.

[173] 92/44/EEC, Art. 10.

[174] In all Member States some degree of rebalancing has been necessary in the course of liberalisation of the telecommunications markets and changes in the social objectives pursued through telecommunication policy.

[175] 92/44/EEC, Recital 17.

[176] 92/44/EEC, Recital 18.

[177] 92/44/EEC, Recital 17; see also ONA requirements discussed at p. 97.

[178] 92/44/EEC, Art. 10(1)(a),(b).

[179] 92/44/EEC, Art. 10(c).

[180] 92/44/EEC, Art. 10(2).

[181] 92/44/EEC, Art. 10(2),(3).

[182] 92/44/EEC, Art. 10(2).

Tariff cost operation should be achieved by 31 December 1993,[183] and any deferral of compliance must be notified and justified to the Commission.[184]

Other supply requirements

The requirements of the Directive apply to leased lines,[185] subject to some limitations on the services that may be offered on such circuits. In keeping with the Services Directive,[186] this Directive does not extend to voice telephony, nor to telex, mobile radio telephony, paging and satellite services which are not covered by the Services Directive. In addition, Member States may, until 31 December 1992,[187] prohibit service operators from offering leased line capacity for simple resale[188] of packet-switched or circuit-switched data services.[189] After that date Member States may impose certain conditions on the provision of packet-switched or circuit-switched services on leased lines.[190]

In addition to providing for non-discriminatory access to leased lines[191] the Directive seeks to ensure that provision of leased lines to all users is non-discriminatory.[192] An important aspect of implementing this principle is the publication of information on access conditions and terms,[193] to which TOs must adhere. Accordingly, the Directive requires that not only access conditions, including those relating to the connection of terminal equipment to leased lines, but also licensing and authorisation requirements are predetermined and published.[194] Any published access and provision terms must be adhered to by the TOs for a reasonable period.[195]

In further ensuring that there is no discrimination between users of leased lines, there is a requirement for the publication of detailed information about ordering procedures, typical delivery times and repair times and the minimal contractual period that a user is obliged to accept[196] the facility.

Common ordering and billing procedures

The Commission considers one-stop ordering and billing[197] as a desirable means of promoting the use of leased lines throughout the Community.[198] This, however, presents the potential risk of collusion between TOs leading to price fixing, market sharing or the exclusion of other competitors.[199] Therefore, Member States are encouraged to ensure

---

[183] 92/44/EEC, Art. 13.
[184] As defined in 92/44/EEC, Art. 2(2).
[185] 90/388/EEC.
[186] Subject to certain authorisation procedures contained in the Services Directive, 90/388/EEC, Art. 2.
[187] As defined in Art. 2(2) of 92/44/EEC.
[188] 92/44/EEC, Recitals 8 and 9; 90/380/EEC, Art. 3.
[189] 92/44/EEC, Annex I, D(5).
[190] 92/44/EEC, Art. 6.
[191] 92/44/EEC, Recitals 4 and 5.
[192] 92/44/EEC, Recital 3.
[193] 92/44/EEC, Art. 3.
[194] 92/44/EEC, Art. 5.
[195] 92/44/EEC, Recital 5, Art. 4.
[196] As defined in 92/44/EEC, Art. 2(2).
[197] 92/44/EEC, Recital 15.
[198] 92/44/EEC, Recitals 15 and 16.
[199] 92/44/EEC, Art. 9(1).

that such procedures can be put into effect, but strictly subject to the competition rules of the Treaty[200] which would ensure that the TOs do not indulge in anti-competitive practices.

APPLICATION OF ONP TO PACKET-SWITCHED DATA SERVICES

Packet-Switched Data Services[201] was the second area identified in the ONP Directive[202] for specific implementation of ONP. The ONP Directive envisages some preliminary steps[203] to be taken in relation to the specified areas and preparatory to full implementation in respect of them. Among the preparatory steps is the adoption of an appropriate Council Recommendation on supply of technical interfaces, conditions of usage and tariff principles applying to the provision in each Member State of at least one packet-switch data service complying with open network principles.[204] Pursuant to this requirement, Council has issued a Recommendation[205] that each Member State ensure at least one telecommunications organisation[206] would in its territory provide a minimum set of PSDS[207] conforming to recommended harmonised technical characteristics.[208] The Recommendation outlines the standards to be utilised and the service technical characteristics, which are to be implemented by 31 December 1992.[209]

The Recommendation contains information requirements on supply conditions,[210] similar to those for leased lines.[211] It is also recommended that procedures be established for common ordering, whereby intra-Community PSDS entails similar procedures, one stop ordering whereby user can satisfy all PSDS requirements through one supplier, one stop billing and one stop maintenance, ensuring that faults can be rectified through a single organisation with whom the user deals.[212] The usual requirements of transparency, objectivity and independence from application implemented by the user, apply to PSDS tariffs.[213] These should normally comprise an initial connection charge, a periodical rental charge and a usage charge.[214]

Naturally, there are the usual, but broad, criteria for technical characteristics, supply and usage conditions, tariffs, licensing and declaration conditions and conditions for the attachments of terminal equipment[215] which are to be published to users[216] and be made available to the Commission.[217] There is also a reporting requirement on the regulatory

---

[200] PSDS.

[201] 90/387/EEC, Annex I.

[202] 90/387/EEC, Arts 4, 5 and 6.

[203] 90/387/EEC, Annex III, point 3.

[204] Council Recommendation of 5 June 1992 on the harmonised provision of a minimum set of packet-switched data services (PSDS) in accordance with open network provision (ONP) principles, 92/382/EEC, OJ L 200/1, 18 July 1992; the ONP Directive, 92/382/EEC, para. 10.90/387/EEC, Annex III.2, provided for the adoption of a Council Recommendation by 1 July 1991.

[205] 92/382/EEC, para. 1.

[206] 92/382/EEC, Annex I.

[207] 92/382/EEC, Annex I, B and C.

[208] 92/382/EEC, point 4.

[209] 92/44/EEC, Art. 4.

[210] 92/382/EEC, point 5.

[211] 92/382/EEC, point 8.

[212] 92/382/EEC, point 9.

[213] 92/382,EEC, Annex II.

[214] 92/382/EEC, point 3.

[215] Point 12.

[216] Point 11.

[217] 92/382/EEC, point 7.

authorities to keep the Commission informed of the availability of PSDS in their territories.[218] Member States are called on to report[219] network performance of PSDS in their territory, according to certain identified criteria.[220]

IMPLEMENTATION OF ONP IN RESPECT OF ISDN

Council has also issued a Recommendation[221] to implement ONP in respect of ISDN, on broadly similar lines to that relating to PSDS.[222]

ISDN will normally be used to provide both voice telephony and PSDS. Where either of these services are provided by ISDN, in addition to complying with the ONP requirements applying to ISDN, the provision of the services should also conform to the ONP requirements applied to voice telephony and to PSDS respectively.[223] The ISDN offerings are divided into two parts. The first part[224] identifies the minimum set of offerings to be made available in all Member States by 1 January 1994. The second part[225] is to be offered on dates to be published by the telecommunications organisations in each Member State[226] to meet market demand.[227] The minimum offerings correspond to those services identified as commercially viable for ISDN in the Memorandum of Understanding signed by a number of telecommunications organisations in 1989,[228] identified in the ISDN MoU of June 1991.[229]

APPLICATION OF ONP TO VOICE TELEPHONY

Under the ONP Directive,[230] voice telephony service is identified as the fourth area to which ONP should be applied. Having addressed the three first areas of ONP application,[231] as well as the approximation of laws concerning telecommunications terminal equipment and the mutual recognition of their conformity,[232] the Commission has proposed a Directive[233] to implement ONP in relation to voice telephony.

The Proposed Voice Telephony Directive[234] is framed in such a way as to be independent of the technology involved[235] and embraces both analogue and digital

---

[218] 92/382/EEC, Annex III.

[219] Council Recommendation of 5 June 1992 on the provision of harmonised integrated services digital network (ISDN) access arrangements and a minimum set of ISDN offerings in accordance with open network provision (ONP) principles, 92/383/EEC, OJ L 200/10, 220. 18 July 1992.

[221] 92/382/EEC.

[222] See p. 87 92/383/EEC, recitals 25 and 27, Annex I, Part B, note 1.

[223] 92/383/EEC, Annex I, Part A.

[224] 92/383/EEC, Annex I, Part B.

[225] 92/383/EEC, Art. 1(a).

[226] 92/383/EEC, Annex I, Part B.

[227] 92/383/EEC, recital 5.

[228] 92/383/EEC, Annex I.

[229] 90/387/EEC, Art. 4(2), Annex I.

[230] Leased lines, 92/44/EEC; packet- and circuit-switched data services, 92/382/EEC; and ISDN, 92/383/EEC; see pp. 83, 87 and 88 respectively.

[231] 91/263/EEC.

[232] Proposal for a Council Directive on the Application of ONP to Voice Telephony, COM (92) 247, 27 Aug. 1992.

[233] COM (92) 247.

[234] COM (92) 247, Art. 2(1) imports the definitions in the ONP Dir. 90/387/EEC, which by Art. 2(3) and (4) defines telecommunications networks and services in a technologically neutral way. The same applies to the definition of 'fixed public telephone network' given in COM (92) 247, Art. 2(2). See also COM (92) 247, Art. 1(2).

[235] See previous footnote.

networks. The Proposed Voice Telephony Directive also accommodates the different approaches by Member States in the extent to which the provision of voice telephony networks and services are subject to competitive or monopoly provision.[236]

To achieve the objectives of the Community to have an efficient, cost-effective Community-wide telecommunications infrastructure as well as a harmonised voice telephony service, it is necessary for ONP conditions to apply both to networks and to voice telephony services. This is also achieved by the Proposed Voice Telephony Directive in setting out the scope of its application.[237]

As envisaged by the ONP Directive,[238] the Commission prepared a Report[239] relating to the application of ONP to voice telephony and on which it invited public comment.[240] The Report identified the features to be included in the Proposed Voice Telephony Directive to meet three basic goals. These are:[241]

1. to establish the rights of users of the public telephone network in relation to the TOs;
2. to provide service providers and other telecommunications operators equitable and non-discriminatory access to the public telephone network; and
3. to meet the needs of the single market in the provision of European-wide telephony service and to plan and co-ordinate pan-European numbering.

Scope of the Voice Telephony Directive

To achieve these goals within the political and commercial constraints of the Commission, the Proposed Voice Telephony Directive is devised to allow market demand and commercial considerations to drive development of new features and facilities. Therefore, although the Commission considers wide availability of features an important aspect of developing the community telecommunications services market,[242] it specifically makes provision of advanced features 'subject to technical and economic feasibility'.[243]

The Proposed Voice Telephony Directive also emphasises[244] the principle of subsidiarity. The Commission, which works in conjunction with the ONP Committee[245] is intended to have a minimum co-ordination role at the Community level, where this is necessary for establishing a European voice telephony market for the benefit of users. The Proposed Voice Telephony Directive entrusts the primary responsibility for implementing the Directive to the national regulatory authorities.[246] The Proposed Voice Telephony Directive[247] goes to some length in setting out and justifying the role of the Commission under the Proposed Voice Telephony Directive.

---

[236] COM (92) 247, Art. 1(1).
[237] 90/387/EEC, Art. 4(4).
[238] Analysis Report on the Application of ONP to Voice Telephony, OJ C 197/12, 26 July 1991, discussed at the meeting of the ONP Committee on 2 and 3 July 1991.
[239] COM (92) 247, Explanatory Memorandum, para. 3.
[240] COM (92) 247, Explanatory Memorandum, para. 4.
[241] COM (92) 247, Proposed Voice Telephony Dir., Recital 18.
[242] COM (92) 247, Art. 8(1).
[243] COM (92) 247, Explanatory Memorandum, para. 4.
[244] The ONP Committee is established under the ONP Dir. 90/387/EEC, Art. 9(1).
[245] COM (92) 247, Proposed Voice Telephony Dir., Recital 9 and Arts 4–16, 18, 20–22, 24 and 25.
[246] COM (92) 247, Proposed Voice Telephony Dir., Recital 43.
[247] COM (92) 247, Proposed Voice Telephony Dir., Art. 1(2).
[248] COM (92) 247, Proposed Voice Telephony Dir., Arts 1(1) and 3.

The Proposed Voice Telephony Directive does not apply to mobile telephone services. But, to ensure that comprehensive Europe-wide services are achieved, the Proposed Voice Telephony Directive extends to inter-connections between mobile networks and the fixed public telephone networks.[248]

The provisions of the Proposed Voice Telephony Directive apply both within and between Member States.[249] It does not apply to any services or features provided outside the Community.[250]

Harmonisation requirements

In the context of 'universal service' and the right to subscribe to voice telephony service throughout the Community, the Proposed Voice Telephony Directive sets out the conditions for non-discrimination and ensures that these principles are applied to all users.[251] The Proposed Voice Telephony Directive also covers the availability of technical access, tariffs, quality of service and provision time, fair distribution of scarce capacity, repair time[252] and makes provision for information about these matters to be published and made available to users.[253] There are also appropriate provisions dealing with customer proprietary information and the protection of personal data and privacy.[254]

Some Member States continue to grant special or exclusive rights to provide the public telecommunications network and voice telephony services.[255] Where such rights are maintained the Member State is required to ensure that conditions for access to and use of the network are objective and non-discriminatory and to publish them.[256] The information required to be published and the manner and form in which it is to be published are harmonised under the Proposed Voice Telephony Directive.[257] Such harmonisation is necessary in order to ensure the development of single markets for voice telephony services within and between Member States. This is particularly important for service providers in one Member State providing services to users in another Member State.[258]

This end is achieved by the requirement that national regulatory authorities ensure the publication of up-to-date information[259] giving specified categories of information under identified headings.[260]

There are also requirements for targets in relation to the quality of service to be set by the national regulatory authority, as an essential aspect of the service being provided.[261] Clearly there is a relationship between the quality of the service and the tariffs charged.[262]

---

[249] COM (92) 247, Proposed Voice Telephony Dir., Recital 5.
[250] Proposed Voice Telephony Dir., Arts 3, 4, 5 and 9(4). In the context of the Proposed Directive 'users' includes service providers who use the telephone networks and services for the provision of services to third parties; Art. 2(2).
[251] Proposed Voice Telephony Dir., Arts 4, 5 and 22.
[252] Proposed Voice Telephony Dir., Art. 4(1) and (2).
[253] Proposed Voice Telephony Dir., Art. 21(5).
[254] Such rights may be maintained under the Services Dir. 90/388/EEC; see in particular Art. 2; but see p. 96 Joined Cases, C-271/90, 281/90 and 289/90.
[255] 90/388/EEC, Art. 4.
[256] Proposed Voice Telephony Dir., Art. 4, Annex 1.
[257] Proposed Voice Telephony Dir., Recital 8.
[258] Proposed Voice Telephony Dir., Art. 4(1).
[259] Proposed Voice Telephony Dir., Annex 1.
[260] Proposed Voice Telephony Dir., Art. 5.
[261] Proposed Voice Telephony Dir., Recital 10.
[262] Proposed Voice Telephony Dir., Annex 2.

The Commission aims to achieve a convergence of quality of service throughout the Community. To this end specific indicators are identified,[263] ranging from supply time for initial network connection, fault rate and repair time, to availability of public telephone boxes and billing accuracy. These indicators must be measured[264] and the results of the measurements published.[265]

Relationship between users and TOs

The Commission considers that the relationship between users and the TOs should be no different from that of other customers and suppliers of goods and services.[266] Therefore, provisions are contained in the Proposed Voice Telephony Directive with regard to the circumstances and conditions in which TOs can terminate their offerings,[267] giving users the right to dispute the termination date envisaged by the TO.

The national regulatory authorities are also required to ensure that any user contracts provide for compensation and remedies if service quality levels are not met.[268] Any users must have the opportunity to bring proceedings against TOs.[269]

Promotion of services

The Commission considers it desirable to encourage the development of more advanced voice telephony service features, harmonised throughout the Community.[270] The Proposed Voice Telephony Directive identifies two levels of advanced features.[271] In relation to the first set of features,[272] national regulatory authorities are required to secure that these features are provided, subject to technical and economic feasibility.[273]

The second set of features,[274] which are more advanced than the first set, only carry the obligation that national regulatory authorities 'facilitate and encourage' such provision.[275] In both cases network development and market demand are to dictate the timing for the introduction of the features.[276]

This theme of allowing commercial considerations to drive the progress of voice

---

[263] The measurements must be made against established standards in the order of preference set out in the Proposed Voice Telephony Dir., Art. 22, and the measurement methods published; Proposed Voice Telephony Dir., Annex 2, para. 2.

[264] Proposed Voice Telephony Dir., Art. 5(2).

[265] Proposed Voice Telephony Dir., Recital 11.

[266] Proposed Voice Telephony Dir., Art. 6.

[267] Proposed Voice Telephony Dir., Art. 7.

[268] Proposed Voice Telephony Dir., Art. 7(3).

[269] Proposed Voice Telephony Dir., Recital 12.

[270] Proposed Voice Telephony Dir., Annex 3.

[271] Proposed Voice Telephony Dir., Annex 3, para. 1, lists four features, namely duel tone multi-frequency (DTMF) operation, direct dialling in, call transfer and call forwarding.

[272] The technical standards to which such features must conform are to be determined in accordance with the Proposed Voice Telephony Dir., Art. 22.

[273] Proposed Voice Telephony Dir., Annex 3, para. 2, identifies six features, namely, European-wide access to freephone (green) services, European-wide kiosk billing, automatic reverse charging feature, calling line identification, access to operator services in other Member States and access to directory enquiry services in other Member States.

[274] Proposed Voice Telephony Dir., Art. 8(2).

[275] Proposed Voice Telephony Dir., Art. 8(3).

[276] Proposed Voice Telephony Dir., Art. 31(1).

telephony ONP is further reflected in the implementation requirements of the Proposed Voice Telephony Directive. Although Member States are required to comply with the Directive by 1 January 1994,[277] such implementation may be deferred.[278] Any application for deferment must be based on the state of development of the public telephone network in the Member State as well as the conditions of demand.[279] There will, inevitably, be different considerations applicable to the provision of basic voice telephony and to the provision of more advanced services. The requirements of the Proposed Voice Telephony Directive in regard to the provision of the more advanced services should not impede the provision of basic voice telephony service.[280]

Access and interconnections

The Community policy for Community-wide telephone networks will entail interconnections between networks operated by different TOs. Such interconnections will generally be made at points other than network termination points located on the premises of the user. To achieve interconnections of this type, in particular, requires a level of co-operation between TOs. Therefore, agreements for these interconnections are likely to require consideration of Community competition rules and must be made in accordance with the Competition Guidelines[281] issued by the Commission on the application of the competition rules to the telecommunications sector.

While some Member States continue to maintain licensing or declaration procedures for the provision of networks services,[282] these must be compatible with Community law.[283] The Proposed Voice Telephony Directive particularly addresses the interconnection of leased lines and the public telephone network[284] and requires that any restrictions must not be technical but regulatory. In terms of regulatory restrictions, these must be justified on grounds such as the network integrity, inter-operability of services and other defined[285] and published[286] essential requirements.[287]

The Proposed Voice Telephony Directive[288] establishes the conditions for access by service providers to the public telephone networks at points other than the network termination point.[289] It does not specifically require access by service providers at network termination points located on the premises of the service provider or the TO, which is already covered in the ONP Directive.[290]

---

[277] Proposed Voice Telephony Dir., Art. 26.

[278] Proposed Voice Telephony Dir., Art. 26(2).

[279] Proposed Voice Telephony Dir., Recital 13.

[280] OJ C 233/2, 6 Sept. 1991.

[281] See Dir. 90/388/EEC.

[282] These include the ONP Dirs, 90/387/EEC, 92/44/EEC, as well as the competition rules.

[283] Proposed Voice Telephony Dir., Art. 21(3).

[284] Proposed Voice Telephony Dir., Art. 21(5).

[285] Proposed Voice Telephony Dir., Annex 4.

[286] Conforming with ONP Dir. 90/387/EEC.

[287] Proposed Voice Telephony Dir., Art. 9.

[288] As defined in the ONP Dir., 90/387/EEC, Art. 2(4); it can be argued that connections at points other than on the premises of the TO or of the service provider are not 'necessary for access to and efficient communications through' the public network. Furthermore, the scheme of the ONP Dir. and the harmonisation requirements for interfaces do not appear to import an obligation for interconnection being considered here; 90/387/EEC, Art. 4(4)(d) and Annex II.

[289] See previous footnote.

[290] Proposed Voice Telephony Dir., Art. 9(2).

TOs are to be required to permit access at interconnection points without discrimination against their competitors[291] and at tariffs which apply to the TOs themselves.[292] However, TOs may refuse access to the network at such special interconnection points if to do so would adversely affect the integrity of the public network.[293]

Tariffs and user interests

The Proposed Voice Telephony Directive aims at extending to all users the benefits of advanced technology, such as intelligent network architectures, which carry with them the new facilities that may be made available[294] and the benefits from economies, scope and scale. Such benefits are extended to users through cost orientation of tariffs, coupled with Community market in telecommunications services.[295] To ensure that the application of non-discrimination does not hinder service development, the national regulatory authorities are required to balance the interests of service providers and TOs in such a way as to bring the greatest benefit to all users.[296]

The national regulatory authorities are further charged with a balancing role in encouraging co-operation between TOs in setting up Community-wide inter-connectivity of networks and to provide Community-wide voice telephony service.[297] This also requires keeping the Commission informed and full disclosure and publication of information.[298]

Interests of users are maintained through requirements for unbundling of tariffs as required by the competition rules.[299] Whenever possible itemised bills are to be provided on request.[300] These requirements merely expand the general principles of the ONP Directive.[301] The Commission also proposes implementation of cost accounting systems,[302] and suggests the adoption of fully distributed costing.

The Proposed Voice Telephony Directive accommodates[303] arrangements relating to groups of people with special needs, such as the handicapped.

The Commission recognises the commercial desirability of discount schemes as well as the social need for such schemes in certain circumstances. Therefore, the Proposed Voice Telephony Directive[304] accommodates such schemes within the overall principle of cost orientation. Naturally any discount scheme must comply with the competition rules, which also means that they be not linked to other obligations on the user which are not related to the services provided.

In keeping with current general practice, users must be given a choice as to whether or not they are included in directories.[305] Furthermore, as an important element in provid-

---

[291] Proposed Voice Telephony Dir., Art. 11(a).
[292] Proposed Voice Telephony Dir., Arts 9(1) and 21(5)(b).
[293] Proposed Voice Telephony Dir., Arts 8 and 22, Annex 3.
[294] Proposed Voice Telephony Dir., Art. 11, in particular Art. 11(b).
[295] Proposed Voice Telephony Dir., Recital 18, Arts 9(4) and 10(1).
[296] Proposed Voice Telephony Dir., Art. 10.
[297] Proposed Voice Telephony Dir., Art. 10(4) and (5), Recitals 19 and 20.
[298] Proposed Voice Telephony Dir., Art. 11, particularly Art. 11(b),(c) and (d).
[299] Proposed Voice Telephony Dir., Art. 14.
[300] 90/387/EEC; Proposed Voice Telephony Dir., Recital 21.
[301] Proposed Voice Telephony Dir., Art. 12.
[302] Proposed Voice Telephony Dir., Art. 18.
[303] Proposed Voice Telephony Dir., Art. 13.
[304] Proposed Voice Telephony Dir., Art. 15(b).
[305] Proposed Voice Telephony Dir., Art. 15(c).

ing access to the telephone service, directories of users must be available both to those who subscribe to the telephone service and to service providers, on fair and non-discriminatory terms.[306]

Terminal equipment

There is a specific requirement that national regulatory authorities ensure adequate provision of public call boxes both in terms of numbers and geographic coverage.[307] The Commission proposes further harmonisation within the Community in respect of public call boxes by harmonising telephone payment cards which can be used in all Member States.[308] The Commission has already put in hand the development of suitable standards for such payment cards.[309]

There is already in place the terminal Directive[310] approximating the Member States' laws on terminal equipment and providing for mutual recognition of their conformity.[311] Clearly, for a single type of telephone payment card to be usable in all Member States it is also necessary for commercial agreements between TOs.[312] Any such agreements must, of course, conform to the Community competition rules.[313]

Other usage conditions include the connection of terminal equipment to the network[314] and the circumstances in which TOs may restrict or interrupt service to a user.[315]

Numbering

In terms of competition, as well as uniformity across the Community, numbering schemes are a powerful tool. In recognition of this, the Commission make a number of proposals, not least important of which is that national telephone numbers be controlled by the regulatory bodies and their allocation be fair, equitable and timely.[316] At a Community level priority is to be given to the long-term numbering framework.[317] In particular, numbers for freephone, also known as green numbers, are to be harmonised.[318]

Standards

The prohibition of technical restrictions on interconnection between leased lines and public networks is of particular importance to service providers in that anyone connected

---

[306] Proposed Voice Telephony Dir., Art. 16.
[307] Proposed Voice Telephony Dir., Art. 17.
[308] The Commission has given a mandate to CEN-CENELEC to develop a standard.
[309] 91/263/EEC.
[310] See p. 27.
[311] Proposed Voice Telephony Dir., Recital 27.
[312] See p. 16 and guidelines on the competition.
[313] Proposed Voice Telephony Dir., Art. 21(4).
[314] Proposed Voice Telephony Dir., Art. 21(2).
[315] Proposed Voice Telephony Dir., Art. 20(1).
[316] Proposed Voice Telephony Dir., Annex 4. The Community has already taken a number of measures relating to the international prefix 00 and has made proposals for certain Community-wide services; see p 43
[317] Proposed Voice Telephony Dir., Art. 20(4).
[318] 91/263/EEC.

to the public network will be 'capable' of accessing private networks run by service providers.

In conjunction with the rules for free circulation of terminal equipment,[319] it is necessary also to ensure that network termination points, including sockets, are subject to community specifications. There are provisions for the definition of such specifications as well as for any necessary adaptors.[320]

In order to ensure that the transparency of standards is maintained in relation to voice telephony services and standardisation and harmonisation take place to the widest extent, the Proposed Voice Telephony Directive defines a hierarchy in the adoption and application of standards.[321] The provisions are designed to ensure that wherever possible international standards are applied and that new national standards are not developed where harmonised European standards are under development.[322] The existing provisions on information[323] are specifically applied by the Proposed Voice Telephony Directive.[324]

Convergence and dispute resolution

The wider reporting requirements which run throughout the Proposed Voice Telephony Directive are aimed at both harmonising the provision of voice telephony networks and services throughout the Community and to enable the Commission to monitor and oversee convergence at Community level. To this end the Proposed Voice Telephony Directive provides the procedures and the framework for notification of reporting[325] to the Commission and spells out the monitoring role[326] of the Commission. Any effective monitoring is necessarily to be coupled with the ability of the Commission to make necessary adjustments, both in meeting market conditions and technological developments. Accordingly, the Proposed Voice Telephony Directive[327] facilitates the appropriate measures.

The implementation of the Proposed Voice Telephony Directive involves consensus and agreements at varying levels. It is inevitable that these will give rise to disagreements both at national and Community level. In particular, the requirement for inter-connection between networks specifically calls for Commission intervention where agreement cannot be reached between the parties.[328] It is in the interests of all concerned that there be an efficient, inexpensive and responsive mechanism for resolving any disputes. Such a mechanism is provided under the Proposed Voice Telephony Directive,[329] involving the ONP Committee where appropriate.

---

[319] Proposed Voice Telephony Dir., Art. 19.
[320] Proposed Voice Telephony Dir., Art. 22.
[321] Proposed Voice Telephony Dir., Recital 34.
[322] Council Dir. 83/189/EEC, OJ L 109/8, 26 Apr. 1983, as amended by Dir. 88/182/EEC, OJ L 81/75, 26 Mar. 1988.
[323] Proposed Voice Telephony Dir., Art. 22(2).
[324] Proposed Voice Telephony Dir., Art. 24.
[325] Proposed Voice Telephony Dir., Arts 23 and 29.
[326] Proposed Voice Telephony Dir., Arts 27 and 29.
[327] See p. 89 et seq.
[328] Proposed Voice Telephony Dir., Art. 25.
[329] 90/387/EEC.

Data protection and privacy

Under the ONP Directive,[330] the protection of personal data and privacy is regarded as an *essential requirement* on the basis of which certain restrictions may be imposed by Member States. The Proposed Voice Telephony Directive implements the same principle with regard to voice telephony.[331] It is envisaged that in making any determination with regard to any restrictions based on data protection, the Commission consult with bodies involved with data protection and privacy under two other Directives. However, the Directives in question relating to protection of personal data and privacy in the context of public digital telecommunication networks[332] and that relating to harmonisation of Member States' data protection laws[333] have not yet been issued as Directives. But, this need not prevent the issue of the Proposed Voice Telephony Directive, which does not specifically refer to such bodies.[334] The Proposed Voice Telephony Directive envisages a progressive and ongoing process of applying ONP to voice telephony, through flexible regulatory conditions, given the dynamic developments in the sector.[335] The same approach is favoured for technical adjustment.

Implementation and review

The Proposed Voice Telephony Directive envisages compliance by Member States not later than 1 January 1994,[336] subject to deferments on limited grounds.[337] The Commission also proposes a review of the provisions of the Directive on the basis of its implementation up to 1 January 1995.[338]

EXTERNAL AND COMPARATIVE ASPECTS OF COMMUNITY MEASURES

In pursuing its policy of growing cross-border telecommunication services within the Community, the Commission attaches great importance to increased participation of Community service providers in third country markets. In drawing up specific Directives the Commission will take account of reciprocal market opening in other countries. The Commission considers negotiations within the framework of GATT[339] as the preferred means of achieving its objectives with regard to third countries, while also recognising the bilateral discussions between the Community and third countries can also contribute to this process.[340]

---

[330] Proposed Voice Telephony Dir., Art. 21(5)(d).
[331] COM (90) 314-SYN 288, 13 Sept. 1990.
[332] COM (90) 314-SYN 287, 13 Sept. 1990.
[333] However, the references are made to both documents in the Proposed Voice Telephony Dir., Recital 39 but, such references can easily be removed from any final Directive.
[334] Proposed Voice Telephony Dir., Recital 41.
[335] Proposed Voice Telephony Dir., Art. 31(1).
[336] Proposed Voice Telephony Dir., Art. 26.
[337] Proposed Voice Telephony Dir., Art. 30.
[338] General Agreement on Tariffs and Trade.
[339] ONP Dir., 19th, 20th and 21st Recitals.
[340] Council resolution of 30 June 1988, 88/C 257/01.

The Council resolution on the development of the common market for services and equipment[341] identified a major policy goal of the measures on telecommunications to be 'the taking fully into account of the external aspects of Community measures'.[342] The Commission had in mind that the progressive establishment of ONP corresponded to worldwide trends in telecommunications markets, such as the development of Open Network Architecture (ONA) in the United States.[343] However, the scope of the US provisions differ from those of the ONP Directive. The ONA strives to give options to any service provider that needs access to the local facilities of the regional bell operating companies[344] and the inter-exchange facilities of AT&T.[345] To satisfy ONA requirements the RBOCs must unbundle key elements of their networks and offer them on a tariffed basis, thus enabling the service providers to make an *à-la-carte* choice of only the services and facilities that they need. AT&T is not required to unbundle its offerings, but must provide long-distance transport of signalling and information needed for the implementation by RBOCs of their ONA obligations.

The ONP concentrates on the elimination of the differences in network access terms, conditions, interfaces and features within the Community. It also addresses usage conditions and tariff principles, but primarily as a means of achieving equality and symmetry throughout the single market. Unlike the ONA, it is not directed to fostering competition among operators. As competition intensifies, the Commission may well go further towards some of the policies of the ONA, which are more suited to eliminating opportunities for uncompetitive behaviour by dominant network providers.

---

[341] 90/387/EEC, 19th Recital.

[342] Amendment of 64.702 of the Commission's rules and Regulations, see docket number 85–229, 104 FCC 2d 958 (1986) ('The Third Computer Enquiry'); filing and review of Open Network Architecture plans, 4 FCC Rcd 1 (1988), Petitions for Recon. Pending, (ONA Implementation).

[343] RBOCs.

[344] American Telephone and Telegraph Co.

CHAPTER 8
Tariffs

IMPACT OF DOMESTIC AND INTERNATIONAL TARIFFS ON COMPETITION

The creation of the competitive market in telecommunications both within and between Member States would easily be thwarted in the absence of any regulation of tariffs. Domestically a dominant telecommunications organisation could adjust its tariffs in a manner calculated to prevent competition. This is particularly the case where there is a monopoly in the provision of the network infrastructure. In these circumstances the network provider could adjust its tariffs for access to and use of the network to a level at which any competitor service provider would be unable to charge competitive prices for its services.

Alternatively, the dominant service provider may be in a position to provide its services at tariffs which could not be matched by a competitor. Any such strategy would normally involve the dominant provider in either cross-subsidising the relevant activity from its other resources or attributing its underlying costs in a way which would not fully reflect the costs associated with the service in question. The latter is, of course, another form of cross-subsidisation.

These tariff related measures would have a similar effect on the provision of telecommunications infrastructure networks and services between Member States.

In most Member States long-distance call charges are higher than their economic level while, in many cases, exchange line rentals[1] have been lower than their economic level. However, identification of cross-subsidisation is usually difficult to establish in the telecommunications sector because of the large amount of common costs and the arbitrariness of cost accounting procedures for dealing with these costs. The maintenance of this position can assist new entrants, if they are permitted to interconnect with the

---

[1] These are charges for the provision of the exchange lines connecting customers' premises to the public network and are independent of usage.

dominant providers, infrastructure network without contributing to the deficit incurred by the network provider in the provision of exchange lines.[2]

This has a bearing on international call prices. There is a degree of justification for the argument by TOs that international calls use the same exchange as domestic calls, but there is no reason to require that international calls should bear the same proportion of the cost of exchange lines as other calls. Elements influencing the determination of international call prices should take account of the incremental costs of the call and the sensitivity of demand to price changes.

A central issue in the determination of international call charges is the settlement procedure established by the ITU, involving the application of accounting rates.[3] Apart from disparities between accounting rates, there is the additional problem of determining the cost of delivery which involves an allocation of common costs. The accounting rate system created severe anomalies in call charges between Member States,[4] as with virtually all other international calls. One of the factors that has sustained this position is that the imbalance in accounting rates and international call settlements provides a flow of funds to less developed countries, thus providing them with a source of foreign aid.

Regulation of tariffs has a clear impact on the development of the network infrastructure. The ability of network providers to finance modernisation and extension of networks is influenced by tariff policies adopted to fulfil other social and economic objectives. The pursuit of universal service provision has in the past involved, at least in some Member States, keeping tariffs artificially low. The Commission considers such a policy as 'damaging a dynamic source of overall economic growth in the process'.[5] The Commission also observed that major changes in tariff structures taking place in Member States were attributable in part to the differing impact of technological development on the cost of providing long distance traffic and local traffic. This differential arises due to the diminishing importance of distance related costs compared with usage or connection costs, resulting in greater reduction in the cost of providing long distance traffic.[6] Other factors at work are the closer relationship between international tariffs and costs due to increasing international competition. Competition, together with fair and open access by users, has also forced TOs to provide clearer definition of tariff principles.

Observing the differences between tariffs within and between Member States and the impact of the accounting rates and K-factors, the Green Paper echoes the Council Recommendation[7] that tariffs for all services should be less distance dependent. Any value added by the network should be charged independently of the use of the carrier capabilities of the network.[8]

The tariff principles advocated by the Commission include:

1. Tariffs should be based on costs. In rebalancing tariffs necessitated by this principle, a consistent trade-off between universal service and tariff policies would be necessary.

---

[2] This position obtained in the United Kingdom before 1991 and continues to apply in some cases; see generally Prof. Bryan Carsberg, ITU Forum 91, p. 9.

[3] The accounting rates are the amounts charged by an operator for the domestic delivery of international calls, payable by an operator in another country with whom the call originated.

[4] For example, a call from Italy to the UK would cost twice as much as the same call from the UK to Italy.

[5] COM (87) 290 final, pp. 50 and 79.

[6] COM (87) 290 final, p. 29.

[7] 86/659/EEC of 22 Dec. 1986.

[8] COM (87) 290 final, p. 81.

2. The convergence of intra-Community and international tariffs clearing the way for a European tariff zone.
3. Tariff principles should be built into the open network provision. This in turn would involve unbundling of tariffs to achieve fair access.[9]

Although the harmonisation of tariff structures forms an essential part of the Commission's policy aimed at creating a single market in telecommunications services, it is not the intent of the Commission to eradicate tariff differences between service providers. Indeed, the freedom of service providers to compete on prices is an essential element of achieving a competitive market within the Community.[10]

Both CCITT and CEPT have reviewed their Recommendations with regards to international charges, in part due to pressure from the Commission. In particular CEPT has revised and abolished its Recommendation[11] imposing a 30 per cent surcharge on service providers for the use of international leased circuits.[12]

IMPLEMENTATION OF TARIFF PRINCIPLES

The main strands of the Commission's tariff policy are cost orientation and transparency. The first involves basing tariffs on the costs associated with the provision of the relevant service. This does not necessarily imply a requirement that tariffs reflect costs plus a predetermined margin. However, as between various services the principle involves tariffs bearing a relationship to the cost associated with each service. It also involves the sensitivity of costs to various factors also being reflected in tariffs. For example, if the cost of provision does not alter with distance, the tariff for the service will also be expected to be distance-independent. Transparency requires that service and network providers provide to users sufficient information for the user to ascertain the basis of charges and to challenge the tariffs when they do not conform to the appropriate principles.

The Commission has secured the introduction of tariff principles as a part of the harmonising process, by means of incorporation in Directives and Recommendations. An early example of the application of tariff principles relates to pan-European cellular digital land-based mobile communications.[13] The Council has made detailed Recommendations to be implemented by various dates from 1991 to 1995.[14]

The tariff considerations[15] which the TOs are invited to consider incorporate the principles of departure from distance dependence. It is recommended that tariffs should be based on the duration of the use of the radio channels. This was justified on grounds of the scarcity of frequency resources. In its resolution of 30 June 1988,[16] the Council declared[17] as a major policy goal in telecommunications policy, the 'definition of common tariff principles and the encouragement of co-operation between network

---

[9] See p. 71 et seq.

[10] Price agreements between providers of services and goods constitutes serious breaches of Art. 85 of the Rome Treaty; see for example, PVC Commission Decision 89/190/EEC, OJ L 74/1, 17 Mar. 1989; case 123/85, BNIC v Clair [1985] ECR 391.

[11] PGT/10.

[12] See Commission press release IP(90) 188, 6 Mar. 1990.

[13] *Council Recommendation of 25 June 1987 on Co-ordinated Introduction of Public Pan-European Cellular Digital Land-based Mobile Communications in the Community*, 87/371/EEC, OJ L 196/81, 17 July 1987.

[14] 87/371/EEC, para. 1.

[15] 87/371/EEC, Annex, para. 7.

[16] 88/C 257/01, OJ C 257/1, 4 Oct. 1988.

[17] 88/C 257/01, para. 3.

operators and others, as far as compatible with Community competition rules;[18] one of the aims of this should be a clear definition of efficient pricing principles throughout the Community while ensuring general service for all[19]'. Another element of the tariff policy is the elimination of discrimination in the provision of services. Accordingly, the Services Directive[20] provides that there be 'no discrimination either in the conditions of use or in the *charges*[21] payable'.

The central instrument giving effect to the Community tariff principles is the ONP Directive.[22] The importance of tariff principles in the context of ONP conditions has already been discussed.[23] The reference framework for ONP conditions[24] elaborates on the basic principles harmonised for tariff principles. Tariffs must:[25]

1. Be based on objective criteria.

   The intention is that tariffs throughout the Community should be based on harmonised principles and ensure the universal service. The actual level of tariffs continues to be a matter for national regulation by Member States. In the context of services which are subject to special or exclusive rights, objectivity implies cost orientation.[26]

2. Be transparent and published.[27]

   Associated with this concept of transparency, is the need for unbundling of services and tariffs so that users can make competitive choices. The ONP Directive specifically refers to extra services which provide additional features, which must be charged separately from carriage and inclusive features.

3. Be non-discriminatory and guarantee equality of access and treatment of users.

It is, of course, always permissible to take account of fluctuations in demand in setting tariffs, as long as these are justifiable commercially and conform to the general principles.[28]

The Council Recommendation on radio paging[29] highlights some of the specific tariff considerations[30] which arise in relation to radio-based services. It recommends that in establishing principles of charging for a European service account should be taken of 'cross charging between national operators for the handling of roaming traffic[31] and of the network technicalities'. Roaming traffic also arises in other radio-based services, notably in the case of cellular digital mobile communications, but the Council Recommendation on mobile communications[32] makes no specific reference to the handling of such traffic in the context of tariffs.

---

[18] See p. 16.
[19] See p. 62.
[20] 90/388/EEC, Art. 6.
[21] Emphasis added.
[22] 90/387/EEC.
[23] See p. 85.
[24] 90/387/EEC, Art. 4(4)(d), Annex II.
[25] 90/387/EEC, Art. 3(1).
[26] 90/387/EEC, Annex II, s. 3.
[27] See p. 71 et seq; 90/387/EEC, Art. 3(1) and Annex II, s. 3.
[28] 90/387/EEC, Annex II, s. 3.
[29] 90/543/EEC, OJ L 310/23, 9 Nov. 1990.
[30] 90/543/EEC, Annex, para. 6.
[31] Roaming occurs where the customer of one network provider can obtain a service through the network of another provider. This generally occurs where the network to which the customer subscribes does not extend to a location at which the customer requires the service at a given time. In these circumstances the operators enter into arrangements for handling roaming traffic originating with the customer of another operator.
[32] 87/371/EEC; see p. 41.

The radio paging Recommendation also sets an upper limit on tariffs to users of a European radio paging service. These are to be no higher than user cost 'of current services of the same type'.[33] This raises a few questions. First, it is not clear whether user cost of services is to be determined at the date of the Recommendation[34] or when the European service is introduced. Also, the expression 'the same type' is somewhat vague and may be argued to mean services within European reach. However, the Commission's intention is probably to refer to the nature of the services as opposed to the extent of coverage. This would fit in with the general principle that, where possible, tariffs should be independent of distance.

Council Recommendation on DECT[35] makes very brief reference to tariff considerations[36] that requires the timely identification of methods of charging and accounting between operators.

The Council Directive applying ONP to leased lines[37] provides the clearest and most extensive elaboration of tariff principles. The Directive refers to and explains the tariff principles of the ONP Directive[38] in the context of leased lines.[39] The Directive enumerates the principles already discussed[40] and provides the basis for harmonised tariff principles by specifying that the same principles must be used by all telecommunications organisations in arriving at their tariffs for leased lines.[41] The Directive declares a prejudice in favour of flat rate periodic rentals except where costs would justify a departure from this type of tariff.

The elements that are expected to contribute to a tariff are costs, ascertained on the basis of fair sharing of the costs of the resources utilised, and a reasonable return on investment, taking into account funds needed for the development of the telecommunications infrastructure.[42] The need for transparency is reinforced by the requirement to use transparent cost accounting systems which can be independently verified.[43]

These principles are incorporated into the Directive[44] through the requirements for publication and notification[45] to the Commission. The Directive further secures that the tariffs are independent of the use to which leased lines are put by the user[46] and defines the elements which go into making up the tariffs.[47] Furthermore, the basis for the allocation and determination of costs[48] is provided.

---

[33] 90/543/EEC, para. 6.
[34] 9 Oct. 1990.
[35] Council Recommendation of 3 June 1991 on the Co-ordinated Introduction of Digital Cordless European Telecommunications (DECT) into the Community, 91/288/EEC, OJ L 134/47, 8 June 1991.
[36] 91/288/EEC, Annex, para. 6.
[37] 92/44/EEC.
[38] 90/387/EEC.
[39] 92/44/EEC, Recital 17.
[40] These were that tariffs for leased lines must be:
  1. based on objective criteria and must follow the principle of cost orientation, taking into account the reasonable time needed for rebalancing;
  2. transparent and properly published;
  3. sufficiently unbundled in accordance with the competition laws of the Treaty;
  4. non-discriminatory and guaranteed equality of treatment.
  See p. 85.
[41] 92/44/EEC, Recital 17.
[42] Recital 18.
[43] Recital 19.
[44] Art. 3(1).
[45] Art. 3(2), Annex I, para. B.
[46] Art. 10(1)(a).
[47] Art. 10(1)(b).
[48] Art. 10(2).

CHAPTER 9

Spectrum Management

THE INTERNATIONAL TELECOMMUNICATIONS UNION

As noted already,[1] the major purpose and focus of the International Telecommunications Union is the promotion of international co-operation to maintain and improve the rational use of telecommunications on an international level.[2] The attainment of these objectives involves the ITU in the management of the frequency spectrum. The ITU discharges this function through the International Frequency Registration Board,[3] which is responsible for maintaining the Register of spectrum assignments. The ITU, primarily through the IFRB, enforces the regime for the avoidance of *harmful interference* between radiocommunications services.

All Member States are also members of the ITU and bound by its rules and Regulations.[4] Even in the absence of any legal requirement to submit to the frequency management role, Member States would find it difficult to conduct radiocommunications activities without central international management of the spectrum resource. However, the achievement of a Community-wide telecommunications market also requires further co-ordination at Community level.

In certain specific areas the Community has sought to impose frequency spectrum discipline. These include satellite and mobile communications services and systems. The

---

[1] See p. 18.
[2] The International Telecommunications Convention, Art. 4(1) provides: 'The purposes of the Union are:
   (a) To maintain and extend international co-operation between all Members of the Union for the improvement and rational use of telecommunications of all kinds, as well as to promote and to offer technical assistance to developing countries in the field of telecommunications;
   (b) To promote the development of technical facilities and their most efficient operation with a view to improving the efficiency of telecommunication services, increasing their usefulness and making them, so far as possible, generally available to the public;
   (c) To harmonise the actions of nations in the attainment of those ends.'
[3] IFRB.
[4] But see p. 20 et seq.

Community rules in these areas are addressed in the relevant Paragraphs. However, it may be useful to summarise those rules here.

MOBILE RADIO COMMUNICATIONS SYSTEMS

Radio paging systems

The Council Recommendation on the introduction of pan-European public radio paging[5] specifies the requirement as to efficient use of the spectrum,[6] access to the system and outlines for the receiver specifications, radio subsystem, system implementation and the service and facilities which should be supported by the system.[7]

The Recommendation specifies that radio paging systems be suitable for operation over the frequency band range 169.4 MHz to 169.8 MHz. Each channel is recommended to be 25 KHz.

GMS mobile systems

In 1987 the Council effectively recommended the adoption of the GSM[8] for the public pan-European cellular digital land-based mobile communication systems,[9] defining the frequency bands within which the systems should operate.[10] There are two frequency band recommended for GSM systems. These are 890–915 MHz and 935–960 MHz.

DECT systems

As with other Recommendations in this area, the DECT Recommendations[11] identify the frequency band which should be available for DECT as well as other general characteristics of the standard, including tariff considerations.[12] The recommended DECT frequencies are 1880–1900 MHz.[13]

Mobile communications services

Clearly, in relation to any mobile communications service the allocation and availability of suitable frequencies on a Community-wide basis is of central importance.[14] Therefore,

---

[5] Council Recommendation 90/543/EEC, Annex, para. 1.

[6] Spectrum usage and grade of service should be comparable to systems based on CCIR radio paging code number 1 (Pocsag).

[7] 90/543/EEC, Annex, paras 1–5.

[8] Group Speciale Mobile.

[9] Council Recommendation of 25 June 1987 on the co-ordinated introduction of public pan-European cellular digital land-based mobile communications in the Community, 87/371/EEC, OJ L 196/81, 17 July 1987.

[10] 87/371/EEC, Annex, para. 1 at 83.

[11] 91/288/EEC, OJ L 144/47, 8 June 1991.

[12] 91/288/EEC, OJ L 144/47, 8 June 1991, Annex, paras 1–6.

[13] In conformity with Dir. 91/287/EEC.

[14] Council Dir. on frequency bands to be reserved for co-ordinated introduction of public pan-European cellular digital land-based mobile communications in the Community, 87/372/EEC, Recital 4.

both these features had to be addressed concurrently in the Community initiative to facilitate introduction of cellular mobile communications.[15] Nevertheless, it is logical that the Commission wished first to ensure the availability of relevant frequency bands. The Commission, therefore, proposed a Directive to be adopted by the Council[16] [17] which was approved by Parliament[18] and subsequently issued.[19] [20]

The Directive requires Member States to ensure that 25 MHz within each band from 905 to 914 MHz and from 950 to 959 MHz, are reserved exclusively for cellular digital mobile communications by 1 January 1991.[21] They are further required to ensure there are the necessary plans to enable such services to occupy the bands 890–915 and 935–960 MHz as quickly as possible.[22]

European Radiocommunications Office

The increasing trend towards the development of radio communications services has highlighted the significance of spectrum management and allocation, in achieving Community objectives in telecommunications. Although the ITU regulation of radio frequencies operates at an international level, it is intended to prevent harmful interference between the services of one country and another. However, on a Community level, a further objective is pursued, in order that services may be provided throughout the Community while taking into account particularly persons on the move in the Community.[23] For mobile services, the choice of frequencies also has a direct impact on standards as well as the size of the market for radio equipment.[24]

There is clearly a role for the management of spectrum at a Community and preferably a European level.[25] In recognition of this need, CEPT reached a decision[26] to create a European Radiocommunications Office.[27] The Community seized the occasion to support the establishment of the ERO[28] and to outline its goals in relation to the management of the radio spectrum.

The main Community objectives are:[29]

1. to ensure sufficient frequency spectrum for new services through strengthening European co-operation;
2. seeking early allocation of spectrum for mobile and satellite applications;

---

[15] Frequencies allocated for mobile communications systems also had an impact on the definition of standards for the network and mobile terminal.

[16] Proposal for a Council Dir. on the frequency bands to be made available for the co-ordinated introduction of public pan-European digital mobile communications in the Community, submitted to the Council on 9 Feb. 1987.

[17] Com (87) 35 Final OJ C 69/9, 17 Mar. 1987.

[18] Opinion of the European Parliament of 10 Apr. 1987, OJ C 125/159, 11 May 1987.

[19] Council Dir. of 25 June 1987 on the frequency bands to be reserved for the co-ordinated introduction of public pan-European cellular digital land-based mobile communications in the Community.

[20] 87/372/EEC, OJ L 196/85, 17 July 1987.

[21] 87/372/EEC, Art. 1(1).

[22] 87/372/EEC, Art. 1(2).

[23] 90/C 166/02, Recital 2.

[24] 90/C 166/82, Recitals 6 and 7.

[25] 90/C 166/02, Recital 5.

[26] 90/C 166/02, para. 6.

[27] ERO.

[28] Council resolution of 28 June 1990 on the strengthening of the Europe-wide co-operation on radio frequencies, in particular with regard to services with a pan-European dimension, 90/C 166/02, OJ C 166/4, 7 July 1990; para. 7.

[29] 90/C 166/02, paras 1–4.

3. promoting efficient use of frequency, particularly in the setting of standard;
4. developing a unified European stance within the ITU.

The Community will participate in ERO to further these aims. It is debateable that a more general role will have to be performed by ERO to facilitate the smooth running of radiocommunications within Europe.

CHAPTER 10

Data Protection

DATA PROTECTION REGULATION AND IMPACT ON COMPETITION

In pursuing its policy to create a single European telecommunications market and to open telecommunication services to competition, the Commission has recognised a number of factors which may justify Member States in departing from the rigours of this policy. These reasons are not confined to matters such as national security, but extend to 'non-economic reasons in the general interest which may cause a Member State to restrict access to the public telecommunications network or public telecommunications services',[1] which are collectively termed '*essential requirements*'. One *essential requirement* is data protection.

Access to data is increasingly dependent on the use of the telecommunications infrastructure. Conversely, restrictions on access to data and its processing can have an impact on telecommunications services that may be provided. This in turn can limit competition in such services both within and between Member States.

Data can be broadly divided into four categories. These are: personal data, business data, technical data and organisational data. It is self-evident that these categories are not mutually exclusive and data within one category may include also data falling within one or more other categories. Therefore, data in that sense, can cover the whole range of economic activity. If Member States who are permitted to regulate telecommunications infrastructures and services to protect data in the general sense, not only would the telecommunications market be affected but they could severely distort virtually all aspects of trade between Member States.

The various Directives and resolutions including reference to data protection in the context of telecommunications do not provide a definition of 'data'. The Services Directive[2] provides that:

---

[1] Services Dir., 90/388/EEC, Art. 1(1).
[2] 90/388/EEC, Art. 1(1).

Data protection may include protection of personal data, and confidentiality of information transmitted or stored, as well as the protection of privacy.

This definition is far from exhaustive and in itself does not provide sufficient indication of the limitations of data protection in the context of *essential requirements*. There is some assistance in the recitals[3] where it is provided:[4]

Data protection means measures taken to warrant the confidentiality of communications and the protection of personal data.

The services Green Paper[5] refers to data protection as 'a shorthand formula for the protection of an individual's rights and fundamental freedoms and in particular his [or] her rights to privacy, with regard to automatic processing of personal data relating to him [or] her'. This is similar to the definition used by the Council of Europe in its Convention on data protection.[6] Therefore, it can be assumed that references to data protection by the Commission in the context of telecommunications do not extend beyond what may be termed 'personal data'.

For the reasons already indicated,[7] even if data protection in the context of essential requirements is confined to personal data, a conflict can arise between the interests of a Member State in safeguarding personal data and the development of a common market in telecommunication services. This would run contrary not only to the Commission's policy in telecommunications, but also to the goal of establishing a Community-wide information market as expressed by the Commission in the Green Paper:[8]

One important economic, political and cultural advantage for Europe of advanced Europe-wide telecommunications derives from the possibilities created for the enhanced exchange and free flow of information. This advantage can only be fully materialised with the development of a common market for information.
Adequate telecommunications infrastructures and services are a condition *sine-qua-non* for the free expression and free flow of information in the Community in the future. The provision of telecommunications network infrastructure and telecommunications services will provide the conduit within which information can flow. The provision of information services in a free market for information content are indispensable requirements for putting telecommunications network infrastructures and telecommunications services to best use.

This clearly requires harmonised data protection legislation within the Community which might be achieved by either ratifying or acceding to the Council of Europe Convention,[9] or a new Directive on the subject.[10]

Currently the most relevant international document affecting the protection of personal data by Member States is the Council of Europe Convention.[11]

---

[3] 90/388/EEC, Recitals 8 and 9.

[4] Recital 9.

[5] COM (87), 290 final, p. 142, para. 3.2.1.

[6] Convention for the Protection of Individuals with Regard to Automatic Processing of Personal Data, Council of Europe, Strasbourg, 28 Jan. 1981, Art. 1.

[7] See above.

[8] COM (87) 290 final, p. 139, para. 3.

[9] Council of Europe Data Protection Convention, Arts 22 and 23, provide for ratification by Member States and accession by non-Member States.

[10] This would be based on the Commission Recommendation 91/679/EEC and the European Parliament Resolution of 9 Mar. 1982; in July 1990 the Commission submitted its proposals for a Directive to harmonise data protection laws, Proposal for a Council Directive Concerning the Protection of Individuals in Relation to the Processing of Personal Data, 90/C 277/03, OJ C 277/3, 5 Nov. 1990.

[11] Although all Member States are signatories to the Convention, not all have yet ratified the Convention; as of Feb. 1992 only Denmark, France, Germany, Luxembourg, Spain and the UK had ratified the Convention.

COUNCIL OF EUROPE CONVENTION ON DATA PROTECTION

The Convention requires that State Parties provide under their domestic law protection to individuals[12] in respect of whom personal data[13] is automatically processed.[14] Chapter II of the Convention sets out the basic protections which must be provided by each Party under its domestic law.[15] These include ensuring that personal data is obtained, processed and stored fairly and lawfully and is not kept for longer than legitimately needed.[16] Personal data should also be safeguarded against unauthorised interference and there needs to be special safeguards in respect of sensitive information such as racial origin, political opinions, health or similar data.[17]

Perhaps the most important safeguard provided under the Convention[18] is the ability of data subjects to discover whether and what possible data is held about them and to secure corrections to the data so held.

Nevertheless, a Party can derogate from some of the provisions[19] of the Convention where this is 'a necessary measure in a democratic society in the interests of:

(a) protecting state security, public safety, the monetary interests of the State or the suppression of criminal offences;

(b) protecting the data subject or the rights and freedoms of others'.[20]

The Explanatory Report which accompanies the text of the Convention makes it clear that the derogations permitted under these provisions are not to be construed as giving States undue wide leeway.[21] In particular:

The term 'monetary interests of the State' covers all the different means of financing a State's policies. Accordingly, the term refers in particular to tax collection requirements and exchange controls.[22]

However, it may be concluded that a State Party may not justify exceptions to the requirements of the Convention on the basis of general economic policy and, in the present context, aimed at restricting trade with other countries. The Convention specifically addresses trans-border data flows[23] and provides that:

A party shall not for the sole purpose of the protection of privacy, prohibit or subject to special authorisation trans-border flows of personal data going to the territory of another Party.[24]

---

[12] Parties may extend the application of the Convention to persons other than individuals, including associations, companies or corporations; Art. 3(2) b).

[13] 'Personal data' means any information relating to an identified or identifiable individual ('data subject'); Art. 2(a).

[14] 'Automatic processing' includes the following operations if carried out in whole or in part by automated means: storage of data, carrying out of logical and/or arithmetical operations on those data, their alteration, erasure, retrieval or dissemination; Art. 2(c). It follows that access to and retrieval of data by means of a telecommunications system could amount to 'automatic processing'.

[15] Council of Europe Data Protection Convention, Art. 4.

[16] Council of Europe Data Protection Convention, Art. 5.

[17] Council of Europe Data Protection Convention, Arts 6 and 7.

[18] Council of Europe Data Protection Convention, Art. 8.

[19] Council of Europe Data Protection Convention, Arts 5, 6 and 8.

[20] Council of Europe Data Protection Convention, Art. 9(2)

[21] Explanatory Report, para. 56.

[22] Explanatory Report, para. 57.

[23] Explanatory Report, Chapter III, Art. 12.

[24] Explanatory Report, Art. 12(2).

On the face of it, this provision may suggest that general domestic economic policy may justify restriction of trans-border data flows between Parties. However, the Explanatory Report[25] makes it clear that a Party can prohibit certain transfers of personal data, but these must be applied equally to transfers within its territory as well as across its borders. It further provides that:

> The expression 'for the sole purpose of the protection of privacy' adds an important clarification, namely that a Contracting State may not invoke this Convention to justify interference with trans-border data flows for reasons which have nothing to do with the protection of privacy (for example, hidden trade barriers).

As between Member States, even in the absence of the specific provisions of the Convention on trans-border data flows, the Community competition rules could be invoked to ensure that, at least between Parties to the Convention, trans-border data flows are not restricted. This reasoning could also extend to the interpretation of 'data protection' in the context of *essential requirements*.

PROTECTION OF DATA IN DIGITAL TELECOMMUNICATIONS SYSTEMS

The Commission has proposed a Directive[26] specifically aimed at protecting personal data and privacy in the context of public digital telecommunications networks. This proposal followed references in several Community telecommunications measures to the need for Community action on data protection and privacy, and particularly in the Council Recommendation on the co-ordinated introduction of ISDN.[27] The Council[28] has also identified the protection of data as a major policy goal. The European Parliament has also called for measures[29] to ensure that 'legislative proposals on opening up telecommunications markets . . . are accompanied by action at Community level relating to the protection of personal data'.

The proposed Directive set out to create a harmonised approach to the protection of personal data in order that the development of telecommunications services and systems not be hampered within the Community. It aims at achieving a basic level of protection for subscribers in a digital environment by limiting the data processing stored in the context of public telecommunications operations to the bare minimum required and providing the subscriber with control over the accuracy and the divulgence of personal data accumulated by telecommunications organisations. The Directive is primarily concerned with voice telephony, although it also addresses other services.

Scope and application

The proposed Directive applies to the collection, storage and processing of personal data by telecommunications organisations.[30] This application is confined to the provision of

---

[25] Explanatory Report, para. 67.
[26] Proposal for a Council Dir. Concerning the Protection of Personal Data and Privacy in the Context of Public Digital Telecommunications Networks, in particular the Integrated Services Digital Network (ISDN) and Public Digital Mobile Networks, 90/C 277/04, OJ C277/4, 5 Nov. 1990.
[27] 86/659/EEC; see p. 38.
[28] Council Resolution of 30 June 1988, OJ C 257/1, endorsing the action programme of the Commission in the Green Paper, COM 87, 290 final.
[29] Resolution of 14 Dec. 1988.
[30] 90/C 277/04, Art. 2(1).

public telecommunications services in public digital telecommunications networks which include ISDN and public digital mobile networks.[31] Such collection, storage and processing of personal data can only be justified for the purposes of providing the intended service and may in particular not be used to give telecommunications organisations any undue competitive advantage over other service providers.[32]

The subscriber is entitled to obtain details of personal data held about him and to require its correction[33] and to have such information safeguarded against unauthorised access.[34] There are also safeguards with regard to the confidentiality of billing and traffic data, including itemised call statements.[35]

There are extensive provisions regarding calling line identification and the ability to override such identification.[36] Similarly, there are specific requirements in relation to call forwarding,[37] in particular, the recipient of a forwarded call should be informed that he is receiving a forwarded call and the caller must be informed of the fact that his call is being forwarded to another location.[38] Telecommunications organisations are also required to secure that telephone calls cannot be recorded without the other party's being informed of the fact of recording.[39]

Telecommunications organisations are required to ensure that data concerning the uses of teleshopping or videotext services is not such as to enable a profile of the subscriber to be established.[40] They are also expected to prevent future communications to subscribers from providers of unsolicited goods or services.[41]

Limitations of proposals

This Proposed Directive came under extensive criticism from all quarters.[42] The Proposed Directive is primarily concerned with the protection of individuals against the abuse of Personal Data which can be easily collated within a digitalised telecommunication system. Such systems make it particularly easy to gather information about the identification of both subscribers engaged in a call.

However, the achievement of objectives of the Proposed Directive require measures in different fields. Some of these are specifically related to data protection, but others concern telecommunications regulation and equipment standards. The Proposed Directive makes no clear distinction between these areas and the measures that need to be taken in respect of each.

Further, and perhaps a more important drawback of the Proposed Directive, is that it is not always clear who should bear responsibility for many of its proposed provisions. This is further highlighted in the comments which follow on each of the Articles of the Proposed Directive.

---

[31] Ibid.
[32] 90/C 277/04, Arts 4 and 5.
[33] 90/C 277/04, Art. 6.
[34] 90/C 277/04, Arts 7 and 8.
[35] 90/C 277/04, Arts 9, 10 and 11.
[36] 90/C 277/04, Arts 12 and 13.
[37] 90/C 277/04, Art. 14.
[38] This latter feature has been removed from the call forwarding service provided by BT as a result of subscriber pressure. The feature undoubtedly diminishes the utility of call forwarding facilities.
[39] 90/C 277/04, Art. 15.
[40] 90/C 277/04, Art. 16.
[41] 90/C 277/04, Art. 17.
[42] Including from the author of the present work, Submission to the DTI on EC Commission Proposed Dir. on Data Protection in Digital Telecommunications Network, July 1990.

It is recognised[43] that many of the provisions of the Proposed Directive are relevant also to services based on analogue networks. It is inconsistent with this reality to confine the applications of the provisions of the Proposed Directive to analogue networks only when digital networks have not yet been implemented. It is unlikely that any Member State will have digital networks exclusively, at least for many years to come.

The first reference[44] to 'implemented' is misleading, as network implementation will be by telecommunications organisations and not Member States.

The definition[45] of *telecommunications organisation* is also considered to be too narrow. In many Member States general licences are already or will soon be issued, permitting any organisation to provide a large variety of telecommunication services through the medium of public or private telecommunication networks. All such organisations are potentially capable of collating the type of Personal Data which the Proposed Directive aims to protect. This is particularly true of re-sellers of capacity provided by operators of public telecommunication networks. The exclusion of such organisations and their networks and services from the Proposed Directive puts them at a competitive advantage over those to which the Proposed Directive applies.

The absolute prohibition[46] against the use of Personal Data to compile classifications and the like may be too restrictive. This should be possible with the consent of an appropriate authority within each Member State.

On a technical point, the use of the word 'individual'[47] is unnecessary and serves only to confuse.

The ambit of certain clauses[48] is much more limited than those encompassed in the principles previously set out,[49] and may be inadequate to enable telecommunications organisations to provide certain mobile services to subscribers. For example, in a Telepoint system the location of a subscriber making a call or logging-in at a particular station is necessary to provide the service. The storage of such Personal Data goes beyond what is necessary *to conclude, amend or terminate the contract with the telecommunications organisation*.

The provision of *end-to-end encryption service* in mobile telecommunications systems would be impracticable and, where possible, could be prohibitively expensive.[50] Such an obligation would require telecommunications organisations to offer a scrambling service to each customer. The state of the art techniques demand greater bandwidth for each communication. Furthermore, for scrambling to be effective it would need to be specific to each set of two handsets, so that the subscriber would need to choose the terminals with which he wanted to have this type of *secure* communication. Therefore, there would only be a limited and previously designated population of handsets with which each subscriber could be in *secure* communication. The administrative and technical difficulties of achieving this would make the system more expensive to run and would be of extremely limited value to subscribers.[51]

In some areas[52] the wording is ambiguous and may be understood to suggest that all itemised call statements should be produced *without the last 4 digits* of the called sub-

---

[43] 90/C 277/04, Art. 2.
[44] 90/C 277/04, para. 2, Art. 2.
[45] 90/C 277/04, Art. 3.
[46] 90/C 277/04, Art. 4.
[47] 90/C 277/04, para. 2, Art. 4.
[48] 90/C 277/04, Art. 5, para. 1.
[49] 90/C 277/04, Art. 4.
[50] 90/C 277/04, Art. 8.
[51] The recording of the time the call starts and finishes is permitted under 90/C 277/04, Art. 10.
[52] 90/C 277/04, Art. 11.

scribers. However, the intention is understood to be to provide a measure of privacy to the subscriber receiving the itemised call statement and it should be only at his request that the last 4 digits are omitted. Otherwise, any itemised call statement may be rendered pointless if the subscriber cannot identify the specific call for which he is billed.

The specification of terminal equipment and of the network is affected.[53] Administrative duties are also imposed on the network operator. Both the network standards which will be necessary and the additional obligations will add to the cost of operating the network and providing service. Again these burdens are specifically to be borne only by telecommunications organisations operating digital networks. It would be more appropriate for such requirements, if necessary, to apply to SPC.

The provisions of the facilities[54] will also have an impact on the bandwidth required to operate the network. The exact extent of the obligations is unclear and who bears those obligations. For example, there may be a number of ways in which the objective[55] may be achieved. This could be either through the design of the network or facilities solely within the terminal equipment. Furthermore, certain areas[56] appear to be *permissive* and not *mandatory*. If that is the intention, then there appears to be no purpose served by their inclusion in a Directive.

It also appears to be unnecessary to provide that a subscriber be able to limit acceptance of incoming calls to those identifying the callers' number. The subscriber will in all cases have the choice whether or not to respond to a call and can refrain from responding to a call where the caller's number is not displayed. To make this an obligation which may be imposed on the telecommunications organisation is unnecessary and difficult to implement by the organisation.

The obligation[57] is technically difficult to discharge, if indeed it is possible at all. Furthermore, operators of analogue systems can argue that certain stipulations of the Directive[58] exempt them from the requirements of others.[59] Therefore, the telecommunications organisations operating the digital network will be under an obligation to provide a service of a higher standard to the analogue subscriber than he would receive from the network to which he is connected.

If the controls addressed[60] are intended to be effected through the network there are a large number of practical and technical difficulties which would prevent its implementation. These controls[61] would also benefit from greater clarity, for example by substituting the words 'third party' for the words 'this party'.

The facility to forward calls is entirely within the control of the *called subscriber* and the telecommunications organisation has no means of ascertaining whether the third party has consented. To set up an authorisation machinery which could record and control the forwarding of calls would be totally impractical. Also, the addition of a signal to forwarded calls would greatly complicate what in essence is a simple switching operation.

It must also be recognised that where call forwarding has occurred within a private network which is then conveyed by a network of a telecommunications organisation it will not conform to these requirements. This could result in complaints from the third parties

---

[53] 90/C 277/04, Art. 12.
[54] Required under 90/C 277/04, Art. 12.
[55] Expressed in 90/C 277/04, Art. 12, the first para. of para. 1.
[56] 90/C 277/04, Art. 12, the second para. of para. 1 and part of the first para. of para. 2.
[57] Contained in 90/C 277/04, Art. 12, para. 3.
[58] 90/C 277/04, Art. 2.
[59] 90/C 277/04, Art. 12.
[60] 90/C 277/04, Art. 14.
[61] Ibid.

to whom calls have been forwarded and the telecommunications would not be in a position to identify such calls.

Certain provisions[62] are cumbersome and unnecessary, particularly where the third party is able to identify the number of the originator of the call which has been forwarded to him. Other requirements[63] can clearly only be met by appropriate terminal equipment and it must be made clear that the telecommunications organisation has no responsibility in this regard. Any obligation by the telecommunications organisation[64] would be impossible to discharge.

Where the telecommunications organisation is not the service provider it cannot ensure that specific requirements[65] are met. In the light of earlier clauses[66] the reference to telecommunications organisation[67] is redundant and may be construed to impose obligations on the organisation which it cannot meet.

The obligations on the telecommunications organisation[68] are open to the same objections as those in earlier clauses.[69] Furthermore, both domestic and international law prohibit the telecommunications organisation from intercepting and monitoring the content and nature of the calls. Without the ability to do so the telecommunications organisation will have no means of excluding certain types of calls.

A further obstacle to enforcement against telecommunications organisation is that such organisations are under legal obligation, both domestic and international, to provide their services to whoever requests them, including those engaged in providing services or goods, and cannot lawfully withdraw the service from them. Interference with particular goods may also be a denial of the freedom of speech.

Nowhere in the Proposed Directive is there specific identification of the *risks for the privacy of the user*. Without such identification services to which the Proposed Directive may be applied[70] remains an unsatisfactorily open question.

The greatest impact of the Proposed Directive is on telecommunications organisations[71] and it is essential that they be represented on any committee advising the Commission on the issues raised in the Proposed Directive.

---

[62] Ibid., particularly those under para. 1.
[63] 90/C 277/04, Art. 15.
[64] Ibid.
[65] 90/C 277/04, Art. 16.
[66] 90/C 277/04, Arts 4 and 5.
[67] 90/C 277/04, Art. 16.
[68] 90/C 277/04, Art. 17.
[69] 90/C 277/04, Art. 16.
[70] 90/C 277/04, Art. 19.
[71] 90/C 277/04, Art. 22.

CHAPTER 11

Promotion of European Telecommunications Industry

ECONOMIC IMPORTANCE OF TELECOMMUNICATIONS SECTOR

There are two facets to the economic significance of the telecommunications sector within the Community. First, an efficient and effective advanced network infrastructure is essential to the integration and development of a single European market. An efficient communications system, and increasingly a telecommunications system, is a requirement of all economies, including manufacturing and service based economies. While economies become more information based and information dependent, the role and importance of communications will continue to increase.

As economies around the world mature and follow the same trends as those in Europe, Japan and the United States, the demand for telecommunications equipment and services provided by European companies will increase. The Commission's Action Programme[1] has been devised with the object of promoting investment and development of the European telecommunications industry. To further this objective the Commission, *inter alia*, established a number of specific projects with defined objectives. This Action Programme in telecommunications, within the mandate given by Council, was developed on the basis of the Commission's view of the requirements for advanced infrastructure and service development.[2] In the Commission's view, such development required a combination of:

1. Research and Development,[3] in areas where technology still needs to be developed and 'pre-normative' work needs to be undertaken;
2. agreement on standards, in areas where technological feasibility and capability has

---

[1] The European Council agreed on the main elements of a Community telecommunications policy, including the objective of developing advanced telecommunications services and networks by actions at Community level, on 17 Dec. 1984.
[2] Green Paper, COM(87) 290, p. 114.
[3] R&D.

115

been established but agreement on specifications is needed to create the necessary economies of scale and scope;[4]

3. investment in areas where the economic and technological basis has been established.

In addition to the programmes which are discussed below, the Community makes, by its financial instruments, a substantial contribution to telecommunications investment.[5]

FRAMEWORK PROGRAMME FOR RESEARCH AND TECHNOLOGICAL DEVELOPMENT

From the early 1980s the Commission has encouraged a cohesive approach to research and technological development throughout the Community, particularly at the early precompetitive stages of the development of high technology. An initial framework programme was established for the period 1984 to 1987 followed by a second framework programme extending to 1991.[6] These programmes were intended in particular to encourage SMEs, research centres and universities.

This policy is continued in the third framework programme 1990 to 1994.[7] The programme furthers the intentions of the Single European Act[8] to strengthen the scientific and technological base of European industry in order that it may become more competitive at an international level.[9]

The Community activities under the framework programmes are focused on specific objectives and are intended to add value to work carried out at national and other levels.[10] Projects within the framework programme are carried out in co-operation with third countries[11] and in particular by those countries who are members of the European Co-operation in the Field of Scientific and Technical Research.[12]

The activities falling within the third framework programme,[13] to be funded under the programme[14] include in particular information and communications technologies.[15]

Research and development programmes

The Action Programme addresses the development of particular parts of the regions within the Community. The following is a brief description of the various programmes in progress

---

[4] The issue of standards is addressed in Chap. 5.

[5] In 1985 loans for telecommunications investment by the European Investment Bank and the New Community Lending Instrument (NIC) totalled 572 million ecu. Total contributions from the European Regional Fund, within the framework of its annual operations were 162 million ecu.

[6] Council Resolution of 25 July 1983 on framework programmes for Community research, development and demonstration activities and a first framework programme 1984–87, OJ C 208/1, 4 Aug. 1983; 87/516 Euratom EEC, OJ L 302/1, 24 Oct. 1987 as amended by Decision 88/193/EEC, Euratom, OJ L 89/35, 6 Apr. 1988.

[7] Council Decision of 23 Apr. 1990 concerning the framework programme of Community activities in the field of research and technological development (1990–94), 90/221/Euratom, EEC, OJ L 117/28, 8 May 1990.

[8] EEC Treaty, Art. 130.

[9] 90/221/Euratom, EEC, recital 1.

[10] 90/221/Euratom, EEC, recitals 9 and 10, Art. 2(4) and Annex III.

[11] 90/221/Euratom, EEC, recitals 19 and 20 and Annex II.

[12] COST.

[13] 90/221/Euratom, EEC, Art. 1(2).

[14] 90/221/Euratom, EEC, Art. 1(3), Art. 3 and Annex IV.

[15] 90/221/Euratom, EEC, Art. 1(2)(1).

The RACE programmme

Initially the RACE[16] programme was established[17] for a definition phase lasting 18 months.[18] The overall objective of RACE is the introduction of Integrated Broadband Communications[19] taking into account the evolving ISDN and national introduction strategies, resulting in a Community-wide service by 1995. RACE engages the co-operation of all those involved, including the TOs and users of telecommunications equipment and services. Inevitably, it involves the elaboration of common standards and specifications.[20] An underlying objective of RACE is to define standards and conditions prior to implementation of IBC, in order that a unified single market in the appropriate key technologies is developed. This would avoid the need for subsequent harmonisation.

The definition phase of RACE consisted of two parts.[21] Phase 1 comprised analytical work in formulation of a reference model for IBC. Part 2 was directed towards evaluation and exploration of the technology by means of projects carried out under contracts with network operators, research establishments and other appropriate bodies within the Community. The Part 2 projects were only partly funded out of the general budget of European communities.[22] Such projects were normally at least 50 per cent funded by the contractors.[23]

The Council Decision[24] broadly described the two parts of the definition phase, and provided for the Commission representative serving on the committee[25] overseeing the activities under the Decision, to make proposals for the measures to be taken in implementing the Decision objectives.[26] An indication of such measures was contained in the Commission's original proposal[27] which lead to the Council Decision.[28]

Three groups carried out the basic design of the European broadband network and services by elaborating an IBC reference model:

1. Groupe Speciale Large Bande[29] of CEPT, established their permanent team in Darmstadt and defined the standards and requirements for the networks;
2. manufacturers, research laboratories and the TOs carried out the work on terminals under shared cost contracts; and
3. SOG-T/GAP carried out the work on services.

At the conclusion of the definition phase, the RACE Management Committee called on the Commission and the Council to take the necessary decisions to ensure that the greater project continued and the follow up work carried out.[30] Thus, the Council issued a

---

[16] R & D Programme in Advance Communications Technologies for Europe (RACE).

[17] Council Decision of 25 July 1985 on a Definition Phase for a Community Action in the Field of Telecommunications Technologies: RACE, 85/372/EEC, OJ L 210/24, 7 Aug. 1985.

[18] 84/372/EEC, Art. 1(1); the 18 month period commenced on 1 July 1985.

[19] IBC.

[20] COM (87) 290 final, p. 116.

[21] 85/372/EEC, Art. 2(1).

[22] 85/372/EEC, Art. 4(1).

[23] 87/372/EEC, Art. 2(2); the Community budget contribution to Part 2 was estimated at 14 million ecu, Art. 4(2).

[24] 85/372/EEC, Annex.

[25] 85/372/EEC, Art. 6(1).

[26] 85/372/EEC, Art. 7(2).

[27] Commission proposal for a Council Decision on a preparatory action for a Community research and development programme in the field of telecommunication technologies: RACE, COM (85) 113 final, 85/C 148/07, OJ C 148/5, 18 June 1985.

[28] 85/C 148/07, Annex.

[29] GSLB.

[30] Council Decision of 14 December 1987 on a Community programme in the field of telecommunications technologies: RACE, 88/28/EEC, Recital 17.

Decision[31] to adopt the RACE programme for a further five year period.[32] This Decision was in part based on the new political basis provided by the Single European Act for the development of scientific and technological strategies to promote industrial competitiveness of the Community.[33]

The new RACE programme consists of 3 parts.[34] Part I consists of developing 'functional specifications, systems and operations research' to enable Open Systems-Conformity[35] standards, concepts and Conventions. This also encompasses analytical work which is necessary to establish inter-operability of IBC[36] equipment and services. Part II calls for conduct of co-operative R&D on the key technologies required for low cost realisations of IBC equipment and services. Such co-operation focuses on the pre-competitive stage of development. Part III, grandly entitled Pre-normative Functional Integration, involves simulated tests and research experiments leading to standardisation proposals. It is designed to test the technologies developed under RACE in conjunction with ESPRIT, national programmes and international projects which come together as an integral part of an IBC system.[37]

The extended RACE programme again provides opportunities for contractors from industry and research establishments and other relevant institutions to have a proportion of the costs of their work falling within the scope of the RACE programme to be financed by the Community.[38] For the five-year term of the programme the Council estimated the Community contribution to amount to 550 million ecu.

Advanced telecommunications services for the less-favoured regions: STAR programme

Advances in telecommunications in the 1980s provided means of communication whose cost was not directly dependent on distance.[39] This development in telecommunications had particular significance for the less-favoured regions of the Community for diminishing the disadvantages faced by them due to their distance from main concentrations of population and economic activity. To overcome such disadvantage the Community instituted a programme[40] to encourage the provision in these less-favoured regions of a wide range of advanced telecommunications services which were considered essential to attract new companies to the regions and to keep existing enterprises competitive with those in the more central regions.[41]

---

[31] 88/28/EEC, OJ L 16/35, 21 Jan. 1988.

[32] 88/28/EEC, Art. 1(1); the 5-year period commenced 1 June 1987.

[33] 88/28/EEC, Recital 11.

[34] 88/28/EEC, Art. 2.

[35] Open Systems-Conformity is an international standardisation effort to achieve inter-operability of equipment and services from different suppliers, operators and service providers.

[36] These are advanced telecommunications services relying on high performance infrastructure.

[37] 88/28/EEC, Annex II.

[38] 88/28/EEC, Art. 3; normally the institutions are expected to meet at least 50% of the total expenditure involved, Art. 3(1).

[39] Resolution of 13 June 1986 closing the procedure for consultation of the European Parliament on the proposal from the Commission of the European Communities to the Council for a Regulation instituting a Community programme for the development of certain less-favoured regions of the Community by improving access to advanced telecommunications services (STAR Programme), doc A 2-60/86, OJ C 176/189, 14 July 1986, para. 1.

[40] Council Regulation EEC number 3300/86 of 27 October 1986 instituting a Community programme for the development of certain less-favoured regions of the Community by improving access to advance telecommunications services (STAR) programme, OJ L 305/1, 31 Oct. 1986.

[41] Doc A2-60/86, para. 2.

The STAR programme was an application of the Regulation covering the European Regional Development Fund.[42] The ERDF Regulation provides for funding Community programmes which help to solve serious socio-economic problems in some regions, by allowing a better link between regional development objectives and other Community goals, in this case developing an integrated and advanced telecommunications network in the Community.[43]

The STAR programme did not offer aid directly to the suppliers of telecommunications equipment. It was designed to stimulate both the supply of and the demand for equipment and services in advanced telecommunications in regions where without such action normal demand would not stimulate the required level of private investment.

The STAR programme only benefits regions that satisfy a number of specific conditions,[44] which include remote geographic locations, unfavourable economic circumstances compared to the Community as a whole and the lack of adequate telecommunications services, particularly advanced services for the productive sector. The Regulation[45] identifies regions in Spain, France, Greece, Ireland, Italy, Portugal and the United Kingdom which qualify to benefit from the STAR programme. The programme is financed jointly by Member States concerned and the general budget of the European communities through the ERDF. The assistance from the ERDF could not exceed 55 per cent of the total public expenditure taken into account in the programme.[46]

The equipment and services in respect of which the programme applies are broadly identified.[47] There is particular emphasis[48] on assistance for small and medium-sized enterprises.[49]

Member States were required to submit programmes to benefit from the STAR programme within six months of the Regulation coming into force.[50] The programme lasted for 5 years, until 31 October 1991.

Each of the relevant countries proposed an intervention programme for implementing the STAR programme, approved by Commission Decisions.[51]

As observed in the Green Paper[52] the STAR programme provided support for telecommunications in the less favoured regions through:

1. substantial contributions to investment in telecommunications network infrastructure;
2. finance for the development of telecommunications service centres, especially for SMEs;
3. support, especially to SMEs, for the use of terminals, modems and other equipment;
4. other promotional measures including technical assistance.

---

[42] ERDF; Council Regulation 1787/84, Art. 7(4).

[43] Council Regulation 3300/86, Recital 1, Arts 1 and 2; COM (87) 290 final, p. 119.

[44] Regulation 3300/86, Art. 3(1).

[45] Regulation 3300/86, Art. 3(2).

[46] Regulation 3300/86, Art. 5(1); in the case of Portugal, the maximum rate of contribution by the fund was 70% until 31 Dec. 1990, Art. 5(2).

[47] Regulation 3300/86, Art. 4.

[48] Regulation 3300/86, Art. 4(2).

[49] SME.

[50] Regulation 3300/86, Art. 8; the Regulation came into force on 1 Nov. 1986.

[51] Greece, 88/55/EEC, OJ L 30/33, 2 Feb. 1988; Spain, 88/56/EEC, OJ L 30/34, 2 Feb. 1988; France, 88/57/EEC, OJ L 30/35, 2 Feb. 1988; Ireland, 88/58/EEC, OJ L 30/36, 2 Feb. 1988; Italy, 88/59/EEC, OJ L 30/37, 2 Feb. 1988; Portugal, 88/60/EEC, OJ L 30/38, 2 Feb. 1988; UK, 88/61/EEC, OJ L 30/39, 2 Feb. 1988; all these Commission Decisions were made on 22 Oct. 1987 validating the intervention programmes until 31 Oct. 1991.

[52] COM (87) 290 final, p. 119.

The extent to which the STAR programme has achieved these objectives remains to be seen. The programme did not finance Conventional telecommunications equipment[53] which could come under other ERDF measures.[54]

Trade electronic data interchange systems (TEDIS)

The conduct of all trade requires substantial exchange of data between the partners involved, in the form of product or service specifications, price lists, orders, delivery schedules, invoices and the like. Much of this exchange of information takes place across borders and internationally, often also involving customs declarations and authorisations. Electronic data interchange[55] replaces these traditionally paper transactions which are time-consuming and costly,[56] by more rapid and efficient transfer of business messages directly between computers. Many industry sectors and trade associations saw the benefits of EDI and started to develop trade exchange data information systems,[57] which were inevitably patchy and often incompatible.

Recognising the significance of TEDIS both in terms of the competitiveness of the European economies[58] and in terms of providing opportunities for new value-added telecommunication services, the Commission proposed a programme for harmonised development of TEDIS.[59]

The advantages of promoting TEDIS also benefited the development of the telecommunications sector which in itself makes an important economic contribution. In turn, efficient information interchange benefits the manufacturing and other service industries. The spread of TEDIS would assist in the formation of the Community single market, harmonise economic development across the Community. It would particularly help overcome the disadvantages of firms in remote areas, who would be in a position to respond more quickly and efficiently to the needs of their customers.

Therefore, the Council set up[60] a two-year preparatory phase[61] on standardisation, promotion and development of other conditions necessary for the establishment of a compatible TEDIS within the Community. The preparatory phase was intended to develop a strategy for the full programme phase of TEDIS. The TEDIS programme was based on the existing Community framework[62] for standardisation in telecommunications and information technology, which aimed at establishing standards and common technical specifications to facilitate information exchange throughout the Community by removing barriers created by incompatibilities due to lack of precise standards. One of the aims of the TEDIS programme was to strengthen competitiveness and enable users and suppliers of equipment and services to benefit from the full advantages of EDI.

The preparatory phase was designed to meet the special features of information technology standardisation. In particular:

---

[53] Doc 82–60/86, para. 8.
[54] Between 1975 and 1985 the ERDF funded investments related to conventional telecommunications to the tune of 1,000 million ecu.
[55] EDI.
[56] EID has been estimated to save up to 10% of the cost of exporting the goods and 10–15% of the final transport costs; COM (87) 290 final, p. 121.
[57] TEDIS.
[58] EDI systems were already becoming better established and more sophisticated in the US.
[59] COM (86) 662 final, 1 Dec. 1986.
[60] Council Decision of 5 October 1987 Introducing a Communications Network Community Programme on Trade, Electronic Data Interchange Systems (TEDIS), 87/499/EEC, OJ L 285/35, 8 Oct. 1987.
[61] 87/499/EEC, Art. 2.
[62] Council Decision 87/95/EEC, OJ L 36/31, 7 Feb. 1987.

1. the complexity of the technical specifications and the precision required for data interchange and systems inter-operability;
2. the need to halt the development of incompatible trade EDI systems; and
3. the need for international standards which are credible for practical use.

The TEDIS programme has close links with the CADDIA[63] programme and the CD[64] project and ensures close involvement of industry and commerce to ensure that any system developed is practical and deals also with information exchange between the sectors and customs authorities.[65] To ensure the compatibility of TEDIS the preparatory phase concentrated on activities of common interest for co-ordinated development and on sectoral projects to solve problems which arose during development.

Two particular issues which the TEDIS programme had to address within the context of the Community were the language differences and differing legal requirements among Member States for the production or preservation of paper documents. Therefore, the programme looked at multi-lingual tools such as Eurotra and Systran and the extent to which the laws of Member States had to be harmonised to facilitate the use of TEDIS. In view of the aims of the Commission to facilitate not only trade among Member States but also between the Community and its trading partners, the initial Decision on the TEDIS programme was later amended[66] to allow non-member countries, in particular Member States of the European Free Trade Association,[67] to be associated with the programme. Subsequently, Council approved agreements on systems for electronic transfer of data for commercial use, made between the Community and Austria,[68] Finland,[69] Iceland,[70] Norway,[71] Sweden[72] and Switzerland.[73]

The preparatory phase of TEDIS, concluded in 1989, provided the basis for further examination and progress towards the development of pan-European networks. Therefore, a second phase of the TEDIS programme was instituted[74] for a three-year period,[75] to create the conditions for such pan-European networks. This phase of the TEDIS programme was in particular to be dovetailed[76] with programmes in related fields.[77] Estimated funds of 25 million ecu have been earmarked for the three-year programme.[78]

---

[63] Co-operation in Automation of Data and Documentation for Imports/Exports and the Management and Financial Control of the Agriculture Markets.

[64] Co-ordinated Development.

[65] Much of the paperwork generated within the Community is the result of requirements by various administrations. The Commission initiated the CADDIA programme to reduce the complexity and cost of such paperwork. The CD project, which is a distinct section within the CADDIA programme, deals specifically with the requirements of customs authorities.

[66] Council Decision 89/241/EEC, OJ L 97/46, 11 Apr. 1989.

[67] EFTA.

[68] 89/689/EEC, OJ L 400/1, 30 Dec. 1989.

[69] 89/690/EEC, OJ L 400/6, 30 Dec. 1989.

[70] 89/691/EEC, OJ L 400/11, 30 Dec. 1989.

[71] 89/692/EEC, OJ L 400/16, 30 Dec. 1989.

[72] 89/693/EEC, OJ L 400/21, 30 Dec. 1989.

[73] 89/694/EEC, OJ L 400/26, 30 Dec. 1989.

[74] Council Decision of 22 July 1991 establishing the second phase of the TEDIS programme, 91/385/EEC, OJ L 208/66, 30 July 1991.

[75] 91/385/EEC, Art. 1(1); the 3-year programme commenced on 1 July 1991, 91/385/EEC, Art. 9.

[76] 91/385/EEC, recital 7.

[77] The relevant programmes are those relating to Research and Technological Development in Communications Technology (1990–94), Programme of Research and Technological Development in the Field of Telematics Systems of General Interest (1990–94) and the Programme for Information Technology (1990–94); 91/385/EEC, recital 7.

[78] 91/385/EEC, Recital 10, Art. 1(2).

The ambit of the second phase was also to extend to non-Member States and particularly to EFTA countries.[79]

The second phase of the programme encompasses a number of measures[80] intended to ensure the establishment of EDI systems 'to the best effect'.[81] The Council Decision[82] recognises the importance of co-ordinating the TEDIS programme with the Community policy on ONP and the information market as well as the CADDIA programme and the CD project.

The measures to be taken under the second phase relate to:[83]

1. Standardisation of EDI messages. The preferred standard for messages is EDI-FACT.[84] The standardisation work envisaged involves co-ordination with the work of the EDIFACT Board for Western Europe and the promotion of EDIFACT as an international standard.[85]

2. Specific EDI needs as regards telecommunications. This involves proposals to improve technical interconnectivity between EDI users and co-ordination with the requirements of ONP and the encouragement for increased use of ISDN for EDI.[86]

3. Legal aspects of EDI. This ranges from matters such as electronic signatures for EDI messages and protection of data and confidentiality to the needs for harmonisation of European legislation to facilitate the use of EDI.[87]

4. Security of EDI messages. This covers the whole range of security matters including procedures and standards relating to EDI security, quantification of risks to security and the security aspects of multi-service environments.[88]

5. Multi-sector and Europe-wide products. To avoid the development of differing incompatible EDI systems, sectoral projects for EDI are to be co-ordinated and the development of inter-sectoral projects encouraged. Furthermore, the use of EDI throughout Europe including in non-Member States and particularly in the Mediterranean and in Central and Eastern Europe are to be promoted.[89]

6. Analysis of the impact of EDI on company management. The economic, management and organisational impact of introducing EDI are to be studied, with particular regard to SMEs.[90]

7. Information campaigns. The spread of EDI is to be monitored by surveys and campaigns to be run in order to increase the acceptability and the use of EDI, again with particular emphasis on SMEs.[91]

Within this framework the detailed work programme is determined by the Commission in consultation with a special committee set up under the TEDIS programme.[92] At the

---

[79] 91/385/EEC, Art. 5.
[80] 91/385/EEC, Art. 3.
[81] 91/385/EEC, Art. 2.
[82] 91/385/EEC, Art. 4.
[83] 91/385/EEC, Art. 3.
[84] Electronic Data Interchange For Administration, Commerce and Transport, promoted by the United Nations.
[85] 91/385/EEC, Annex 1, para. 1.
[86] 91/385/EEC, Annex 1, para. 2.
[87] 91/385/EEC, Annex 1, para. 3.
[88] 91/385/EEC, Annex 1, para. 4.
[89] 91/385/EEC, Annex 1, para. 5.
[90] 91/385/EEC, Annex 1, para. 6.
[91] 91/385/EEC, Annex 1, para. 7.
[92] 91/385/EEC, Art. 6; for work programmes with a value of more than 200,000 ecu a slightly modified procedure applies, Art. 7.

end of the TEDIS programme an assessment will be made of the influence of the TEDIS programme in respect of each of the measures above.[93]

Research programmes in communications technologies and in telematic systems

In 1990 the Council adopted[94] a programme of research[95] in communications technology, telematics systems and information technology[96] from 1990 to 1994. The third framework programme provides the framework for the specific research and technological development activities in each of these areas.[97] Pursuant to the third framework programme, the Council adopted specific research and technological development programmes in the field of communications technologies[98] and telematic systems[99] to run from 7 June 1991 to the end of 1994.[100] The aim of both programmes is to strengthen the scientific and technological basis of European industry in advanced technology, to encourage it to become more competitive at the international level,[101] and to ensure harmonised development throughout the Community. As with the TEDIS programme, the ambit of both these programmes extends to non-Member States,[102] but organisations from such countries which participate in projects under the programme cannot benefit from the financing provided by the Community.[103]

The communication technology programme concentrates on IBC system functions, extending the work of the RACE I programme. It covers intelligence in networks, including techniques of information transfer and possibly artificial intelligence, mobile and personal communications. Both development of third generation integrated mobile communication systems and their inter-connection with IBC and radio networks are addressed. The programmes on image and data communications, builds on work done under RACE and concentrates on digital HDTV[104] integrated services technologies, contributing to the definition of common functional specification for new communication services and multi-media-systems. The programme extends to information security technologies, addressing all aspects of service quality, security and reliability necessary for establishing trustworthiness of electronically communicated information. Advanced communication experiments, intended to be a pathfinder for future technology and service developments, are to be conducted. Infrastructure and inter-working tests will be carried out, as well as experiments and trials to determine operational verification of IBC services.[105]

---

[93] 91/385/EEC, Art. 8 and Annex II.

[94] Decision 90/221/Euratom, EEC, OJ L 117/28, 8 May 1990.

[95] The third framework programme.

[96] See also the reference to these programmes in the TEDIS programme.

[97] The programmes relating to communications technology and to telematics systems are most directly relevant to a discussion of telecommunications regulation. The programme in information technology is not considered here.

[98] Council Decision of 7 June 1991 adopting a specific research and technological development programme in the field of communication technologies 1990–94), 91/352/EEC, OJ L 192/8, 16 July 1991.

[99] Council Decision of 7 June 1991 adopting a specific programme of research and technological development in the field of telematic systems in areas of general interest 1990–94), 91/353/EEC, OJ L 192/18, 16 July 1991.

[100] 91/352/EEC, Art. 1; 91/353/EEC, Art. 1.

[101] 91/352/EEC, recital 6; 91/353/EEC, recital 7.

[102] Art. 8(1); under both Decisions the Commission is empowered to negotiate international agreements with member countries of COST, and in particular members of EFTA.

[103] Art. 8(2).

[104] High Definition Television.

[105] 91/352/EEC, recital 9, Art. 1, Annex I.

The telematic systems programme concentrates on certain areas of public services which are of general interest.[106] Notably, it is intended to support the establishment of trans-European networks between administrations, facilitating exchange of electronic information particularly relevant to the completion of the single market. These relate to matters such as free movement of goods, services and capital and of persons.[107] Other objectives of this programme are to contribute to the integration of transport services, stimulate development of harmonised application of information and communication technologies in health care and library facilities, promote and facilitate flexible and distance learning (Delta) and extend the availability of telematic services to rural areas.[108]

An important feature of the telematics programme is the work undertaken to develop linguistic technology.[109] This work is aimed at overcoming one of the major barriers to Europe-wide telematic systems, due to differences in language and terminology. However, of the total Community budget allocated to the programme[110] only about 6 per cent is to be devoted to this part of the programme.[111]

---

[106] 91/353/EEC, Recital 9, Art. 1.
[107] 91/353/EEC, Annex I, Area 1; this includes exchange of information between customs authorities, social services and other administrative agencies. The work under this programme dovetails with other work under the INSIS, CADDIA, TEDIS, Esprit and RACE programmes.
[108] 91/353/EEC, Annex I.
[109] Annex I, Area 6.
[110] 376.2 million ecu; 91/353/EEC, Art. 2 and Annex II.
[111] 22.5 million ecu.

CHAPTER 12

Future Direction of Telecommunications Policy

COMMUNITY OBJECTIVES

The telecommunications Green Paper[1] identified the objectives for the achievement of a Community-wide open market in telecommunications services. These objectives were integrated into the 1992 programme and included the fundamental aim for the full application of the competition rules to the sector. Underlying and inherent in the objectives identified by the Green Paper was the creation of a trans-European network.

The Commission has repeatedly emphasised the particular and important role tele-communications plays in creating a prosperous and dynamic economy. Telecommunications is also seen as an important sector in stimulating the economic activity of peripheral regions which suffer the specific handicap of distance from business centres.[2] The Commission considers that the development of the environment to create such a network has to be considered a major objective. The Community has made the creation of trans-European Networks an overriding policy objective for the sector.[3] The Community is, therefore, committed to a system of open and competitive markets which entail promoting inter-connection and inter-operability of national networks to which users and competitors have access.

To achieve a European-wide network there is a need both for harmonisation and liberalisation. The condition alone to provide services will not guarantee Community-wide services because of the technical divergence between Member States' national networks; harmonisation measures are necessary to ensure inter-operability. This need also underlines the continuing necessity to pursue the measures inherent in the telecom-munications policy outlined in the Green Paper.[4]

---

[1] COM (87) 290.
[2] See From the Single Act to Maastricht and Beyond, COM (92) 2000, 11 Feb. 1992.
[3] This objective has been included in Title XII of the Treaty of Political Union.
[4] COM (87) 290; see also p. 11 et seq.

THE 1992 REVIEW

In the course of 1992 the Commission conducted its review[5] to assess the current situation in the telecommunications sector, and to make proposals for furthering its telecommunications policy.

In the last round of telecommunications directives adopted in 1990[6] the Commission explicitly recognised the need for a reassessment of the situation in the telecommunications sector and called for a review[7] during 1992. In particular, the Commission proposed to re-examine any remaining special or exclusive rights on the provision of services.[8]

In the Review the Commission reassesses the basic assumption for the maintenance of the major exception, namely the maintenance of exclusive or special rights for the (public) voice telephone service, are still valid. These assumptions, underline the Services Directive[9] question. The Commission in particular examines whether:[10]

- the opening of voice telephony to competition could threaten the financial stability of the telecommunications organisations; and
- the restrictions do not affect the development of trade to such an extent as would be contrary to the interests of the Community.

The Review concentrates on simple resale of voice telephony *to the public*[11] as restrictions on the provision of other services are already covered under the Services Directive.[12] The ONP Directive[13] calls for a review of the progress made on harmonisation and an assessment of any remaining restrictions on access to telecommunications networks and services. This latter directive also requires the review to deal with the impact of any restrictions on the operation of the internal telecommunications market and to propose measures for their removal.

The Services Directive[14] permits the continued maintenance of exclusive of special rights for the provision of voice telephony service on the basis that 'opening-up of voice telephony to competition could threaten the financial stability of the telecommunications organisations'. In competition terms[15] the maintenance of such a financial stability is of relevance to the extent that it is necessary 'in the provision and exploitation of a universal network, i.e. one having general geographical coverage, and being provided to any service provider or user upon request within a reasonable period of time. The financial resources for the development of the network shall derive mainly from the operation of the telephony service'.[16] In exploring the options[17] in the Review, the Commission does not 'call into question the need to maintain, and perhaps even extend, universal access

---

[5] 1992 Review of the Situation in the Telecommunications Services Sector, communication by the Commission, 21 Oct. 1992, 'Review'.

[6] Services Dir., 90/388/EEC, and ONP Dir., 90/387/EEC.

[7] 90/387/EEC, Art. 8; 90/388/EEC, Art. 10.

[8] 90/388/EEC, Recital 22.

[9] The Review, s. 1.1.

[10] The current position is that the provision of services to closed user groups must be permitted and that simple resale for data communications must be permitted from 1 Jan. 1993, with a possibility of deferment to 1 Jan. 1996; see p. 130 et seq.

[11] 90/387/EEC, Art. 8.

[12] 90/388/EEC, Recital 18.

[13] Rome Treaty, Art. 90(2).

[14] 90/388/EEC, Recital 18.

[15] The Review considers four options: Review, s. 4.2 and see p. 131 et seq

[16] Review, s. 1.

[17] Review, s. 2.2.3.

to the voice telephone service and network'.[18] Currently voice telephony service and related subscription revenues account for nearly 90 per cent of total revenues of Member States' telecommunications organisations.[19]

The Review outlines developments in telecommunications policy[20] within the Community[21] and internationally.[22] It then sets the political context[23] within which the Review is set and must be considered. While the Commission reaffirms its own and the Council's[24] commitment to establishing trans-European networks to reinforce economic and social cohesion,[25] there are three elements that will influence future approaches to telecommunications policy.

First, the concept of *'bottle necks'* has entered into the Commission's vocabulary in this area.[26] The concept is akin to that of the FCC[27] which, in its regulatory approach, concentrates on factors and activities which impede the open and competitive operation of the communications market. The Commission's concept of bottle necks is somewhat from that of the FCC, but also serves to focus the Commission activity on the most important of the issues hampering the development of open and competitive market within the Community.

The second new factor is the Commission's particular focus on Central and Eastern Europe. The Review states:[28]

Telecommunications have a major role to play for the integration of the Community, European competitiveness and European cohesion, all of them major policy goals for the Community.

At the same time, the dramatic changes in Central and Eastern Europe, the increases in the Community's external role have given some emphasis to the urgency of developing trans-European networks. *The Community's telecommunications policy must now be seen in the context of the new wider European dimension.*[29]

Third, and significantly, the Review specifically addresses *'subsidiarity'*. In stating its approach,[30] the Commission gives its view of subsidiarity. In this context the Commission sees its obligation as having to consider whether the objectives of any action it proposes can adequately be achieved by Member States. Nevertheless, the Commission will take action where this is necessary to liberalise and harmonise the market. Perhaps, the position is best summarised in their Review statement.[31]

The 1987 Green Paper on telecommunications set out lines of action for creating a common market in telecommunications. This Review continues and develops that approach, *envisaging the minimum action necessary at the Community level*[32] in order to remove obstacles to the provision of the widest possible rate of telecommunications sources. Within the framework

---

[18] Review, s. 2.2.
[19] Review, s. 2.2.2.
[20] Review, s. 2.3.
[21] Review, s. 2.4.
[22] Council Conclusions on Trans-European Networks, adopted on 31 Mar. 1992.
[23] Review, s. 2.4.
[24] Review, s. 2.4, p. 16.
[25] Federal Communications Commission of the United States.
[26] Review, s. 2.4, p. 16.
[27] Emphasis added.
[28] Review, para. 2.2.1.
[29] Review, s. 2.2.1.
[30] Emphasis added.
[31] 90/388/EEC.
[32] Review, s. 1.1, p. 5.

thus created at Community level, Member States will continue to determine their own telecommunications policies.

This assertion of subsidiarity provides Member States with wider scope to argue against detailed regulation of telecommunications by the Commission. However, the development of a Community-wide telecommunications network is unlikely to be achieved without harmonisation and liberalisation at the Commission level.

The Review identifies the major bottle necks[33] which continue to distort the telecommunications market and hamper the development of trans-European networks and services. The Review identifies a number of factors which continue to contribute to this lack of progress.

1. Tariffs

Although the ONP Directive[34] requires the application of objective criteria and cost orientation to tariffs, tariffs in the Community have not been adequately adjusted.[35] This has resulted not only in high tariffs for communications within the Community, but international call charges continue to be disproportionately high. The Review asserts that calls across national borders, even within the Community, are up to three times the cost of the most expensive national long distance call. There is also an absence of appropriate off-peak charges.[36] Furthermore, calls between Member States continue to be direction dependent, in some cases charges for calls from Member State A to Member State B being twice that of an equivalent call from Member State B to Member State A.

2. Traffic diversion

As a result of high international tariffs, there is growing use of automatic 'call-me-back' equipment enabling large users in particular to originate the calls at the low-tariff end of an international circuit.[37] This practice is particularly prevalent in calls between the Community and the United States, where tariffs are generally lower than those in Member States. The Review foresees continuing increase in the use of traffic diversion so long as significant tariff differentials remain. Clearly, the practice will lead to a loss of revenue by Community TOs.[38]

3. New network and service offerings

Under this heading the review[39] addresses two distinct issues. First, it observes the lack of progress in the introduction of new technology based networks, save for mobile com-

---

[33] In this context 'bottle neck' refers to matters which prevent or inhibit the development of telecommunications in the Community; the Review, s. 3.2. The Commission identifies as bottle necks:
1. The lack of trans-European structures; and
2. Continuing special and exclusive rights granted to TOs.

[34] 90/387/EEC, Annex II.

[35] Review, s. 3.2.1.

[36] Calls across national frontiers, the 'frontier effect', increases to as high as six times the cost of national calls, thus having a disproportionately penal effect on residential users.

[37] Review, s. 3.2.2.

[38] This assumes that the international accounting settlement procedures do not proportionately compensate the high tariff operator.

[39] Review, s. 3.2.3.

munications. In particular, there has been a little progress in ISDN which was subject of early attention from the Commission.[40]

Second, it is observed that the provision of the basic infrastructure and services in some Member States have waiting lists of several years. This observation highlights the weakness of the argument for exclusive rights based on the provision of universal service. Clearly, such rights have demonstrably failed to guarantee a universal service.

4. High speed lines

The review[41] also highlights the difficulty in many Member States to obtain high speed circuits. There is also significant disparity between the cost of such circuits between Member States.[42]

5. Commission proposals

The Commission in the Review has assessed the current remaining difficulties against this objective of creating a single market and achieving full integration of economic activity within the community.[43] The review comes to the conclusion that 'the telecommunications services sector has not adapted quickly enough. Clearly, this situation is increasingly unacceptable since it impedes progress towards the objectives of the Community.' The Commission sees the remaining difficulties, particularly the 'frontier effect',[44] as barriers to its progress. The Review also asserts that trans-European networks are a necessary ingredient of the competitiveness of Community businesses.

The solutions proposed by the Commission in the Review[45] are aimed at:[46]

1. providing effective solutions to the bottle necks and the difficulties bringing them about;
2. changing the structure and perspective of the telecommunications sector in order to achieve full integration of economic activity, the creation of trans-European networks, including removal of the 'frontier-effect';[47] and
3. compatibility with objectives specific to telecommunications services, identified in the Review.[48]

The Review identifies a number of Commission objectives which the solutions proposed by the Review must meet. There are six such objectives:

1. *Growth and efficiency*
   To serve the needs of business, the Commission will pursue the establishment of integrated high speed networks for voice, data and image.[49]

---

[40] See p. 12.
[41] Review, s. 3.2.4.
[42] Prices for two Mbit/S circuits can vary from up to tenfold between Member States.
[43] Review, s. 3.3.
[44] The "frontier effect" refers to the imbalance between national long-distance tariffs and international tariffs between Member States. This effect results in charges for calls to other Member States being between 2.5 and 6 times as much as national calls within a Member State over the same distance; Review, section 3.2.1.
[45] Review, s. 4.
[46] Review, s. 4.1.
[47] Review, s. 3.3.
[48] Review, ss 4.1.1 to 4.1.6.
[49] Review, s. 4.1.1.

2. *Universal service*

The Commission considers the establishment of universal cost-effective trans-European telecommunications networks and services of central importance to the vitality of the single market.[50] The Commission believes that universal service is vital and can be cost-effectively provided by the introduction of technology.[51] The Commission considers it desirable that all TOs can participate in the new liberalised markets.[52] This appears to suggest that the Commission does not consider the exclusion of TOs from certain markets[53] desirable.

3. *Tariffs*

The Commission emphasises the need for objective criteria and cost orientation of tariffs, including those for intra-Community telephony.[54]

4. *Regional and social cohesion*

The Commission high intra-community tariffs a barrier to the progress of less-developed regions of the Community.[55] In addition, the lack of infrastructure and services in these regions also contributed to hamper their development. Therefore, in addition to these tariff objectives, the Commission considers it important to continue its aid and R&D programmes to assist these regions.[56]

5. *International services*

The ambitions of the Commission with regard to a larger Europe, as well as the development of Community telecommunications internationally, lead to the conclusion that universal service must extend beyond Community borders.[57] Clearly, the GATT agreement is of central importance in this context.

6. *Liberalisation and harmonisation*

In pursuing its policy in telecommunications it is of vital importance that the Commission continues its harmonisation measures to ensure inter-operability necessary to the creation of Community-wide network and services.[58]

Action proposed by the Commission

Against this background, the Commission considers four basic options[59] for actions to be undertaken in order to meet the identified difficulties and satisfy the objectives discussed.

Option 1

The first option would be to maintain the *status quo*, in effect bringing to an end the liberalisation process of the Green Paper.

The only significant advantage of this course would be one of certainty and stability. The regulatory framework would already be in place and no new initiatives would be required. However, this option would not resolve the 'tariff bottle neck'. Nor would it

---

[50] Review, s. 4.1.2.
[51] Review, s. 4.1.1.
[52] Review, s. 4.1.2.
[53] Such as cable TV.
[54] Review, s. 4.1.3.
[55] Review, s. 4.1.4.
[56] Review, s. 4.3.2.
[57] Review, s. 4.1.5.
[58] Review, s. 4.1.6.
[59] Review, s. 4.2.

encourage further growth of the sector based on studies[60] conducted for the Commission, in the absence of liberalisation, telephony services in the Community would grow at the rate of 3 per cent to 4 per cent in real terms a year. This is significantly less than projected growth for Japan and the United States and would result in unfavourable consequences for the Community telecommunications equipment industry.

Partly on the basis that this option would result in the Community market falling behind those of the United States and Japan,[61] this option was rejected. Additional reasons for its rejection are that it is not conducive to the provision of universal service, with its associated impact on regional and social cohesion.[62] The review argues that in order to achieve a trans-European network, a significant measure of co-operation between TOs is necessary. Such co-operation would only be compatible with the Community competition rules[63] in a more competitive market environment, which is not foreseen under this option. In the absence of a sufficient number of competitors in the market, co-operation agreements would operate to strengthen the dominant position of the TOs.

Further, it is not certain that the exclusive or special rights reserved to TOs for telephony[64] can be preserved, even without further new initiative from the Commission. This would be on the basis that the changing environment for telecommunications would erode the justification for the exclusion of voice telephony from the application of Community competition rules.[65]

Option 2

The Commission could remove the bottle necks, including the high intra-Community tariffs, through direct regulation of tariffs and investments.

Any regulation of tariffs would necessarily imply fixing the framework for investment decisions.[66] Also, effective measures to control tariffs and impose cost orientation would involve extensive administrative and regulatory measures. Nevertheless, the review fairly observes that even if cost orientation is achieved, in the current environment these would reflect monopoly costs which would in general tend to be higher than those achieved in an efficient competitive market.

However, intra-Community tariffs as well as other problems identified in the Review could be resolved by tariff control, including measures such as price capping.

The Commission rejects this option on the duel basis that it is not conducive to promoting efficiency and would require extensive regulation at national and community levels.[67]

---

[60] Telecommunications Issues and Options 1992–2010: Study prepared for the Commission, Oct. 1991; Performance of the Telecommunications Sector up to 2010 Under Different Regulatory and Market Options: Study prepared for the Commission, Feb. 1992.

[61] Review, s. 4.2, p. 29.

[62] Review, s. 4.2, p. 26.

[63] See p. 10 et seq.

[64] See 90/388/EEC, and p. 62.

[65] See p. 60 et seq.

[66] The Review, s. 4.2, p. 26.

[67] The Review, s. 4.2, p. 29. The Commission asserts that the growth paths for this option are close to those of Option 1; Review, s. 4.2, p. 27.

Option 3

The most all-embracing measure that the Commission could take would be to fully liberalise all voice telephony.[68] This would include international calls between Member States and between Member States and third countries, as well as national calls.[69]

This approach has obvious attractions. Primarily, it would act as a catalyst in the achievement of the Commission's objectives in the economic and social cohesion of the Community. The Commission studies project that such a course would result in growth rates of 6 per cent to 7 per cent in real terms annually, having commensurate impact on the equipment industry.

Both the impact on the equipment supply industry and the services market would put the European industry at a significant advantage in world markets. Nevertheless, the Commission has decided against such full liberalisation on the slightly dubious grounds that its policy has always been one of gradual introduction of competition and this option would depart from that policy.[70] A more significant objection to immediate full liberalisation is the differences that continue to exist between Member States. In particular, tariffs for telephony are not yet aligned with costs in all Member States. The tendency is for international tariffs to be higher than justifiable on cost grounds, the reverse being true in the case of national calls. Access charges are similarly distorted in many Member States. The Commission takes the view that application of this Option 3 would force rapid realignment of tariffs with costs resulting in disruption in the market.

Option 4

To meet the objections raised in relation to Option 3, the Commission proposes and favours an intermediate course. Under this proposal immediate introduction of competition will be limited to voice telephony between Member States.[71]

The Commission emphasises that the full liberalisation of intra-Community public telephony service would carry with it the implication that sufficient inter-connection points[72] are provided to create competition from service providers and include the liberalisation of the supporting infrastructure.[73] Other necessary ingredients for this option are the introduction of measures to permit full and effective entry, such as appropriate connection charges and the ability to physically interconnect.[74]

This option will clearly require further harmonisation where liberalising this particular part of the telecommunications market. Also, there will be scope for co-operation agreements in the more competitive environment.

The Commission has naturally argued the case for Option 4 in much greater detail. In its review this particular course overcomes one of the most serious bottle necks, namely

---

[68] Review, s. 4.2.
[69] This option would be introduced together with ONP regulations to ensure inter-connection and universal access to the network.
[70] The Review, s. 4.2, p. 30.
[71] The Review, s. 4.2.
[72] This would be subject to intra-connection agreements and, where appropriate, licensing conventions consistent with community law.
[73] The supporting infrastructure would include long-distance point-to-point fibre-optic links and appropriate equipment necessary to provide transport of telephone services.
[74] The Review, s. 4.2, p. 29. The Review states that appropriate access charges may include a contribution to the costs of maintaining the universal service.
[75] The Review quotes Council's affirmation that such networks should be introduced "in the framework of the system of open competitive markets . . ." to reinforce economic and social cohesion; COM (92) 2000, 11 Feb. 1992.

the "frontier effect", while being consistent with the policy of gradual liberalisation. The Commission also argues that Option 4 will facilitate the establishment of trans-European networks.[75]

In the Review, the Commission closely argues that its preferred course of action does not compromise the universal service obligations of TOs. It bases this argument on the relatively small part of the total traffic and revenues of the TOs represented by intra-Community voice.[76] The Commission further argues that because of the growth of international traffic[77] is higher than purely national traffic,[78] liberalisation would lead to accelerated volume growth. Consequently, it is argued, this will compensate TOs for any loss of volume share. Other Commission arguments that the financial viability of the TOs would not be affected by this proposal are:

1. competition between TOs stimulated by liberalisation would result in gains in the growing markets of other Member States, thus compensating the monopoly operators for any loss in their share of the home market;
2. co-operative agreements would result in capacity adding competitive effects;
3. the TOs would obtain additional revenue from new entrants who would operate, at least, partially, on the TOs infrastructures;
4. new entrants with their own infrastructures would nevertheless have to pay an excess charge for inter-connection to the networks of the TOs.

Curiously, all of these arguments would be sustainable in relation to Option 3. The probable key to the Commission's motivation for preferring liberalisation of intra-Community voice telephony only, lies in the political acceptability of this course.

SUPPORT FOR FURTHER LIBERALISATION FROM MEMBER STATES

With increasing momentum from the Commission, there has grown further and more open resistance from some Member States to the pace and, in some instances, the level of competition being introduced into the telecommunications sector. It is clear from the line-up of Member States in the challenges to the exercise of its powers by the Commission that France, Italy, Spain and Belgium are more resistant to change than some of the other Member States.

It is not always true that those Member States with strong domestic telecommunications entities have a greater preference for increased competition. Both France Telecom and Telefonica are substantial players in the sector. It is perhaps more relevant to look to the domestic economic and social structure of the Member States for clues to the policy towards Community liberalisation.

As has been observed by the French Minister,[79] domestic competition is not a prerequisite of the achievement of a Community-wide telecommunications network and

---

[76] Intra-Community voice represents 1% of total traffic and 4–5% of total revenues. The latter is based on collection revenue plus net settlement income from intra-Community telephony. There are significant differences in traffic flows and revenue structures of Member States TOs, leading to significant variations in the revenue contribution from intra-Community calls. With one exception, excluding extra-Community international traffic, share of total telecommunications services revenue in a Member State represented by intra-Community telephony ranges from 3% to 14%; the Review, s. 4.2, p. 28.

[77] Including intra-Community traffic.

[78] This is estimated at 14% a year for international traffic and 5–6% a year for total traffic.

[79] Budapest, October 1992.

services. What is not addressed by that argument, however, is the compatibility of the *status quo* with Community competition rules.

Nevertheless, the Commission is in slight retreat, giving emphasis to subsidiarity and showing signs of reluctance to press more controversial reforms of the telecommunications market. This is no less evident in the Commission's preferred Option under the 1992 Review.

APPENDIX 1

Council Directive of 24 July 1986 on the initial stage of the mutual recognition of type approval for telecommunications terminal equipment

(86/361/EEC)

THE COUNCIL OF THE EUROPEAN COMMUNITIES.

Having regard to the Treaty establishing the European Economic Community, and in particular Article 100 thereof.

Having regard to the proposal from the Commission.

Having regard to the opinion of the European Parliament[1].

Having regard to the opinion of the Economic and Social Committee[2].

Whereas the mutual recognition of type approval for telecommunications terminal equipment features in the Commission communication to the Council of 18 May 1984 on telecommunications, in the Council recommendations of 12 November 1984 concerning the implementation of 12 November in the field of telecommunications and the first phase of opening up access to public telecommunications contracts, and in the Council conclusions of 17 December 1984 concerning a Community telecommunications policy;

Whereas the market in telecommunications terminal equipment and use of the full potential of the new telecommunications services are of considerable importance for the economic development of the Community;

Whereas it is absolutely essential to establish or consolidated a specifically European industrial potential in the technologies concerned;

Whereas it is highly desirable to make rapid progress towards establishing a common market in this sector, in particular in order to offer the industry an improved base for its operations and to facilitate the adoption of a joint position with respect to third countries;

Whereas the mutual recognition of type approval for telecommunications terminal equipment constitutes a major step towards the creation of an open and unified market for such equipment;

Whereas, since situations differ and technical and administrative constraints exist in the Member States, progress towards this objective should be made in stages;

Whereas in particular the mutual recognition of conformity tests on mass produced terminal equipment should constitute an initial stage of the mutual recognition of type approval for such equipment.

Whereas such an approach must be based on the definition of common technical specifications based on international standards and specifications and on the harmonization of general technical requirements for testing, measuring and approval procedures in the areas of telecommunications and information technology;

Whereas a general standardization programme is being implemented in the field of information technology in compliance with the Standards Code of the General Agreement on Tariffs and Trade (GATT);

---

[1] OJ No C 36, 17. 2. 1986, p. 55.
[2] OJ No C 303, 25. 11. 1985, p. 2.

Whereas there is a need for a more comprehensive framework to be drawn up in preparation for a second stage which would create an open and unified market in telecommunications terminal equipment, bearing in mind that for the telecommunications this has to include both the free movement of equipment and unimpeded connection to networks, in accordance with the harmonized requirements;

Whereas Council Directive 73/23/EEC of 19 February 1973 on the harmonization of the laws of the Member States relating to electrical equipment designed for use within certain voltage limits[3] and Council Directive 83/189/EEC of 28 March 1983 laying down a procedure for the provisions of information in the field of technical standards and regulations[4] are applicable, *inter alia*, to the field of telecommunications and information technology;

Whereas the Memorandum of Understanding between the European Conference of Postal and Telecommunications Administrations (CEPT) and the Commission concerning standards and type approval for telecommunications equipment and the general guidelines agreed with the Joint European Standards Institution CEN-CENELEC henceforth make it possible to entrust specialized technical harmonization work to those bodies;

Whereas the mechanism introduced by certain CEPT administrations, including those of the Community Member States, under the agreement drawn up at Copenhagen on 15 November 1985, incorporates a formal adoption procedure and an undertaking to implement certain CEPT recommendations, which are then designed as 'NETS' (Normes européennes de télécommunications);

Whereas it is necessary to set up a Committee, with the task of assisting the Commission in implementing this Directive and in progressively implementing the mutual recognition of type approval for terminal equipment.

HAS ADOPTED THIS DIRECTIVE:

Article 1

The Member States shall implement the mutual recognition of the results of tests of conformity with common conformity specifications for mass-produced telecommunications terminal equipment in accordance with the detailed rules set out in this Directive.

Article 2

For the purposes of the Directive:

1. 'telecommunications administrations' means the administrations or private operating agencies recognized in the Community and providing public telecommunications services;

2. 'terminal equipment means equipment directly or indirectly connected to the termination of a public telecommunications network to send, process or receive information;

3. 'technical specifications' means a specification contained in a document which lays down the characteristics of a product such as levels of quality, performance, safety or dimensions, including the requirements applicable to the product as regards terminology, symbols, testing and test methods, packaging, marking and labelling;

4. 'international technical specification in telecommunications' means the technical specification of all or some characteristics of a product, recommended by such organizations as the Comité international télégraphique et téléphonique (CCITT) or the CEPT;

5. 'common technical specification' means a technical specification drawn up with a view to uniform application in all Member States of the Community;

6. 'standard' means a technical specification adopted by a recognized standards body for repeated or continuous application, compliance with which is not compulsory;

---

[3] OJ No L 77, 26. 3. 1973, p. 29.
[4] OJ No L 109, 26. 4. 1983, p. 8.

7. 'international standard' means a standard adopted by a recognized international standards body;

8. 'approved testing laboratory' means a laboratory the conformity of which the accreditation system established by the CEPT in close cooperation with specialized organizations and any relevant national accreditation organizations has been verified, with particular relevance to the relevant ISO guides, by the appropriate Member State or a body recognized as competent by that State and which is approved by that Member State or body recognized as competent for conducting conformity tests on terminal equipment;

9. 'certificate of conformity' means the document certifying that a product or service conforms to given standards or technical specifications;

10. 'type approval of terminal equipment' means the confirmation delivered by the competent authority of a Member State that a particular terminal equipment type is authorized or recognized as suitable to be connected to a particular public telecommunications network;

11. 'conformity specification' means a document giving a precise and full description of the technical characteristics of the relevant terminal equipment (such as safety, technical parameters, functions and procedures and service requirements) together with a precise definition of the tests and test methods enabling the conformity of the terminal equipment with the prescribed technical characteristics to be verified;

12. 'type approval specification' means a specification setting out the full and precise requirements that must be satisfied by terminal equipment to be granted type approval. It includes the conformity specification and also administrative requirements and, where appropriate, requirements concerning quality control operations to be carried out during the manufacture of the equipment;

13. 'common conformity specification' means a conformity specification used in all the Community Member States by the authority competent for testing the conformity of terminal equipment. It also includes, where appropriate, requirements made necessary in a given State by historical network peculiarities or established national provisions concerning the use of radio frequencies;

14. 'common type approval specification' means a type approval specification which is used in' all the Community Member States by all the authorities empowered to grant type approval for terminal equipment. It includes the common conformity specification and also administrative requirements and, where appropriate, requirements concerning quality control operations to be carried out during the manufacture of the equipment;

15. 'NET (Norme européenne de télécommunications) is an approved technical specification recommendation of the CEPT or part or parts thereof which the signatories of the Memorandum of Understanding established at the meeting of Directors-General of CEPT Administrations, in Copenhagen on 15 November 1985, adopted in accordance with the procedures set down in that Memorandum;

16. 'mutual recognition of the results of conformity tests on terminal equipment' means a situation where, when an approved laboratory or the competent authority in a Member State issues a certificate, accompanied by test data and identification details, stating that a terminal is in conformity with a common conformity specification or a part thereof, that certificate is recognized in the other Member States, so that if the terminal in question is the subject of an application for type approval in another Member State, it no longer has to be subject to the tests for verifying conformity with that specification, or with the part of that specification concerning the tests carried out;

17. 'essential requirements' means those aspects of common conformity specifications of such importance as to necessitate compliance as a matter of legal obligation for the implementation of the mutual recognition of the results of conformity tests on terminal equipment as an integral part of the type approval procedure. These essential requirements are at present;

— user safety in so far as this requirement is not covered by Directive 72/23/EEC,
— safety of employees of public telecommunications network operators in so far as this requirement is not covered by Directive 73/23/EEC,
— protection of public telecommunications network from harm,
— interworking of terminal equipment, in justified cases.

Article 3

The Council, acting in accordance with the rules of the Treaty on a proposal from the Commission, shall supplement as necessary the list of essential requirements and shall make them more specific where necessary for certain products.

Article 4

The Commission shall:

1. draw up each year, after consulting the Committee referred to in Article 5 and with due regard to the general programme of standardization in the information technology sector;

   — a list international standards and international technical specifications in telecommunications to be harmonized,
   — a list terminal for which common conformity specifications should be drafted as a matter of priority, on the basis above all of the essential requirements,
   — a timetable for this work;

2. request the CEPT to draw up the common conformity specifications in the form of NETs, within the specified time limits; in so doing the later shall, when appropriate, consult other specialized standardization organizations such as the European Committee for Standardization (CEN) and the European Committee for Electrotechnical Standardization (CENELEC).

Article 5

1. In carrying out the tasks referred to in Article 4, the Commission shall be assisted by a Committee, which shall be the Working Party of Senior Officials on Telecommunications. The members of the Committee may be assisted by experts or advisers according to the nature of the question under discussion. The Committee shall be chaired by a Commission representative.

2. Apart from the cases listed in this Directive, the Commission shall consult the Committee on:

(a) the broad objectives and the future needs of the telecommunications standardization policy;
(b) problems raised by the approval of testing laboratories, and in particular the accreditation system referred to in Article 2 (8) and any amendment to that system which may appear necessary;
(c) the effect of technological progress on specification work already under way and the possible need to give a new or revised mandate to the CEPT.

At the request of its Chairman or of a Member State, the Committee may consider any question relating to the implementation of this Directive.

3. The Committee shall adopt its own rules of procedure.

4. The Secretariat of the Committee shall be provided by the Commission.

Article 6

1. For the purposes of this Directive, a 'NET' shall be regarded as the equivalent of the common conformity, specification.

References to NETs shall be published in the *Official Journal of the European Communities*.

2. Without prejudice to the cases referred to in Article 8, the competent authorities of the Member States shall not have any further tests carried out in respect of a particular type of terminal equipment where results of tests carried out in accordance with Article 7 have given rise to the issue of a certificate of conformity with the relevant common conformity specification, the references to

which are published in the *Official Journal of the European Communities*. Such certificate of conformity shall be recognized for the purpose of type approval of the terminal equipment in question.

3. The common conformity specifications shall be used in all Member States by the competent authorities for any verification demanded for type approval purposes of the relevant terminal equipment.

The procedure for exceptions referred to in Article 7 (4) may also be applied by the competent authorities of the Member States in respect of the first subparagraph.

Article 7

1. Member States shall inform the Commission of the authority or authorities competent in their territory to issue type approval for terminal equipment. The Commission shall publish a list of these authorities in the *Official Journal of the European Communities*.

2. Member States shall send the Commission a list of the laboratories which they have approved, or which have been approved by bodies recognized by them as competent, for the purpose of verifying the conformity of terminal equipment with the common conformity specifications. They shall regularly submit a report on the activities of these laboratories in the field covered by this Directive. Such lists and reports shall be transmitted to the Committee referred to in Article 5 for information.

3. For the purposes of Article 6, the certificate of conformity issued by the approved laboratory which has carried out the tests must be accompanied by the data obtained from the measurements performed during the conformity tests, all the information necessary for practice identification of the terminal equipment on which the tests were made and a precise indication of the common conformity specification, or part thereof, used for the tests.

4. Member States shall ensure that telecommunications administrations use common conformity specifications when purchasing terminal equipment covered by such specifications except in the following cases:

(a) where the equipment is to replace equipment connected to the network before the adoption of common conformity specification and is to the same technical specification as the equipment it replaces, or where, during any transition period between two systems, which is accepted as necessary and which is defined within the NET, a Member State needs to add a limited number of pieces of equipment complying with the specification of the first system. In both cases, the Commission shall be informed when such a waiver is invoked and kept informed of the number of pieces of equipment involved; this information shall be given to the Committee referred to in Article 5;

(b) where a careful consultation of the market – i.e. including the publication of a call for declarations of interest in the *Official Journal of the European Communities* – shows there is no offer at economically acceptable conditions for such terminal equipment complying with those common conformity specifications. In this case, on the basis of an unavoidable need, a Member State may, for a limited period of time, apply only a part of the characteristics set out in the common conformity specifications. The Member State shall inform the Commission immediately and also state what departures from the common conformity specification it intends to permit. The Commission shall consult the Committee referred to in Article 5 as a matter of urgency and may request the CEPT to revise the particular common conformity specification. In addition, the Committee shall review the situation at least every six months during the period when this waiver is applied.

In the event that a request for revision is not made to the CEPT then his waiver shall cease when another Member State presents evidence to the Committee that terminal equipment conforming to that common conformity specification has been connected to its public telecommunication networks on a normal commercial basis.

However, a Member State may have the waiver extended provided that the Commission, on the advice of the Committee referred to in Article 5, agrees that the technical and economic conditions are sufficiently different in the two Member States as to warrant such as extension.

5. The Member States shall consult within the Committee referred to in Article 5, so as to create conditions of fair competition for carrying out the same series of conformity tests in all the approved laboratories.

Article 8

1. A Member State may, after examining the common conformity specification and the test results, suspend recognition of a certificate of conformity issued for the purpose of type approval;

(a) if it discovers shortcomings regarding the application of the common conformity specification;

(b) if it discovers that the common conformity specification itself fails to meet the essential requirements which it is supposed to cover.

It is exercises this option, the Member State concerned shall immediately inform the Commission and the other Member States, stating the reasons for its decision.

2. Where the decision of the Member State concerns the electrical safety of users of terminal equipment, the procedures set out in Article 9 of Directive 73/23/EEC shall apply.

3. If the reasons given for the Member State's decision are as described in paragraph 1 (a), the Commission shall immediately consult the Member States concerned. If no agreement is reached without four weeks, the Commission shall seek the opinion of one of the approved laboratories notified in accordance with Article 7 which is based outside the territory of the Member States concerned. The Commission shall communicate the opinion of this laboratory to all the Member States, which may submit the comments to it within a period of one month.

After taking note of any such comments the Commission shall, if necessary, formulate appropriate recommendations or opinions.

If in preparing its opinion a laboratory consulted unavoidable incurs expenditure, which may if necessary include additional tests, the Commission will defray that expenditure on production of documentary evidence. If, however, further to an opinion a decision to suspend recognition of a certificate of conformity is not maintained, the Member State which took it shall reimburse the Commission, in accordance with the procedures for payment then negotiated with the Member State.

4. If the reasons invoked in support of the Member State's decision are as described in paragraph 1 (b), the Commission shall refer the matter to the Committee referred to in Article 5, which shall express its opinion as a matter or urgency. On the basis of that opinion the Commission shall decide whether or not to withdraw the common specification in question from the list published in the *Official Journal of the European Communities*. If it withdraws the specification, the Commission shall inform the CEPT and may entrust it with a further brief.

5. If a Member State considers that terminal equipment which has already been approved does not meet one or more of the essential requirements, it may revoke the type approval granted and shall in that case immediately apply the procedures set out in paragraphs 1 and 2.

Article 9

The Commission shall examine the detailed rules for the second stage of the establishment of a market in telecommunications terminal equipment without internal frontiers covering, in particular, the implementation of mutual recognition of type approval for terminal equipment. To this end it shall submit proposals to the Council within a period of two years following the implementation of this Directive.

Article 10

This Directive shall not prejudice the application of Directive 83/189/EEC.

Article 11

1. Member State shall introduce the measures necessary to comply with this Directive within a period of not more than one year following adoption thereof. It shall forthwith inform the Commission thereof.

2. Member States shall ensure that the Commission is informed of the main provisions of national law which they adopt in the field governed by this Directive.

Article 12

This Directive is addressed to the Member States.

Done at Brussels, 24 July 1986.

For the Council
The President
A. CLARK

APPENDIX 2

Council Decision of 22 December 1986 on standardization in the field of information technology and telecommunications

(87/95/EEC)

THE COUNCIL OF THE EUROPEAN COMMUNITIES,

Having regard to the Treaty establishing the European Economic Community, and in particular Article 235 thereof,

Having regard to the proposal from the Commission,

Having regard to the opinion of the European Parliament[1],

Having regard to the opinion of the Economic and Social Committee[2],

Whereas the standards applicable in the field of information technology and the activities necessary for their preparation must, in particular, take account of:

— the complexity of the technical specifications and the precision required to ensure the exchange of information and data and the compatible operating of systems;
— the need to ensure rapid publication of standards so that undue delays do not result in the early obsolescence of texts that have been overtaken by the speed of technological change;
— the need to encourage the application of international standards of exchange of information and data on a basis which will establish their credibility from the standpoint of practical implementation;
— the economic importance of the role played by standardization in contributing to the creation of a Community market in this field;

Whereas Directive 83/189/EEC[3] enables the Commission, the Member States and the standards institutions to be informed of the intentions of standards institutions to draw up or amend a standard, and whereas, under the terms of that Directive, the Commission may establish terms of reference for work on standardization of common interest to be undertaken jointly and at an early stage;

Whereas that Directive does not contain all the provisions necessary for the implementation of a Community policy on standardization in the field of information technology and telecommunications;

Whereas the increasing amount of technical overlap between the different fields of standardization, particularly in the case of information technology and telecommunications, is such as to justify close cooperation between standards institutions, which should collaborate in order to deal with these matters of common interest;

Whereas agreements have been recently concluded by the Commission within the framework of the Memorandum of Understanding signed with the European Conference of Postal and Telecommunications Administrations (CEPT) and in the context of the general guidelines approved with the joint standardization organization European Committee for Standardization/European Committee for Electrotechnical Standardization (CEN/CENELEC);

Whereas Directive 86/361/EEC[4] sets out programmes for work on common technical specifications (corresponding to Normes Européennes de Télécommunication (NETs)) for this field by the

---

[1] OJ No C 36, 17. 2. 1986, p. 55.
[2] OJ No C 303, 25. 11. 1985, p. 2.
[3] OJ No L 109, 26. 4. 1983, p. 8.
[4] OJ No L 217, 5. 8. 1986, p. 21.

European Conference of Postal and Telecommunications Administrations in consultation, where appropriate, with the European Committee for Standardization and the European Committee for Electrotechnical Standardization;

Whereas the field of public procurement orders is suitably placed to encourage wider acceptance of open systems interconnection information and data exchange standards through reference to them in purchasing;

Whereas it is necessary to trust a committee with the task of assisting the Commission in its pursuance and management of the objectives and activities laid down by the Decision,

HAS DECIDED AS FOLLOWS:

Article 1

For the purposes of this Decision:

1. *'technical specifications'* means a specification contained in a document which lays down the characteristics required of a product, such as levels of quality, performance, safety or dimensions, including the requirements applicable to the product as regards terminology, symbols, testing and test methods, packaging, marketing or labelling;

2. *'common technical specifications'* means a technical specification drawn up with a view to uniform application in all the Member States of the Community;

3. *'standard'* means a technical specification approved by a recognized standards body or repeated or continuous application, compliance with which is not compulsory;

4. *'international standard'* means a standard adopted by a recognized international standards body;

5. *'Draft International Standard (DIS)'* means a draft standard adopted by a recognized international standards body;

6. *'international technical specification in telecommunications'* means the technical specification of all or some characteristics of a product, recommended by such organizations as the Comité international télégraphique et téléléphonique (CCITT) or the CEPT;

7. *'European standard'* means a standard which has been approved pursuant to the statutes of the standards bodies with which the Community has concluded agreements;

8. *'European pre-standard'* means a standard adopted under the reference (EPS) in accordance with the statutory rules of the standards bodies with which the Community has concluded agreements;

9. *'functional standard'* means a standard worked out to yield a complex function required to ensure systems interoperability and generally obtained by the linking together of several existing reference standards and adopted in accordance with the statutory rules of standards bodies;

10. *'functional specification'*: the specification which defines, in the field of telecommunications, the application of one or more open system interconnection standards in support of a specific requirement for communication between information technology systems (standards recommended by such organizations as the 'Comité international télégraphique et téléphonique' (CCITT) or the (CEPT);

11. *'technical regulation'* means the technical specifications, including the recent administrative provisions, the observance of which is compulsory, *de jure* or *de facto*, in the case of marketing or use in a Member State or a major part thereof, except those laid down by local authorities;

12. *'certification of conformity'* means the activity whereby the conformity of a product or service to given standards or other technical specifications is certified by means of a certificate or mark of conformity;

13. *'information technology'* means the systems, equipment, components and software required to

ensure the retrieval, processing and storage of information in all centres of human activity (home, office, factory, etc.), the application of which generally requires the use of electronics or similar technology;

14. *'public procurement orders'* means those:

— defined in Article 1 of Directive 77/62/EEC[5];

— concluded for the supply of equipment relating to information technology and telecommunications, irrespective of the sector of activity of the contracting authority;

15. *'telecommunications authorities'* means recognized authorities or private enterprises in the Community which provide public telecommunications services.

Article 2

In order to promote standardization in Europe and the preparation and applications of standards in the field of information technology and functional specifications in the field of telecommunications, the following measures, subject to Article 3 (2) and Article 4, shall be implemented at Community level:

(a) regular, at least annual, determination on the basis of international standards, draft international standards or equivalent documents, of the priority standardization requirements with a view to the preparation of work programmes and the commissioning of such European standards and functional specifications as may be deemed necessary to ensure the exchange of information and data and systems interoperability;

(b) on the basis of international standardization activities:

— the European standards institutions and specialized technical bodies in the information technology and telecommunications sector shall be invited to establish European standards, European prestandards or telecommunications functional specifications having recourse, if necessary, to the drafting of functional standards, to ensure the precision required by users for exchange of information and data and systems interoperability. Such bodies shall base their work on international standards, draft international standards or international technical specifications in telecommunications. Where an international standard, draft international standard or international technical specification in telecommunications offers clear provisions allowing its uniform application, these provisions will be adopted unaltered in the European standard, European prestandard, or telecommunication functional specification. Only where such clear provisions do not exist in the international standard, draft international standard or international technical specification in telecommunications, the European standard, European prestandard, or telecommunication functional specification will be written to clarify or, where necessary, supplement the international standard, draft international standard or international technical specification in telecommunications while avoiding divergence from it;

— the same bodies shall be invited to prepare technical specifications which may form the basis of European standards or European prestandards in the absence of, or as a contribution to the production of, agreed international standards for the exchange of information and data and systems interoperability;

(c) measures to facilitate the application of the standards and functional specifications, in particular by means of coordinating Member States' activities in:

— the verification of the conformity of products and services to the standards and functional specifications on the basis of test requirements specified;

— the certification of conformity to standards and functional specifications in accordance with properly harmonized procedures.

---

[5] OJ No L 13, 15. 1. 1977, p. 1.

(d) promotion of the application of standards and functional specifications relating to information technology and telecommunications in public sector orders and technical regulations.

Article 3

1. The specific objectives of the measures proposed are described in the Annex to this Decision.

2. This Decision shall cover:

— standards in the field of Information Technology as set out in Article 5

— functional specifications for the services specifically offered over public telecommunications networks for exchange of information and data between information technology systems.

3. This Decision shall not cover:

— common technical specifications for terminal equipment connected to the public telecommunications networks, which are covered by Directive 86/361/EEC

— specifications for the equipment forming any part of the telecommunications networks themselves.

Article 4

In determining requirements as regards standardization and in drawing up a work programme for standardization and the preparation of functional specifications, the Commission shall refer in particular to the information communicated to it pursuant to Directive 83/189/EEC.

The Commission, after consulting the Committee provided for in Article 7, shall entrust the technical work to the competent European standards organizations or specialised bodies (CEN, CENELEC and CEPT) requesting them, if necessary, to draw up corresponding European standards or functional specifications. The mandates to be given to these organizations shall be referred for agreement to the Committee provided for under Article 5 of Directive 83/189/EEC in accordance with the procedures of the said Directive. No mandate shall be issued which overlaps with any part of work programmes commenced or drawn up under Directive 86/361/EEC.

Article 5

1. Taking account of the differences between existing national procedures, Member States shall take the necessary steps to ensure that reference is made to:

— European standards and European prestandards as described in Article 2 (b);

— international standards when accepted in the country of the contracting authority;

in public procurement orders relating to information technology so that these standards are used as the basis for the exchange of information and data for systems interoperability.

2. In order to provide end-to-end compatibility, Member States shall take the necessary steps to ensure that their telecommunications administrations use functional specifications for the means of access to their public telecommunication networks for those services specifically intended for exchange of information and data between information technology systems which themselves use the standards mentioned in paragraph 1.

3. Application of this Article shall take account of special circumstances as outlined below which may justify the use of standards and specifications other than those provided for in this Decisions:

— the need for operational continuity in existing systems, but only as part of clearly defined and recorded strategies for subsequent transition to international or European standards or functional specifications;

— the genuinely innovative nature of certain projects;

— where the standard or functional specification in question is technically inadequate for its purpose on the grounds that it does not provide the appropriate means of achieving information and data exchange or systems interoperability, or that the means (including testing) do not exist to establish satisfactorily conformity of a product to that standard or functional specification or where, in the case of European Pre-Standards, these lack the necessary stability for application. It shall be open to other Member States to demonstrate to the Committee referred to in Article 7 that equipment conforming to the standard had been used satisfactorily, and that use of this waiver was not justified;

— where, after careful consultation of the market, it is found that important reasons related to cost-effectiveness make use of the standard or functional specification in question in appropriate. It would be open to other Member States to demonstrate to the Committee referred to in Article 7 that equipment conforming to that standard had been used satisfactorily on a normal commercial basis, and that use of this waiver was not justified.

4. In addition, Member States may require reference, on the same basis as in paragraph 1, to draft international standards.

5. Contracting authorities relying upon paragraph 3 shall record their reasons for doing so, if possible, in the initial tender documents issued in respect of the procurement, and in all cases shall record these reasons in their internal documentation and shall supply such information on request to tendering companies and to the Committee referred to in Article 7 whilst respecting commercial confidentiality. It shall also be possible for complaints about use of derogations referred to in paragraph 3 to be made direct to the Commission.

6. The Commission shall ensure that the provisions of this Article are applied in the case of all Community projects and programmes, including public procurement orders financed from the Community budget.

7. Contracting authorities, if they consider it necessary, may apply other specifications to contracts of a value lower than 100 000 ECU, provided that these purchases will not prevent the use of the standards mentioned in paragraphs 1 and 2 in any contract of a greater value than the sum mentioned in this paragraph. The need for the derogation or the level of the threshold established in this paragraph will be revised within three years of the bringing into application of this Decision.

Article 6

When drafting or amending technical regulations in areas covered by this Decision, Member States shall refer to the standards referred to in Article 5 whenever these meet in an appropriate fashion the required technical specifications of the regulation.

Article 7

1. An advisory committee, called the 'Senior Officials Group on standardization in the field of Information Technology' shall assist the Commission in its pursuance of the objectives and its management of the activities laid down by the Decision. It shall consist of representatives appointed by the Member States, who may call on the assistance of experts or advisers: its chairman shall be a representative of the Commission. For telecommunication issues the competent committee is the 'Senior Officials Group for Telecommunications' provided for in Article 5 of Directive 86/361/EEC.

2. The Commission shall consult the Committee when determining Community priorities, implementing measures referred to in the Annex, when dealing with matters concerning the verification of conformity to standards, monitoring the implementation of Article 5 and other matters relating to standardization in the field of information technology and telecommunications, or other fields in which these overlap. It shall also consult the Committee on the report referred to in Article 8.

3. The Commission shall coordinate the activities of these Committees with the Committee provided for in Article 5 of Directive 83/189/EEC in particular where there is a potential overlap in issuing requests to European standards institutions under this Decision and that Directive.

4. Any questions regarding the implementation of this Decision may be submitted to the Committee at the request of the Chairman or a Member State.

5. The Committee shall meet at least twice a year.

6. The Committee shall adopt its own rules of procedure.

7. The Secretariat of the Committee shall be provided by the Commission.

Article 8

Every two years the Commission shall submit a progress report to the European Parliament and the Council on standardization activities in the information technology sector. This report shall refer to the implementing arrangements adopted within the Community, the results obtained, the application of these results in public procurement contracts and national regulations, and, in particular, their practical significance for certification.

Article 9

This Decision shall not prejudice the application of Directive 83/189/EEC and Directive 86/361/EEC.

Article 10

This Decision shall be brought into application one year from the date of its publication in the *Official Journal of the European Communities*.

Article 11

This Decision is addressed to the Member States.

Done at Brussels, 22 December 1986.

> *For the Council*
> *The President*
> G. SHAW

ANNEX

MEASURES FOR STANDARDIZATION IN THE FIELD OF INFORMATION TECHNOLOGY AND TELECOMMUNICATIONS

1. **Aims**

   (a) to contribute to the integration of the internal Community market in the information technology and telecommunications sector;

   (b) to improve the international competitiveness of Community manufacturers by allowing for greater market uptake in the Community of equipment manufactured to recognize European and international standards;

   (c) to facilitate the exchange of information throughout the Community, by reducing the obstacles created by incompatibles arising from the absence of standards or their lack of precision;

   (d) to ensure that user requirements are taken into account by giving users greater freedom to assemble their systems in a manner guaranteeing operating compatibility and, consequently, improved performance at a lower cost;

   (e) to promote the application of standards and functional specifications in public sector orders.

2. **Description of measures and activities to be undertaken**

2.1. *Preparation of work programmes and definition of priorities*

   The drawing-up of work programmes and assignment of priorities taking account of Community requirements and the economic impact of these activities from the standpoint of users, producers and telecommunications administrations. The tasks to be performed at this level may include, in particular:

2.1.1. gathering detailed information on the basis of national and international programmes, presentation of that information in a form which facilitates comparative analysis and preparation of the summaries required for the work of the Committee;

2.1.2. the dissemination of that information, the examination of requirements and the consultation of interested parties;

2.1.3. synchronization of the work programmes with international standardization activities;

2.1.4. the management of work programmes;

2.1.5. the preparation of reports describing the execution of the activities and the practical results of their implementation.

2.2. *The execution of standardization activities in the field of information technology*

Execution of the work programmes necessitates the implementation of a series of activities, responsibility for which is generally entrusted to CEN/CENELEC and to the CEPT and which correspond to the different stages of activity that must be completed in order to ensure the credibility of standards.

These activities include:

2.2.1. the refinement of international standards in an effort to remove the ambiguities and options that distort the function of standards designed to guarantee the exchange of information and the compatible operation of systems;

2.2.2. the drafting of prestandards in cases justified by the excessive delays of international standardization procedures, or of standards required in the Community context in the absence of international standards;

2.2.3. the definition of the conditions to be fulfilled in order to establish complete conformity to a standard;

2.2.4. the preparation of test standards or test specifications included in the standards and the organization of procedures and structures to enable test laboratories to check conformity to those standards on a properly harmonized basis.

2.3. *Activities affecting the telecommunications sector*

The standardization measures which concern the telecommunications sector include two types of activity:

— the drafting of functional specifications, based on international or European standards/specifications where they exist, for the means of access to public telecommunication networks for those services specifically intended for exchange of information and data between information technology systems. This technical work comes under the harmonization activities carried out in the telecommunications section and is entrusted to CEPT following the procedures described in Directive 86/361/EEC,

— the work to be carried out in the field common to information technology and to telecommunications requires increased cooperation between the competent technical bodies (i.e. CEN/CENELEC/CEPT). It should raise the degree of convergence so that the standards and functional specifications can be applied in as many ways as possible and in a harmonized manner following the procedure described in Directive 83/189/EEC.

2.4. *Complementary measures*

This part of the programme covers the following measures:

2.4.1. specific metrological activities relating to:

— promotion of the development of test and validation instruments and formal description techniques,

— support for the case of references, particularly in the case of applications requiring the use of functional standards based on a number of standards in combination;

2.4.2. the promotion of the preparation of manuals giving guidance on the application of standards for the final user;

2.4.3. the promotion of demonstrations in respect of the operating compatibility achieved as a result of the application of a standard. The main aim of this action will be to make the test and metrological instruments defined in 2.4.1. available for use in different projects and to ensure that development standards are experimented with;

2.4.4. the promotion of arrangements that go beyond the framework of industrial standardization, depend on agreements concluded in particular fields of professional activity and contribute to the efficient exchange of information (travel agency transactions, automation of money transactions, computerization of customs documents, robotics, office automation, micro-computing, etc.);

2.4.5. studies and projects relating specifically to standardization in the field of information technology.

3. **Measures relating to the application of standards in the public procurement sector**

Determination of the most efficient methods of ensuring the rapid application of the standards and technical specifications within the context of the present Decision while assuring appropriate linking with activities depending on Directive 77/62/EEC[6].

---

[6] OJ No L 13, 15. 1. 1977, p. 1.

APPENDIX 3

Council Recommendation of 25 June 1987 on the coordinated introduction of public pan-European cellular digital land-based mobile communications in the Community

(87/371/EEC)

THE COUNCIL OF THE EUROPEAN COMMUNITIES,

Having regard to the Treaty establishing the European Economic Community, and in particular Article 235 thereof,

Having regard to the proposal from the Commission[1],

Having regard to the opinion of the European Parliament[2],

Whereas Council Regulation 84/549/EEC[3] calls for the introduction of services on the basis of a common harmonized approach in the field of telecommunications;

Whereas the resources offered by modern telecommunications networks should be utilized to the full for the economic development of the Community;

Whereas mobile radio services are the only means of contacting users on the move and the most efficient means for those users to be connected to the public telecommunications networks;

Whereas the land-based mobile communications systems currently in use in the Community are largely incompatible and do not allow users on the move in vehicles, boats, trains or on foot throughout the Community, including inland or coastal waters to reap the benefits of European-wide services and European-wide markets;

Whereas the change-over to the second generation cellular digital mobile communications system will provide a unique opportunity to establish truly pan-European mobile communications;

Whereas the European Conference of Postal and Telecommunications Administrations (CEPT) has set up a special Working Group, referred to as GSM (Groupe Spécial Mobile), for planning all system aspects of a second-generation cellular mobile radio infrastructure;

Whereas such a future system, offering both voice and data services, is to be based on digital technique, thereby facilitating compatibility with the general digital environment that will evolve with the coordinated introduction of the Integrated Services Digital Network (ISDN) in accordance with recommendation 86/659/EEC[4];

Whereas a coordinated policy for the introduction of a pan-European cellular digital mobile radio service will make possible the establishment of a European market in mobile and portable terminals which will be capable of creating, by virtue of its size, the necessary development conditions to enable undertakings established in Community countries to maintain and improve their presence on world markets;

Whereas it is necessary to work out rapidly all agreements necessary to allow unrestricted access to mobile communications and free circulation of mobile terminals throughout the Community for the European user;

---

[1] OJ No C 69, 17. 3. 1987, p. 5.
[2] OJ No C 125, 11. 5. 1987, p. 159.
[3] OJ No L 298, 16. 11. 1984, p. 49.
[4] OJ No L 382, 31. 12. 1986, p. 36.

Whereas the rapid implementation of Council Directive 86/361/EEC of 24 July 1986 on the initial stage of the mutual recognition of type approval for telecommunications terminal equipment[5] will make an important contribution towards this goal;

Whereas consideration should be given to Council Directive 83/189/EEC of 28 March 1983 laying down a procedure for the provision of information in the field of technical standards and regulations[6] and the Council 87/95/EEC of 22 December 1986 on standardization in the field of information technology and telecommunications[7], and to any other proposal that the Commission may make;

Whereas it is appropriate to make use of the potential of the Community's existing financial instruments in order to promote the development of Community's infrastructure;

Whereas special attention should be paid to the urgent requirement of certain users for pan-European land-based communications;

Whereas the Commission will in the future submit other proposals in the field of mobile communications, including radio-paging systems;

Whereas the implementation of such a policy will lead to closer cooperation, at Community level, between the telecommunications industry, on the one hand, and the telecommunications administrations and the recognized private operating agencies offering public mobile telecommunications services, hereinafter referred to as 'telecommunications administrations' on the other;

Whereas a favourable opinion has been delivered by the Senior Officials Group on Telecommunications (SOG-T), according to which the detailed recommendations drawn by the Analysis and Forecasting Group (GAP) provide a strategic basis for the development of public mobile communications in the Community enabling European users on the move to communicate efficiently and economically; .

Whereas favourable opinions on these recommendations have been delivered by the telecommunications administrations, by the European Conference of Postal and Telecommunications Administrations (CEPT) and by telecommunications equipment manufacturers in the Member States;

Whereas the envisaged measures will allow the economic benefit and rapidly increasing market potential of public mobile communications to be fully realized in the Community;

Whereas the Treaty has not provided the necessary powers, others than those of Article 235,

HEREBY RECOMMENDS:

1. that the telecommunications administrations implement the detailed recommendations concerning the coordinated introduction of public pan-European cellular digital land-based mobile communications in the Community as described in the Annex;

2. that, in so doing, they give special consideration to:

   (a) the choice of the transmission system and network interfaces;
   (b) the time schedule set out in the Annex;
   (c) the start of service at the latest from 1991 onwards, with geographical coverage and penetration objectives compatible with commercial strategies;

3. that the telecommunications administrations continue the cooperation within the European Conference of Postal and Telecommunications Administrations (CEPT), particularly concerning the objectives and time schedule set out in the Annex for the completion of the specifications of the pan-European cellular digital mobile communications system;

---

[5] OJ No L 217, 5. 8. 1986, p. 21.
[6] OJ No L 109, 26. 4. 1983, p. 8.
[7] OJ No L 36, 7. 2. 1987, p. 31.

4. that the telecommunications administrations plan for a gradual evolution from the existing public mobile radio systems to the pan-European cellular mobile communications system so as to ensure a transition which meets the needs of users, telecommunications administrations and undertakings established within Community countries;

5. that Member State Governments and telecommunications administrations rapidly complete the technical arrangements necessary to allow unrestricted access to cellular digital mobile communications;

6. that the Community's financial instruments take this recommendation into account within the framework of their interventions, particularly as regards investments required for the implementation of the pan-European cellular digital mobile communications system and that the Community's technological research and development programmes do likewise as regards the development of the required technological base;

7. that Member State Governments invite the telecommunications administrations to carry out this recommendation;

8. that Member State Governments inform the Commission at the end of each year, form the end of 1987 onwards, of the measures taken and problems encountered in the course of implementing this Recommendation. The progress of work will be examined by the Commission with the Senior Officials Group on Telecommunications (SOG-T) set up by the Council on 4 November 1983.

Done at Luxembourg, 25 June 1987.

For the Council
The President
H. DE CROO

ANNEX

1. General requirements

The future pan-European cellular digital mobile communications system should fulfil the following general requirements:

— be suitable for use in the 890–915 and 935–960 MHz frequency bands to be made available for the pan-European cellular digital mobile communications system;
— permit a traffic flow (measured in $E/KM^8/MHz$) greater than, or equal to, existing networks, bearing in mind the scarcity of the bandwidth resource allowed for these systems;
— provide the user with a voice transmission quality at least equal to that of the existing systems;
— allow for efficient use of hand-held terminals by encouraging competition amongst manufacturers;
— to be sufficiently flexible to facilitate the introduction of new services related to ISDN.

The cost of the system should be considered in terms of the cost of the fixed infrastructure to be met by the telecommunications administrations, taking into account both urban and rural areas, and the cost of the mobile equipment. All these costs should be within affordable limits and in any case must not exceed the cost of existing public mobile telephone systems working in the 900 MHz band. Since the cost of the mobile communication equipment will constitute the main portion of the total cost, it is preferable for the mobile equipment cost (for quantities in excess of 100 000) to be lower than that for mobile equipment used in existing public mobile telephone systems working in the 900 MHz band.

2. Choice of transmission system

The transmission mode for the pan-European mobile system should be digital. The basis for the final choice of the technical option common to all the member States (radio subsystem multiple access method) within the digital mode was established by the telecommunications administrations in May 1987, on the basis of work carried out by CEPT (European Conference of Postal and Telecommunications Administrations) and particularly its special group for mobile communications, referred to as GSM (Groupe Spécial Mobile).

3. Network architecture

The principles of the network structure and the definition and allocation of functions between the various system components – Mobile Stations (MS), Base Stations (BS), and Mobile Switching Centres (MSC) – should be defined by the middle of 1987. In the course of this work, the appropriate interfaces between the various system components (MS-BS-MSC) should be completely defined for all Open Systems Interconnections Standards (OSI) layers applicable to the relevant services, and for all applications using those interfaces (call processing functions, maintenance, etc.). The system must be able to support geographically co-located cellular digital mobile radio operators.

4. Mobile interfaces to be specified in detail by the end of 1987

(a) S. reference point, with B (N Kbits/s) + D (N' Kbits/s) structure (N and N' to be defined;

(b) Interface between MS and BS;

(c) Interface between BS and MSC.

A minimum set of man/machine interface specifications (control procedures) should be established.

5. Mobile services to be specified in detail by the end of 1987 and available for provision in all Member States starting from 1991, with hand-over and national/international roaming

Although, initially, voice telephony capabilities will constitute the most important service required, the mobile system must nevertheless be open to an overall evolution towards ISDN services[8]. Therefore, the following mobile service should be specified in detail by the end of 1987 and available in all Member States starting from 1991:

(a) *Bearer services*

— Non-transparent bearer service for speech;
— Transparent bearer service for data transmission at N Kbit/s switched in the network at 64 Kbits/s (N to be defined).

(b) *Basic services*

— Hand-over;
— National/international roaming.

(c) *Teleservices*

Telephony at 3,1 kHz (corresponding to N Kbit/s on B channel. N is to be defined).

(d) *Supplementary services*

— Calling line identification;
— Advice of call duration;
— Speech encryption.

This list may be added to by CEPT.

---

[8] OJ No C 157, 24. 6. 1986, p. 3.

6. **Signalling**

User access signalling (subscriber signalling) should be defined along the principles of the existing CEPT recommendations for ISDN, and should be able to permit supplementary services of ISDN/PSTN.

Network and inter-network signalling process should be defined in the framework of the SS No 7 in such a way that international roaming and hand-over facilities are safeguarded.

7. **Tariff considerations**

The telecommunications administrations are invited to consider within the CEPT framework the following tariff principles:

— given the scarcity of frequency resources, the service should be charged basically according to the duration of the radio channel use;
— the tariffs should take into account the current trend towards less distance dependence.

By the end of 1987, the basic framework of charging principles should be identified, so that the network implications can be identified and resolved in an appropriate manner.

8. **Geographical coverage**

The introduction date of the pan-European cellular digital mobile communications system should be 1991 at the latest. Major urban areas should be covered by 1993 at the latest. The main links between these areas should be covered by 1995 at the latest.

Further, the telecommunications administration should collaborate in studying these respective priorities for coverage, in order to stimulate the maximum pan-European traffic as early as possible. This should take into account the needs of users in vehicles on Major European routes, and the needs of air travellers located between city centres and international airports.

APPENDIX 4

Council Directive of 25 June 1987 on the frequency bands to be reserved for the coordinated introduction of public pan-European cellular digital land-based mobile communications in the Community

(87/372/EEC)

THE COUNCIL OF THE EUROPEAN COMMUNITIES,

Having regard to the Treaty establishing the European Economic Community, and in particular Article 100 thereof,

Having regard to the proposal from the Commission[1],

Having regard to the opinion of the European Parliament[2],

Whereas recommendations 84/549/EEC[3] calls for the introduction of services on the basis of a common harmonized approach in the field of telecommunications;

Whereas the resources offered by modern telecommunications networks should be utilized to the full for the economic development of the Community;

Whereas mobile radio services are the only means of contacting users on the move and the most efficient means for those users to be connected to public telecommunications networks;

Whereas mobile communications depend on the allocation and availability of frequency bands in order to transmit and receive between fixed-base stations and mobile stations;

Whereas the frequencies and land-based mobile communications systems currently in use in the Community vary widely and do not allow all users on the move in vehicles, boats, trains, or on foot throughout the Community, including on inland or coastal waters, to reap the benefits of European-wide services and European-wide markets;

Whereas the change-over to the second generation cellular digital mobile communications system will provide a unique opportunity of establishing truly pan-European mobile communications;

Whereas the European Conference of Postal and Telecommunications Administrations (CEPT) has recommended that frequencies 980–915 and 935–960 MHz be allocated to such a system, in accordance with the International Telecommunications Union (ITU) Radio Regulations allocating such frequencies to mobile radio services use as well;

Whereas parts of these frequency bands are being used or are intended for use by certain Member States for interim systems and other radio services;

Whereas the progressive availability of the full range of the frequency bands set out above will be indispensable for the establishment of truly pan-European mobile communications;

Whereas the implementation of Council recommendation 87/371/EEC of 25 June 1987 on the coordinated introduction of public pan-European cellular digital land-based mobile communications in the Community[4], aiming at starting a pan-European system by 1991 at the latest, will allow the speedy specification of the radio transmission path;

Whereas on the basis of present technological and market trends it would appear to be realistic to envisage the exclusive occupation of the 890–915 and 935–960 MHz frequency bands by the pan-European system within 10 years of 1 January 1991;

---

[1] OJ No C 69, 17. 3. 1987, p. 9.
[2] OJ No C 125, 11. 5. 1987, p. 159.
[3] OJ No L 298, 16. 11. 1984, p. 49.
[4] See page 81 of this Official Journal.

Whereas Council Directive 86/361/EEC of 24 July 1986 on the initial stage of the mutual recognition of type approval for telecommunications terminal equipment[5] will allow the rapid establishment of common conformity specifications for the pan-European cellular digital mobile communications system;

Whereas the report on public mobile communications drawn up by the Analysis and Forecasting Group (GAP) for the Senior Officials Group on Telecommunications (SOG-T) has drawn attention to the necessity for the availability of adequate frequencies as a vital pre-condition for pan-European cellular mobile communications;

Whereas favourable opinions on this report have been delivered by the telecommunications administrations, by the European Conference of Postal and Telecommunications Administrations (CEPT) and the telecommunications equipment manufacturers in the Member States,

HAS ADOPTED THIS DIRECTIVE:

Article 1

1. Member States shall ensure that the 905–914 and 950–959 MHz frequency bands or equivalent parts of the bands mentioned in paragraph 2 are reserved exclusively[6] for a public pan-European cellular digital mobile communications service by 1 January 1991.

2. Member States shall ensure that the necessary plans are prepared for the public pan-European cellular digital mobile communications service to be able to occupy the whole of the 890–915 and 935–960 MHz bands according to commercial demand as quickly as possible.

Article 2

The Commission shall report to the Council on the implementation of the Directive not later than the end of 1996.

Article 3

For the purposes of this Directive, a public pan-European cellular digital land-based mobile communications service shall mean a public cellular radio service provided in each of the Member States to a common specification, which includes the feature that all voice signals are encoded into binary digits prior to radio transmission, and where users provided with a service in one Member State can also gain access to the service in any other Member State.

Article 4

1. Member States shall bring into force the provisions necessary to comply with this Directive within 18 months of its notification[7]. They shall forthwith inform the Commission thereof.

2. Member States shall communicate to the Commission the text of the provisions of national law which they adopt in the field governed by this Directive.

Article 5

This Directive is addressed to the Member States.

Done at Luxembourg, 25 June 1987.

For the Council
The President
H. DE CROO

---

[5] OJ No L 217, 5. 8. 1986, p. 21.
[6] With the exception of the use of these frequencies for point-to-point connections existing when the Directive enters into force provided they do no interfere with the public pan-European cellular digital mobile communications service and do not prevent its establishment or extension.
[7] This Directive was notified to the Member States on 26 June 1987.

APPENDIX 5

Council Decision of 5 October 1987 introducing a communications network Community programme on trade electronic data interchange systems (TEDIS)

(87/499/EEC)

THE COUNCIL OF THE EUROPEAN COMMUNITIES,

Having regard to the Treaty establishing the European Economic Community, and in particular Article 235 thereof,

Having regard to the proposal from the Commission,

Having regard to the opinion of the European Parliament[1],

Having regard to the opinion of the Economic and Social Committee[2],

Whereas the Community has, in particular, as its task, by establishing a common market and progressively approximating the economic policies of Member States, to promote throughout the Community a harmonious development of economic activities and closer relations between the States belonging to it;

Whereas, when they met in Stuttgart, Athens and Fontainebleau, the Heads of State or of Government emphasized the importance of telecommunications as a vital driving force for economic growth and social development;

Whereas the European Parliament, in evaluating the situation and development of telecommunications, emphasized the key role of the latter in the future political, social and economic development of the Community (debates of the European Parliament on telecommunications 1983, Leonardi report, Albert and Ball report of 1982);

Whereas, on 17 December 1984, the Council approved the main features of a Community Policy on telecommunications, including the aim of improving advanced telecommunications services and networks through Community projects;

Whereas the telecommunications sector is of great economic importance as regards both its own industrial activities and its contribution to efficient information interchange throughout the Community;

Whereas there are specific aspects to information technology standards and the work needed to produce them; whereas this is the case in particular as regards:

— the complexity of the technical specifications and the precision needed for data interchange and systems inter-operability,
— the urgent need for standards in order to prevent totally incompatible (trade) electronic data interchange systems being developed,
— the need to ensure that international standards are implemented on a basis that makes them credible for practical use;

Whereas a general programme of information technology and telecommunications standardization is being implemented;

Whereas Council Decision No 87/95/EEC of 22 December 1986 on standardization in the field of information technology and telecommunications[3] is intended to establish in these sectors a general

---

[1] OJ No C 246, 14. 9. 1987, p. 92.
[2] OJ No C 105, 21. 4. 1987, p. 1.
[3] OJ No L 36, 7. 2. 1987, p. 31.

framework for drawing up standards or common technical specifications so as to facilitate information exchange throughout the Community by breaking down the barriers created by the incompatibilities that stem from the absence of standards or their lack of precision;

Whereas, under the CD project and under the CADDIA programme[4], action is to be taken to ensure close cooperation with commercial and industrial interest so as to provide appropriate communications and information exchange interfaces between commercial and industrial systems and those of customs administrations;

Whereas the above mentioned objective can be achieved only between the establishment of close cooperation between commercial and industrial interests in different industries so as to ensure the necessary compatibility of trade electronic data interchange systems;

Whereas the CD project requires that consideration be given to the aspects concerning the security, protection and privacy of data in respect of imports, exports and intra-Community trade supplied to, held by, or in the course of transmission between the Commission, customs administrations and commercial circles;

Whereas the above questions form part of a much wider issue, the protection of information in the context of trade electronic data interchange between information systems, and whereas it is essential to ensure consistency between the measures taken and the CD project and those implemented in the industrial context;

Whereas the Commission's White paper on completing the internal market underlines the importance of the development of new cross-border services and the part that telecommunications networks based on common standards can play in creating a market free of obstacles at Community level;

Whereas there are guidelines contained in the Green paper of 30 June 1987 on the development of the common market for telecommunications services and equipment;

Whereas trade electronic data interchange can increasingly help to strengthen the competitiveness of European companies in manufacturing and services;

Whereas there is at present a rapid increase in public and private efforts at both national and international level to bring into service within companies, groups and industries trade electronic data interchange systems that are not compatible with each other;

Whereas the diverse and piecemeal approaches to trade electronic data interchange adopted within a country or more generally a firm, group of firms or industry are likely to lead to the establishment of incompatible systems unable to communicate with each other and to prevent both users and suppliers of equipment and services from benefiting to the full from the advantages offered by the development of trade electronic data interchange;

Whereas, to ensure that these trade electronic data interchange systems be able to communicate, it is necessary to adopt a programme containing an initial set of activities of common interest needed for the coordinated development of trade electronic data interchange and a further set of activities more closely linked to sectoral projects so as to attempt to solve in a coordinated fashion the common problems encountered during their development;

Whereas initially it is necessary to carry out activities and studies so as to establish and develop the conductive conditions necessary for the coordinated development of trade electronic data exchange;

Whereas, in the light of the results and experience obtained, it will be necessary to define the aims and details of a possible second phase offering support for pilot projects and continuing some of the activities that have been started;

Whereas the Treaty has not provided the necessary powers to this end, other than those of Article 235,

---

[4] OJ No L 33, 8. 2. 1986, p. 28.

HAS DECIDED AS FOLLOWS:

Article 1

A communications network Community programme on trade electronic data interchange systems (TEDIS) in trade, industry and administration, hereafter referred to as the 'programme', is hereby set up.

Article 2

The programme shall be implemented in accordance with this Decision. It shall cover a period of two years.

Article 3

The aims of the programme are:

1. coordination at Community level of work going on in the various Member States on the development of trade electronic data interchange systems:

2. to alert potential users;

3. to alert European hardware and software manufacturers to the opportunities offered by electronic data interchange;

4. logistic support for European sectoral groups;

5. consideration of the specific requirements of trade electronic data interchange within Member States and between the Member States and the Community in telecommunications and standardization policies; carrying-out of preparatory work for that purpose;

6. help in the setting-up of conformance testing centres for software and hardware used in trade electronic data interchange systems;

7. to seek solutions to legal problems that might inhibit the development of trade electronic data interchange and to see to it that restrictive telecommunications regulations cannot hamper the development of trade electronic data interchange;

8. to study security requirements for trade electronic data interchange systems so as to guarantee confidentiality of messages transmitted;

9. to study specific problems caused by the multiplicity of languages in the Community and, to this end, to examine the possibility, for the purposes of multilingualism, of using the results obtained or expected under the machine translation programmes Systran and Eurotra;

10. to study the advisability of promoting the development of the specialized software needed for trade electronic data exchange;

11. to list existing or potential sectoral projects on trade electronic data interchange and to make a comparative analysis of them;

12. identification of special requirements emerging during the implementation of trade electronic data interchange systems that could be met more easily with Community assistance;

13. to make a particular study of the assistance that could be given to small and medium-sized businesses to help them to take an active part in trade electronic data interchange;

14. to give thought to possible support for pilot projects the gradual implementation of which would be likely to encourage solutions, capable of being generalized, to problems of common interest encountered by most trade electronic data interchange systems.

Article 4

The programme shall be implemented in coordination with the existing or planned policies and activities in the Community on telecommunications, the information market, standardization and multilingualism, and in particular with the CADDIA programme and the CD project, so as to ensure the necessary interaction with the specific requirements of trade electronic data interchange.

Article 5

Contracts for the programme shall be concluded with enterprises, including small and medium-sized enterprises, research establishments and other bodies established in the Community.

Article 6

1 The Community shall contribute to the programme within the limits of the appropriations entered each year for that purpose in the general budget of the European Communities.

2. The amount estimated necessary to cover the Community's contribution to the carrying-out of the programme is 5.3 million ECU for the duration of the programme.

Article 7

The Commission shall see to it that the programme is carried out satisfactorily and shall take the appropriate implementing measures.

Article 8

The Commission shall submit to the Council by 1 January 1990 at the latest a report on the execution of the work defined in this Decision and if necessary, a proposal for further measures.

Article 9

This Decision shall take effect on 1 January 1988.

Done at Luxembourg, 5 October 1987.

For the Council
The President
N. WILHJELM

APPENDIX 6

Council Decision of 14 December 1987 on a Community programme in the field of telecommunications technologies – research and development (R&D) in advanced communications technologies in Europe (RACE programme)

(88/28/EEC)

THE COUNCIL OF THE EUROPEAN COMMUNITIES,

Having regard to the Treaty establishing the European Economic Community, and in particular Article 130Q (2) thereof,

Having regard to the proposal from the Commission[1],

In cooperation with the European Parliament[2],

Having regard to the opinion of the Economic and Social Committee[3],

Whereas the Community has as its task, by establishing a common market and progressively approximating the economic policies of Member States, *inter alia*, to promote throughout the Community a harmonious development of economic activities and closer relations between the States belonging to it;

Whereas the Heads of State and of Government, meeting in Stuttgart, Athens, Fontainebleau and Brussels, emphasized the importance of telecommunications as a major source for economic growth and social development;

Whereas the European Parliament, in its assessment of the situation and development of tele-communications, stressed the key role of telecommunications for the future political, social and economic development of the Community;

Whereas on 17 December 1984 the Council agreed on the main elements of a Community tele-communications policy in the field of advanced telecommunications services and networks involving actions at Community level;

Whereas, with the emergence of new services and the progressive convergence of tele-communications, data processing and wider public services, the trend is towards a Europe-wide integrated broadband network (Integrated Broadband Communications (IBC) capable of sup-porting a wide range of customers and service providers;

Whereas developments in telecommunications will benefit the international competitiveness of the European economies in general and of the telecommunications industries in particular;

Whereas the option selected for advanced telecommunications technologies must be such that it does not increase regional disparities in the Community; whereas the development of common specifications for equipment and services is necessary but not sufficient to prevent further diver-gences in the regional development;

Whereas the development of IBC offers a wide range of opportunities for small and medium sized companies in the manufacture of equipment and in the provision of specialized services within the Community;

---

[1] OJ No C 304, 28. 11. 1986, p. 2.
[2] OJ No C 281, 19. 10. 1987, p. 113. Decision of 18 November 1987not yet published in the Official Journal.
[3] OJ No C 68, 16. 3. 1987, p. 22.

Whereas, in response to the requirement of using fully the economic and market potential of telecommunications, the Commission has submitted a programme of action which has been recognized by the Council as a base for further work;

Whereas cooperation in R&D and the development of standards can make a major contribution, notably by facilitating the evolution towards future IBC in terms of transnational connections and also at regional and local levels;

Whereas the 'Single European Act' provides a new political and legal base for the development of a scientific and technological strategy with particular importance being given to the goal of promoting industrial competitiveness;

Whereas the Research Council on 4 June 1985 recognized the importance of the rapid establishment of a definition phase for the RACE programme, in order to prepare a general European framework for the development of advanced systems of communications for the future and to promote technological and industrial cooperation;

Whereas the Council adopted by Decision 85/372/EEC[4] the RACE definition phase of 18 months on which to base the Decision for the main programme by the end of 1986;

Whereas, by Decision 87/516/Euratom/EEC[5], the Council adopted a framework programme of Community activities in the field of research and technological development (1987 to 1991) providing for research to be undertaken leading towards a large market and an information and communications society, including telecommunications;

Whereas the constitution or consolidation of a specifically European industrial potential in the technologies concerned is an urgent necessity; whereas its beneficiaries must be network operators, research establishments, undertakings, including small and medium-sized undertakings and other bodies established in the Community which are best suited to attain these objectives;

Whereas the RACE definition phase has produced the requisite conclusions;

Whereas the RACE Management Committee has carried out an assessment and called for the necessary decisions to be taken in time to ensure the follow-up of the work;

Whereas it is in the Community's interest to consolidate the scientific and financial basis of European research by means of the involvement to a greater extent of participants from European third countries in certain Community programmes and particularly in programmes involving cooperation in research and development of telecommunications technology;

Whereas consistency with ESPRIT is essential since both programmes benefit from each other;

Whereas it is essential to ensure consistency with Eureka, other European transnational cooperation and national actions;

Whereas during the RACE main phase numerous decisions may have to be taken which are extremely relevant to consumers, whether private individuals or businesses, such as those concerning the desired level of confidentiality and privacy of data transfer;

Whereas one fundamental concern which has emerged from the RACE definition phase is the need for attention to be paid to consumer-oriented aspects of future telecommunications services; whereas quality requirements and costs are associated problems in respect of which ongoing decisions will have to be made during the RACE main phase; whereas, therefore, the European Parliament should be kept informed of developments;

Whereas the implementation of concerted actions in the COST framework is an essential element to complement industrially-oriented R&D projects;

Whereas the Scientific and Technical Research Committee (CREST) has expressed its opinion;

---

[4] OJ No L 210, 7. 8. 1985, p. 24.
[5] OJ No L 302, 24. 10. 1987, p. 1.

Whereas, on the basis of results achieved, the programme may be extended for a second period of five years, following a proposal from the Commission,

HAS ADOPTED THIS DECISION

Article 1

1. A Community programme in the field of telecommunications technologies (RACE) is adopted for an initial period of five years commencing 1 June 1987.

2. The programme is designed, in concertation with public and private actions in the field of telecommunications technologies, undertaken at national and international level, to promote the competitiveness of the Community's telecommunications industry, operators and service providers in order to make available to the final users, at minimum cost and with minimum delay, the services which will sustain the competitiveness of the European economy over the coming decades and contribute to maintaining and creating employment in the Community.

Article 2

The programme summary and objectives, as set out in more detail in Annex II, shall consist of three parts:

Part I: IBC development and implementation strategies

Shall comprise work required for the development of functional specifications, systems and operations research towards the definition of proposals for Open Systems-conformity[6] standards, concepts and conventions and analytical work serving the objective of establishing interoperability for IBC[7] equipment and services. This work is to be carried out by appropriate organizations, groups and other bodies including, where required, contract work;

Part II: IBC technologies

Shall comprise R&D cooperation in IBC technologies at the precompetitive stage;

Part III: Prenormative functional integration

Shall comprise prenormative and precompetitive R&D relating to cooperation in the realization of an 'open verification environment' designed to assess functions, operational concepts and experimental equipment with respect to functional specifications and standardization proposals arising from the work in Part I.

Article 3

1. Projects relating to the programme shall be executed, where required, by means of shared-cost contracts. Contractors shall be expected to bear a substantial proportion of the costs, which should normally be at least 50% of the total expenditure.

2. The proposals for projects shall, as a rule, be submitted in reply to an open invitation to tender and involve the participation of at least two independent industrial partners not all established in the same Member State. The invitation to tender shall be published in the *Official Journal of the European Communities*.

3. In exceptional cases concerning projects indispensable for implementing key requirements of the workplan:

— where a proposal would involve

   (i)   unreasonable burdens on the participants, particularly small and medium-sized under-takings and research establishments,

---

[6] Open Systems-conformity stands for an international standardization effort to make equipment and service from different suppliers, operators and service providers inter-operable.

[7] IBC – Integrated Broadband Communication, which stands for advanced telecommunications services relying on high performance infrastructure.

(ii) only one independent industrial partner,

(iii) more than one independent industrial partner established in the same Member State, or

— where an open tendering procedure would be unjustified on grounds of cost or efficiency, or
— where the amount of the Community's contribution to the cost does not exceed 1 million ECU,

it may be decided, in accordance with the procedures laid down in Article 8, to depart from the general provisions set out in paragraphs (1) and (2) of this Article.

4. The contracts shall be concluded with network operators, research establishments, undertakings, including small and medium-sized undertakings, and other bodies established in the Community.

Article 4

Where framework agreements for scientific and technical cooperation between non-member European countries and the European Communities have been concluded, organizations and undertakings established in these countries may, in accordance with the procedures laid down in Articles 3 and 8, become partners to a project undertaken within the programme.

Article 5

1. The funds estimated as necessary for the Community contribution to the implementation of the programme amount to 550 million ECU over five years, including expenditure on a staff whose costs shall not exceed 4,5% of the Community's contribution.

2. The internal and indicative allocation of these funds is set out in Annex I.

Article 6

1. The Commission shall ensure that the programme is properly performed and establish the appropriate implementation measures.

2. The Commission shall ensure that procedures are set up to allow for appropriate cooperation with COST activities related to the areas of research covered by the programme, by ensuring regular exchanges of information between the Committee referred to in Article 7 and the relevant COST Management Committees.

3. The Commission shall establish for each year and update as required a draft workplan defining the detailed objectives, the type of projects and actions to be undertaken and the corresponding financial plans. The Commission shall keep the European Parliament informed on progress of the annual workplans.

4. The procedure laid down in Article 8 shall apply to:

— the establishment and updating of the annual workplan referred to in paragraph 3 of this Article,
— any departure from the general conditions laid down in Article 3 (1) and (2),
— the evaluation of work undertaken in respect of each part of the programme by appropriate organizations, groups and other bodies,
— the assessment of proposed projects for the implementation of Parts I and III and the Community financial contribution for a project when this contribution is in excess of 2,5 million ECU,
— the assessment of proposed projects for the implementation of Part II and the Community financial contribution for a project when this contribution is in excess of 5 million ECU,
— the participation in any project by European organizations and enterprises not established in the Community.

5. The Commission may consult the Committee referred to in Article 7, and shall consult it at the request of the representatives of at least four Member States on any matter falling within the scope of this decision.

Article 7

The Commission shall be assisted in the performance of its tasks by a Management Committee, hereinafter referred to as 'the Committee'. The Committee, consisting of two representatives of each Member State, shall be set up by the Commission on the basis of nominations by the Member States.

Members of the Committee may be assisted by experts or advisors depending on the nature of the issue under consideration.

The Committee shall be chaired by a Commission representative.

The proceedings of the Committee shall be confidential. The Committee shall adopt its own rules of procedure. The secretarial services shall be provided by the Commission.

Article 8

1. Where the procedure laid down in this Article is to be followed, the Chairman shall refer the matter to the Committee, either on his own initiative or at the request of one of its members.

2. Under this procedure, the representative of the Commission, who acts as Chairman, shall submit to the Committee the draft of the measures to be adopted. The Committee shall deliver an opinion within a time limit which shall normally be one month and shall in no case exceed two months. The opinion shall be delivered by the majority specified in Article 148 (2) of the Treaty for decisions which the Council is required to adopt on a proposal from the commission, the votes of the representatives of the Article States being weighted as indicated in that Article. The Chairman shall not vote.

3. The Commission shall adopt the intended measures when they are in accordance with the Committee's opinion.

Where the proposed measures are not in accordance with the Committee's opinion, or if no opinion is delivered, the Commission shall forthwith submit to the Council a proposal. The Council shall act by qualified majority.

If the Council has not acted within a period of two months from the date on which the matter was referred to it, the proposed measures shall:

— be adopted by the Commission for matters falling under the third, fourth and fifth indents of Article 6 (4),
— be adopted by the Commission, save where the Council has decided against the said measures by simple majority for matters falling under the first, second and sixth indents of Article 6 (4).

Article 9

1. The programme shall be reviewed after 30 months on the basis of an evaluation of the results achieved in relation to the precise objectives set out in Annex II to this Decision. The Commission shall inform the Council and European Parliament of the results of this review.

2. After the completion of the first five-year period of the programme, the Commission shall, after consulting the committee, send to the Member States and the European Parliament a report on the performance and results of the programme.

Article 10

With regard to the coordination activities provided for in Article 1 (2), the Member States and the Commission shall exchange all appropriate information to which they have access and which they are free to disclose concerning activities in the areas covered by this Decision, whether or not planned or carried out under their authority.

Information shall be exchanged according to a procedure to be defined by the Commission after consulting the Committee and shall be treated as confidential at the suppliers' request.

Article 11

This Decision shall apply from 1 June 1987.

Article 12

This Decision is addressed to the Member States.

Done at Brussels, 14 December 1987.

For the Council
The President
U. ELLEMANN-JENSEN

ANNEX I

INDICATIVE INTERNAL ALLOCATION OF FUNDS

(Million ECU)

PART I: IBC DEVELOPMENT AND IMPLEMENTATION STRATEGIES	60
I.1. IBC strategies	14
I.2. IBC realization (Systems analysis and functional specifications)	28
I.3. IBC usage	10
I.4. Common operational environment	8
PART II: IBC TECHNOLOGIES	332
II.1. Techniques for IBC systems functions	94
II.2. IBC programming infrastructure	49
II.3. Usability engineering	12
II.4. Technologies enabling network evolution	177
PART III: PRENORMATIVE FUNCTIONAL INTEGRATION	113
III.1. Verification tools	63
III.2. Development of IBC application pilot schemes	50
Personnel costs	25
Administrative costs	20
Total	550

ANNEX II

RACE PROGRAMME SUMMARY AND OBJECTIVES[8]

The goal of RACE is to make a major contribution to the objective of the:

'Introduction of Integrated Broadband Communication (IBC) taking into account the evolving Integrated Services Digital network (ISDN) and national introduction strategies, progressing to Community-wide services by 1995'.

The general objectives of RACE are, in this light:

---

[8] OJ No L 217, 5. 8. 1986, p. 21.

(a) to promote the Community's telecommunications industry so as to ensure that it maintains a strong position at European and world levels in a context of rapid technological change;

(b) to enable the European network operators to confront under the best possible conditions the technological and service challenges with which they will be faced;

(c) to enable a critical minimum number of the Member States of the Community to introduce commercially viable IBC services by 1996;

(d) to offer opportunities to service providers to improve cost-performance and introduce new or enhanced information services which will both earn revenue in their own right and give indispensable support to other productive sectors of the Community;

(e) to make available to the final users, at a cost and on a timescale at least as favourable as in other major western countries, the services which will sustain the competitiveness of the European economy over the next decades and contribute to maintaining and creating employment in the Community;

(f) to accompany the formation of a Community internal market for all IBC related telecommunications equipment and services based on agreed European or international standards as an indispensable basis for sustained strength on the world markets;

(g) to contribute to regional development within the Community with the support of the development of common functional specifications for equipment and services permitting the less-developed regions to benefit fully from the efforts of Member States piloting the telecommunications developments in the Community.

In order to achieve the objectives described, the RACE programme would be structured into three main parts with each project containing verifiable objectives to be met and reported on.

PART I: IBC DEVELOPMENT AND IMPLEMENTATION STRATEGIES

relating to the development of functional specifications, the systems and operations research towards the definition of proposals for IBC standards, concepts and conventions conforming to an open systems approach, and the analytical work serving the objective of establishing interoperability for IBC equipment and services.

PART II: IBC TECHNOLOGIES

covering the technological cooperation in precompetitive R&D addressing key requirements of new technology for the low-cost realization of IBC equipments and services.

PART III: PRENORMATIVE FUNCTIONAL INTEGRATION

relating to prenormative cooperation in the realization of an 'open verification environment' designed to assess functions, operational concepts and experimental equipment and applications with respect to functional specifications and standardization proposals arising from the work in Part I.

The corresponding work areas, tasks and approaches are specified in detail in the RACE workplan which is under preparation and will be submitted separately.

This work is to be carried out by industry, academics and telecommunication operators. The latter are expected to finance independently the work falling within their domain.

The following sections provide a description of the scope and nature of the work to be undertaken.

PART I: IBD DEVELOPMENT AND IMPLEMENTATION STRATEGIES

Objectives

The main objectives of the work under Part I are to achieve, throughout the introduction and further enhancement of IBC:

— a common understanding of the evolution towards introduction of IBC and its implications including market research and promotion of the IBC concept and services in Europe and internationally,

— a common definition and understanding of the IBC system and subsystems, between all main actors concerned,
— guidelines for the functional specifications of the IBC system and the development of integrated services,
— a framework in which to identify the technology requirements and to assess the implications of technological advances and the evolution of service demands in RD&E (Research, Development and Engineering),
— a tool for the evaluation of cost-effectiveness of various technological solutions, implementation schemes and evolutionary routes starting from the given situation,
— mechanisms for analysing and assessing, at an early stage, the requirements for standardization proposals and functional specifications in order to facilitate and accelerate the emergence of international standards.

Scope

To meet these standards, Part I would comprise two major areas of activity:

— maintenance and further development of the European Reference Model for Integrated Broadband Communication, defined in its initial form during the RACE definition phase,
— systems analysis and engineering work to transform the concepts derived in the Reference Model into systems and subsystems and functional specifications.

I.1 IBC strategies

IBC is a broad field of activities which requires the dedicated work of many independent participants. They all need to be able to situate their respective work in the context of evolving objectives, conditions and rapid technological change and demand.

I.2 IBC realization

The Reference Model work of point I.1 represents a major concertation exercise to produce consensus views on the evolution towards IBC and its broad functional specifications for IBC systems, subsystems and services, and to provide a two-way link between the Reference Model and other RACE activities. The required systems analysis will be carried out under this point.

I.3 IBC usage

The economic impact of IBC will depend heavily on the nature of the applications supported by iBC networks, the modes of presentation to the users, the facilities available to users and other important parameters related to the ergonomy of telecommunications usage. This work area will concern these elements to the extent that they are related to work under I.1 and I.2.

I.4 Common operational environment

The convergence and transition to IBC represents a major problem in managing the complexity of the technical issues. This does require a specific effort which is the objective of the work under this heading.

PART II: IBC TECHNOLOGIES

Objective

The objective of this part is to carry out cooperative R&D on the key technologies required for low-cost-realizations of IBC equipment and services. In particular, success for the IBC depends critically on the cost of the local loop optimal components being within affordable limits of domestic subscribers. This presents RACE with a key objective of providing the technology which in association with standardization will reduce the costs in mass production by a factor of 100 over today's typical costs of comparable components. Part II will be system-driven and specifically related to the functional specifications derived by Part I.

Scope

The scope of the work will include the research, test and experimentation needed to explore the techno-economic characteristics of the new technologies relevant to IBC.

II.1. Techniques for IBC system functions

Objective

The use of advanced technology for cost-efficient implementation of IBC. The work will focus on functions which, due to their generalized use, form a key cost factor.

II.2. IBC programming infrastructure

Objective

Based on advances in software technology in general, as they result from fundamental work done elsewhere, the objective here is to realize major advance in telecommunication software infrastructure so as to master the complexity of systems integration and the associated requirements of network reliability and efficiency.

II.3. Usability engineering

Objective

The objective is to advance the technological aspects of man-machine interface and human factors so as to facilitate IBC user acceptance linked to ergonomy and cognitive facilities of IBC equipment.

II.4. Technologies enabling network evolution

Objective

The objective of the R&D is to exploit key enabling technologies to realize advanced evolutionary subsystems, systems and networks.

PART III: PRENORMATIVE FUNCTIONAL INTEGRATION

Objective

The work is aimed at the validation of standardization concepts and prenormative work as deriving from work done in other parts of RACE. The parts of the IPC system or subsystems will be tested by means of simulation of research-experimentation with particular reference to the needs of technological work in preparation of standardization proposals.

Prenormative functional integration serves several important functions. It will:

— permit the verification of concepts, standardization options, reliability, security, as well as other key functional characteristics by simulation and testing at the research stage,
— contribute to the reduction of risks for development and implementation by permitting the evaluation of the functional features by operators, industry and, where applicable, service providers and users,
— provide a mechanism for demonstrating interoperability features and compliance to standards and specifications.

Scope[9]

The scope of the work is to:

---

[9] The work invisaged within this part of the RACE programme is not expected to have the nature of demonstration projects or field trials. Such trials or prototype installations will be required before operational implementation of a harmonized set of IBC services can be undertaken but are beyond the scope and scale of effort under consideration for the RACE programme.

— test new technology, and devices from projects in Part II RACe, Esprit, relevant national programmes, international projects as an integral part of an IBC system to evaluate its functionalities and techno-economic performance characteristics,
— explore relevant performance parameters and confirm the feasibility of meeting the relevant requirements of the functional entities and applications as defined within Part I activities.

III.1. Verification tools

Objective

Work here is intended to develop verification tools related to make up operational IBC components of subsystems in order to verify design concepts, functional groups or protocols. The goal is to contribute to refinement of functional specification and/or standard proposals.

III.2. Development of IBC application pilot schemes

Objective

Early introduction of IBC services will require the diminution of the uncertainties and risks associated with new services. A key element to this is the early development of experimental situations where service providers, network operators and users are placed in conditions where IBC experimental products can be tested by users and service providers. The objective of the work in this area is to contribute to the development of such experimental situations and the exploitation of the results so as to speed up Community-wide understanding of the characteristics of IBC commercial exploitation.

APPENDIX 7

Commission Directive of 16 May 1988 on competition in the markets in telecommunications terminal equipment

(88/301/EEC)

THE COMMISSION OF THE EUROPEAN COMMUNITIES,

Having regard to the Treaty establishing the European Economic Community, and in particular Article 90 (3) thereof,

Whereas:

1. In all the Member States, telecommunications are, either wholly or partly, a State monopoly generally granted in the form of special or exclusive rights to one or more bodies responsible for providing and operating the network infrastructure and related services. Those rights, however, often go beyond the provision of network utilization services and extend to the supply of user terminal equipment for connection to the network. The last decades have seen considerable technical developments in networks, and the pace of development has been especially striking in the area of terminal equipment.

2. Several Member States have, in response to technical and economic developments, reviewed their grant of special or exclusive rights in the telecommunications sector. The proliferation of types of terminal equipment and the possibility of the multiple use of terminals means that users must be allowed a free choice between the various types of equipment available if they are to benefit fully from the technological advances made in the sector.

3. Article 30 of the Treaty prohibits quantitative restrictions on imports from other Member States and all measures having equivalent effect. The grant of special or exclusive rights to import and market goods to one organization can, and often does, lead to restrictions on imports from other Member States.

4. Article 37 of the Treaty states that 'Member States shall progressively adjust any State monopolies of a commercial character so as to ensure that when the transitional period has ended no discrimination regarding the conditions under which goods are procured and marketed exists between nationals of Member States.

   The provisions of this Article shall apply to any body through which a Member State, in law or in fact, either directly or indirectly supervises, determines or appreciably influences imports or exports between Member States. These provisions shall likewise apply to monopolies delegated by the State to others.' Paragraph 2 of Article 37 prohibits Member States from introducing any new measure contrary to the principles laid down in Article 37 (1).

5. The special or exclusive rights relating to terminal equipment enjoyed by national telecommunications monopolies are exercised in such a way as, in practice, to disadvantage equipment from other Member States, notably by preventing users from freely choosing the equipment that best suits their needs in terms of price and quality, regardless of its origin. The exercise of these rights is therefore not compatible with Article 37 in all the Member States except Spain and Portugal, where the national monopolies are to be adjusted progressively before the end of the transitional period provided for by the Act of Accession.

6. The provision of installation and maintenance services is a key factor in the purchasing or rental of terminal equipment. The retention of exclusive rights in this field would be tantamount to retention of exclusive marketing rights. Such rights must therefore also be abolished if the abolition of exclusive importing and marketing rights is to have any practical effect.

7. Article 59 of the Treaty provides that 'restrictions on freedom to provide services within the Community shall be progressively abolished during the transitional period in respect of nationals of Member States who are established in a State of the Community other than that of the person for whom the services are intended.' Maintenance of terminals is a service within the meaning of Article 60 of the Treaty. As the transitional period has ended, the service in question, which cannot from a commercial point of view be dissociated from the marketing of the terminals, must be provided freely and in particular when provided by qualified operators.

8. Article 90 (1) of the Treaty provides that 'in the case of public undertakings and undertakings to which Member States grant special or exclusive rights, Member States shall neither enact nor maintain in force any measure contrary to the rules contained in this Treaty, in particular to those rules provided for in Article 7 and Articles 85 to 94.'

9. The market in terminal equipment is still as a rule governed by a system which allows competition in the common market to be distorted; this situation continues to produce infringements of the competition rules laid down by the Treaty and to affect adversely the development of trade to such an extent as would be contrary to the interests of the Community. Stronger competition in the terminal equipment market requires the introduction of transparent technical specifications and type-approval procedures which meet the essential requirements mentioned in Council Directive 86/361/EEC[1] and allow the free movement of terminal equipment. In turn, such transparency necessarily entails the publication of technical specifications and type approval procedures. To ensure that the latter are applied transparently, objectively and without discrimination, the drawing-up and application of such rules should be entrusted to bodies independent of competitives in the market in question. It is essential that the specifications and type approval procedures are published simultaneously and in an orderly fashion. Simultaneous publication will also ensure that behaviour contrary to the Treaty is avoided. Such simultaneous, orderly publication can be achieved only by means of a legal instrument that is binding on all of the Member States. The most appropriate instrument to this end is a directive.

10. The Treaty entrusts the Commission with very clear tasks and gives it specific powers with regard to the monitoring of relations between the Member States and their public undertakings and enterprises to which they have delegated special or exclusive rights, in particular as regards the elimination of quantitative restrictions and measures having equivalent effect, discrimination between nationals of Member States, and competition. The only instrument, therefore, by which the Commission can efficiently carry out the tasks and powers assigned to it, is a Directive based on Article 90 (3).

11. Telecommunications bodies or enterprises are undertakings within the meaning of Article 90 (1) because they carry on an organized business activity involving the production of goods or services. They are either public undertakings or private enterprises to which the Member States have granted special or exclusive rights for the importation, marketing, connection, bringing into service of telecommunications terminal equipment and/or maintenance of such equipment. The grant and maintenance of special and exclusive rights for terminal equipment constitute measures within the meaning of that Article. The conditions for applying the exception of Article 90 (2) are not fulfilled. Even if the provision of a telecommunications network for the use of the general public is a service of general economic interest entrusted by the State to the telecommunications bodies, the abolition of their special or exclusive rights to import and market terminal equipment would not obstruct, in law or in fact, the performance of that service. This is all the more true given that Member States are entitled to subject terminal equipment to type-approval procedures to ensure that they conform to the essential requirements.

---

[1] OJ No L 217, 5. 8. 1986, p. 21.

12. Article 86 of the Treaty prohibits as incompatible with the common market any conduct by one or more undertakings that involve an abuse of a dominant position within the common market or a substantial part of it.

13. The telecommunications bodies hold individually or jointly a monopoly on their national telecommunications network. The national networks are markets. Therefore, the bodies each individually or jointly hold a dominant position in a substantial part of the market in question within the meaning of Article 86.

The effect of the special or exclusive rights granted to such bodies by the State to import and market terminal equipment is to:

— restrict users to renting such equipment, when it would often be cheaper for them, at least in the long term, to purchase this equipment. This effectively makes contracts for the use of networks subject to acceptance by the users of additional services which have no connection with the subject of the contracts,

— limit outlets and impede technical progress since the range of equipment offered by the telecommunications bodies is necessarily limited and will not be the best available to meet the requirements of a significant proportion of users.

Such conduct is expressly prohibited by Article 86 (d) and (b), and is likely significantly to affect trade between Member States.

At all events, such special or exclusive rights in regard to the terminal equipment market give rise to a situation which is contrary to the objective of Article 3 (f) of the Treaty, which provides for the institution of a system ensuring that competition in the common market is not distorted, and requires *a fortiori* that competition must not be eliminated. Member States have an obligation under Article 5 of the Treaty to obtain from any measure which could jeopardize the attainment of the objectives of the Treaty, including Article 3 (f).

The exclusive rights to import and market terminal equipment must therefore be regarded as incompatible with Article 86 in conjunction with Article 3, and the grant or maintenance of such rights by a Member State is prohibited under Article 90 (1).

14. To enable users to have access to the terminal equipment of their choice, it is necessary to know and make transparent the characteristics of the termination points of the network to which the terminal equipment is to be connected. Member States must therefore ensure that the characteristics are published and that users have access to termination points.

15. To be able to market their products, manufacturers of terminal equipment must know what technical specifications they must satisfy. Member States should therefore formalize and publish the specifications and type-approval rules, which they must notify to the Commission in draft form, in accordance with Council Directive 83/189/EEC[2]. The specifications may be extended to products imported from other Member States only insofar as they are necessary to ensure conformity with the essential requirements specified in Article 2 (17) of Directive 86/361/EEC that can legitimately be required under community law. Member States must, in any event, comply with Articles 30 and 36 of the Treaty, under which an importing Member State must allow terminal equipment legally manufactured and marketed in another Member State to be imported on to its territory, and may only subject it to such type-approval and possibly refuse approval for reasons concerning conformity with the abovementioned essential requirements.

16. The immediate publication of these specifications and procedures cannot be considered in view of their complexity. On the other hand, effective competition is not possible without such publication, since potential competitors of the bodies or enterprises with special or exclusive rights are aware of the precise specifications with which their terminal equipment must comply and of the terms of the type-approval procedures and hence their cost and

---

[2] OJ No L 109, 28. 3. 1983, p. 8.

duration. A deadline should therefore be set for the publication of specifications and the type-approval procedures. A period of two-and-a-half years will also enable the telecommunications bodies with special or exclusive rights to adjust to the new market conditions and will enable economic operators, especially small and medium-sized enterprises, to adapt to the new competitive environment.

17. Monitoring of type-approval specifications and rules cannot be entrusted to a competitor in the terminal equipment market in view of the obvious conflict of interest. Member States should therefore ensure that the responsibility for drawing up type-approval specifications and rules is assigned to a body independent of the operator of the network and of any other competitor in the market for terminals.

18. The holders of special or exclusive rights in the terminal equipment in question have been able to impose on their customers long-term contacts preventing the introduction of free competition from having a practical effect within a reasonable period. Users must therefore be given the right to obtain a revision of the duration of their contracts.

HAS ADOPTED THIS DIRECTIVE:

Article 1

For the purposes of this Directive:

— 'terminal equipment' means equipment directly or indirectly connected to the termination of a public telecommunications network to send, process or receive information. A connection is indirect if equipment is placed between the terminal and the termination of the network. In either case (direct or indirect), the connection may be made by wire, optical fibre or electromagnetically.

Terminal equipment also means receive-only satellite stations not reconnected to the public network of a Member State.

— 'undertaking' means a public or private body, to which a Member State grants special or exclusive rights for the importation, marketing, connection, bringing into service of telecommunications terminal equipment and/or maintenance of such equipment.

Article 2

Member States which have granted special or exclusive rights within the meaning of Article 1 to undertakings shall ensure that those rights are withdrawn.

They shall, not later than three months following the notification of this Directive, inform the Commission of the measures taken or draft legislation introduced to that end.

Article 3

Member States shall ensure that economic operators have the right to import, market, connect, bring into service and maintain terminal equipment. However, Member States may:

— in the absence of technical specifications, refuse to allow terminal equipment to be connected and brought into service where such equipment does not, according to a reasoned opinion of the body referred to in Article 6, satisfy the essential requirements laid down in Article 2 (17) of Directive 86/361/EEC,

— require economic operators to possess the technical qualifications needed to connect, bring into service and maintain terminal equipment on the basis of objective, non-discriminatory and publicly available criteria.

Article 4

Member States shall ensure that users have access to new public network termination points and that the physical characteristics of these points are published not later than 31 December 1988.

Access to public network termination points existing at 31 December 1988 shall be given within a reasonable period to any user who so requests.

Article 5

1. Member States shall, not later than the date mentioned in Article 2, communicate to the Commission a list of all technical specifications and type-approval procedures which are used for terminal equipment, and shall provide the publication references.

Where they have not as yet been published in a Member State, the latter shall ensure that they are published not later than the dates referred to in Article 8.

2. Member States shall ensure that all other specifications and type-approval procedures for terminal equipment are formalized and published. Member States shall communicate the technical specifications and type-approval procedures in draft form to the Commission in accordance with Directive 83/189/EEC and according to the timetable set out in Article 8.

Article 6

Member States shall ensure that, from 1 July 1989, responsibility for drawing up the specifications referred to in Article 5, monitoring their application and granting type-approval is entrusted to a body independent of public or private undertakings offering goods and/or services in the tele-communications sector.

Article 7

Member States shall take the necessary steps to ensure that undertakings within the meaning of Article 1 make it possible for their customers to terminate, with maximum notice of one year, leasing or maintenance contracts which concern terminal equipment subject to exclusive or special rights at the time of the conclusion of the contracts.

For terminal equipment requiring type-approval, Member States shall ensure that this possibility of termination is afforded by the undertakings in question no later than the dates provided for in Article 8. For terminal equipment not requiring type approval, Member States shall introduce this possibility no later than the date provided for in Article 2.

Article 8

Member States shall inform the Commission of the draft technical specifications and type-approval procedures referred to in Article 5 (2);

— not later than 31 December 1988 in respect of equipment in category A of the list in Annex I,
— not later than 30 September 1989 in respect of equipment in category B of the list in Annex I,
— not later than 30 June 1990 in respect of equipment in category C of the list in Annex I.

Member States shall bring these specifications and type-approval procedures into force after expiry of the procedure provide for by Directive 83/189/EEC.

Article 9

Member States shall provide the Commission at the end of each year with a report allowing it to monitor compliance with the provisions of Articles 2, 3, 4, 6 and 7.

An outline of the report is attached as Annex II.

Article 10

The provisions of this Directive shall be without prejudice to the provisions of the instruments of accession of Spain and Portugal, and in particular Articles 48 and 208 of the Act of Accession.

Article 11

This Directive is addressed to the Member States.

Done at Brussels, 16 May 1988.

For the Commission
Peter SUTHERLAND
Member of the Commission

ANNEX I

List of terminal equipment referred to in Article 8

Category

Additional telephone set; private automatic branch exchanges (PABXs):   A

Models: A

Telex terminals: B

Data-transmission terminals: B

Mobile telephones: B

Receive-only satellite stations not connected to the public network of a Member State: B

First telephone set: C

Other terminal equipment: C

ANNEX II

Outline of the report provided for in Article 9

Implementation of Article 2

1. Terminal equipment for which legislation is being or has been modified.

By category of terminal equipment:

   — date of adoption of the measure or,
   — date of introduction of the bill or,
   — date of entry into force of the measure.

2. Terminal equipment still subject to special or exclusive rights:

   — type of terminal equipment and rights concerned.

Implementation of Article 3

—terminal equipment, the connection and/or commissioning of which has been restricted,
— technical qualifications required, giving reference of their publication.

Implementation of Article 4

— references of publications in which the physical characteristics are specified,
— number of existing network termination points,

— number of network termination points now accessible.

Implementation of Article 6

— independent body or bodies appointed.

Implementation of Article 7

— measures put into force, and
— number of terminated contracts.

APPENDIX 8

Council Resolution of 27 April 1989 on standardization in the field of information technology and telecommunications

(89/C 117/01)

THE COUNCIL HEREBY INVITES:

— the Member States:

to nominate without delay the national standardization bodies which will participate in the procedures for the adoption of ETSI (European Telecommunication Standard Institute) standards in so far as they have not yet done so;

— ETSI and Cen-Cenelec: (European Committee for Standardization – European Committee for Electrotechnical Standardization);

(a) to quickly conclude a cooperation agreement within the ITSTC (Information Technology Steering Committee) framework;

(b) to consult with a view to forming a single European standardization in which each of the present standardization bodies would preserve its individual identity,

— the administrations, the public network operators, the industry, research institutes and users who are members of ETSI:

(a) to make available to ETSI the experts required to carry out its programme of work;

(b) to ensure that any pre-standardization and standardization work is carried out at a common level from the earliest possible stage in the work,

— the Commission:

(a) to contribute to the coherent development of ETSI and lend it its support, in particular in the programme of work related to the Community telecommunications policy;

(b) to report to it as and when necessary on the operation and progress made by ETSI[1].

---

[1] The proceedings of CEN-Cenelec are the subject of Commission reports in accordance with Council Decision 87/95/EEC of 22 December 1986 on standardization in the field of information technology and telecommunications OJ No L 36, 7. 2. 1987, p. 31.

APPENDIX 9

Council Directive of 3 May 1989 on the approximation of the laws of the Member States relating to electromagnetic compatibility

(89/336/EEC)

THE COUNCIL OF THE EUROPEAN COMMUNITIES,

Having regard to the treaty establishing the European Economic Community, and in particular Article 100a thereof,

Having regard to the proposal from the Commission[1],

In cooperation with the European Parliament[2],

Having regard to the opinion of the Economic and Social Committee[3],

Whereas it is necessary to adopt measures with the aim of progressively establishing the internal market over a period expiring on 31 December 1992; whereas the internal market comprises an area without internal frontiers in which the free movement of goods, persons, services and capital is ensured;

Whereas Member States are responsible for providing adequate protection for radio-communications and the devices, apparatus and systems whose performance may be degraded by electromagnetic disturbance produced by electrical and electronic apparatus against the degradation caused by such disturbances;

Whereas Member States are also responsible for ensuring that electric energy distribution networks are protected from electromagnetic disturbance which can affect them and, consequently, equipment fed by them;

Whereas Council Directive 86/361/EEC of 24 July 1986 on the initial stage of the recognition of type-approval for telecommunications terminal equipment[4] covers in particular the signals emitted by such equipment when it is operating normally and the protection of public telecommunications networks from harm; whereas it is therefore still necessary to provide adequate protection for these networks, including the equipment connected to them, against temporary disturbances caused by signals of an accidental nature that may be emitted by this equipment;

Whereas in some Member States, mandatory provisions define in particular the permissible electromagnetic disturbance levels that this equipment is liable to cause and its degree of immunity to such signals; whereas these mandatory provisions do not necessarily lead to different protection levels from one Member State to another but do, by their disparity, hinder trade within the Community;

Whereas the national provisions ensuring such protection must be harmonized in order to guarantee the free movement of electrical and electronic apparatus without lowering existing and justified levels of protection in the Member States;

Whereas Community legislation as it stands at present provides that, notwithstanding one of the fundamental rules of the Community, namely the free movement of goods, barriers to intra-Community trade resulting from disparities in national laws on the marketing of products have to be accepted in so far as those provisions may be recognized as necessary to satisfy essential requirements; whereas the harmonization of laws in the case in point must therefore be confined to

---

[1] OJ No C 322, 2. 12. 1987, p. 4.
[2] OJ No C 262, 10. 10. 1988, p. 82 and OJ No C 69, 20. 3. 1989, p. 72.
[3] OJ No C 134, 24. 5. 1988, p. 2.
[4] OJ No L 217, 5. 8. 1986, p. 21.

those provisions needed to comply with the protection requirements relating to electromagnetic compatibility; whereas these requirements must replace the corresponding national provisions;

Whereas this Directive therefore defines only protection requirements relating to electromagnetic compatibility; whereas, to facilitate proof of conformity with these requirements, it is important to have harmonized standards at European level concerning electromagnetic compatibility, so that products complying with them may be assumed to comply with the protection requirements; whereas these standards harmonized at European level are drawn up by private bodies and must remain non-binding texts; whereas for that purpose the European Committee for Electrotechnical Standardization (CENELEC) is recognized as the competent body in the field of this Directive for the adoption of harmonized standards in accordance with the general guidelines for cooperation between the Commission and the European Committee for Standardization (CEN) and CENELEC signed on 13 November 1984; whereas, for the purposes of this directive, a harmonized standard is a technical specification (European standard or harmonization document) adopted by CENELEC upon a remit from the Commission in accordance with the provisions of Council directive 83/189/ EEC of 28 March 1983 laying down a procedure for the provision of information in the field of technical standards and regulations[5], as last amended by Directive 88/182/EEC[6], and pursuant to the abovementioned general guidelines;

Whereas, pending the adoption of harmonized standards for the purposes of this Directive, the free movement of goods should be facilitated by accepting, as a transitional measure, on a Community level, apparatus complying with the national standards adopted, in accordance with the Community inspection procedure ensuring that such national standards meet the protection objectives of this Directive;

Whereas the EC declaration of conformity concerning the apparatus constitutes a presumption of its conformity with this Directive; whereas this declaration must take the simplest possible form;

Whereas, for apparatus covered by Directive 86/361/EEC, in order to obtain efficient protection as regards electromagnetic compatibility, compliance with the provisions of this Directive should nevertheless be certified by marks or certificates of conformity issues by bodies notified by the Member States; whereas, to facilitate the mutual recognition of marks and certificates issued by these bodies, the criteria to be taken into consideration for appointing them should be harmonized;

Whereas it is nevertheless possible that equipment might disturb radiocommunications and tele-communications networks; whereas provision should therefore be made for a procedure to reduce this hazard;

Whereas the Directive applies to the appliances and equipment covered by Directives 76/889/ EEC[7] and 76/890/EEC[8] which relate the approximation of the laws of the Member States relating to radio interference caused by electrical household appliances, portable tools and similar equipment and to the suppression of radio interference with regard to fluorescent lighting luminaires fitted with starters; whereas those Directive should therefore be repealed,

HAS ADOPTED THIS DIRECTIVE:

Article 1

For the purposes of this Directive:

1. 'apparatus' means all electrical and electronic appliances together with equipment and installations containing electrical and/or electronic components.

2. 'electromagnetic disturbance' means any electromagnetic phenomenon which may degrade the performance of a device, unit of equipment or system. An electromagnetic disturbance

---

[5] OJ No L 109, 26. 4. 1983, p. 8.
[6] OJ No L 81, 26. 3. 1988, p. 75.
[7] OJ No L 336, 4. 12. 1976, p. 1.
[8] OJ No L 336, 4. 12. 1976, p. 22.

may be electromagnetic noise, an unwanted signal or a change in the propagation medium itself.

3. 'immunity' means the ability of a device, unit of equipment or system to perform without degradation of quality in the presence of an electromagnetic disturbance.

4. 'electromagnetic compatibility' means the ability of a device, unit of equipment or system to function satisfactorily in its electromagnetic environment without introducing intolerable electromagnetic disturbances to anything in that environment.

5. 'competent body' means any body which meets the criteria listed in Annex II and is recognized as such.

6. 'EC type-examination certificate' is a document in which a notified body referred to in Article 10 (6) certifies that the type of equipment examined complies with the provisions of this directive which concern it.

Article 2

1. This Directive applies to apparatus liable to cause electromagnetic disturbance or the performance of which is liable to be affected by such disturbance.

It defines the protection requirements and inspection procedures relating thereto.

2. In so far as protection requirements specified in this Directive are harmonized, in the case of certain apparatus, by specific Directives, this Directive shall not apply or shall cease to apply with regard to such apparatus or protection requirements upon the entry into force of those specific Directives.

3. Radio equipment used by radio amateurs within the meaning of Article 1, definition 53, of the radio regulations in the International Telecommunications Convention, shall be excluded from the scope of this Directive, unless the apparatus is available commercially.

Article 3

Member States shall take all appropriate measures to ensure that apparatus as referred to in Article 2 may be placed on the market or taken into service only if it complies with the requirements laid down by this Directive when it is properly installed and maintained and when it is used for the purposes for which it is intended.

Article 4

The apparatus referred to in Article 2 shall be so constructed that:

(a) the electromagnetic disturbance it generates does not exceed a level allowing radio and telecommunications equipment and other apparatus to operate as intended;
(b) the apparatus has an adequate level of intrinsic immunity of electromagnetic disturbance to enable it to operate as intended.

The principal protection requirements are set out in Annex III.

Article 5

Member States shall not impede for reasons relating to electromagnetic compatibility the placing on the market and the taking into service of their territory of apparatus covered by this Directive which satisfies the requirements thereof.

Article 6

1. The requirements of this Directive shall not prevent the application in any Member State of the following special measures:

(a) measures with regard to the taking into service and use of the apparatus taken for a specific site in order to overcome an existing or predicted electromagnetic compatibility problem;

(b) measures with regard to the installation of the apparatus taken in order to protect the public telecommunications networks or receiving or transmitting stations used for safety purposes.

2. Without prejudice to Directive 83/189/EEC, Member States shall inform the Commission and the other Member States of the special measures taken pursuant to paragraph 1.

3. Special measures that have been recognized as justified shall be contained in an appropriate notice made by the Commission in the *Official Journal of the European Communities*.

Article 7

1. Member States shall presume compliance with the protection requirements referred to in Article 4 in the case of apparatus which is in conformity;

(a) with the relevant national standards transposing the harmonized standards, the reference numbers of which have been published in the *Official Journal of the European Communities*. Member States shall publish the reference numbers of such national standards;

(b) or with the relevant national standards referred to in paragraph 2 in so far as, in the areas covered by such standards, no harmonized standards exist.

2. Member States shall communicate to the Commission the texts of their national standards, as referred to in paragraph 1 (b), which they regard as complying with the protection requirements referred to in Article 4. The Commission shall forward such texts forthwith to the other Member States. In accordance with the procedure provided for in Article 8 (2), it shall notify the Member States of those national standards in respect of which there is a presumption of conformity with the protection requirements referred to in Article 4.

Member States shall publish the reference numbers of those standards. The Commission shall also publish them in the *Official Journal of the European Communities*.

3. Member States shall accept that where the manufacturer has not applied, or has applied only in part, the standards referred to in paragraph 1, or where no such standards exist, apparatus shall be regarded as satisfying the protection requirements has been certified by the means of attestation provided for in Article 10 (2).

Article 8

1. Where a Member State or the Commission considers that the harmonized standards referred to in Article 7 (1) (a) do not entirely satisfy the requirements referred to in Article 4, the Member State concerned or the Commission shall bring the matter before the Standing Committee set up by Directive 83/189/EEC, hereinafter referred to as 'the Committee', giving the reasons therefor. The Committee shall deliver an opinion without delay.

Upon receipt of the Committee's opinion, the Commission shall inform the Member States as soon as possible whether or not it is necessary to withdraw in whole or in part those standards from the publications referred to in Article 7 (1) (a).

2. After receipt of the communication referred to in Article 7 (2), the Commission shall consult the Committee. Upon receipt of the latter's opinion, the Commission shall inform the Member States as soon as possible whether or not the national standard in question shall enjoy the presumption of conformity and, if so, that the references thereof shall be published nationally.

If the Commission or a Member State considers that a national standard no longer satisfies the necessary conditions for presumption of compliance with the protection requirements referred to in Article 4, the Commission shall consult the Committee, which shall give its opinion without delay. Upon receipt of the latter's opinion, the Commission shall inform the Member States as soon as possible whether or not the standard in question shall continue to enjoy a presumption of conformity and, if not, that it must be withdrawn in whole or in part from the publications referred to in Article 7 (2).

Article 9

1. Where a Member State ascertains that apparatus accompanied by one of the means of attestation provided for in Article 10 does not comply with the protection requirements referred to in Article 4, it shall take all appropriate measures to withdraw the apparatus from the market, prohibit its placing on the market or restrict its free movement.

The Member State concerned shall immediately inform the Commission of any such measure, indicating the reasons for its decision and, in particular, whether non-compliance is due to:

(a) failure to satisfy the protection requirements referred to in Article 4, where the apparatus does not meet the standards referred to in Article 7 (1);
(b) incorrect application of the standards referred to in Article 7 (1);
(c) shortcomings in the standards referred to in Article 7 (1) themselves.

2. The Commission shall consult the parties concerned as soon as possible. If the Commission finds, after such consultations, that the action is justified, it shall forthwith so inform the Member State that took the action and the other Member States.

Where the decision referred to in paragraph 1 is attributed to shortcomings in the standards, the Commission, after consulting the parties, shall bring the matter before the Committee within two months if the Member State which has taken the measures intends to uphold then, and shall initiate the procedures referred to in Article 8.

3. Where apparatus which does not comply is accompanied by one of the means of attestation referred to in Article 10, the competent Member State shall take appropriate action against the author of the attestation and shall inform the Commission and the other Member States thereof.

4. The Commission shall ensure that the Member States are kept informed of the progress and outcome of this procedure.

Article 10

1. In the case of apparatus for which the manufacturer has applied the standards referred to in Article 7 (1), the conformity of apparatus with this Directive shall be certified by an EC declaration of conformity issued by the manufacturer or his authorized representative established within the Community. The declaration shall be held at the disposal of the competent authority for ten years following the placing of the apparatus on the market.

The manufacturer or his authorized representative established within the Community shall also affix the EC conformity mark to the apparatus or else to the packaging, instructions for use or guarantee certificate.

Where neither the manufacturer nor his authorized representative is established within the Community, the above obligation to keep the EC declaration of conformity available shall be the responsibility of the person who places the apparatus on the Community market.

The provisions governing the EC declaration and the EC mark are set out in Annex I.

2. In the case of apparatus for which the manufacturer has not applied, or has applied only in part, the standards referred to in Article 7 (1) or failing such standards, the manufacturer or his authorized representative established within the Community shall hold at the disposal of the relevant competent authorities, as soon as the apparatus is placed on the market, a technical construction file. This file shall describe the apparatus, set out the procedures used to ensure conformity of the apparatus with the protection requirements referred to in Article 4 and include a technical report or certificate, one or other obtained from a competent body.

The file shall be held at the disposal of the competent authorities for ten years following the placing of the apparatus on the market.

Where neither the manufacturer nor his authorized representative is established within the Community, this obligation to keep a technical file available shall be the responsibility of the person who places the apparatus on the Community market.

The conformity of apparatus with that described in the technical file shall be certified in accordance with the procedure laid down in paragraph 1.

Member States shall presume, subject to the provisions of this paragraph, that such apparatus meets the protection requirements referred to in Article 4.

3. Where the standards referred to in Article 7 (1) are not yet in existence, and without prejudice to the provisions of paragraph 2 of this Article, the apparatus concerned may, on a transitional basis until 31 December 1992 at the latest, continue to be governed by the national arrangements in force on the date of adoption of this Directive, subject to the compatibility of such arrangements with the provisions of the Treaty.

4. Conformity of apparatus covered by Article 2 (2) of Directive 86/361/EEC with the provisions of this Directive shall be certified in accordance with the procedure laid down in paragraph 1 once the manufacturer or his authorized representative established within the Community has obtained an EC type-examination certificate concerning this apparatus issued by one of the notified bodies referred to in paragraph 6 of this Article.

5. The conformity of apparatus designed for the transmission of radiocommunications, as defined in the International Telecommunication Union Convention, with the provisions of this Directive shall be certified in accordance with the procedure laid down in paragraph 1 once the manufacturer or his authorized representative established within the Community has obtained an EC type-examination certificate concerning this apparatus issued by one of the notified bodies referred to in paragraph 6 below.

This provision shall not apply to the above apparatus where it is designed and intended exclusively for radio amateurs within the meaning of Article 2 (3).

6. Each Member State shall notify the Commission and the other Member States of the competent authorities referred to in this Article and of the bodies responsible for issuing the EC type-examination certificates referred to in paragraphs 4 and 5. The Commission shall publish a list of these authorities and bodies, for information purposes, in the *Official Journal of the European Communities* and shall ensure that the list is updated.

Such notification shall state whether those bodies are competent for all apparatus covered by this Directive or whether their responsibility is limited to certain specific areas.

Member States shall apply the criteria listed in Annex II for the assessment of the bodies to be notified.

Bodies which comply with the assessment criteria fixed by the relevant harmonized standards shall be presumed to comply with the aforementioned criteria.

A Member State which has notified a body must withdraw approval if it finds that the body no longer meets the criteria listed in Annex II. It shall forthwith inform the Commission and the other Member States thereof.

Article 11

Directive 76/889/EEC and Directive 76/890/EEC shall be repealed as from 1 January 1992.

Article 12

1. By 1 July 1991, Member States shall adopt and publish the laws, regulations and administrative provisions necessary to comply with this Directive. They shall inform the Commission thereof.

They shall apply these provisions as from 1 January 1992.

2. Member States shall communicate to the Commission the texts of the provisions of national law which they adopt in the field covered by this Directive.

Article 13

This Directive is addressed to the Member States.

Done at Brussels, 3 May 1989.

for the Council
The President
P. SOLBES

ANNEX I

1. EC declaration of conformity

The EC declaration of conformity must contain the following:

— description of the apparatus to which it refers,
— reference to the specifications under which conformity is declared, and, where appropriate, to the national measures implemented to ensure the conformity of the apparatus with the provisions of the Directive,
— identification of the signatory empowered to bind the manufacturer or his authorized representative,
— where appropriate, reference to the EC type-examination certificate issued by a notified body.

2. EC conformity mark

— The EC conformity mark shall const of the letters CE as set out below and the figures of the year in which the mark was affixed.

— This mark should, where appropriate, be accompanied by the distinctive letters used by the notified body issuing the EC type-examination certificate.
— Where apparatus is the subject of other Directives providing for the EC conformity mark, the affixing of the EC mark shall also indicate conformity with the relevant requirements of those other Directives.

ANNEX II

Criteria for the assessment of the bodies to be notified

The bodies designated by the Member States must fulfil the following minimum conditions:

1. availability of personnel and of the necessary means and equipment;

2. technical competence and professional integrity of personnel;

3. independence, in carrying out the tests, preparing the reports, issuing the certificates and performing the verification function provided for in this Directive, of staff and technical personnel in relation to all circles, groups of persons directly or indirectly concerned with the product in question;

4. maintenance of professional secrecy by personnel;

5. possession of civil liability insurance unless such liability is covered by the State under national law.

Fulfilment of the conditions under points 1 and 2 shall be verified at intervals by the competent authorities of the Member States.

ANNEX III

Illustrative list of the principal protection requirements

The maximum electromagnetic disturbance generated by the apparatus shall be such as not to hinder the use of in particular the following apparatus:

(a) domestic radio and television receivers
(b) industrial manufacturing equipment
(c) mobile radio equipment
(d) mobile radio and commercial radiotelephone equipment
(e) medical and scientific apparatus
(f) information technology equipment
(g) domestic appliances and household electronic equipment
(h) aeronautical and marine radio apparatus
(i) educational electronic equipment
(j) telecommunications networks and apparatus
(k) radio and television broadcast transmitters
(l) lights and fluorescent lamps.

Apparatus, and especially the apparatus referred to in (a) to (l), should be constructed in such a way that it has an adequate level of electromagnetic immunity in the usual electromagnetic compatibility environment where the apparatus is intended to work so as to allow its unhindered operation taking into account the levels of disturbance generated by apparatus complying with the standards laid down in Article 7.

The information required to enable use in accordance with the intended purpose of the apparatus must be contained in the instructions accompanying the apparatus.

APPENDIX 10

Commission Decision of 3 May 1990 amending the lists of standardization institutions set out in the Annex to Council Directive 83/189/EEC

(90/230/EEC)

THE COMMISSION OF THE EUROPEAN COMMUNITIES,

Having regard to the Treaty establishing the European Economic Community,

Having regard to Council Directive 83/189/EEC of 28 March 1983 laying down a procedure for the provision of information in the field of technical standards and regulations[1], as last amended by Directive 88/182/EEC[2], and in particular Article 2 (1) thereof,

Having regard to the opinion of the Standard Committee set up pursuant to Article 5 of Directive 83/189/EEC,

Whereas Article 2 (1) of Directive 83/189/EEC provides that the Commission may amend or supplement the lists of standardization institutions supplied in the Annex to the Directive of the basis of communication from the Member States;

Whereas communications from several Member States require the updating of the said lists,

HAS ADOPTED THIS DECISION:

Article 1

The list set out in the Annex to Directive 83/189/EEC shall be replaced by the list set out in the Annex to this Decision.

Article 2

This Decision is addressed to the Member States.

Done at Brussels, 3 May 1990.

For the Commission
Martin BANGEMANN
Vice-President

---

[1] OJ No L 109, 26. 4. 1983, p. 8.
[2] OJ No L 81, 26. 3. 1988, p. 75.

ANNEX

LIST 1

Standards institutions

1. AENOR (Spain):
   Asociatión Española de Normalizacín y
   Certifcación,
   C/Fernández de la Hoz, no 52,
   E-28010 Madrid;

2. AFNOR (France):
   Association française de normalisation,
   Tour Europe – Cedex 7,
   F-92080 Paris La Défense;

   UTE (France):
   Union technique de l'électricté (UTE),
   Cedex 64,
   F-92052 Paris La Défense;

3. BSI (United Kingdom):
   British Standards Institution,
   2, Park Street,
   Uk-London W1A 2BS;

   BEC (United Kingdom):
   British Electrotechnical Committee,
   British Standards Institution,
   2, Park Street,
   UK-London W1A 2BS;

4. DS (Denmark):
   Danks Standardiseringsrad,
   Aurehøjvej 12
   Postboks 77,
   DK-2900 Hellerup 12;

   DEK (Denmark):
   Dansk Elektrotecknisk Komité (DEK),
   Strandgade, 36 st.,
   DK-1401 Kobenhavn K;

5. DIN (Germany):
   DIN Deutsches Institut für Normung eV,
   Burggrafenstraße 6,
   Postfach 1107,
   D-1000 Berlin 30;

   DKE (Germany):
   Deutsche Elektrotechnische Komission
   im
   DIN und VDE (DKE),
   Stresemannallee 15,
   D-6000 rankfurt am Main 70;

6. ELOT (Greece):
   Hellenic Organization for Standardization

(ELOT),
Acharnon St, 313,
GR-11145 Athens;

7. IBN/BIN (Belgium):
   Institut belge de normalization (IBN),
   Belgisch Instituut voor Normalisatie
   (BIN),
   29, avenue de la Brabançonne/
   Brabançonnelaan,
   B-1040 Bruxelles/Brussel;

   CEB/BEC (Belgium):
   Comité electrotechnique Belge (CEB),
   Belgisch Elektrotechnisch Comité (BEC),
   3, Galerie Ravenstein, boîte 11,
   3, Ravensteingalerij, bus 11,
   B-1000 Bruxelles/Brussel;

8. IPQ (Portugal):
   Instituto Porguês da Qualidade,
   Rua José Estêvão, 83 A,
   P-1199 Lisboa Codex;

9. ITM (Luxembourg):
   Inspection du travail et des mines,
   26, rue Zithe – BP 27,
   L-2010 Luxembourg;

   Service de l'Énergie de l'État,
   34, avenue Marie-Thérèse,
   BP 10,
   L-2010 Luxembourg;

10. NSAI (Ireland):
    National Standards Authority of Ireland,
    Glasnevin,
    IRL-Dublin 9;

    ETCI (Ireland):
    Electro-Technical Council of Ireland
    (ETCI),
    National Standards Authority of Ireland,
    Glasnevin,
    IRL-Dublin 9;

11. NNI (Netherlands):
    Nederlands Normalisatie Instituut,
    Postbus 5059,
    NL-2600 GB Delft;

    NEC (Netherlands):
    Nederlands Elektrotechnisch Comité

(NEC),
Kalfjeslaan 2,
Postbus 5059,
NL-2600 AA Delft;

12. UNI (Italy:
Ente Nazionale italiano di unificazione,
Piazza Armando Diaz 2,
I-20123 Milano,

CEI (Italy):
Comitato Elettrotecnico Italiano (CEI),
Viale Monza 259,
I-20126 Milano;

13. CEN:
Comité Européen de normalisation,
2, rue Bréderode, boîte 5,
B-1000 Bruxelles;

CENELEC
Comité Européen de normalision
électrotechnique,
2, rue Bréderode, boîte 5,
B-1000 Bruxelles.

LIST 2

National standards institutions in the Member States of the European Community

(Same as those in List 1 except for CEN and CENELEC)

APPENDIX 11

Council Directive of 28 June 1990 on the establishment of the internal market for telecommunications services through the implementation of open network provision

(90/387/EEC)

THE COUNCIL OF THE EUROPEAN COMMUNITIES,

Having regard to the Treaty establishing the European Economic Community, and in particular Article 100a thereof,

Having regard to the proposal from the Commission[1],

In cooperation with the European Parliament[2],

Having regard to the opinion of the Economic and Social Committee[3],

Whereas Article 8 a of the Treaty stipulates that the internal market shall comprise an area without internal frontiers in which the free movement of services is ensured, in accordance with the provisions of the Treaty;

Whereas the Commission submitted a Green paper on the development of the common market for telecommunications services and equipment, dated 30 June 1987, and a communication on the implementation of that Green paper up to 1992, dated 9 February 1988;

Whereas the Council adopted on 30 June 1988 a resolution on the development of the common market for telecommunications services and equipment up to 1992[4];

Whereas the full establishment of a Community-wide market in telecommunications services will be promoted by the rapid introduction of harmonized principles and conditions for open network provision;

Whereas, since situations differ and technical and administrative constraints exist in the Member States, this objective should be realized in stages;

Whereas the conditions of open network provision must be consistent with certain principles and must not restrict access to networks and services except for reasons of general public interest, hereinafter referred to as 'essential requirements';

Whereas the definition and application of such principles and essential requirements must take full account of the fact that any restrictions of the right to provide services within and between Member States must be objectively justified, must follow the principle of proportionality and must not be excessive in relation to the aim pursued;

Whereas the conditions of open network provision must not allow for any additional restrictions on the use of the public telecommunications network and/or public telecommunications services except those restrictions which may be derived from the exercise of special or exclusive rights granted by Member States and which are compatible with Community law;

Whereas tariff principles should be clearly laid down to ensure fair and transparent conditions for all users;

Whereas this entire directive must be read in the light of Annex III which lays down a work programme for the first three years;

---

[1] OJ No C 39, 16. 2. 1989, p. 8.
[2] OJ No C 158, 26. 6. 1989, p. 300, OJ No C 149, 18. 6. 1990.
[3] OJ No C 159, 16. 6. 1989, p. 37.
[4] OJ No C 257, 4. 10. 1988, p. 1.

Whereas the establishment of harmonized conditions of open network provision must be a progressive process and must be prepared with the assistance of a committee composed of representatives of the Member States, which consults the representatives of the telecommunications organizations, the users, the consumers, the manufacturers and the service providers; whereas this process must also be open to all parties concerned and therefore sufficient time must be given for public comment;

Whereas the Community-wide definition of harmonized technical interfaces and access conditions must be based on the definition of common technical specifications based on international standards and specifications;

Whereas work to be undertaken in this area must take full account, *inter alia*, of the framework resulting from the provisions of Council Directive 83/189/EEC of 28 March 1983 laying down a procedure for the provision of information in the field of technical standards and regulations[6], as last amended by Directive 88/182/EEC[6], Council Directive 86/361/EEC of 24 July 1986 on the initial stage of the mutual recognition of type approval for telecommunications terminal equipment[7] and Council Decision 87/95/EEC of 22 December 1986 on standardization in the field of information technology and telecommunications[8];

Whereas the formal adoption on 12 February 1988 of the statutes of the European Telecommunications Standards Institute (ETSI) and of the associated internal rules has created a new mechanism for producing European telecommunications standards;

Whereas the Council in its resolution of 27 April 1989 on standardization in the field of information technology and telecommunications[9] supported the work of ETSI and invited the Commission to contribute to the coherent development of ETSI and lend it its support;

Whereas the Community-wide definition and implementation of harmonized network termination points establishing the physical interface between the network infrastructure and users' and other service providers' equipment will be an essential element of the overall concept of open network provision;

Whereas Commission Directive 88/301/EEC of 16 May 1988 on competition in the markets in telecommunications terminal equipment[10] requires Member States to ensure that users who so request are given access to network termination points within a reasonable time period;

Whereas one of the principal aims of the establishment of an internal market in telecommunications services must be the creation of conditions to promote the development of Europe-wide services;

Whereas, in its abovementioned resolution of 30 June 1988, the Council considered the taking fully into account of the external aspects of Community measures on telecommunications to be a major policy goal;

Whereas the Community attaches very great importance to the continued growth of cross-border telecommunications services, to the contribution that telecommunications services provided by companies, firms or natural persons established in a Member State may make to the growth of the Community market, and to the increased participation of Community service providers in third country markets; whereas it will therefore be necessary, as specific Directives are drawn up, to ensure that these objectives are taken into account with a view to reaching a situation where the progressive realization of the internal market for telecommunications services will, where appropriate, be accompanied by reciprocal market opening in other countries;

---

[5] OJ No L 109, 26. 4. 1983, p. 8.
[6] OJ No L 81, 26. 3. 1988, p. 75.
[7] OJ No L 217, 5. 8. 1986, p. 21.
[8] OJ No L 36, 7. 2. 1987, p. 31.
[9] OJ No C 117, 11. 5. 1989, p. 1.
[10] OJ No L 131, 27. 5. 1988, p. 73.

Whereas this result should be achieved preferably through multilateral negotiations in the framework of GATT, it being understood that bilateral discussions between the Community and third countries may also contribute to this process;

Whereas this Directive should not address the problems of mass media, meaning problems linked to broadcasting and distribution of television programmes via telecommunications means, in particular cable television networks, which need special consideration;

Whereas neither should this Directive address the question of communication via satellite for which, according to the abovementioned Council resolution of 30 June 1988, a common position should be worked out;

Whereas the Council, on the basis of a report which the Commission is to submit to the European Parliament and the Council, and in accordance with Article 100b of the Treaty, will review, during 1992, any remaining conditions for access to telecommunications services which have not been harmonized, the effects of these conditions on the workings of the internal market for telecommunications services, and the extent to which this market needs to be further opened up,

HAS ADOPTED THIS DIRECTIVE:

Article 1

1. This Directive concerns the harmonization of conditions for open and efficient access to and use of public telecommunications networks and, where applicable, public telecommunications services.

2. The conditions referred to in paragraph 1 are designed to facilitate the provision of services using public telecommunications networks and/or public telecommunications services, within and between Member States, and in particular the provision of services by companies, firms or natural persons established in a Member State other than that of the company, firm or natural person for whom the services are intended.

Article 2

For the purposes of this Directive:

1. 'telecommunications organizations' means public or private bodies, to which a Member State grants special or exclusive rights for the provision of a public telecommunications network and, where applicable, public telecommunications services.

   For the requirements of this Directive, Member States shall notify the Commission of the bodies to which they have granted special or exclusive rights;

2. 'special or exclusive rights' means the rights granted by a Member State or a public authority to one or more public or private bodies through any legal, regulatory or administrative instrument reserving them the right to provide a service or undertake an activity;

3. 'public telecommunications network' means the public telecommunications infrastructure which permits the conveyance of signals between defined network termination points by wire, by microwave, by optimal means or by other electromagnetic means;

4. — 'telecommunications services' means services whose provision consists wholly or partly in the transmission and routing of signals on a telecommunications network by means of telecommunications processes, with the exception of radio broadcasting and television;
   — 'public telecommunications services' means telecommunications services whose supply Member States have specifically entrusted *inter alia* to one or more telecommunications organizations;

5. 'network termination point' means all physical connections and their technical access specifications which form part of the public telecommunications network and are necessary for access to and efficient communication through that public network;

6. 'essential requirements' means the non-economic reasons in the general interest which may cause a Member State to restrict access to the public telecommunications network or public

telecommunications services. These reasons are security of network operations, maintenance of network integrity and, in justified cases, interoperability of services and data protection.

Data protection may include protection of personal data, the confidentiality of information transmitted or stored as well as the protection of privacy;

7. 'voice telephony' means the commercial provision for the public or direct transport of real-time speech via the public switches network or networks such that any user can use equipment connected to a network termination point to communicate with another user of equipment connected to another termination point;

8. 'telex service' means the commercial provision for the public of direct transport of telex messages in accordance with the relevant 'Comité consultatif international télégraphique et téléphonique' (CCITT) recommendation via the public switched network or networks, whereby any users can use equipment connected to a network termination point to communicate with another user using another termination point;

9. 'packet- and circuit-switched data services' means the commercial provision for the public of direct transport of data via the public switched network or networks such that any equipment connected to a network termination point can communicate with equipment connected to another termination point;

10. 'open network provision conditions' means the conditions, harmonized according to the provisions of this Directive, which concern the open and efficient access to public telecommunications networks and, where applicable, public telecommunications services and the efficient use of those networks and services.

Without prejudice to their application on a case-by-case basis, the open network provision conditions may include harmonized conditions with regard to:

— technical interfaces, including the definition and implementation of network termination points, where required,
— usage conditions, including access to frequencies where required,
— tariff principles;

11. 'technical specifications', 'standards' and 'terminal equipment' are given the same meaning for those terms as in Article 2 of Directive 86/361/EEC.

Article 3

1. Open network provision conditions must comply with a number of basic principles set out hereafter, namely that:

— they must be based on objective criteria,
— they must be transparent and published in an appropriate manner,
— they must guarantee equality of access and must be non-discriminatory, in accordance with Community law.

2. Open network provision conditions must not restrict access to public telecommunications networks or public telecommunications services, except for reasons based on essential requirements, within the framework of Community law, namely:

— security of network operations,
— maintenance of network integrity,
— interoperability of services, in justified cases,
— protection of data, as appropriate.

In addition, the conditions generally applicable to the connection of terminal equipment to the network shall apply.

3. Open network provision conditions may not allow for any additional restrictions on the use of the public telecommunications networks and/or public telecommunications services except the

restrictions which may be derived from the exercise of special or exclusive rights granted by Member States and which are compatible with Community law.

4. The Council, acting in accordance with Article 100a of the Treaty, may, if necessary, modify the points set out in paragraphs 1 and 2.

5. Without prejudice to the specific Directives provided for in Article 6 and in so far as the application of the essential requirements referred to in paragraph 2 of this Article may cause a Member State to limit access to one of its public telecommunications networks or services, the rules for uniform application of the essential requirements, in particular concerning the interoperability of services and the protection of data, shall be determined, where appropriate, by the Commission, in accordance with the procedure laid down in Article 10.

Article 4

1. Open network provision conditions shall be defined in stages under the procedure set out hereafter.

2. Open network provision conditions shall concern the areas selected in accordance with the list in Annex 1.

The Council, acting in accordance with Article 100a of the Treaty, may, if necessary, modify this list.

3. Using the list referred to in paragraph 2, the Commission shall draw up a work programme each year, under the procedure laid down in Article 9.

4. For the work programme referred to in paragraph 3, the Commission shall:

(a) initiate detailed analysis, in consultation with the committee referred to in Article 9, and draw up reports on the results of this analysis;
(b) invite, by publication of a notice to that effect in the *Official Journal of the European Communities*, public comment by all parties concerned on the reports on the detailed analysis provided for in subparagraph (a). The period for submitting such comment shall be not less than three months from the date of publications of the said notice:
(c) request, where appropriate, the European Telecommunications Standards Institute (ETSI) to draw up European standards, taking account of international standardization as a basis for setting up, where required, within specified time limits, harmonized technical interfaces and/or service features. In so doing, ETSI shall coordinate, in particular, with the Joint European Standards Institution CEN/Cenelec;
(d) draw up proposals for open network provision conditions in accordance with Article 3 and with the open network provision reference framework described in Annex II.

5. For 1990, 1991 and 1992 a work programme shall be drawn up in order to implement the guidelines in Annex III.

Article 5

1. Reference to European standards drawn up as a basis for harmonized technical interfaces and/ or service features for open network provision according to Article 4 (4) (c) shall be published in the *Official Journal of the European Communities* as suitable for open network provision.

2. The standards mentioned under paragraph 1 shall carry with them the presumption:

(a) that a service provider who complies with those standards fulfils the relevant essential requirements, and
(b) that a telecommunications organization which complies with those standards fulfils the requirement of open and efficient access.

3. If the implementation of European standards within the meaning of Article 5 (2) appears inadequate to ensure the interoperability of transfrontier services in one or more Member States, reference to European standards may be made compulsory under the procedure laid down in

Article 10, to the extent strictly necessary to ensure such interoperability and to improve freedom of choice for users. The procedure provided for in this paragraph may in no way affect the implementation of Articles 85 and 86 of the Treaty.

4. Where a Member State or the Commission considers that the harmonized standards mentioned under paragraph 1 do not correspond to the objective of open and efficient access, in particular the basic principles and the essential requirements referred to in Article 3, the Commission or the Member State concerned shall bring the matter before the committee referred to in Article 9, giving the reasons therefore. The committee shall deliver an opinion without delay.

5. In the light of the committee's opinion and after consultation of the standing committee set up by Directive 83/189/EEC, the Commission shall inform the Member States whether or not it is necessary to withdraw references to those standards from the *Official Journal of the European Communities*.

Article 6

Following the completion of the procedures set out in Articles 4 and 5, and acting in accordance with Article 100a of the Treaty, the Council shall adopt specific Directives establishing open network provision conditions including a time schedule for implementing them.

Article 7

The Council, acting in accordance with Article 100a of the Treaty, taking Article 8c of the Treaty into consideration, shall, where required, adopt measures for harmonizing declaration and/or licensing procedures for the provision of services via public and/or licensing procedures for the provision of services via public telecommunications networks, with a view to establishing conditions in which there would be mutual recognition of declaration and/or licensing procedures.

Article 8

During 1992 the Council, on the basis of a report which the Commission shall submit to the European Parliament and the Council, shall review progress on harmonization and any restrictions on access to telecommunications networks and services still remaining, the effects of those restrictions on the operation of the internal telecommunications market, and measures which could be taken to remove these restrictions, in conformity with Community law, taking account of technological development and in accordance with the procedure provided for under Article 100b of the Treaty.

Article 9

1. The Commission shall be assisted by a committee of an advisory nature composed of the representatives of the Member States and chaired by the representative of the Commission.

The committee shall, in particular, consult the representatives of the telecommunications organizations, the users, the consumers, the manufacturers and the service providers. It shall lay down its rules of procedure.

2. The representative of the Commission shall submit to the committee a draft of the measures to be taken. The Committee shall deliver its opinion on the draft, within a time limit which the chairman may lay down according to the urgency of the matter, if necessary by taking a vote.

The opinion shall be recorded in the minutes; in addition, each Member State shall have the right to ask to have its position recorded in the minutes.

The Commission shall take the utmost account of the opinion delivered by the committee. It shall inform the committee of the manner in which its opinion has been taken into account.

Article 10

1. Notwithstanding the provisions of Article 9, the following procedure shall apply in respect of the matters covered by Article 3 (5) and Article 5 (3).

2. The representative of the Commission shall submit to the committee a draft of the measures to be taken. The committee shall deliver its opinion on the draft within a time limit which the chairman may lay down according to the urgency of the matter. The opinion shall be delivered by the majority laid down in Article 148 (2) of the Treaty in the case of decisions which the Council is required to adopt on a proposal from the Commission. The votes of the representatives of the Member States within the Committee shall be weighted in the manner set out in that Article. The chairman shall not vote.

3. The Commission shall adopt the measures envisaged if they are in accordance with the opinion of the committee.

4. If the measures envisaged are not in accordance with the opinion of the committee, or if no opinion is delivered, the Commission shall, without delay, submit to the Council a proposal relating to the measures to be taken. The Council shall act by a qualified majority.

If on the expiry of a period of three months from the date of referral to the Council, the Council has not acted, the proposed measures shall be adopted by the Commission.

Article 11

1. So Member States shall bring into force the laws, regulations and administrative provisions necessary in order to comply with this Directive before 1 January 1991 at the latest. They shall forthwith inform the Commission thereof.

2. Member States shall communicate to the Commission the texts of the provisions of national law which they adopt in the field governed by this Directive.

Article 12

This Directive is addressed to the Member States.

Done at Luxembourg, 28 June 1990.

For the Council
The President
M. GEOGHEGAN-QUINN

ANNEX I

Areas for which open network provision conditions may be drawn up in accordance with Article 4

Area shall be selected from the following list in accordance with the procedures laid down in Article 4:

1. leased lines;

2. packet- and circuit-switched data services;

3. Integrated Services Digital Network (ISDN);

4. voice telephony service;

5. telex service;

6. mobile services, as applicable;

subject to further study,

7. new types of access to the network, such as access, under certain conditions, to the circuits connecting subscriber premises to the public network exchange ('data over voice') and access to the network's new intelligent functions, according to progress on definition and technological development;

8. access to the broadband network, according to progress on definition and technological development.

ANNEX II

Reference framework for drawing up proposals on open network provision conditions in accordance with Article 4 (4) (d)

Proposals on open network provision conditions as defined in Article 2 (10) should be drawn up in accordance with the following reference framework:

1. *Common principles*

   In drawing up the conditions described in this Annex, due account will be taken of the relevant rules of the Treaty.

   Open network provision conditions shall be drawn up in such a way as to facilitate the service providers' and users' freedom of action without unduly limiting the telecommunications organizations' responsibility for the functioning of the network and the best possible condition of communications channels.

   Member States may, in accordance with Community law, take any measure enabling the telecommunications organizations to develop the new opportunities deriving from open network provision.

2. *Harmonized technical interfaces and/or service features*

   In drawing up open network provision conditions the following scheme should be taken into account for the definition of technical interfaces at appropriate open network termination points:

   — for existing services and networks, existing interfaces should be adopted;
   — for entirely new services or the improvement of existing services, existing interfaces should also be adopted, as far as feasible. When existing interfaces are not suitable, enhancements and/or new interfaces will have to be specified;
   — for networks that are still to be introduced, but for which the standardization programme has already commenced, open network provision requirements falling within the terms of Article 3 should be taken into account when specifying new interfaces.

   Open network provision proposals must, wherever possible, be in line with the ongoing work in the European Conference of Postal and Telecommunications Administrations (CEPT), CCITT, ETSI and CEN-Cenelec.

   Work undertaken in this area shall take full account of the framework resulting from the provisions of Council Directive 83/189/EEC of 28 March 1983 laying down a procedure for the provision of information in the field of technical standards and regulations[11], as last amended by Directive 88/182/EEC[12], Council Directive 86/361/EEC of 24 July 1986 on the initial stage of the mutual recognition of type approval for telecommunications terminal equipment[13] and Council Decision 87/95/EEC of 22 December 1986 on standardization in the field of information technology and telecommunications[14].

   Additional features will be identified where required. They may be classified as:

   — inclusive if they are provided in association with a specific interface and included in the standard offering,

---

[11] OJ No L 109, 26. 4. 1983, p. 8.
[12] OJ No L 81, 26. 3. 1988, p. 75.
[13] OJ No L 217, 5. 8. 1986, p. 21.
[14] OJ No L 36, 7. 2. 1987, p. 31.

— optional if they can be requested as an option with regard to a specific open network provision offering.

Work shall include the drawing up of proposals for time schedules for the introduction of interfaces and service features, taking account of the state of development of telecommunications networks and services in the Community.

3. *Harmonized supply and usage conditions*

Supply and usage conditions shall identify conditions of access and of provision of services, as far as required.

They may include as applicable:

(a) supply conditions such as:

— maximum provision time (delivery period),
— quality of service, in particular the quality of transmission,
— maintenance,
— network malfunction reporting facilities;

(b) usage conditions such as:

— conditions for resale of capacity,
— conditions for shared use,
— conditions for interconnection with public and private networks.

Usage conditions may include conditions regarding access to frequencies, as applicable, and measures concerning protection of personal data and confidentiality of communications, where required.

Harmonized tariff principles

Tariff principles must be consistent with the principles set out in Article 3 (1).

These principles imply, in particular, that:

— tariffs must be based on objective criteria and especially in the case of services and areas subject to special or exclusive rights must in principle be cost-oriented, on the understanding that the fixing of the actual tariff level will continue to be the province of national legislation and is not the subject of open network provision conditions. When these tariffs are determined, one of the aims should be the definition of efficient tariff principles throughout the Community while ensuring a general service for all,
— tariffs must be transparent and must be properly published,
— in order to leave users a choice between the individual service elements and where technology so permits, tariffs must be sufficiently unbundled in accordance with the competition rules of the Treaty. In particular, additional features introduced to provide certain specific extra services must, as a general rule, be charged independently of the inclusive features and transportation as such.
— tariffs must be non-discriminatory and guarantee equality of treatment.

Any charge for access to network resources or services must comply with the principles set out above and with the competition rules of the Treaty and must also take into account the principle of fair sharing in the global cost of the resources used and the need for a reasonable level of return on investment.

There may be different tariffs, in particular to take account of excess traffic during peak periods and lack of traffic during off-periods, provided that the tariff differentials are commercially justifiable and do not conflict with the above principles.

ANNEX III

Guidelines for implementation of the framework Directive up to 31 December 1992

In an initial phase, and without prejudice to the procedures laid down in Article 4 (2) and (3), work to be undertaken in 1990, 1991 and 1992 concerning Articles 4, 5 and 6 will implement the following priorities:

1. adoption of specific Directives pursuant to Article 6 covering leased lines and the voice telephony service;

2. implementation by 1 January 1991 of harmonized technical interfaces and/or service features for packet-switched data services and ISDN (Integrated Services Digital Network); reference to such interfaces and features may be made compulsory before that date in accordance with the procedure set out in Article 5 (3);

3. adoption by the Council by 1 July 1991, acting on a proposal from the Commission, of a recommendation on the supply of technical interfaces, conditions of usage and tariff principles applying to provision of packet-switched data switches complying with open network principles; this recommendation would in particular call on Member States to ensure that at least one such service was provided on their territory;

4. adoption by the Council on 1 January 1992, acting on a proposal from the Commission, of a similar recommendation on ISDN;

5. examination in 1992, with a view to its adoption, on a proposal from the Commission, of a specific Directive on packet-switched data services. The proposal should take into account the initial results of the implementation of the recommendation referred to in point 3;

6. subsequent examination of a proposal for a Directive on ISDN. That proposal should also take into account the initial results of the implementation of the recommendation referred to in point 4.

APPENDIX 12

Commission Directive of 28 June 1990 on competition in the markets for telecommunications services

(90/388/EEC)

THE COMMISSION OF THE EUROPEAN COMMUNITIES,

Having regard to the Treaty establishing the European Economic Community, and in particular Article 90 (3) thereof,

Whereas:

(1) The improvement of telecommunications in the Community is an essential condition for the harmonious development of economic activities and a competitive market in the Community, from the point of view of both service providers and users. The Commission has therefore adopted a programme, set out in its Green paper on the development of the common market for telecommunications services and equipment and in its communication on the implementation of the Green paper by 1992, for progressively introducing competition into the telecommunications market. The programme does not concern mobile telephony and paging services, and mass communication services such as radio for television. The Council, in its resolution of 30 June 1988[1], expressed broad support for the objectives of this programme, and in particular the progressive creation of an open Community market for telecommunications services. The last decades have seen considerable technological advances in the telecommunications sector. These allow an increasingly varied range of services to be provided, notably data transmission services, and also make it technically and also make it technically and economically possible for competition to take place between different service providers.

(2) In all the Member States the provision and operation of telecommunications networks and the provision of related services are generally vested in one or more telecommunications organizations holding exclusive or special rights. Such rights are characterized by the discretionary powers which the State exercises in various degrees with regard to access to the market for telecommunications services.

(3) The organizations entrusted with the provision and operation of the telecommunications network are undertakings within the meaning of Article 90 (1) of the Treaty because they carry on an organized business activity, namely the provision of telecommunications services. They are either public undertakings or private enterprises to which the State has granted exclusive or special rights.

(4) Several Member States, while ensuring the performance of public service tasks, have already revised the system of exclusive or special rights that used to exist in the telecommunications sector in their country. In all cases, the system of exclusive or special rights has been maintained in respect of the provision and operation of the network. In some Member States, it has been maintained for all telecommunications services, while in others such rights cover only certain services. All Member States have either themselves imposed or allowed their telecommunications administrations to impose restrictions on the free provision of telecommunications services.

(5) The granting of special or exclusive rights to one or more undertakings to operate the network derives from the discretionary power of the State. The granting by a Member State of such rights inevitably restricts the provision of such services by other undertakings to or from other Member States.

---

[1] OJ No C 257, 4. 10. 1988, p. 1.

(6)   In practice, restrictions on the provision of telecommunications services within the mean-
      ing of Article 59 to or from other Member States consist mainly in the prohibition on
      connecting leased lines by means of concentrators, multiplexers and other equipment to
      the switched telephone network, in imposing access charges for the connection that are
      out of proportion to the service provided, in prohibiting the routing of signals to or from
      third parties by means of leased lines or applying volume sensitive tariffs without eco-
      nomic justification or refusing to give service providers access to the network. The effect
      of the usage restrictions and the excessive charges in relation to net cost is to hinder the
      provision to or from other Member States of such telecommunications services as:

      — services designed to improve telecommunications functions, e.g. conversion of the
        protocol, code, format or speed,
      — information services providing access to data bases,
      — remote data-processing services,
      — message storing and forwarding services, e.g. electronic mail,
      — transaction services, e.g. financial transactions, electronic commercial data transfer,
        teleshopping and telereservations,
      — teleaction services, e.g. telemetry and remote monitoring.

(7)   Articles 55, 56 and 66 of the Treaty allow exceptions on non-economic grounds to the
      freedom to provide services. The restrictions permitted are those connected, even occa-
      sionally, with the exercise of official authority, and those connected with public policy,
      public security or public health. Since these are exceptions, they must be interpreted
      restrictively. None of the telecommunications services is connected with the exercise of
      official authority involving the right to use undue powers compared with the ordinary
      law, privileges of public power or a power of coercion over the public. The supply of
      telecommunication services cannot in itself threaten public policy and cannot affect public
      health.

(8)   The Court of Justice case law also recognizes restrictions on the freedom to provide
      services if they fulfil essential requirements in the general interest and are applied without
      discrimination and in proportion to the objective. Consumer protection does not make it
      necessary to restrict freedom to provide telecommunications services since this objective
      can also be attained through free competition. Nor can the protection of intellectual
      property be invoked in this connection. The only essential requirements derogating from
      Article 59 which could justify restrictions on the use of the public network are the main-
      tenance of the integrity of the network, security of network operations and in justified
      cases, interoperability and data protection. The restrictions imposed, however, must be
      adapted to the objectives pursued by these legitimate requirements. Member States will
      have to make such restrictions known to the public and notify them to the Commission
      to enable it to assess their proportionality.

(9)   In this context, the security of network operations means ensuring the availability of the
      public network in case of emergency. The technical integrity of the public network means
      ensuring its normal operation and the interconnection of public networks in the commu-
      nity on the basis of common technical specifications. The concept of interoperability of
      services means complying with such technical specifications introduced to increase the
      provision of services and the choice available to users. Data protection means measures
      taken to warrant the confidentiality of communications and the protection of personal
      data.

(10) Apart from the essential requirements which can be included as conditions in the licen-
      sing or declaration procedures, Member States can include conditions regarding public-
      service requirements which constitute objective, non-discriminatory and transparent trade
      regulations regarding the conditions of permanence, availability and quality of the service.

(11) When a Member State has entrusted a telecommunications organization with the task of
      providing packet or circuit switched data services for the public in general and when this

service may be obstructed because of competition by private providers, the Commission can allow the Member State to impose additional conditions for the provision of such a service, with respect also to geographical coverage. In assessing these measures the Commission in the context of the achievement of the fundamental objectives of the Treaty referred to in Article 2 thereof, including that of strengthening the Community's economic and social cohesion as referred to in Article 130a, will also take into account the situation of those Member States in which the network for the provision of the packet or circuit switched services is not yet sufficiently developed and which could justify the deferment for these Member States until 1 January 1996 of the date for prohibition on the simple resale of leased line capacity.

(12) Article 59 of the Treaty requires the abolition of any other restriction on the freedom of nationals of Member States who are established in a Community country to provide services to persons in other Member States. The maintenance or introduction of any exclusive or special right which does not correspond to the abovementioned criteria is therefore a breach of Article 90 in conjunction with Article 59.

(13) Article 86 of the Treaty prohibits as incompatible with the common market any conduct by one or more undertakings that involves an abuse of a dominant position within the common market or a substantial part of it. Telecommunications organizations are also undertakings for the purposes of this Article because they carry out economic activities, in particular the service they provide by making telecommunications networks and services available to users. This provision of the network constitutes a separate services market as it is not interchangeable with other services. On each national market the competitive environment in which the network and the telecommunications services are provided is homogeneous enough for the Commission to be able to evaluate the power held by the organizations providing the services on these territories. The territories of the Member States constitute distinct geographical markets. This is essentially due to the existing difference between the rules governing conditions of access and technical operation, relating to the provision of the network and of such services. Furthermore, each Member State market forms a substantial part of the common market.

(14) In each national market the telecommunications organizations hold individually or collectively a dominant position for the creation and the exploitation of the network because they are the only ones with networks in each Member State covering their whole territory of those States and because their governments granted them the exclusive right to provide this network either alone or in conjunction with other organizations.

(15) Where a state grants special or exclusive rights to provide telecommunications services to organizations which already have a dominant position in creating and operating the network, the effect of such rights is to strengthen the dominant position by extending it to services.

(16) Moreover, the special or exclusive rights granted to telecommunications organizations by the State to provide certain telecommunications services mean such organizations:

(a) prevent or restrict access to the market for these telecommunications services by their competitors, thus limiting consumer choice, which is liable to restrict technological progress to the detriment of consumers;

(b) compel network users to use the services subject to exclusive rights, and thus make the conclusion of network utilization contracts dependent on acceptance of supplementary services having no connection with the subject of such contracts.

Each of these types of conduct represents a specific abuse of a dominant position which is likely to have an appreciable effect on trade between Member States, as all the services in question could in principle be supplied by providers from other Member States. The structure of competition within the common market is substantially changed by them. At all events, the special or exclusive rights for these services give rise to a situation which is contrary to the objective in Article 3 (f) of the Treaty, which provides for the institution of a system ensuring that competition in the common market is not distorted, and requires *a fortiori* that competition must not be eliminated. Member States have an obligation under Article 5 of the Treaty to abstain from any measure which could jeopardize the attainment of the objectives of the Treaty, including that of Article 3 (f).

(17)   The exclusive rights to telecommunications services granted to public undertakings or undertakings to which Member States have granted special or exclusive rights for the provision of the network are incompatible with Article 90 (1) in conjunction with Article 86.

(18)   Article 90 (2) of the Treaty allows derogation from the application of Articles 59 and 86 of the Treaty where such application would obstruct the performance, in law or in fact, of the particular task assigned to the telecommunications organizations. This task consists in the provision and exploitation of a universal network, i.e. one having general geographical coverage, and being provided to any service provider or user upon request within a reasonable period of time. The financial resources for the development of the network still derive mainly from the operation of the telephone service. Consequently, the opening-up of voice telephony to competition could threaten the financial stability of the telecommunications organizations. The voice telephony service, whether provided from the present telephone network or forming part of the ISDN service, is currently also the most important means of notifying and calling up emergency services in charge of public safety.

(19)   The provision of leased lines forms an essential part of the telecommunications organizations' tasks. There is at present, in almost all Member States, a substantial difference between charges for use of the data transmission service on the switched network and for use of leased lines. Balancing those tariffs without delay could jeopardise this task. Equilibrium in such charges must be achieved gradually between now and 31 December 1992. In the meantime it must be possible to require private operators not to offer to the public a service consisting merely of the resale of leased line capacity, i.e. including only such processing, switching of data, storing, or protocol conversion as is necessary for transmission in real time. The Member States may therefore establish a declaration system through which private operators would undertake not to engage in simple resale. However, no other requirement may be imposed on such operators to ensure compliance with this measure.

(20)   These restrictions do not affect the development of trade to such an extent as would be contrary to the interests of the Community. Under these circumstances, the restrictions are compatible with Article 90 (2) of the Treaty. This may also be the case as regards the measures adopted by Member States to ensure that the activities of private service providers do not obstruct the public switched-data service.

(21)   The rules of the Treaty, including those on competition, apply to telex services; however, the use of this service is gradually declining throughout the Community owing to the emergence of competing means of telecommunication such as telefax. The abolition of current restrictions on the use of the switched telephone network and leased lines will allow telex messages to be retransmitted. In view of this particular trend, an individual approach is necessary. Consequently, this Directive should not apply to telex services.

(22)   The Commission will in any event reconsider in the course of 1992 the remaining special or exclusive rights on the provision of services taking account of technological development and the evolution towards a digital infrastructure.

(23)   Member States may draw up fair procedures for ensuring compliance with the essential requirements without prejudice to the harmonization of the latter at Community Level within the framework of the Council Directives on open network provision (ONP). As regards data-switching, Member States must be able, as part of such procedures, to

require compliance with trade regulations from the standpoint of conditions of permanence, availability and quality of the service, and to include measures to safeguard the task of general economic interest which they have entrusted to a telecommunications organization. The procedures must be based on specific objective criteria and be applied without discrimination. The criteria should in particular be justified and proportional to the general interest objective, and be duly motivated and published. The Commission must be able to examine them in depth in the light of the rules on free competition and freedom to provide services. In any event, Member States that have not notified the Commission of their planned licensing criteria and procedures within a given time may no longer impose any restrictions on the freedom to provide data transmission services to the public.

(24)   Member States should be given more time to draw up general rules on the conditions governing the provision of packet- or circuit-switched data services for the public.

(25)   Telecommunications services should not be subject to any restriction, either as regards free access by users to the services, or as regards the processing of data which may be carried out before messages are transmitted through the network or after messages have been received, except where this is warranted by an essential requirement in proportion to the objective pursued.

(26)   The digitization of the network and the technological improvement of the terminal equipment connected to it have brought about an increase in the number of functions previously carried out within the network and which can now be carried out by users themselves with increasingly sophisticated terminal equipment. It is necessary to ensure that suppliers of telecommunications services, and notably suppliers of telephone and packet or circuit-switched data transmission services enable operators to use these functions.

(27)   Pending the establishing of Community standards with a view to an open network provision (ONP), the technical interfaces currently in use in the Member States should be made publicly available so that firms wishing to enter the markets for the services in question can take the necessary steps to adapt their services to the technical characteristics of the networks. If the Member States have not yet established such technical interfaces, they should do so as quickly as possible. All such draft measures should be communicated to the Commission in accordance with Council Directive 83/189/EEC[2], as last amended by Directive 88/182/EEC[3].

(28)   Under national legislation, telecommunications organizations are generally given the function of regulating telecommunications services, particularly as regards licensing, control of type-approval and mandatory interface specifications, frequency allocation and monitoring of conditions of use. In some cases, the legislation lays down only general principles governing the operation of the licensed services and leaves it to the telecommunications organizations to determine the specific operating conditions.

(29)   This dual regulatory and commercial function of the telecommunications organizations has a direct impact on firms offering telecommunications services in competition with the organizations in question. By this bundling of activities, the organizations determine or, at the very least, substantially influence the supply of services offered by their competitors. The delegation to an undertaking which has a dominant position for the provision and exploitation of the network, of the power to regulate access to the market for telecommunication services constitutes a strengthening of that dominant position. Because of the conflict of interests, this is likely to restrict competitors' access to the markets in telecommunications services and to limit users' freedom of choice. Such arrangements may also limit the outlets for equipment for handling telecommunications messages and, con-

---

[2] OJ No L 109, 26. 4. 1983, p. 8.
[3] OJ No L 81, 26. 3. 1988, p. 75.

sequently, technological progress in that field. This combination of activities therefore constitutes an abuse of the dominant position of telecommunications organizations within the meaning of Article 86. If it is the result of a State measure, the measure is also incompatible with Article 90 (1) in conjunction with Article 86.

(30) To enable the commission to carry out effectively the monitoring task assigned to it by Article 90 (3), it must have available certain essential information. That information must in particular give the Commission a clear view of the measures of Member States, so that it can ensure that access to the network and the various related services are provided by each telecommunications organization to all its customers on non-discriminatory tariff and other terms. Such information should cover:

— measures taken to withdraw exclusive rights pursuant to this Directive,
— the conditions on which licenses to provide telecommunications services are granted.

The Commission must have such information to enable it to check, in particular, that the users of the network and services, including telecommunications organizations where they are providers of services, are treated equally and fairly.

(31) The holders of special or exclusive rights to provide telecommunications services that will in future be open to competition have been able in the past to impose long-term contracts on their customers. Such contracts would in practice limit the ability of any new competitors to offer their services to such customers and of such customers to benefit from such services. Users must therefore be given the right to terminate their contracts within a reasonable length of time.

(32) Each Member State at present regulates the supply of telecommunications services according to its own concepts. Even the definition of certain services differs from one Member State to another. Such differences cause distortions of competition likely to make the provision of cross-frontier telecommunications services more difficult for economic operators. This is why the Council, in its resolution of 30 June 1988, considered that one of the objectives of a telecommunications policy was the creation of an open Community market for telecommunication services, in particular through the rapid definition, in the form of Council Directives, of technical conditions, conditions of use and principles governing charges for an open network provision (ONP). The Commission has presented a proposal to this end to the Council. Harmonization of the conditions of access is not however the most appropriate means of removing the barriers to trade resulting from infringements of the Treaty. The Commission has a duty to ensure that the provisions of the Treaty are applied effectively and comprehensively.

(33) Article 90 (3) assigns clearly-defined duties and powers to the Commission to monitor relations between Member States and their public undertakings and undertakings to which they have granted special or exclusive rights, particularly as regards the removal of obstacles to freedom to provide services, discrimination between nationals of the Member States and competition. A comprehensive approach is necessary in order to end the infringements that persist in certain Member States and to give clear guidelines to those Member States that are reviewing their legislation so as to avoid further infringements. A Directive within the meaning of Article 90 (3) of the Treaty is therefore the most appropriate means of achieving that end,

HAS ADOPTED THIS DIRECTIVE:

Article 1

1. For the purposes of this Directive:

— 'telecommunication organizations' means public or private bodies, and the subsidies they control, to which a Member State grants special or exclusive rights for the provision of a public telecommunications network and, when applicable, telecommunications services.

— 'special or exclusive rights' means the rights granted by a Member State or a public authority to one or more public or private bodies through any legal, regulatory or administrative instrument reserving them the right to provide a service or undertake an activity,
— 'public telecommunications network' means the public telecommunications infrastructure which permits the conveyance of signals between defined network termination points by wire, by microwave, by optimal means or by other electromagnetic means,
— 'telecommunications services' means services whose provision consists wholly or partly in the transmission and routing of signals on the public telecommunications network by means of telecommunications processes, with the exception of radio-broadcasting and television,

'network termination point' means all physical connections and their technical access specifications which form part of the public telecommunications network and are necessary for access to and efficient communication through that public network,

— 'essential requirements' means the non-economic reasons in the general interest which may cause a Member State to restrict access to the public telecommunications network or public telecommunications services. These reasons are security of network operations, maintenance of network integrity, and, in justified cases, interoperability of services and data protection.

Data protection may include protection of personal data, the confidentiality of information transmitted or stored as well as the protection of privacy,

— 'voice telephony' means the commercial provision for the public of direct transport and switching of speech in real-time between public switched network termination points, enabling any user to use equipment connected to such a network termination point in order to communicate with another termination point,
— 'telex service' means the commercial provision for the public of direct transmission of telex messages in accordance with the relevant Comité consultatif international télégraphique et télélephonique (CCITT) recommendation between public switched network termination points, enabling any user to use equipment connected to such a network termination point in order to communicate with another termination point,
— 'packet- and circuit-switched data services' means the commercial provision for the public of direct transport of data between public switched network termination points, enabling any user to use equipment connected to such a network termination point in order to communicate with another termination point,
— 'simple resale of capacity' means the commercial provision on leased lines for the public of data transmission as a separate service, including only such switching, processing, data storage or protocol conversion as is necessary for transmission in real time to and from the public switched network.

2. This Directive shall not apply to telex, mobile radiotelephony, paging and satellite services.

Article 2

Without prejudice to Article 1 (2), Member States shall withdraw all special or exclusive rights for the supply of telecommunications services other than voice telephony and shall take the measures necessary to ensure that any operator is entitled to supply such telecommunications services.

Member States which make the supply of such services subject to a licensing or declaration procedure aimed at compliance with the essential requirements shall ensure that the conditions for the grant of licenses are objective, non-discriminatory and transparent, that reasons are given for any refusal, and that there is a procedure for appealing against any such refusal.

Without prejudice to Article 3, Member States shall inform the Commission no later than 31 December 1990 of the measures taken to comply with this Article and shall inform it of any existing regulations or of plans to introduce new licensing procedures or to change existing procedures.

Article 3

As regards packet- or circuit-switched data services, Member States may, until 31 December 1992, under the authorization procedures referred to in Article 2, prohibit economic operators from offering leased line capacity for simple resale to the public.

Member States shall, no later than 30 June 1992, notify to the commission at the planning stage any licensing or declaration procedure for the provision of packet- or circuit-switched data services for the public which are aimed at compliance with:

— essential requirements, or
— trade regulations relating to conditions of permanence, availability and quality of the service, or
— measures to safeguard the task of general economic interest which they have entrusted to a telecommunications organization for the provision of switched data services, if the performance of that task is likely to be obstructed by the activities of private service providers.

The whole of these conditions shall form a set of public-service specifications and shall be objective, non-discriminatory and transparent.

Member States shall ensure, no later than 31 December 1992, that such licensing or declaration procedures for the provision of such services are published.

Before they are implemented, the Commission shall verify the compatibility of these projects with the Treaty.

Article 4

Member States which maintain special or exclusive rights for the provision and operation of public telecommunications networks shall take the necessary measures to make the conditions governing access to the networks objective and non-discriminatory and publish them.

In particular, they shall ensure that operators who so request can obtain leased lines within a reasonable period, that there are no restrictions on their use other than those justified in accordance with Article 2.

Member States shall inform the Commission no later than 31 December 1990 of the steps they have taken to comply with this article.

Each time the charges for leased lines are increased, Member States shall provide information to the Commission on the factors justifying such increases.

Article 5

Without prejudice to the relevant international agreements, Member States shall ensure that the characteristics of the technical interfaces necessary for the use of public networks are published by 31 December 1990 at the latest.

Member States shall communicate to the Commission, in accordance with Directive 83/189/EEC, any draft measure drawn up for this purpose.

Article 6

Member States shall, as regards the provision of telecommunications services, and existing restrictions on the processing of signals before their transmission via the public network or after their reception, unless the necessity of these restrictions for compliance with public policy or essential requirements is demonstrated.

Without prejudice to harmonized Community rules adopted by the Council on the provision of an open network, Member States shall ensure as regards service providers including the telecommunications organizations that there is no discrimination either in the conditions of use or in the charges payable.

Member States shall inform the Commission of the measures taken or draft measures introduced in order to comply with this Article by 31 December 1990 at the latest.

Article 7

Member States shall ensure that from 1 July 1991 the grant of operating licenses, the control of type approval and mandatory specifications, the allocation of frequencies and surveillance of usage conditions are carried out by a body independent of the telecommunications organizations.

They shall inform the Commission of the measures taken or draft measures introduced to that end no later than 31 December 1990.

Article 8

Member States shall ensure that as soon as the relevant special or exclusive rights have been withdrawn, telecommunications organizations make it possible for customers bound to them by a contract with more than one year to run for the supply of telecommunications services which was subject to such a right at the time it was concluded to terminate the contract at six months' notice.

Article 9

Member States shall communicate to the Commission the necessary information to allow it to draw up, for a period of three years, at the end of each year, an overall report on the application of this Directive. The Commission shall transmit this report to the Member States, the Council, the European Parliament and the Economic and Social Committee.

Article 10

In 1992, the Commission will carry out an overall assessment of the situation in the tele-communications sector in relation to the aims of this Directive.

In 1994, the Commission shall assess the effects of the measures referred to in Article 3 in order to see whether any amendments need to be made to the provisions of that Article, particularly in the light of technological evolution and the development of trade within the Community.

Article 11

This Directive is addressed to the Member States.

Done at Brussels, 28 June 1990.

For the Commission
Leon BRITTAN
Vice-President

APPENDIX 13

Council Directive of 17 September 1990 on the procurement procedures of entities operating in the water, energy, transport and telecommunications sectors

(90/531/EEC)

THE COUNCIL OF THE EUROPEAN COMMUNITIES,

Having regard to the Treaty establishing in the European Economic Community and in particular the last sentence of Article 57 (2), Article 66, Article 100a and Article 113 thereof,

Having regard to the proposal from the Commission[1],

In cooperation with the European Parliament[2],

Having regard to the opinion of the Economic and Social Committee[3],

Whereas the measures aimed at progressively establishing the internal market, during the period up to 31 December 1992, need to be taken; whereas the internal market consists of an area without internal frontiers in which free movement of goods, persons, services and capital is guaranteed;

Whereas the European Council has drawn conclusions concerning the need to bring about a single internal market;

Whereas restrictions on the free movement of goods and on the freedom to provide services in respect of supply contracts awarded in the water, energy, transport and telecommunications sectors are prohibited by the terms of Articles 30 and 59 of the Treaty;

Whereas Article 97 of the Euratom Treaty prohibits any restrictions based on nationality as regards companies under the jurisdiction of a Member State where they desire to participate in the construction of nuclear installations of a scientific or industrial nature in the Community;

Whereas these objectives also require the coordination of the procurement procedures applied by the entities operating in these sectors;

Whereas the White Paper on the completion of the internal market contains an action programme and a timetable for opening up public procurement markets in sectors which are currently excluded from Council Directive 71/305/EEC of 26 July 1971 concerning the coordination of procedures for the award of public works contracts[4], as last amended by Council Directive 89/440/EEC[5], and Council Directive 77/62/EEC of 21 December 1976 coordinating procedures for the award of public supply contracts[6], as last amended by Directive 88/295/EEC[7];

Whereas among such excluded sectors are those concerning the provision of water, energy and transport services and, as far as Directive 77/62/EEC is concerned, the telecommunications sector;

Whereas the main reason for their exclusion was that entities providing such services are in some cases governed by public law, in others by private law;

Whereas the need to ensure a real opening-up of the market and a fair balance in the application of procurement rules in these sectors requires that the entities to be covered must be identified on a different basis than by reference to their legal status;

---

[1] OJ No C 264, 16. 10. 1989, p. 22.
[2] OJ No C 158, 26. 6. 1989, p. 258 and OJ No C 175, 16. 7. 1990, p. 78.
[3] OJ No C 139, 5. 6. 1989, pp. 23 and 31.
[4] OJ No L 185, 16. 8. 1971, p. 5.
[5] OJ No L 210, 21. 7. 1989, p. 1.
[6] OJ No L 13, 15. 1. 1977, p. 1.
[7] OJ No L 127, 20. 5. 1988, p. 1.

Whereas, in the four sectors concerned, the procurement problems to be solved are of a similar nature, so permitting them to be addressed in one instrument;

Whereas, among the main reasons why entities operating in these sectors do not purchase on the basis of Community-wide competition is the closed nature of the markets in which they operate, due to the existence of special or exclusive rights granted by the national authorities, concerning the supply to, provision or operation of, networks for providing the service concerned, the exploitation of a given geographical area for a particular purpose, the provision or operation of public tele-communications networks or the provision of public telecommunications services;

Whereas the other main reason for the absence of Community-wide competition in these areas results from various ways in which national authorities can influence the behaviour of these entities, including participation in their capital and representation in the entities' administrative, managerial or supervisory bodies;

Whereas this Directive should not extend to activities of those entities which either fall outside the sectors of water, energy and transport services or outside the telecommunications sector, or which fall within those sectors but nevertheless are directly exposed to competitive forces in markets to which entry is unrestricted;

Whereas it is appropriate that these entities apply common procurement procedures in respect of their activities relating to water; whereas certain entities have been covered up to now by the Directives 71/305/EEC and 77/62/EEC in respect of their activities in the field of hydraulic engineering projects, irrigation, land drainage or the disposal and treatment of sewage;

Whereas, however, procurement rules of the type proposed for supplies of goods are inappropriate for purchases of water, given the need to procure water from sources near the area it will be used;

Whereas, when specific conditions are fulfilled, exploitation of a geographical area with the aim of exploring for or extracting oil, gas, coal or other solid fuels may be made subject to alternative arrangements which will enable the same objective of opening up contracts to be achieved; whereas the Commission must ensure that these conditions are complied with by the Member States who implement these alternative arrangements;

Whereas the Commission has announced that it will propose measures to remove obstacles to cross-frontier exchanges of electricity by 1992; whereas procurement rules of the type proposed for supplies of goods would not make it possible to overcome existing obstacles to the purchases of energy and fuels in the energy sector; whereas, as a result, it is not appropriate to include such purchases in the scope of this Directive, although it should be borne in mind that this exemption will be re-examined by the Council on the basis of a Commission report and Commission proposals;

Whereas Regulations (EEC) No 3975/87[8] and (EEC) No 3976/87[9], Directive 87/601/EEC[10] and Decision 87/602/EEC[11] are designed to introduce more competition between the entries offering air transport services to the public and it is therefore not appropriate for the time being to include such entities in the scope of this Directive although the situation ought to be reviewed at a later stage in the light of progress made as regards competition;

Whereas, in view of the competitive position of Community shipping, it would be inappropriate for the greater part of the contracts in this sector to be subject to detailed procedures; whereas the situation of shippers operating sea-going ferries should be kept under review; whereas certain inshore and river ferry services operated by public authorities should no longer be excluded from the scope of Directives 71/305/EEC and 77/62/EEC;

Whereas it is appropriate to facilitate compliance with provisions relating to activities not covered by this Directive;

[8] OJ No L 374, 31. 12. 1987, p. 1.
[9] OJ No L 374, 31. 12. 1987, p. 9.
[10] OJ No L 374, 31. 12. 1987, p. 12.
[11] OJ No L 374, 31. 12. 1987, p. 19.

Whereas this Directive should not apply to procurement contracts which are declared secret or may affect basic State security interests or are concluded according to other rules set up by existing international agreements or international organizations;

Whereas the Community's or the Member States' existing international obligations must not be affected by the rules of this Directive;

Whereas products, works or services must be described by reference to European specifications; whereas, in order to ensure that a product, work or service fulfils the use for which it is intended by the contracting entity, such reference may be complemented by specifications which do not change the nature of the technical solution or solutions set out in the European specification;

Whereas the principles of equivalence and of mutual recognition of national standards, technical specifications and manufacturing methods are applicable in the field of application of this Directive;

Whereas, when the contracting entities define by common award with tenderers the deadlines for receiving tenders, they shall comply with the principle of non-discrimination, and whereas, if there is no such agreement, it is necessary to lay down suitable provisions;

Whereas it could prove useful to provide for greater transparency as to the requirements regarding the protection and conditions of employment applicable in the Member State in which the works are to be carried out;

Whereas it is appropriate that national provisions for regional development requirements to be taken into consideration for the award of public words contracts should be made to conform to the objectives of the Community and be in keeping with the principles of the Treaty;

Whereas contracting entities must not be able to reject abnormally low tenders before having requested in writing explanations as to the constituent elements of the tender;

Whereas, within certain limits, preference should be given to an offer of Community origin where there are equivalent offers of third country origin;

Whereas this Directive should not prejudice the position of the Community in any current or future international negotiations;

Whereas, based on the results of such international negotiations, this Directive should be extendable to offers of third country origin, pursuant to a Council Decision;

Whereas the rules to be applied by the entities concerned should establish a framework for sound commercial practice and should leave a maximum of flexibility;

Whereas, as a counterpart for such flexibility and in the interest of mutual confidence, a minimum level of transparency must be ensured and appropriate methods adopted for monitoring the application of this Directive;

Whereas it is necessary to adapt Directives 71/305/EEC and 77/62/EEC to establish well-defined fields of application; whereas the scope of Directive 71/305/EEC should not be reduced, except as regards in the water and telecommunications sectors; whereas the scope of Directive 77/62/EEC should not be reduced, except as regards certain contracts in the water sector; whereas the scope of Directives 71/305/EEC and 77/62/EEC should not, however, be extended to contracts awarded by carriers by land, air, sea, inshore or inland waterway which, although carrying out economic activities of an industrial or commercial nature, belong to the State administration and are carried out only for reasons of public service should be covered by those Directives;

Whereas this Directive should be re-examined in the light of experience;

Whereas the opening up of contracts, on 1 January 1993, in the sectors covered by this Directive might have an adverse effect upon the economy of the Kingdom of Spain; whereas the economies of the Hellenic Republic and the Portuguese Republic will have to sustain even greater efforts;

whereas it is appropriate that these Member States be granted adequate additional periods to implement this Directive,

HAS ADOPTED THIS DIRECTIVE:

TITLE I

General provisions

Article 1

for the purposes of this Directive:

1. 'public authorities' shall mean the State, regional or local authorities, bodies governed by public law, or associations formed by one or more of such authorities or bodies governed by public law.

    A body is considered to be public law where it:

    — is established for the specific purpose of meeting needs in the general interest, not being of a commercial or industrial nature, and
    — has legal personality, and
    — is financed for the most part by the State, or regional or local authorities, or other bodies governed by public law, or is subject to management supervision by those bodies, or has an administrative, managerial or supervisory board more than half of whose members are appointed by the State, regional or local authorities, or other bodies governed by public law;

2. 'public undertaking' shall mean any undertaking over which the public authorities exercise directly or indirectly a dominant influence by virtue of their ownership of it, their financial participation therein, or the rules which govern it. A dominant influence on the part of the public authorities shall be presumed when these authorities, directly or indirectly, in relation to an undertaking:

    — hold the major of the undertaking's subscribed capital, or
    — control the majority of the votes attaching to shares issued by the undertaking, or
    — can appoint more than half of the members of the undertaking's administrative, managerial or supervisory body;

3. 'supply and works contracts' shall mean contacts for pecuniary interest concluded in writing between one of the contracting entities referred to in Article 2 and a supplier or contractor and which have as their object:

    (a) in the case of supply contracts, the purchase, lease, rental or hire-purchase, with or without options to buy, of products or of software services. These contracts may in addition cover siting and installation operations.

    Software services shall be covered by this definition where they are procured by a contracting entity exercising and activity defined in Article 2 (2) (d) and are for use in the operation of a public telecommunications network or are intended to be used in a public telecommunications service as such;

    (b) in the case of works contracts, either the execution, or both the execution and design or the realization, by whatever means, of building or civil engineering activities referred to in Annex XI. These contracts may, in addition, cover supplies and services necessary for their execution.

    Contracts which include the provision of services other than those referred to in (a) and (b) shall be regarded as supply contracts if the total value of supplies, including siting and installation operations necessary for the execution of the contract and of software services within the meaning of subparagraph (a), is greater than the value of the other services covered by the contract;

4. 'framework agreement' shall mean an agreement between one of the contracting entities defined in Article 2 and one or more suppliers or contractors, the purpose of which is to establish the terms, in particular with regard to the prices and, where appropriate, the quantity envisaged, governing the contracts to be awarded during a given period;

5. 'tenderer' shall mean a supplier or contractor who submits a tender and 'candidate' shall mean a person who has sought an invitation to take part in a restricted or negotiated procedure;

6. 'open, restricted and negotiated procedures' shall mean the award procedures applied by contracting entities whereby:

   (a) in the case of open procedures, all interested suppliers or contractors may submit tenders;

   (b) in the case of the restricted procedures, only candidates invited by the contracting entity may submit tenders;

   (c) in the case of negotiated procedures, the contracting entity consults suppliers or contractors of its choice and negotiates the terms of the contract with one or more of them;

7. 'technical specifications' shall mean the technical requirements contained in particular in the tender documents, defining the characteristics of a set of works, material, product or supply, and enabling a piece of work, a material, a product or a supply to be objectively described in a manner such that it fulfils the use for which is it intended by the contracting entity. These technical prescriptions may include quality, performance, safety or dimensions, as well as requirements applicable to the material, product, or supply as regards quality assurance, terminology, symbols, testing and test methods, packaging, marking or labelling. In the case of works contracts, they may also include rules for the design and costing, the test, inspection and acceptance conditions for works and methods or techniques of construction and all other technical conditions which the contracting entity is in a position to prescribe under general or specific regulations, in relation to the finished works and to the materials or parts which they involve;

8. 'standard' shall mean a technical specification approved by a recognized standardizing body for repeated and continuous application, compliance with which is in principle not compulsory;

9. 'European standard' shall mean a standard approved by the European Committee for Standardization (CEN) or by the European Committee for Electrotechnical standardization (CENELEC) as a 'European Standard (EN)' or 'Harmonization Document (HD)', according to the common rules of those organizations, or by the European Telecommunications Standards Institute (ETSI) according to its own rules as a 'European Telecommunications Standard (ETS)';

10. 'common technical specification' shall mean a technical specification drawn up in accordance with a procedure recognized by the Member States which a view to uniform application in all Member States and published in the *Official Journal of the European Communities*;

11. 'European technical approval' shall mean a favourable technical assessment of the fitness for use of a product for a particular purpose, based on fulfilment of the essential requirements for building works, by means of the inherent characteristics of the product and the defined conditions of application and use, as provided for in Council Directive 89/106/EEC of 21 December 1988 for the approximation of laws, regulations and administrative provisions of the Member States relating to construction products[12]. European technical approval shall be issued by an approval body designated for this purpose by the Member State;

12. 'European specification' shall mean a common technical specification, a European technical approval or a national standard implementing a European standard;

---

[12] OJ No L 40, 11. 2. 1989, p. 12.

13. 'public telecommunications network' shall mean the public telecommunications infrastructure which enables to be conveyed between defined network termination points by wire, by microwave, by optical means or by other electromagnetic means.

'Network termination point' shall mean all physical connections and their technical access specifications which form part of the public telecommunications network and are necessary for access to, and efficient communication through, that public network;

14. 'public telecommunications services' shall mean telecommunications services the provision of which the Member States have specifically assigned notably to one or more telecommunications entities.

'Telecommunications services' shall mean services the provision of which consists wholly or partly in the transmission and routing of signals on the public telecommunications network by means of telecommunications processes, with the exception of radio-broadcasting and television.

Article 2

1. This Directive shall apply to contracting entities which:

(a) are public authorities or public undertakings and exercise one of the activities referred to in paragraph 2;

(b) or, when they are not public authorities or public undertakings, have as one of their activities any of those referred to in paragraph 2 or any combination thereof and operate on the basis of special or exclusive rights granted by a competent authority of a Member State.

2. Relevant activities for the purposes of this Directive shall be:

(a) the provision or operation of fixed networks intended to provide a service to the public in connection with the production, transport or distribution of:

   (i)   drinking water, or
   (ii) electricity, or
   (iii) gas or heat,

or the supply of drinking water, electricity, gas or heat to such networks;

(b) the exploitation of a geographical area for the purpose of

   (i)   exploring for or extracting oil, gas, coal or other solid fuels, or
   (ii) the provision of airport, maritime or inland port or other terminal facilities to carriers by air, sea or inland waterway;

(c) the operation of networks providing a service to the public in the field of transport by railway, automated systems, tramway, trolley bus, bus or cable.

As regards transport services, a network shall be considered to exist where the service is provided under operating conditions laid down by a competent authority of a Member State, such as conditions on the routes to be served, the capacity to be made available or the frequency of the service;

(d) the provision or operation of public telecommunications networks or the provision of one or more public telecommunications services.

3. For the purpose of applying paragraph 1 (b), special or exclusive rights shall mean rights deriving from authorizations granted by a competent authority of the Member State concerned, by law, regulation or administrative action, having as their result the reservation for one or more entities of the exploitation of an activity defined in paragraph 2.

A contracting entity shall be considered to enjoy special or exclusive rights in particular where:

(a) for the purpose of constructing the networks or facilities referred to in paragraph 2, it may take advantage of a procedure for the expropriation or use of property or may place network equipment on, under or over the public highway;

(b) in the case of paragraph 2 (a), the entity supplies with drinking water, electricity, gas or heat a network which is itself operated by an entity enjoying special or exclusive rights granted by a competent authority of the Member State concerned.

4. The provision of bus transport services to the public shall not be considered to be a relevant activity within the meaning of paragraph 2 (c) where other entities are free to provide those services, either in general or in a particular geographical area, under the same conditions as the contracting entities.

5. The supply of drinking water, electricity, gas or heat to networks which provide a service to the public by a contracting entity other than public authority shall not be considered as a relevant activity within the meaning of paragraph 2 (a) where:

(a) in the case of drinking water or electricity:

— the production of drinking water or electricity by the entity concerned takes place because its consumption is necessary for carrying out an activity other than that referred to in paragraph 2, and

— supply to the public network depends only on the entity's own consumption and has not exceeded 30% of the entity's total production of drinking water or energy, having regard to the average for the preceding three years, including the current year;

(b) in the case of gas or heat:

— the production of gas or heat by the entity concerned is the unavoidable consequence of carrying on an activity other than that referred to in paragraph 2, and

— supply to the public network is aimed only at the economic exploitation of such production and amounts to not more than 20% of the entity's turnover having regard to the average for the preceding three years, including the current year.

6. The contracting entities listed in Annexes I to X shall fulfil the criteria set out above. In order to ensure that the lists are as exhaustive as possible, Member States shall notify the Commission of amendments to their lists. The Commission shall revise Annexes I to X in accordance with the procedure in Article 32.

Article 3

1. Member States may request the Commission to provide that exploitation of geographical areas for the purpose of exploring for, or extracting, oil, gas, coal or other solid fuels shall not be considered to be an activity defined in Article 2 (2) (b) (i) and that entities shall not be considered as operating under special or exclusive rights within the meaning of Article 2 (3) (b) by virtue of carrying on one or more of these activities, provided that all the following conditions are satisfied with respect to the relevant national provisions concerning such activities:

(a) at the time when authorization to exploit such a geographical area is requested, other entities shall be free to seek authorization for that purpose under the same conditions as the contracting entities;

(b) the technical and financial capacity of entities to engage in particular activities shall be established prior to any evaluation of the merits of competing applications for authorization;

(c) authorization to engage in those activities shall be granted on the basis of objective criteria concerning the way in which it is intended to carry out the exploitation for extraction, which shall be established and published prior to the requests and applied in a non-discriminatory manner;

(d) all conditions and requirements concerning the carrying out or termination of the activity, including provisions on operating obligations, royalties, and participation in the capital or revenue of the entities, shall be established and made available prior to the requests for authorization being made and then applied in a non-discriminatory manner; every change concerning these conditions and requirements shall be applied to all the entities concerned, or else amendments must be made in a non-discriminatory manner; however, operating obligations need not be established until immediately before the authorization is granted; and

(e) contracting entities shall not be required by any law, regulation, administrative requirement, agreement or understanding to provide information on a contracting entity's intended or actual sources of procurement, except at the request of national authorities and exclusively with a view to the objectives mentioned in Article 36 of the Treaty.

2. Member States which apply the provisions of paragraph 1 shall ensure, through the conditions of the authorization or other appropriate measures, that any entity:

(a) observes the principles of non-discrimination and competitive procurement in respect of the award of supplies and works contracts, in particular as regards the information that the entity makes available to undertakings concerning its procurement intentions;

(b) communicates to the Commission, under conditions to be defined by the latter in accordance with Article 32, information relating to the award of contracts.

3. As regards individual concessions or authorizations granted before the date on which Member States apply this Directive in accordance with Article 37, paragraphs 1 (a), (b) and (c) shall not apply, provided that at that date other entities are free to seek authorization for the exploitation of geographical areas for the purpose of exploring for or extracting oil, gas, coal or other solid fuels, on a non-discriminatory basis and in the light of objective criteria. Paragraph 1 (d) shall not apply as regards conditions or requirements established, applied or amended before the date referred to above.

4. A Member State which wishes to apply paragraph 1 shall inform the Commission accordingly. In doing so, it shall inform the Commission of any law, regulation or administrative provision, agreement or understanding relating to compliance with the conditions referred to in paragraphs 1 and 2.

The Commission shall take a decision in accordance with the procedure laid down in Article 32 (4) to (7). It shall publish its decision, giving its reasons, in the *Official Journal of the European Communities*.

it shall forward to the Council each year a report on the implementation of this Article and review its application in the framework of the report provided for in Article 36.

Article 4

1. When awarding supply or works contracts, the contracting entities shall apply procedures which are adapted to the provisions of this Directive.

2. Contracting entities shall ensure that there is no discrimination between different suppliers or contractors.

3. In the context of provision of technical specification to interested suppliers and contractors, of qualification and selection of suppliers or contractors and of award of contracts, contracting entities may impose requirements with a view to protecting the confidential nature of information which they make available.

4. The provisions of this Directive shall not limit the right of suppliers or contractors to require a contracting entity, in conformity with national law, to respect the confidential nature of information which they make available.

Article 5

1. Contracting entities may regard a framework agreement as a contract within the meaning of Article 1 (3) and award it in accordance with this Directive.

2. Where contracting entities have awarded a framework agreement in accordance with this Directive, they may avail themselves of Article 15 (2) (i) when awarding contracts based on that agreement.

3. Where a framework agreement has not been awarded in accordance with this Directive, contracting entities may not avail themselves of Article 15 (2) (i).

4. Contracting entities may not misuse framework agreements in order to hinder, limit or distort competition.

Article 6

1. This Directive shall not apply to contracts which the contracting entities award for purposes other than the pursuit of their activities as described in Article 2 (2) or for the pursuit of such activities in a non-member country, in conditions not involving the physical use of a network or geographical area within the Community.

2. However, this Directive shall apply to contracts awarded on behalf of the entities which exercise an activity referred to in Article 2 (2) (a) (i) and which:

(a) are connected with hydraulic engineering projects, irrigation or land drainage, provided that the volume of water intended for the supply of drinking water represents more than 20% of the total volume of water made available for these projects or irrigation or drainage installations; or

(b) are connected with the disposal or treatment of sewage.

3. The contracting entities shall notify the Commission at its request of any activities they regard as excluded under paragraph 1. The Commission may periodically publish lists of the categories of activities which it considers to be covered by this exclusion, for information in the *Official Journal of the European Communities*. In so doing, the Commission shall respect any sensitive commercial aspects the contracting entities may point out when forwarding this information.

Article 7

1. The provisions of this Directive shall not apply to contracts awarded for purposes of re-sale or hire to third parties, provided that the contracting entity enjoys no special or exclusive rights to sell or hire the subject of such contracts and other entities are free to sell or hire it under the same conditions as the contracting entity.

2. The contracting entities shall notify the Commission at its request of all the categories of products they regard as excluded under paragraph 1. The Commission may periodically publish lists of the categories of activities which it considers to be covered by this exclusion, for information in the *Official Journal of the European Communities*. In so doing, the Commission shall respect any sensitive commercial aspects the contracting entities may point out when forwarding this information.

Article 8

1. This Directive shall not apply to contracts which contracting entities exercising an activity described in Article 2 (2) (d) award for purchases intended exclusively to enable them to provide one or more telecommunications services where other entities are free to offer the same services in the same geographical area and under substantially the same conditions.

2. The contracting entities shall notify the Commission at its request of any services they regard as covered by the exclusion referred to in paragraph 1. The Commission may periodically publish the list of services which it considers to be covered by this exclusion, for information in the *Official Journal of the European Communities*. In so doing, the Commission shall respect any sensitive commercial aspects the contracting entities may point out when forwarding this information.

Article 9

1. This Directive shall not apply to:

(a) contracts which the contracting entities listed in Annex I award for the purchase of water;

(b) contracts which the contracting entities specified in Annexes II, III, IV and V award for the supply of energy or of fuels for the production of energy.

2. The Council shall re-examine the provisions of paragraph 1 when it has before it a report from the Commission together with appropriate proposals.

Article 10

This directive shall not apply to contracts when they are declared to be secret by the Member State, when their execution must be accompanied by special security measures in accordance with the laws, regulations or administrative provisions in force in the Member State concerned or when the protection of the basic security interests of that State so requires.

Article 11

This Directive shall not apply to contracts governed by different procedural rules and awarded:

1. pursuant to an international agreement concluded in conformity with the Treaty between a Member State and one or more third countries and covering supplies or works intended for the joint implementation or exploitation of a project by the signatory States; every agreement shall be communicated to the Commission, which may consult the Advisory Committee for Public Contracts set out by Council Decision 71/306/EEC[13], as last amended by Decision 77/63/EEC[14], or, in the case of agreements governing contracts awarded by entities exercising an activity defined in Article 2 (2) (d), the Advisory Committee on Telecommunications Procurement referred to in Article 31;

2. to undertakings in a Member State or a third country in pursuance of an international agreement relating to the stationing of troops;

3. pursuant to the particular procedure of an international organization.

Article 12

1. This Directive shall apply to contracts whose estimated value, net of VAT, is not less than:

(a) ECU 400 000 in the case of supply contracts awarded by entities exercising an activity defined in Article 2 (2) (a), (b) and (c);

(b) ECU 600 000 in the case of supply contracts awarded by entities exercising an activity defined in Article 2 (2) (d);

(c) ECU 5 million in the case of works contracts.

2. In the case of supply contracts for lease, rental or hire-purchase, the basis for calculating the contract value shall be:

(a) in the case of fixed-term-contracts, where their term is 12 months or less, the estimated total value for the contract's duration, or, where their term exceeds 12 months, the contracts total value including the estimated residual value;

(b) in the case of contracts for an indefinite period or in cases where there is doubt as to the duration of the contracts, the anticipated total instalments to be paid in the first four years.

3. Where a proposed supply contract expressly specifies option clauses, the basis for calculating the contract value shall be the highest possible total purchase, lease, rental or hire-purchase permissible, inclusive of the option clauses.

4. In the case of a procurement of supplies over a given period by means of a series of contracts to be awarded to one or more suppliers or of contracts which are to be renewed, the contract value shall be calculated on the basis of:

---

[13] OJ No L 185, 16. 8. 1971, p. 15.
[14] OJ No L 13, 15. 1. 1977, p. 15.

(a) the total value of contracts which had similar characteristics awarded over the previous fiscal year or 12 months, adjusted where possible for anticipated changes in quantity or value over the subsequent 12 months;

(b) or the aggregate value of contracts to be awarded during the 12 months following the first award or during the whole term of the contract, where this is longer than 12 months.

5. The basis for calculating the value of a framework agreement shall be the estimated maximum value of all the contracts envisaged for the period in question.

6. The basis for calculating the value of a works contract for the purposes of paragraph 1 shall be the total value of the work. 'Work' shall mean the building and engineering activities taken as a whole that are intended to fulfil an economic function by themselves.

In particular, where a supply or work is the subject of several lots, the value of each lot shall be taken into account when assessing the value referred to in paragraph 1. Where the aggregate value of the lots equals or exceeds the value laid down in paragraph 1, that paragraph shall apply to all the lots. However, in the case of works contracts, contracting entities may derogate from paragraph 1 in respect of lots whose estimated value net of VAT is less than ECU 1 million, provided that the aggregate value of those lots does not exceed 20% of the overall value of the lots.

7. For the purposes of paragraph 1, contracting entities shall include in the estimated value of a works contract the value of any supplies or services necessary for the execution of the contract which they make available to the contractor.

8. The value of supplies which are not necessary for the execution of a particular works contract may not be added to that of the contract with the result of avoiding application of this Directive to the procurement of those supplies.

9. Contracting entities may not circumvent this Directive by splitting contracts or usual special methods of calculating the value of contracts.

TITLE II

Technical specifications and standards

Article 13

1. Contracting entities shall include the technical specifications in the general documents or the contract documents relating to each contract.

2. The technical specifications shall be defined by reference to European specifications where these exist.

3. In the absence of European specifications, the technical specifications should as far as possible be defined by reference to other standards having currency within the Community.

4. Contracting entities shall define such further requirements as are necessary to complement European specifications or other standards. In doing so, they shall prefer specifications that indicate performance requirements rather than design or description characteristics unless the contracting entity has objective reasons for considering that such specifications are inadequate for the purposes of the contract.

5. Technical specifications which mention goods of a specific make or source or of a particular process, and which have the effect of favouring or eliminating certain undertakings, shall not be used unless such specifications are indispensable for the subject of the contract. In particular, the indication of trade marks, patents, types, or specific origin or production shall be prohibited; however, such an indication accompanied by the words 'or equivalent' shall be authorized where the subject of the contract cannot otherwise be described by specifications which are sufficiently precise and fully intelligible to all concerned.

6. Contracting entities may derogate from paragraph 2 if:

(a) it is technically impossible to establish satisfactorily that a product conforms to the European specifications;

(b) the application of paragraph 2 would prejudice the application of Council Directive 86/361/ EEC of 24 July 1986 on the initial stage of the mutual recognition of type approval for tele- communications terminal equipment[15], or of Council Decision 87/95/EEC of 22 December 1986 on standardization in the field of information technology and telecommunications[16];

(c) in the context of adapting existing practice to take account of European specifications, use of these specifications would oblige the contracting entity to acquire supplies incompatible with equipment already in use or would entail disproportionate cost or disproportionate technical difficulty. Contracting entities which have recourse to this derogation shall do so only as part of a clearly defined and recorded strategy with a view to a change-over to European specifications;

(d) the relevant European specification is inappropriate for the particular application or does not take account of technical developments which have come about since its adoption. Con- tracting entities which have recourse to this derogation shall inform the appropriate standardizing organization, or any other body empowered to review the European specifica- tion, of the reasons why they consider the European specification to be inappropriate and shall request its revision;

(e) the project is of a genuinely innovative nature for which use of European specifications would not be appropriate.

7. Notices published pursuant to Article 16 (1) (a) shall indicate any recourse to the derogations referred to in paragraph 6.

8. This Article shall be without prejudice to compulsory technical rules insofar as these are compatible with Community law.

Article 14

1. Contracting entities shall make available on demand to suppliers or contractors interested in obtaining a contract the technical specifications regularly referred to in their supply or works contracts or the technical specifications which they intend to apply to contracts covered by periodic information notices within the meaning of Article 17.

2. Where such technical specifications are based on documents available to interested suppliers or contractors, a reference to those documents shall be sufficient.

TITLE III

Procedures for the award of contracts

Article 15

1. Contracting entities may choose any of the procedures described in Article 1 (6), provided, subject to paragraph 2, a call for competition has been made in accordance with Article 16.

2. Contracting entities may use a procedure without prior call for competition in the following cases:

(a) in the absence of tenders or suitable tenders in response to a procedure with a prior call for competition, provided that the original contract conditions have not been substantially changed;

---

[15] OJ No L 217, 5. 8. 1986, p. 21.
[16] OJ No L 36, 7. 2. 1987, p. 31.

(b) where a contract is purely for the purpose of research, experiment, study or development and not for the purpose of ensuring profit or of recovering research and development costs;

(c) when, for technical or artistic reasons, or for reasons connected with protection of exclusive rights, the contract may be executed only by a particular supplier or contractor;

(d) insofar as is strictly necessary when, for reasons of extreme urgency brought about by events unforeseeable by the contracting entities, the time limits laid down for open and restricted procedures cannot be adhered to;

(e) in the case of supply contracts for additional deliveries by the original supplier which are intended either as a partial replacement of normal supplies or installations or as the extension of existing supplies or installations, where a change of supplier would oblige the contracting entity to acquire material having different technical characteristics which would result in incompatibility or disproportionate technical difficulties in operation and maintenance;

(f) for additional works not included in the project initially awarded or in the contract first concluded but which have, through unforeseen circumstances, become necessary for the execution of the contract, on condition that the award is made to the contractor executing the original contract:

— when such additional works cannot be technically or economically separated from the main contract without great inconvenience to the contracting entities,
— or when such additional works, although separable from the execution of the original contract, are strictly necessary to its later stages;

(g) in the case of works contracts, for new works consisting of the repetition of similar works entrusted to the contractor to which the same contracting entities awarded an earlier contract, provided that such works conform to a basic project for which a first contract was awarded after a call for competition. As soon as the first project is put up for tender, notice must be given that this procedure might be adopted and the total estimated cost of subsequent works shall be taken into consideration by the contracting entities when they apply the provisions of Article 12;

(h) for supplies quoted and purchased on a commodity market;

(i) for contracts to be awarded on the basis of a framework agreement, provided that the condition referred to in Article 5 (2) is fulfilled;

(j) for bargain purchases, where it is possible to procure supplies taking advantage of a particularly advantageous opportunity available for a very short space of time at a price considerably lower than normal market prices;

(k) for purchases of goods under particularly advantageous conditions either from a supplier definitely winding up his business activities or from the receivers or liquidators of a bankruptcy, an arrangement with creditors or a similar procedure under national laws or regulations.

Article 16

1. A call for competition may be made:

(a) by means of a notice drawn up in accordance with Annex XII A, B or C; or

(b) by means of a periodic indicative notice drawn up in accordance with Annex XIV; or

(c) by means of a notice on the existence of a qualification system drawn up in accordance with Annex XIII.

2. When a call for competition is made by means of a periodic indicative notice:

(a) the notice must refer specifically to the supplies or works which will be the subject of the contract to be awarded;

(b) the notice must indicate that the contract will be awarded by restricted or negotiated procedure without further publication of a notice of a call for competition and invite interested undertakings to express their interest in writing;

(c) contracting entities shall subsequently invite all candidates to confirm their interest on the basis of detailed information on the contract concerned before beginning the selection of tenderers or participants in negotiations.

3. When a call for competition is made by means of a notice on the existence of a qualification system, tenderers in a restricted procedure or participants in a negotiated procedure shall be selected from the qualified candidates in accordance with such a system.

4. The notices referred to in this Article shall be published in the *Official Journal of the European Communities*.

Article 17

1. Contracting entities shall make known, at least once a year, by means of a periodic indicative notice:

(a) in the case of supply contracts, the total of the contracts for each product area of which the estimated value, taking into account the provisions of Article 12, is equal to or greater than ECU 750 000, and which they intend to award over the following 12 months;

(b) in the case of works contracts, the essential characteristics of the works contracts which the contracting entities intend to award, the estimated value of which is not less than the threshold laid down in Article 12 (1).

2. The notice shall be drawn up in accordance with Annex XIV and published in the *Official Journal of the European Communities*.

3. Where the notice is used as a means of calling for competition in accordance with Article 16 (1) (b), it must have been published not more than 12 months prior to the date on which the invitation referred to in Article 16 (2) (c) is sent. Moreover, the contracting entity shall meet the deadlines laid down in Article 20 (2).

4. Contracting entities may, in particular, publish periodic indicative notices relating to major projects without repeating information previously included in a periodic indicative notice, provided it is clearly stated that such notices are additional notices.

Article 18

1. Contracting entities which have awarded a contract shall communicate to the Commission, within two months of the award of the contract and under conditions to be laid down by the Commission in accordance with the procedure laid down in Article 32, the results of the awarding procedure by means of a notice drawn up in accordance with Annex XV.

2. Information provided under Section I of Annex XV shall be published in the *Official Journal of the European Communities*. In this connection the Commission shall respect any sensitive commercial aspects the contracting entities may point out when forwarding this information in connection with points 6 and 9 of Annex XV.

3. Information provided under Section II of Annex XV must not be published except, in aggregated form, for statistical purposes.

Article 19

1. The contracting entities must be able to supply proof of the date of dispatch of the notices referred to in Articles 15 to 18.

2. The notices shall be published in full in their original language in the *Official Journal of the European Communities* and in the TED data bank. A summary of the important elements of each

notice shall be published in the other official languages of the Community, the original text alone being authentic.

3. The Office for Official Publications of the European Communities shall publish the notices not later than 12 days after their dispatch. In exceptional cases it shall endeavour to publish the notice referred to in Article 16 (1) (a) within five days in response to a request by the contracting entity and provided the notice has been sent to the Office by electronic mail, telex or telefax. Each edition of the *Official Journal of the European Communities* which contains one or more notices shall reproduce the model notice or notices on which the published notice or notices are based.

4. The cost of publication of the notices in the *Official Journal of the European Communities* shall be borne by the Communities.

5. Contracts in respect of which a notice is published in the *Official Journal of the European Communities* pursuant to Article 16 (1) shall not be published in any other way before that notice has been dispatched to the Office for Official Publications of the European Communities. Such publication shall not contain information other than that published in the *Official Journal of the European Communities*.

Article 20

1. In open procedures the time limit for the receipt of tenders shall be fixed by contracting entities at not less than 52 days from the date of dispatch of the notice. This time limit may be shortened to 36 days where contracting entities have published a notice in accordance with Article 17 (1).

2. In restricted procedures and in negotiated procedures with a prior call for competition, the following arrangements shall apply:

(a) the time limit for receipt of requests to participate, in response to a notice published in accordance with Article 16 (1) (a) or in response to an invitation from a contracting entity in accordance with Article 16 (2) (c), shall, as a general rule, be at least five weeks from the data of dispatch of the notice and shall in any case not be less than the time limit for publication laid down in Article 19 (3) plus 10 days;

(b) the time limit for receipt of tenders may be fixed by mutual agreement between the contracting entity and the selected candidates, provided that all tenderers are given equal time to prepare and submit tenders;

(c) where it is not possible to reach agreement on the time limit for the receipt of tenders, the contracting entity shall fix a time limit which shall, as a general rule, be at least three weeks and shall in any case not be less than 10 days from the date of the invitation to tender; the time allowed shall be sufficiently long to take account in particular of the factors mentioned in Article 22 (3).

Article 21

In the contract documents, the contracting entity may ask the tenderer to indicate in his tender any share of the contract he may intend to subcontract to third parties.

This indication shall be without prejudice to the question of the principal contractor's responsibility.

Article 22

1. Provided they have been requested in good time, the contract documents and supporting documents must be sent to the suppliers or contractors by the contracting entities as a general rule within six days of receipt of the application.

2. Provided it has been requested in good time, additional information relating to the contract documents shall be supplied by the contracting entities not later than six days before the final date fixed for receipt of tenders.

3. Where tenders require the examination of voluminous documentation such as lengthy technical specifications, a visit to the site or an on-the-spot inspection of the documents supporting the contract documents, this shall be taken into account in fixing the appropriate time limits.

4. Contracting entities shall invite the selected candidates simultaneously and in writing. The letter of invitation shall be accompanied by the contract documents and supporting documents. It shall include at least the following information:

(a) the address from which any additional documents can be requested, the final date for such requests and the amount and methods of payment of any sum to be paid for such documents;

(b) the final date for receipt of tenders, the address to which they must be sent and the language or languages in which they must be drawn up;

(c) a reference to any tender notice published;

(d) an indication of any document to be annexed;

(e) the criteria for the award of the contract if these are not given in the notice;

(f) any other special condition for participation in the contract.

5. Requests for participation in contracts and invitations to tender must be made by the most rapid means of communication possible. When requests to participate are made by telegram, telex, telefax, telephone or any electronic means, they must be confirmed by letter dispatched before the expiry of the time limit referred to in Article 20 (1) or of the time limit set by contracting entities pursuant to Article 20 (2).

Article 23

1. The contracting entity may state in the contract documents, or be obliged by a Member State so to do, the authority or authorities from which a tenderer may obtain the appropriate information on the obligations relating to the employment protection provisions and the working conditions which are in force in the Member State, region or locality in which the works are to be executed and which shall be applicable to the works carried out on site during the performance of the contract.

2. A contracting entity which supplies the information referred to in paragraph 1 shall request the tenderers or those participating in the contract procedure to indicate that they have taken account, when drawing up their tender, of the obligations relating to employment protection provisions and the working conditions which are in force in the place where the work is to be carried out. This shall be without prejudice to the application of the provisions of Article 27 (5) concerning the examination of abnormally low tenders.

TITLE IV

Qualification, selection and award

Article 24

1. Contracting entities which so wish may establish and operate a system of qualification of suppliers or contractors.

2. The system, which may involve different qualification stages, shall operate on the basis of objective rules and criteria to be established by the contracting entity. The contracting entity shall use European standards as a reference where they are appropriate. The rules and criteria may be updated as required.

3. The rules and criteria for qualification shall be made available on request to interested suppliers or contractors. The updating of these criteria and rules shall be communicated to the interested

suppliers and contractors. Where a contracting entity considers that the qualification or certification system of certain third entities or bodies meet its requirements, it shall communicate to interested suppliers and contractors the names of such third entities or bodies.

4. Contracting entities shall inform applicants of their decision as to qualification within a reasonable period. If the decision will take longer than six months from the presentation of an application, the contracting entity shall inform the applicant, within two months of the application, of the reasons justifying a longer period and of the date by which its application will be accepted or refused.

5. In reaching their decision as to qualification or when the criteria and rules are being updated, contracting entities may not:

— impose conditions of an administrative, technical or financial nature on some suppliers or contractors that are not imposed on others.
— require tests or proof that duplicate objective evidence already available.

6. Applicants whose qualification is refused shall be informed of this decision and the reasons for refusal. The reasons must be based on the criteria for qualification referred to in paragraph 2.

7. A written record of qualified suppliers or contractors shall be kept, and it may be divided into categories according to the type of contract for which the qualification is valid.

8. Contracting entities may bring the qualification of a supplier or contractor to an end only for reasons based on the criteria referred to in paragraph 2. The intention to bring qualification to an end must be notified in writing to the supplier or contractor beforehand, together with the reason or reasons justifying the proposed action.

9. The qualification system shall be the subject of a notice drawn up in accordance with Annex XIII and published in the *Official Journal of the European Communities*, indicating the purpose of the qualification system and the availability of the rules concerning its operation. Where the system is of a duration greater than three years, the notice shall be published annually. Where the system is of a shorter duration, an initial notice shall suffice.

Article 25

1. Contracting entities which select candidates to tender in restricted procedures or to participate in negotiated procedures shall do so according to objective criteria and rules which they lay down and which they shall make available to interested suppliers or contractors.

2. The criteria used may include the criteria for exclusion specified in Article 23 of Directive 71/305/EEC and in Article 20 of Directive 77/62/EEC.

3. The criteria may be based on the objective need of the contracting entity to reduce the number of candidates to a level which is justified by the need to balance the particular characteristics of the contract award procedure and the resources required to complete it. The number of candidates selected must, however, take account of the need to ensure adequate competition.

Article 26

Groupings of suppliers or contractors shall be permitted to tender or negotiate. The conversion of such groupings into a specific legal form shall not be required in order to submit a tender or to negotiate, but the grouping selected may be required so to convert itself once it has been awarded the contract where such conversion is necessary for the proper performance of the contract.

Article 27

1. The criteria on which the contracting requirements shall base the award of contracts shall be:

(a) the most economically advantageous tender, involving various criteria depending on the contract in question, such as: delivery or completion date, running costs, cost-effectiveness, quality, aesthetic and functional characteristics, technical merit, after-sales service and technical assistance, commitments with regard to spare parts, security of supplies and price; or

(b) the lowest price only.

2. In the case referred to in paragraph 1 (a), contracting entities shall state in the contract documents or in the tender notice all the criteria they intend to apply to the award, where possible in descending order of importance.

3. Where the criterion for the award of the contract is that of the most economically advantageous tender, contracting entities may take account of variants which are submitted by a tenderer and meet the minimum specifications required by the contracting entities. Contracting entities shall state in the contract documents the minimum specifications to be respected by the variants and any specific requirements for their presentation. Where variants are not permitted, they shall so indicate in the contract documents.

4. Contracting entities may not reject the presentation of a variant on the sole ground that it was drawn up on the basis of technical specifications defined with reference to European specifications or to national technical specifications recognized as complying with the essential requirements within the meaning of Directive 89/106/EEC.

5. If, for a given contract, tenders appear abnormally low in relation to the services, the contracting entity shall, before it may reject those tenders, request in writing details of the constituent elements of the tender which it considers relevant and shall verify those constituent elements taking account of the explanations received. It may set a reasonable period within which to reply.

The contracting entity may take into consideration explanations which are justified on objective grounds relating to the economy of the construction or production method, or the technical solutions chosen, or the exceptionally favourable conditions available to the tenderer for the execution of the contract, or the originality of the product or the work proposed by the tenderer.

Contracting entities may reject tenders which are abnormally low owing to the receipt of State aid only if they have consulted the tenderer and if the tenderer has not been able to show that the aid in question has been notified to the Commission pursuant to Article 93 (3) of the Treaty or has received the Commission's approval. Contracting entities which reject a tender under these circumstances shall inform the Commission thereof.

Article 28

1. Article 27 (1) shall not apply where a Member State bases the award of contracts on other criteria within the framework of rules in force at the time of adoption of this Directive whose aim is to give preference to certain tenderers provided the rules invoked are compatible with the Treaty.

2. Without prejudice to paragraph 1, this Directive shall not prevent, until 31 December 1992, the application of notional provisions in force on the award of supply or works contracts which have as their objective the reduction of regional disparities and the promotion of job creation in disadvantaged regions or those suffering from industrial decline, provided that the provisions concerned are compatible with the Treaty and with the Community's international obligations.

Article 29

1. This Article shall apply to tenders comprising products originating in third countries with which the Community has not concluded, multilaterally or bilaterally, an agreement ensuring comparable and effective access for Community undertakings to the markets of those third countries. It shall be without prejudice to the obligations of the Community or its Member States in respect of third countries.

2. Any tender made for the award of a supply contract may be rejected where the proportion of the products originating in third countries, as determined in accordance with Council Regulation

(EEC) No 802/68 of 27 June 1968 on the common definition of the concept of the origin of goods[17], as last amended by Regulation (EEC) No 3860/87[18], exceeds 50% of the total value of the products constituting the tender. For the purposes of this Article, software used in the equipment of telecommunication networks shall be considered as products.

3. Subject to paragraph 4, where two or more tenders are equivalent in the light of the award criteria defined in Article 27, preference shall be given to the tenders which may not be rejected pursuant to paragraph 2. The prices of tenders shall be considered equivalent for the purposes of this Article, if the price difference does not exceed 3%.

4. However, a tender shall not be preferred to another pursuant to paragraph 3 where its acceptance would oblige the contracting entity to acquire material having technical characteristics different from those of existing material, resulting in incompatibility or technical difficulties in operation and maintenance or disproportionate costs.

5. For the purposes, in this Article of determining the proportion referred to in paragraph 2 of products originating in third countries, those third countries to which the benefit of the provisions of this Directive has been extended by a Council Decision in accordance with paragraph 1 shall not be taken into account.

6. The Commission shall submit an annual report to the Council (for the first time in the second half of 1991) on progress made in multilateral or bilateral negotiations regarding access for Community undertakings to the markets of third countries in the fields covered by this Directive, on any result which such negotiations may have achieved, and on the implementation in practice of all the agreements which have been concluded.

The Council, acting by a qualified majority on a proposal from the Commission, may amend the provisions of this Article in the light of such developments.

TITLE V

Final provisions

Article 30

1. The value in national currencies of the thresholds specified in Article 12 shall in principle be revised every two years with effect from the date provided for in Directive 77/62/EEC as far as the thresholds for supply and software service contracts are concerned and from the date provided for in Directive 71/305/EEC as far as the threshold for works contracts are concerned. The calculation of such value shall be based on the average daily values of those currencies expressed in ecus over the 24 months terminating on the last day of October preceding the revision with effect from 1 January. The values shall be published in the *Official Journal of the European Communities* at the beginning of November.

2. The method of calculation laid down in paragraph 1 shall be examined pursuant to the provisions of Directive 77/62/EEC.

Article 31

1. The Commission shall be assisted, as regards procurement by the contracting entities exercising an activity defined in Article 2 (2) (d), by a Committee of an advisory nature which shall be the Advisory Committee on Telecommunications Procurement. The Committee shall be composed of representatives of the Member States and chaired by a representative of the Commission.

2. The Commission shall consult this Committee on:

---

[17] OJ No L 148, 28. 6. 1968, p. 1.
[18] OJ No L 363, 23. 12. 1987, p. 30.

(a) amendments to Annex X;

(b) revision of the currency values of the thresholds;

(c) the rules concerning contracts awarded under international agreements;

(d) the review of the application of this Directive;

(e) the procedures described in Article 32 (2) relating to notices and statistical accounts.

Article 32

1. Annexes I to X shall be revised in accordance with the procedure laid down in paragraphs 3 to 7 with a view to ensuring that they fulfil the criteria of Article 2.

2. The conditions for the presentation, dispatch, reception, translation, keeping and distribution of the notices referred to in Articles 16, 17 and 18 and of the statistical reports provided for in Article 34 shall be established, for the purposes of simplification, in accordance with the procedure laid down in paragraphs 3 to 7.

3. The revised Annexes and the conditions referred to in paragraphs 1 and 2 shall be published in the *Official Journal of the European Communities.*

4. The Commission shall be assisted by the Advisory Committee for Public Contracts and, in the case of the revision of Annex X, by the Advisory Committee on Telecommunications Procurement provided for in Article 31 of this Directive.

5. The Commission representative shall submit to the Committee a draft of the decisions to be taken. The Committee shall deliver its opinion on the draft within a time limit which the Chairman may lay down according to the urgency of the matter, if necessary by taking a vote.

6. The opinion shall be recorded in the minutes; in addition, each Member State shall have the right to ask for its position to be recorded in the minutes.

7. The Commission shall take the utmost account of the opinion delivered by the Committee. It shall inform the Committee of the manner in which its opinion has been taken into account.

Article 33

1. Contracting entities shall keep appropriate information on each contract which shall be sufficient to permit them at a later date to justify decisions taken in connection with:

(a) the qualification and selection of contractors or suppliers and award of contracts;

(b) recourse to derogations from the use of European specifications in accordance with Article 13 (6);

(c) use of procedures without prior call for competition in accordance with Article 15 (2);

(d) non-application of Titles II, III and IV in accordance with the derogations provided for in Title I.

2. The information shall be kept for at least four years from the date of award of the contract so that the contracting entity will be able, during that period, to provide the necessary information to the Commission if it so requests.

Article 34

1. The Member States shall ensure that each year, in accordance with the arrangements to be laid down under the procedure provided for in Article 32 (3) to (7), the Commission receives a statistical report concerning the total value, broken down by Member State and each category of activity to which Annexes I to X refer, of the contracts awarded below the thresholds defined in Article 12 which would, if they were not below those thresholds, be covered by this Directive.

2. Arrangements shall be fixed in accordance with the procedure referred to in Article 32 to ensure that:

(a) in the interests of administrative simplification, contracts of lesser value may be excluded, provided that the usefulness of the statistics is not jeopardized;

(b) the confidential nature of the information provided is respected.

Article 35

1. Article 2 (2) of Directive 77/62/EEC is hereby replaced by the following:

'2. This Directive shall not apply to:

(a) contracts awarded in the fields referred to in Articles 2, 7, 8 and 9 of Council Directive 90/531/EEC of 17 September 1990 on the procurement, procedures of entities operating in the water, energy, transport and telecommunications sectors (*) or fulfilling the conditions in Article 6 (2) of the said Directive;

(b) supplies which are declared secret or when their delivery must be accompanied by special security measures in accordance with the laws, regulations or administrative provisions in force in the Member State concerned or when the protection of the basic interests of that State's security so requires.

2. Article 3 (4) and (5) of Directive 71/305/EEC is hereby replaced by the following:

'4. This Directive shall not apply to contracts awarded in the fields referred to in Articles 2, 7, 8 and 9 of Council Directive 90/531/EEC of 17 September 1990 on the procurement procedures of entities operating in water, energy, transport and telecommunications sectors (*) or fulfilling the conditions in Article 6 (2) of the said Directive.

Article 36

Not later than four years after the application of this Directive, the Commission, acting in close cooperation with the Advisory Committee for Public Contracts, shall review the manner in which this Directive has operated and its field of application and, if necessary, make further proposals to adapt it, in the light of developments concerning in particular progress in market opening and the level of competition. In the case of entities exercising an activity defined in Article 2 (2) (d), the Commission shall act in close cooperation with the Advisory Committee on Telecommunications Procurement.

Article 37

1. Member States shall adopt the measures necessary to comply with this Directive by 1 July 1992. They shall forthwith inform the Commission thereof.

2. Member States may stipulate that the measures referred to in paragraph 1 shall apply only from 1 January 1993.

Nevertheless, in the case of the Kingdom of Spain, 1 January 1993 shall be replaced by 1 January 1996. As regards the Hellenic Republic and the Portuguese Republic, 1 January 1993 shall be replaced by 1 January 1998.

3. Council recommendation 84/550/EEC of 12 November 1984 concerning the first phase of opening up access to public recommendations contracts[19] shall cease to have effect as from the date on which this Directive is applied by the Member States.

Article 38

Member States shall communicate to the Commission the text of the main provisions of national law, whether laws, regulations or administrative provisions, which they adopt in the field governed by this Directive.

(*) OJ No L 297, 29. 10. 1990, p. 1.
[19] OJ No L 298, 16. 11. 1984, p. 51.

Article 39

This Directive is addressed to the Member States.

Done at Brussels, 17 September 1990.

For the Council
The President
P. ROMITA

ANNEXES

ANNEX X

OPERATION OF TELECOMMUNICATIONS NETWORKS OR PROVISION OF TELECOMMUNICATIONS SERVICES

BELGIUM

Régie des télégraphes et des téléphones/Regie van Telegrafie en Telefonie.

DENMARK

Kjøbenhauns Telefon Aktieselskab.

Jydsk Telefon.

Fyns Telefon.

Statens Teletjeneste.

Tele Sønderjylland.

GERMANY

Deutsche Bundespost – Telekom.

Mannesmann – Mobilfunk GmbH.

GREECE

OTE/Hellenic Telecommunications Organization.

SPAIN

Compañía Telefónica Nacional de España.

FRANCE

Direction générale des télécommunications.

Transpac.

Telecom service mobile.

Société française de radiotéléphone.

IRELAND

Telecom Éireann.

ITALY

Amministrazione delle poste e delle telecommunicazioni.

Azienda di stato per i servizi telefonici.

Società italiana per l'esercizio telefonico SpA.

Italcable.

Telespazio SpA.

LUXEMBOURG

Administration des postes et télécommunications.

NETHERLANDS

Koninklijke PTT Nederland NV and subsidiaries[20].

---

[20] Except PTT Post BV.

PORTUGAL

Telefones de Lisboa e Porto, SA.

Companhia Portuguesa Rádio Marconi.

Correios e Telecommunicaçoes de Portugal.

UNITED KINGDOM

British Telecommunications plc.

Mercury Communications Ltd.

City of Kingston upon Hull.

Racal Vodafone.

Telecoms Securicor Cellular Radio Ltd (Cellnet).

ANNEX XI

LIST OF PROFESSIONAL ACTIVITIES AS SET OUT IN THE GENERAL INDUSTRIAL CLASSIFICATION OF ECONOMIC ACTIVITIES WITHIN THE EUROPEAN COMMUNITIES

Classes	Groups	Subgroups and items	Description
50			BUILDING AND CIVIL ENGINEERING
	500		General building and civil engineering work (without any particular specification) and demolition work
		500.1	General building and civil engineering work (without any particular specification)
		500.2	Demolition work
	501		Construction of flats, office blocks, hospitals and other buildings, both residential and non-residential
		501.1	General building contractors
		501.2	Roofings
		501.3	Construction of chimneys, kilns and furnaces
		501.4	Water-proofing and damp-proofing
		501.5	Restoration and maintenance of outside walls (repointing, cleaning, etc.)
		501.6	Erection and dismantlement of scaffolding
		501.7	Other specialized activities relating to construction work (including carpentry)
	502		Civil engineering: construction of roads, bridges, railways, etc.
		502.1	General civil engineering work
		502.2	Earth-moving (navvying)
		502.3	Construction of bridges, tunnels and shafts; drillings
		502.4	Hydraulic engineering (rivers, canals, harbours, flows, lochs and dams)
		502.5	Road-building (including specialized construction of airports and runways)

| | 502.6 | Specialized construction work relating to water (i.e. to irrigation land drainage, water supply, sewage disposal, sewerage, etc.) |
| | 502.7 | Specialized activities in other areas of civil engineering |

503		**Installation (fittings and fixtures)**
	503.1	General installation work
	503.2	Gas fitting and plumbing, and the installation of sanitary equipment
	503.3	Installation of heating and ventilating apparatus (central heating, air-conditioning, ventilation)
	503.4	Sound and heat insulation; insulation against vibration
	503.5	Electrical fittings
	503.6	Installation of aerials, lightning conductors, telephones, etc.

504		**Building completion work**
	504.1	General building completion work
	504.2	Plastering
	504.3	Joinery, primarily engaged in the after assembly and/or installation (including the laying of parquet flooring)
	504.4	Painting, glazing and paper-hanging
	504.5	Tiling and otherwise covering floors and walls
	504.6	Other building completion work (putting in fireplaces, etc.)

ANNEX XII

A. OPEN PROCEDURES

1. The name, address, telephone number, telegraphic address, telex and telecopier number of the contracting entity.

2. Nature of the contract (supply or works; where appropriate, state if it is a framework agreement).

3. (a) Place of delivery, or site.

   (b) Nature and quantity of the goods to be supplied;

   or

   the nature and extent of the services to be provided and general nature of the work.

   (c) Indication of whether the suppliers can tender for some and/or all of the goods required.

   If, for works contracts, the work or the contract is subdivided into several lots, the order of size of the different lots and the possibility of tendering for one, for several or for all of the lots.

   (d) Authorization to submit variants.

   (e) For works contracts:

   information concerning the purpose of the work or the contract where the latter also involves the drawing up of projects.

4. Derogation from the use of European specifications, in accordance with Article 13 (6).

5. Time limits for delivery or completion.

6. (a) Name and address of the service from which the contract documents and additional documents may be requested.

   (b) Where appropriate, the amount and terms of payment of the sum to be paid to obtain such documents.

7. (a) The final date for receipt of tenders.

   (b) The address to which they must be sent.

   (c) The language or languages in which they must be drawn up.

8. (a) Where appropriate, the persons authorized to be present at the opening of tenders.

   (b) The date, hour and place of such opening.

9. Where appropriate, any deposits and guarantees required.

10. Main terms concerning financing and payment and/or references to the provisions in which are contained.

11. Where appropriate, the legal form to be taken by the grouping of suppliers or contractors to whom the contract is awarded.

12. Minimum economic and technical conditions required of the supplier or contractor to whom the contract is awarded.

13. Period during which the tenderer is bound to keep open his tender.

14. The criteria for the award of the contract. Criteria other than that of the lowest price shall be mentioned where they do not appear in the contract documents.

15. Other information.

16. Where appropriate, the reference to publication of the periodic information notice in the Official Journal to which the contract refers.

17. Date of dispatch of the notice by the contacting entities.

18. Date of receipt of the notice by the Office for Official Publications of the European Communities (to be supplied by the said Office).

B. RESTRICTED PROCEDURES

1. The name, address, telephone number, telegraphic address, telex and telecopier number of the contracting entity.

2. Nature of the contract (supply or works; where appropriate, state if it is a framework agreement).

3. (a) Place of delivery, or site.

   (b) Nature and quantity of the goods to be supplied;

   or

   the nature and extent of the services to be provided and general nature of the work.

   (c) Indication of whether the suppliers can tender for some and/or all of the goods required.

   If, for works contracts, the work or the contract is subdivided into several lots, the order of size of the different lots and the possibility of tendering for one, for several or for all of the lots.

   (d) Authorization to submit variants.

(e) For works contracts:

information concerning the purpose of the work or the contract where the latter also involves the drawing up of projects.

4. Derogation from the use of European specifications, in accordance with Article 13 (6).

5. Time limits for delivery or completion.

6. Where appropriate, the legal form to be taken by the grouping of suppliers or contractors to whom the contract is awarded.

7. (a) The final date for receipt of requests to participate.

   (b) The address to which they must be sent.

   (c) The language or languages in which they must be drawn up.

8. The final date for dispatch of invitations to tender.

9. Where appropriate, any deposits and guarantees required.

10. Main terms concerning financing and payment and/or references to the texts in which these are contained.

11. Information concerning the supplier's or contractor's position and minimum economic and technical conditions required of him.

12. The criteria for the award of the contract where they are not mentioned in the invitation to tender.

13. Other information.

14. Where appropriate, the reference to publication of the periodic information notice in the Official Journal to which the contract refers.

15. Date of dispatch of the notice by the contracting entities.

16. Date of receipt of the notice by the Office for Official Publications of the European Communities (to be supplied by the said Office).

C. NEGOTIATED PROCEDURES

1. The name, address, telephone number, telegraphic address, telex and telecopier number of the contracting entity.

2. Nature of the contract (supply or works; where appropriate, state if it is a framework agreement).

3. (a) Place of delivery, or site.
   (b) Nature and quantity of the goods to be supplied;

   or

   the nature and extent of the services to be provided and general nature of the work.

   (c) Indication of whether the suppliers can tender for some and/or all of the goods required.

   If, for works contracts, the work or the contract is subdivided into several lots, the order of size of the different lots and the possibility of tendering for one, for several or for all of the lots.

   (d) For works contracts:

   information concerning the purpose of the work or the contract where the latter also involves the drawing up of projects.

4. Derogation from the use of European specifications, in accordance with Article 13 (6).

5. Time limit for delivery or completion.

6. Where appropriate, the legal form to be taken by the grouping 'of suppliers or contractors to whom the contract is awarded.

7. (a) The final date for receipt of tenders.

   (b) The address to which they must be sent.

   (c) The language or languages in which they must be drawn up.

8. Where appropriate, any deposits and guarantees required.

9. Main terms concerning financing and payment and/or references to the texts in which these are contained.

10. Information concerning the supplier's or contractor's position and minimum economic and technical conditions required of him.

11. Where appropriate, the names and addresses of suppliers or contractors already selected by the contracting entity.

12. Where applicable, date(s) of previous publications in the *Official Journal of the European Communities*.

13. Other information.

14. Where appropriate, the reference to publication of the periodic information notice in the Official Journal to which the contract refers.

15. Date of dispatch of the notice by the contracting entities.

16. Date of receipt of the notice by the Office for Official Publications of the European Communities (to be supplied by the said Office).

ANNEX XIII

NOTICE ON THE EXISTENCE OF A QUALIFICATION SYSTEM

1. Name, address, telephone number, telegraphic address, telex and telecopier number of the contracting entity.

2. Purpose of the qualification system.

3. Address where the rules concerning the qualification system can be obtained (if different from the address mentioned under 1.).

4. Where applicable, duration of the qualification system.

ANNEX XIV

PERIODIC INFORMATION NOTICE

A. *For supply contracts:*

   1. Name, address, telephone number, telegraphic address, telex and telecopier number of the contracting entity or the service from which additional information may be obtained.

   2. Nature and quantity or value of the services or products to be supplied.

3. (a) Estimated date of the commencement of the procedures of the award of the contract(s) (if known).

   (b) Type of award procedure to be used.

4. Other information (for example, indicate if a call for competition will be published later).

5. Date of dispatch of the notice by the contracting entities.

6. Date of receipt of the notice by the Office for Official Publications of the European Communities (to be supplied by the said Office).

B. *For works contracts:*

1. The name, address, telegraphic address, telephone, telex and telecopier number of the contracting entity.

2. (a) The site.

   (b) The nature and extent of the services to be provided, the main characteristics of the work or of the lots by reference to the work.

   (c) An estimate of the cost of the service to be provided.

3. (a) Type of award procedure to be used.

   (b) The date scheduled for initiating the award procedures in respect of the contract or contracts.

   (c) The date scheduled for the start of the work.

   (d) Planned time table for completion of the work.

4. Terms of financing of the work and of price revision.

5. Other information (for example, indicate if a call for competition will be published later).

6. Date of dispatch of the notice by the contracting entities.

7. Date of receipt of the notice by the Office for Official Publications of the European Communities (to be supplied by the said Office).

ANNEX XV

NOTICE ON CONTRACTS AWARDED

II. INFORMATION FOR PUBLICATION IN THE *OFFICIAL JOURNAL OF THE EUROPEAN COMMUNITIES*

1. Name and address of the contracting entity.

2. Nature of the contract (supply or works; where appropriate, state if it is a framework agreement).

3. At least a summary indication of the nature of the products, works or services provided.

4. (a) Form of the call for competition (notice on the existence of a qualification procedure; periodic information notice; call for tenders).

   (b) Reference of publication of the notice in the *Official Journal of the European Communities*.

   (c) In the case of contracts awarded without a prior call for competition, indication of the relevant provision of Article 15 (2).

5. Award procedure (open, restricted or negotiated).

6. Number of tenders received.

7. Date of award of the contract.

8. Price paid for bargain purchases under Article 15 (2) (j).

9. Name and address of successful supplier(s) or contractor(s).

10. State, where appropriate, whether the contract has been, or may be, sub-contracted.

11. Optional information:

    — value and share of the contract which may be sub-contracted to third parties.
    — award criteria,
    — price paid (or range of prices).

II. INFORMATION NOT INTENDED FOR PUBLICATION

12. Number of contracts awarded (where an award has been split between more than one supplier).

13. Value of each contract awarded.

14. Country of origin of the product or service (EEC origin or non-Community origin; if the latter, broken down by third country).

15. Was recourse made to the exceptions to the use of European specifications provided for under Article 13 (6). If so, which?

16. Which award criteria was used (most economically advantageous: lowest price: criteria permitted under Article 28)?

17. Was the contract awarded to a bidder who submitted a variant, in accordance with Article 27 (3)?

18. Were any tenders excluded on the grounds that they were abnormally low, in accordance with Article 27 (5)?

19. Date of transmission of the notice by the contracting entities.

STATEMENT

concerning Article 15 of Directive 90/531/EEC

The Council and the Commission state that in open and restricted procedures all negotiation with candidates or tenderers on fundamental aspects of contracts, variations in which are likely to distort competition, and in particular on prices, shall be ruled out; however, discussions with candidates or tenderers may be held but only for the purpose of clarifying or supplementing the content of their tenders or the requirements of the contracting entities and provided this does not involve discrimination.

APPENDIX 14

Council Recommendation of 9 October 1990 on the coordinated introduction of Pan-European land-based public radio paging in the Community

(90/543/EEC)

THE COUNCIL OF THE EUROPEAN COMMUNITIES,

Having regard to the Treaty establishing the European Economic Community, and in particular Article 235 thereof,

Having regard to the proposal from the Commission[1],

Having regard to the opinion of the European Parliament[2],

Having regard to the opinion of the Economic and Social Committee[3],

Whereas, by Recommendation 84/549/EEC[4], the Council calls for the introduction of services on the basis of a common harmonized approach in the field of telecommunications;

Whereas the resources offered by modern telecommunications networks should be utilized to the full for the economic development of the Community;

Whereas paging services are a particularly efficient communications method for alerting and/or sending messages to people on the move;

Whereas the land-based public paging systems currently in use in the Community do not in general allow people on the move throughout the Community to reap the benefits of European-wide paging services and European-wide markets;

Whereas the European Telecommunication Standards Institute (ETSI) has instructed the technical Committee (PS) to specify all system aspects of a more advanced public radio paging system code named European Radio Messaging System (ERMES);

Whereas the introduction of ERMES being specified by ETSI will provide a unique opportunity of establishing a truly pan-European paging service;

Whereas a coordinated policy for the introduction of a pan-European land-based public radio paging service will make it possible to establish a European market in mobile terminals (paging receivers) which will be capable of creating, by virtue of its size, service features and costs, the necessary development conditions to enable undertakings to maintain and improve their presence in world markets;

Whereas it is essential to ensure extensive use of frequency agile type receivers;

Whereas it is necessary to allow unrestricted access to radio paging services and free circulation of paging receivers throughout the Community;

Whereas in this context Community law and in particular the competition rules should be respected;

Whereas the implementation of Council Directive 86/361/EEC of 24 July 1986 on the initial stage of the mutual recognition of type approval for telecommunications terminal equipment[5] will make an important contribution towards this goal;

---

[1] OJ No C 43, 23. 2. 1990, p. 6.
[2] OJ No C 15, 22. 1. 1990, p. 87.
[3] OJ No C 298, 27. 11. 1989, p. 27.
[4] OJ No L 298, 16. 11. 1984, p. 49.
[5] OJ No L 217, 5. 8. 1986, p. 21.

Whereas consideration should be given to Council Directive 83/189/EEC of 28 March 1983 laying down a procedure for the provision of information in the field of technical standards and regulations[6] and to Council Decision 87/95/EEC of 22 December 1986 on standardization in the field of information technology and telecommunications[7];

Whereas it is appropriate to make use of the potential of the Community's financial instruments in order to promote the development of the telecommunications infrastructure in the Community;

Whereas consideration should be given to Council Recommendation 87/371/EEC of 25 June 1987 on the coordinated introduction of public pan-European cellular digital land-based mobile communications in the Community[8] which points out that special attention should be paid to the urgent requirement of certain users for pan-European land-based communications and that the Commission will in the future submit other proposals in the field of mobile communications, including radio paging systems;

Whereas the public telecommunications administrations, the recognized private operating agencies and other authorized agencies offering public mobile telecommunications services are hereinafter referred to as 'telecommunications administrations';

Whereas a favourable opinion has been delivered by the Senior Officials Group on Telecommunications (SOG-T), on the basis of the detailed report drawn up by the Analysis and Forecasting Group (GAP) which provides a strategic basis for the development of public mobile communications in the Community with a view to enabling European users on the move to communicate efficiently and economically;

Whereas favourable opinions on this report have been delivered by the telecommunications administrations, by the European Conference of Postal and Telecommunications Administrations (CEPT) and by telecommunications equipment manufacturers in the Member States;

Whereas the envisaged measures will allow the economic benefit and rapidly increasing market potential of public radio paging to be fully realized in the Community;

Whereas the Treaty does not provide, for the action concerned, powers other than those of Article 235,

HEREBY RECOMMENDS:

1. that the telecommunications administrations implement with due respect for Community law the detailed recommendations as described in the Annex concerning the coordinated introduction of pan-European land-based public radio paging in the Community. For the purposes of this Recommendation, 'pan-European land-based public radio paging service' shall mean a public radio paging service based on a terrestrial infrastructure in the Member States in accordance with a common specification which allows persons wishing to do so to send and/or to receive alert and/or numeric or alphanumeric messages anywhere within the coverage of the service in the Community;

2. that the telecommunications administrations continue the cooperation within the CEPT and, with the collaboration of manufacturers and users, within ETSI, particularly concerning the objectives and time schedule set out in the Annex for the completion of the specifications and service implementation of the pan-European land-based public radio paging system;

3. that the telecommunications administrations plan for a gradual evolution from existing radio paging systems to the pan-European land-based public radio paging system so as to ensure a transition which meets the needs of users, telecommunications administrations and manufacturers;

---

[6] OJ No L 109, 26. 4. 1983, p. 8.
[7] OJ No L 36, 7. 2. 1987, p. 31.
[8] OJ No L 196, 17. 7. 1987, p. 81.

4. that Member State Governments and telecommunications administrations complete the technical arrangements from the implementation of the means of call routing and processing, so that tone and/or numeric or alphanumeric messages can be sent from anywhere in the Community to a radio paging receiver anywhere in the geographical coverage of the Ermes service by 31 December 1992 at the latest;

5. that the Commission take appropriate initiatives, within the framework of application of existing Directives, to encourage the completion of the specifications and the implementation of the pan-European land-based radio paging system, within the time schedule set out in the Annex;

6. that the Community's financial instruments take this Recommendation into account within the framework of their interventions, particularly as regards capital investments required for the implementation of the infrastructure for the pan-European land-based public radio paging system;

7. that the telecommunications administrations prepare and sign by July 1990 at the latest a memorandum of understanding on the implementation of pan-European land-based public radio paging;

8. that Member State Governments inform the Commission at the end of each year, from the end of 1990 onwards, of the measures taken and problems encountered in the course of implementing this Recommendation. The progress of work will be examined by the Commission and the Senior Officials Group on Telecommunications (SOG-T); that the European Parliament be regularly informed.

Done at Luxembourg, 9 October 1990.

For the Council
The President
P. ROMITA

ANNEX

ANALYSIS OF THE REQUIREMENTS FOR THE COORDINATED INTRODUCTION OF PAN-EUROPEAN LAND-BASED PUBLIC PAGING IN THE COMMUNITY

1. GENERAL REQUIREMENTS

The future pan-European public radio paging system should fulfil the following general requirements:

— be suitable for operation over the whole frequency band range 169,4 MHz to 169,8 MHz with 25 KHz radio channels;
— permit an increase in the number of paging users which can be supported per paging area per unit of spectrum and for the same grade of service compared to systems based on CCIR Radio Paging Code No 1 (Pocsag), assuming the same mix of tone, numeric and alphanumeric pagers;
— permit easy access via PSTN, PSS, Videotex terminals, telex and other forms of direct access such as via ISDN;
— permit simultaneous operation of two or more independent systems in the same geographic area and permit several independent systems in areas where several national boundaries meet.

Access facilities should be provided for a calling party to initiate a paging request from service areas anywhere in the Community in the most cost effective and easy manner.

2. CHOICE OF RADIO SUBSYSTEM

Considerable experience in designing, manufacturing and operating public radio paging systems already exists in Europe. Much of this experience derives from the successful development and exploitation of the European Pocsag paging code (now CCIR Radio Paging Code No 1) by manufacturers and telecommunications administrations. This accumulated experience and knowledge should speed the task of selecting a suitable radio subsystem for the pan-European paging system. On the basis of the work underway within ETSI, the system specification should be decided by June 1990. The radio subsystem specification covers the modulation method, channel coding, the radio system structure and the pager's radio identity code structure (RIC).

3. THE PAGING RECEIVER SPECIFICATION

The specification of the paging receiver will cover the radio-performance, services and facilities and physical characteristics. The receiver specification should be finalized by June 1990. However, the optimization and commencement of production of prototype paging receivers should begin if possible as soon as the decision is taken on the radio subsystem in September 1989. This will provide a lead time for the testing and production of equipment before the start of service in December 1992 at the latest. This early start to development should be ensured by the close cooperation of manufacturing industry in the system specification in particular with ETSI.

4. SYSTEM IMPLEMENTATION

Telecommunication administrations should be responsible for the implementation of the radio paging system in their countries. The largest proportion of traffic on each national system will be national traffic, but implementation should support full roaming. Furthermore, the system specification should allow flexibility to enable economic implementation both in areas of low traffic density and areas of very high traffic density. To enable the service to commence by 31 December 1992 at the latest, the system specification should be completed by June 1990.

The system specification should include system access, call routing and processing, numbering scheme, and specification of paging network controller.

5. SERVICES AND FACILITIES SPECIFIED AND SUPPORTED BY THE PAN-EUROPEAN RADIO PAGING SYSTEM

The services and facilities specification should be completely specified by December 1989, and should fall into two categories: minimum and additional.

Minimum services and facilities

Minimum services and facilities are those which should be available on each national system and hence the pan-European system as a whole.

Additional services and facilities

The additional services are those which should be provided in open competition allowing for the national conditions for implementing such services. The non-provision of an additional service or facility should not affect in any way the functioning of the pan-European service at a basic level. The provision of an additional service or facility on one national system should not increase the cost of the minimum service on that system, or require an increase in functionality or an increase in cost on any other national system.

6. TARIFF CONSIDERATIONS

The principles of charging for the European service should be established taking full account of the competition rules of the Treaty for the European service, of cross charging between national operators for the handling of roaming traffic and of network technicalities. Administrations should endeavour to ensure that the user cost of the future radio paging service is not higher than that of current services of the same type.

7. GEOGRAPHICAL SERVICE COVERAGE

Administrations should study priorities for service coverage in order to stimulate the maximum pan-European traffic demand at the earliest possible stage compatible with commercial strategies.

The pan-European public radio paging system should be introduced by 31 December 1992 at the latest. The objective is geographical coverage by the service offered in each Member State, which should progressively extend as follows:

— 31 December 1992: start of service,
— January 1994: at least 25% of population,
— January 1995: at least 50% of population,
— January 1997: at least 80% of population.

8. SPECIAL REQUIREMENT

Consideration should be given to providing within the Ermes system the ability to have displayed, on the radio paging receiver, characters in all official Community languages, wherever possible.

APPENDIX 15

Council Directive of 9 October 1990 on the frequency bands designated for the coordinated introduction of pan-European land-based public radio paging in the Community

(90/544/EEC)

THE COUNCIL OF THE EUROPEAN COMMUNITIES,

Having regard to the Treaty establishing the European Economic Community, and in particular Article 100a thereof,

Having regard to the proposal from the Commission[1],

In cooperation with the European Parliament[2],

Having regard to the opinion of the Economic and Social Committee[3],

Whereas, by Recommendation 84/549/EEC[4], the Council calls for the introduction of services on the basis of a common harmonized approach in the field of telecommunications;

Whereas the resources offered by modern telecommunications networks should be utilized to the full for the economic development of the Community;

Whereas radio paging services depend on the allocation and availability of appropriate frequencies in order to transmit and receive between fixed-base stations and radio paging receivers respectively;

Whereas the frequencies and land-based public radio paging systems currently in use in the Community vary widely and do not allow all users on the move to reap the benefits of European-wide services and European-wide-markets;

Whereas the introduction of the more advanced radio paging system codenamed European Radio Messaging System (Ermes) being specified by the European Telecommunications Standards Institute (ETSI) will provide a unique opportunity of establishing a truly pan-European radio paging service;

Whereas the European Conference of Postal and Telecommunications Administrations (CEPT) has identified the unpaired frequency band 169,4-169,8 MHz as the most suitable band for public radio paging; whereas that choice is in accordance with the provisions of the International Telecommunications Union (ITU) Radio Regulations;

Whereas CEPT Recommendation T/R 25-07 on the coordination of frequencies for the European Radio Messaging System has designated the European channels for the ERMES system;

Whereas parts of the frequency based are being used or are intended for use by certain Member States for other radio services;

Whereas the progressive availability of the requisite part of the frequency band set out above will be indispensable for the establishment of a truly pan-European radio paging service;

Whereas some flexibility will be needed in order to take account of different frequency requirements in different Member States; whereas it will be necessary to ensure that such flexibility does not slow down the expansion of a pan-European system;

---

[1] OJ No C 43, 23. 2. 1990, p. 6.
[2] OJ No C 15, 22. 1. 1990, p. 84 and OJ No C 231, 17. 9. 1990, p. 86.
[3] OJ No C 298, 27. 11. 1989, p. 27.
[4] OJ No L 298, 16. 11. 1984, p. 49.

Whereas coordination procedures will have to be established between neighbouring countries as required;

Whereas the implementation of Council Recommendation 90/543/EEC of 9 October 1990 on the coordinated introduction of pan-European land-based public radio paging in the Community[5] will ensure the start of a pan-European system by 31 December 1992 at the latest;

Whereas on the basis of present technological and market trends, it appears realistic to envisage the designation of the 169,4—169,8 MHz frequency band as the band from which frequencies are selected in accordance with commercial requirements for the implementation and expansion of a pan-European radio paging system;

Whereas Council Directive 86/361/EEC of 24 July 1986 on the initial stage of the mutual recognition of type approval for telecommunications terminal equipment[6] will allow the rapid establishment of common conformity specifications for the pan-European land-based public radio paging system;

Whereas the report on public mobile communication drawn up by the Analysis and Forecasting Group (GAP) for the Senior Officials Group for Telecommunications (SOG-T) strongly recommends that telecommunications administrations reach an agreement to use the same radio frequencies for radio paging;

Whereas favourable opinions on this report have been delivered by the telecommunications administrations, by CEPT and by telecommunications equipment manufacturers in the Member States;

Whereas radio paging is a particularly spectrum-efficient communications method for alerting and/ or sending messages to users on the move,

HAS ADOPTED THIS DIRECTIVE:

Article 1

For the purposes of this Directive, 'pan-European land-based public radio paging service shall mean a public radio paging service based on a terrestrial infrastructure in the Member States in accordance with a common specification which allows persons wishing to do so to send and/or to receive alert and/or numeric or alphanumeric messages anywhere within the coverage of the service in the Community.

Article 2

1. Member States shall, in accordance with CEPT Recommendation T/R 25-07 designate in the 169,4 to 169,8 MHz waveband four channels which shall have priority and be protected, and preferably be:

— 169,6 MHz,
— 169,65 MHz,
— 169,7 MHz,
— 169,75 MHz,

for the pan-European land-based public radio paging service by 31 December 1992 at the latest.

2. Member States shall ensure that plans are prepared as quickly as possible to enable the pan-European public radio paging service to occupy the whole of the band 169,4 to 169,8 MHz according to commercial demand.

---

[5] See page 23 of this Official Journal.
[6] OJ No L 217, 5. 8. 1986, p. 21.

Article 3

1. Member States shall bring into force the laws, regulations and administrative provisions necessary to comply with this Directive no later than 18 October 1991. They shall forthwith inform the Commission thereof.

2. Member States shall communicate to the Commission the texts of the provisions of national law which they adopt in the field governed by this Directive.

Article 4

The Commission shall report to the Council on the implementation of this Directive not later than the end of 1996.

Article 5

This Directive is addressed to the Member States.

Done at Luxembourg, 9 October 1990.

For the Council
The President
P. ROMITA

APPENDIX 16

Council Directive of 29 April 1991 on the approximation of the laws of the Member States concerning telecommunications terminal equipment, including the mutual recognition of their conformity

(91/263/EEC)

THE COUNCIL OF THE EUROPEAN COMMUNITIES,

Having regard to the Treaty establishing the European Economic Community, and in particular Article 100a thereof,

Having regard to the proposal from the Commission[1],

In cooperation with the European Parliament[2],

Having regard to the opinion of the Economic and Social Committee[3],

Whereas Directive 86/361/EEC[4] introduced the initial stage of the mutual recognition of type approval for telecommunications terminal equipment and in particular in its Article 9 envisaged a further stage for full mutual recognition of type approval for terminal equipment;

Whereas Decision 87/95/EEC[5] sets out the measures to be implemented for the promotion of standardization in Europe and the preparation and implementation of standards in the field of information technology and telecommunications;

Whereas the Commission has issued a Green Paper on the development of the common market for telecommunications services and equipment proposing to accelerate the introduction of the full mutual recognition of type approval as the measure vital for the development of a competitive Community-wide terminal market;

Whereas the Council, in its resolution of 30 June 1988 on the development of the common market for telecommunications services and equipment up to 1992[6], considers as a major goal in the telecommunications policy the full mutual recognition of type approval for terminal equipment on the basis of the rapid development of common European conformity specifications;

Whereas the terminal equipment sector is a vital part of the telecommunications industry, which is one of the industrial mainstays of the economy in the Community;

Whereas harmonizing conditions for the placing on the market of telecommunications terminal equipment will create the conditions for an open and unified market;

Whereas real, comparable access to third country markets for European manufacturers should preferably be achieved through multilateral negotiations within GATT, although bilateral talks between the Community and third countries may also contribute to this process;

Whereas the Council resolution of 7 May 1985 provides for a new approach to technical harmonization and standards[7];

Whereas the scope of the Directive must be based on a general definition of the term 'terminal equipment' so as to allow the technical development of products;

---

[1] OJ No C 211, 17. 8. 1989, p. 12.
[2] OJ No C 113, 7. 5. 1990; and OJ No C 19, 28. 1. 1991, p. 88.
[3] OJ No C 329, 30. 12. 1989, p. 1.
[4] OJ No L 217, 5. 8. 1986, p. 21.
[5] OJ No L 36, 7. 2. 1987, p. 31.
[6] OJ No C 257, 4. 10. 1988, p. 1.
[7] OJ No C 136, 4. 6. 1985, p. 1.

Whereas Community law in its present form provides – notwithstanding one of the fundamental rules of the Community, namely the free movement of goods – that obstacles to movement within the Community, resulting from disparities in national legislation relating to the marketing of products, must be accepted in so far as such requirements can be recognized as being necessary to satisfy imperative requirements; whereas, therefore, the harmonization of laws in this case must be limited only to those requirements necessary to satisfy the essential requirements relating to terminal equipment; whereas these requirements must replace the relevant national requirements because they are essential;

Whereas the essential requirements must be satisfied in order to safeguard the general interest; whereas these requirements must be applied with discernment to take account of the state of the art at the time of manufacture and economic requirements;

Whereas Council Directive 73/23/EEC of 19 February 1973 on the harmonization of the laws of the Member States relating to electrical equipment designed for use within certain voltage limits[8] and Council Directive 83/189/EEC of 28 March 1983 laying down a procedure for the provision of information in the field of technical standards and regulations[9], as amended by Directive 88/182/EEC[10], are applicable, *inter alia*, to the fields of telecommunications and information technology;

Whereas Council Directive 89/336/EEC of 3 May 1989 on the approximation of the laws of Member States relating to electromagnetic compatibility[11] is applicable, *inter alia*, to the fields of telecommunications and information technology; whereas it is, however, appropriate to delete the provisions of Directive 89/336/EEC in so far as they refer to the definition of telecommunications terminal equipment and to the conformity assessment procedures to be applied for such equipment;

Whereas in respect of the essential requirements and in order to help manufacturers to prove conformity to those requirements, it is desirable to have standards harmonized at European level to safeguard the general interest in the design and manufacture of terminal equipment and in order to allow checks of conformity to those requirements; whereas these standards harmonized at European level are drawn up by private-law bodies and must retain their non-binding status; whereas for this purpose the European Committee for Standardization (CEN), the European Committee for Electrotechnical Standardization (Cenelec) and the European Telecommunications Standards Institute (ETSI), are the bodies recognized as competent to adopt harmonized standards; whereas, within the meaning of this Directive, a harmonized standard is a technical specification (European standard or harmonization document) adopted by one of these bodies, on the basis of a remit from the Commission in accordance with the provision of Directive 83/189/EEC, and in accordance with the general guidelines referred to above;

Whereas in respect of the essential requirements related to interworking with public telecommunications networks, and in cases where it is justified, through such networks, it is in general not possible to comply with such requirements other than by the application of unique technical solutions; whereas such solutions shall therefore be mandatory;

Whereas the proposals for common technical regulations are, as a general rule, drawn up on the basis of harmonized standards, and, in order to ensure an appropriate technical coordination on a broad European basis, of additional consultations, in particular with the Telecommunications Regulations Application Committee (TRAC) set up by members of the European Conference of Postal and Telecommunications Administration (CEPT) in a memorandum of understanding signed in 1991;

Whereas it is essential to ensure that notified bodies are of a high standard throughout the Community and meet minimum criteria of competence, impartiality and financial and other independence from clients;

---

[8] OJ No L 77, 26. 3. 1973, p. 29.
[9] OJ No L 109, 26. 4. 1983, p. 8.
[10] OJ No L 81, 26. 3. 1988, p. 75.
[11] OJ No L 139, 23. 5. 1989, p. 19.

Whereas it is appropriate to set up a committee bringing together parties directly concerned with the implementation of this Directive, in particular the national bodies designated for certifying conformity, to assist the Commission in executing the tasks entrusted to it by this Directive; whereas representatives from the telecommunication organizations, users, consumers, manufacturers, service providers and the trade unions should have the right to be consulted;

Whereas the Member States' responsibility for safety, health and the other aspects covered by the essential requirements on their territory must be recognized in a safeguard clause providing for adequate Community protection procedures;

Whereas the addressees of any decision taken under this Directive must be informed of the reasons for such a decision and the means of appeal open to them;

Whereas measures must be adopted with the aim of progressively establishing the internal market over a period expiring on 31 December 1992; whereas the internal market comprises an area without internal frontiers in which the free movement of goods, persons, services and capital is ensured.

HAS ADOPTED THIS DIRECTIVE:

CHAPTER 1

Scope, placing on the market and free circulation

Article 1

1. This Directive shall apply to terminal equipment.

2. For the purpose of this Directive:

— 'public telecommunications network' means the public telecommunications infrastructure which permits the conveyance of signals between defined network termination points by wire, by microwave, by optical means or by other electromagnetic means.
— 'terminal equipment' means equipment intended to be connected to the public telecommunications network, i.e.:

   (a) to be connected directly to the termination of a public telecommunications network;

      or

   (b) to interwork with a public telecommunications network being connected directly or indirectly to the termination of a public telecommunications network

in order to send, process or receive information.

The system of connection may be wire, radio, optical or other electromagnetic system,

— 'technical specification' means a specification contained in a document which lays down the characteristics required of a product such as levels of quality, performance, safety or dimensions, including the requirements applicable to the product as regards terminology, symbols, testing and test methods, packaging, marking and labelling.
— 'standard' means a technical specification adopted by a recognized standards body for repeated or continuous application, compliance with which is not compulsory.

3. The intended purpose of the equipment, shall be declared by the manufacturer or supplier of the equipment. However, terminal equipment within the meaning of paragraph 2 which makes use of a system of communication employing the radio frequency spectrum is presumed to be intended for connection to the public telecommunications network.

Article 2

1. Notwithstanding Article 1, equipment which is capable of being connected to the public telecommunications network, but is not intended for such a purpose, shall be accompanied by a manufacturer's or supplier's declaration, the model of which is to be found in Annex VIII and by

the operating manual. At the time of placing the equipment on the market for the first time, a copy of such documentation shall be transmitted to the notified body referred to in Article 10 (1) in the Member State where this first placing on the market takes place. In addition, such equipment shall be subject to the provisions of Article 11 (4).

2. The manufacturer or supplier shall be prepared to justify once, at the request of any notified body referred to in Article 10 (1), the intended purpose of such equipment on the basis of its relevant technical characteristics, its functions and indications of the market segment it is intended for.

Article 3

1. Member States shall take all appropriate measures to ensure that terminal equipment may be placed on the market and put into service only if it complies with the requirements laid down in this Directive when it is properly installed and maintained and used for its intended purpose.

2. Member States shall also take all appropriate measures to ensure that equipment referred to in Article 2 may be placed and allowed to remain on the market only if it complies with the requirements laid down by this Directive for this equipment and may not be connected to the public telecommunications network within the meaning of Article 1 (2).

3. Member States shall also take all appropriate measures to ensure that terminal equipment or equipment referred to in Article 2 is disconnected from the public telecommunications network if it is not used for its intended purpose. Member States may moreover take all appropriate measures, according to their national laws, to prevent connection to the public telecommunications network of terminal equipment that is not used in conformity with its intended purpose.

Article 4

Terminal equipment shall satisfy the following essential requirements:

(a) user safety, in so far as this requirement is not covered by Directive 73/23/EEC;

(b) safety of employees of public telecommunications networks operators, in so far as this requirement is not covered by Directive 73/23/EEC;

(c) electromagnetic compatibility requirements in so far as they are specific to terminal equipment;

(d) protection of the public telecommunications network from harm;

(e) effective use of the radio frequency spectrum, where appropriate;

(f) interworking of terminal equipment with public telecommunications network equipment for the purpose of establishing, modifying, charging for, holding and clearing real or virtual connection;

(g) interworking of terminal equipment via the public telecommunications network, in justified cases.

The cases where terminal equipment supports:

(i) reserved service according to Community law;

(ii) a service which the Council has decided that there should be Community-wide availability,

are considered as justified cases and the requirements concerning this interworking are determined in accordance with the procedure provided for in Article 14.

In addition, after consultation of representatives of the bodies referred to in Article 13 (3) and taking due account of the result of these consultations, the Commission may propose that this essential requirement is recognized as being justified for other terminal equipment in accordance with the procedure provided for in Article 14.

Article 5

Member States shall not impede the placing on the market and the free circulation and use on their territory of terminal equipment which complies with the provisions of this Directive.

Article 6

1. Member States shall presume compliance with the essential requirements referred to in Article 4 (a) and (b) in respect of terminal equipment which is in conformity with the national standards implementing the relevant harmonized standards, the references of which have been published in the *Official Journal of the European Communities*. Member States shall publish the references of such national standards.

2. The Commission shall, in accordance with the procedure laid down in Article 14, adopt:

— as a first step, the measure identifying the type of terminal equipment for which a common technical regulation is required, as well as the associated scope statement for that regulation, with a view to its transmission to the relevant standardization bodies,
— as a second step, once they have been prepared by the relevant standardization bodies, the corresponding harmonized standards, or parts thereof, implementing the essential requirements referred to in Article 4 (c) to (g) which shall be transformed into common technical regulations, compliance with which shall be mandatory and the reference of which shall be published in the *Official Journal of the European Communities*.

Article 7

Where a Member State or the Commission considers that the harmonized standards referred to in Article 6 exceed or do not entirely meet the essential requirements referred to in Article 4, the Commission or the Member State concerned shall bring the matter before the Committee referred to in Article 13, hereinafter referred to as 'the Committee', giving the reasons therefore. The Committee shall deliver an opinion as soon as possible.

In the light of the Committee's opinion and after consultation of the standing Committee set up by Directive 83/189/EEC, the Commission shall inform the Member States whether or not it is necessary to withdraw reference to those standards and any related technical regulations from the *Official Journal of the European Communities* and shall take the necessary steps to correct the shortcomings noted in the standards.

Article 8

1. Where a Member State finds that terminal equipment bearing the markings under the provision laid down in Chapter III does not comply with the relevant essential requirements when properly used in accordance with the purpose intended by the manufacturer, it shall take all appropriate measures to withdraw such products from the market or to prohibit or restrict their being placed on the market.

The Member State concerned shall immediately inform the Commission of any such measure indicating the reasons for its decision, and in particular whether non-compliance is due to:

(a) incorrect application of the harmonized standards or common technical regulations referred to in Article 6;

(b) shortcomings in the harmonized standards or common technical regulations referred to in Article 6 themselves.

2. The Commission shall enter into consultation with the parties concerned as soon as possible. Where, after such consultation, the Commission finds that any measure as referred to in paragraph 1 is justified it shall immediately so inform the Member State that took the action and the other Member States. Where the decision referred to in paragraph 1 is attributed to shortcomings in the harmonized standards or common technical regulations, the Commission, after consulting the parties concerned, shall bring the matter before the Committee within two months if the Member

State which has taken the measure intends to maintain them, and shall initiate the procedure referred to in Article 7.

3. Where terminal equipment which does not comply with the relevant essential requirements bears the CE mark the competent Member State shall take appropriate action against whomsoever has affixed the mark and shall inform the Commission and the other Member States thereof.

4. The Commission shall keep the Member State informed of the progress and outcome of this procedure.

CHAPTER II

Conformity assessment

Article 9

1. According to the choice of the manufacturer or his authorized representative established within the Community, terminal equipment shall be subject to either the EC type-examination, as described in Annex I, or to the EC declaration of conformity, as described in Annex IV.

2. An EC type-examination as described in Annex I shall be accompanied by a declaration issued according to the EC declaration of conformity to type procedure as described in Annex II or Annex III.

3. The records and correspondence relating to the procedure referred to in this Article shall be in an official language of the Member State where the said procedure will be carried out, or in a language acceptable to the notified body involved.

4. Article 10 (4) of Directive 89/336/EEC is hereby deleted.

Article 10

1. Member States shall notify to the Commission the bodies established in the Community and their identifying symbols, which they have designated for carrying out the certification, product checks, and associated surveillance tasks pertaining to the procedures referred to in Article 9. Member States shall apply the minimum criteria, set out in Annex V, for the designation of such bodies. Bodies that satisfy the criteria fixed by the relevant harmonized standards shall be presumed to satisfy the criteria set out in Annex V.

2. Member States shall inform the Commission of test laboratories established in the Community which they have designated for carrying out tests pertaining to the procedures referred to in Article 9. Notified bodies shall apply the criteria fixed by the appropriate parts of the relevant harmonized standards for the designation of such laboratories.

3. The Commission shall publish the list of notified bodies and the list of test laboratories together with the tasks for which they have been designated in the *Official Journal of the European Communities* and shall ensure that this list is kept up to date.

4. A Member State has designated a notified body or a test laboratory under paragraph 1 or 2 shall annul the designation if the notified body or the test laboratory no longer meets the relevant criteria for designation. It shall immediately inform the other Member States and the Commission accordingly and withdraw the notification. Where a Member State or the Commission considers that a notified body or a test laboratory designated by a Member State does not meet the relevant criteria the matter shall be brought before the Committee referred to in Article 13, which shall give its opinion within three months; in the light of the Committee's opinion the Commission shall inform the Member State concerned of any changes needed if that notified body of test laboratory is to retain its recognized status.

5. In order to facilitate the determination of conformity of terminal equipment with technical regulations and standards, the notified bodies shall recognize documentation issued by third country relevant bodies, when agreements between the Community and the third country concerned have been concluded on the basis of a mutually satisfactory understanding.

6. The notified bodies referred to in Article 10 (1), when issuing an EC type-examination certificate as referred to in Annex I, followed by the appropriate document referred to in Annex II or III, or a decision on quality assurance assessment as referred to in Annex IV, issue at the same time an administrative approval for the connection of the concerned terminal equipment to the public telecommunications network.

CHAPTER III

CE mark of conformity and inscriptions

Article 11

1. The marking of terminal equipment complying with this Directive shall consist of the CE mark consisting of the symbol 'CE', followed by the identifying symbol of the notified body responsible and a symbol indicating that the equipment is intended and is suitable to be connected to the public telecommunications network. The CE mark and these two symbols are shown in Annex VI.

2. The affixing of marks which are likely to be confused with the marks of conformity specified in Annex VI shall be prohibited.

3. Terminal equipment shall be identified by the manufacturer by means of type, batch and/or serial numbers and by the name of the manufacturer and/or supplier responsible for placing it on the market.

4. Equipment manufacturers or suppliers who place on the market equipment as referred to in Article 2 shall affix the symbol specified in Annex VII in such a way that it follows the CE mark and visually forms an integral part of the total marking.

Article 12

Where it is established that the marking referred to in Article 11 (1) has been affixed to terminal equipment which:

— does not conform to an approved type,
— conforms to an approved type which does not meet the essential requirements applicable to it,

or, where the manufacturer has failed to fulfil his obligations under the relevant EC declaration of conformity,

the notified body shall withdraw the EC type-examination certificate referred to in Annex I, the EC quality system approval decision referred to in Annex III or the EC quality system approval decision as referred to in Annex IV, notwithstanding any decisions taken under Article 8.

CHAPTER IV

Committee

Article 13

1. The Commission shall be assisted by a Committee of an advisory nature composed of the representatives of the Member States and chaired by the representative of the Commission. The Committee shall be called the Approvals Committee for Terminal Equipment (ACTE).

2. The representative of the Commission shall submit to the Committee a draft of the measure to be taken. The Committee shall deliver its opinion on the draft, within a time limit which the chairman may lay down according to the urgency of the matter, if necessary by taking a vote.

The opinion shall be recorded in the minutes; in addition, each Member State shall have the right to ask to have its position recorded in the minutes.

The Commission shall take the utmost account of the opinion delivered by the Committee. It shall inform the Committee of the manner in which its opinion has been taken into account.

3. The Commission will periodically consult the representative of the telecommunications organizations, the consumers, the manufacturers, the service providers and trade unions and will inform the Committee on the outcome of such consultations, with a view to taking due account of the outcome.

Article 14

1. Notwithstanding Article 13 (1) and (2), the following procedure shall apply for matters covered by Articles 4 (g) and 6 (2).

2. The representative of the Commission shall submit to the Committee established in Article 13 a draft of the measures to be taken as referred to in Articles 4 (g) and 6 (2). The Committee shall deliver its opinion on the draft within a time limit which the chairman may lay down according to the urgency of the matter. The opinion shall be delivered by the majority laid down in Article 148 (2) of the Treaty in the case of decisions which the Council is required to adopt on a proposal from the Commission. The votes of the representatives of the Member States within the Committee shall be weighted in the manner set out in that Article. The chairman shall not vote.

3. The Commission shall adopt the measures envisaged if they are in accordance with the opinion of the Committee.

4. If the measures envisaged are not in accordance with the opinion of the Committee, or if no opinion is delivered, the Commission shall, without delay, submit to the Council a proposal relating to the measure to be taken. The Council shall act by qualified majority. If, within three months from the date of referral to it, the Council has not acted, the proposed measure shall be adopted by the Commission.

CHAPTER V

Final and transitional provisions

Article 15

The Commission shall draw up every second year a report on the implementation of this Directive, including progress on drawing up the relevant harmonized standards and on transforming them into technical regulations, as well as any problems that have arisen in the course of implementation. The report will also outline the activities of the Committee, and assess progress in achieving an open competitive market for terminal equipment at Community level consistent with the essential requirements referred to in Article 4.

Article 16

1. Directive 86/361/EEC is hereby repealed, with effect from 6 November 1992. References made to the repealed Directive shall be construed as being made to this Directive.

2. Notwithstanding paragraph 1 and Article 10 (2), Member States may designate as test laboratories such bodies which have been notified under Directive 86/361/EEC, without applying the criteria of Article 10 (2) for a period of 18 months after the effective date of repeal of Directive 86/361/EEC, it being understood that these laboratories will continue to observe the criteria for which they were notified.

3. Notwithstanding paragraph 1, any type approval granted by Member States in accordance with Directive 86/361/EEC may remain valid under the legislation of the Member States within the criteria of validity appropriate to the original approval.

4. Notwithstanding paragraph 1, measures adopted under Directive 86/361/EEC shall be submitted to the Committee under the procedure of Article 14 for possible transposition into common technical regulations.

Article 17

1. Member States shall take the measure necessary to comply with this Directive not later than 6 November 1992. They shall forthwith inform the Commission thereof.

When Member States adopt these measures, they shall contain a reference to this Directive or shall be accompanied by such reference on the occasion of their official publication. The methods of making such a reference shall be laid down by the Member States.

2. Member States shall inform the Commission of the main provisions of domestic law which they adopt in the field governed by this Directive.

Article 18

This Directive is addressed to the Member States.

Done at Luxembourg, 29 April 1991.

For the Council
The President
R. GOEBBELS

ANNEX I

EC TYPE-EXAMINATION

1. EC type-examination is that part of the procedure whereby a notified body ascertains and attests that a specimen, representative of the production envisaged, meets the provisions of the Directive that apply to it.

2. The application for the EC type-examination shall be lodged by the manufacturer or his authorized representative established within the Community with a notified body of his choice.

    The application shall include:

    — the name and address of the manufacturer and, if the application is lodged by the authorized representative, his name and address in addition,
    — a written declaration that the same application has not been lodged with any other notified body,
    — the technical documentation, as described in point 3.

    The applicant shall place at the disposal of the notified body a specimen, representative of the production envisaged and hereinafter called 'type'[12]. The notified body may request further specimens if needed for carrying out the test programme.

3. The technical documentation shall enable the conformity of the product with the essential requirements of the Directive to be assessed. It shall, as far as relevant for such assessment, cover the design, manufacture and operation of the product.

    For example, the documentation shall contain as far as is relevant for assessment:

    — a general type-description sufficient to identify the product preferably by provision of photographs,
    — design and manufacturing drawings and lists of components, sub-assemblies, circuits, etc.,
    — descriptions and explanations necessary for the understanding of said drawings and lists and the operation of the product,

---

[12] A type may cover several versions of the product provided that the differences between the versions do not affect the level of safety and the other requirements concerning the performance of the product.

— a list of the standards referred to in Article 6, applied in full or in part, and descriptions of the solutions adopted to meet the essential requirements of the Directive when the standards referred to in Article 6 have not been applied,

— results of examinations carried out, etc.,

— test reports,

— proposed user information or handbook.

4. The notified body shall:

4.1. examine the technical documentation, verify that the type has been manufactured in conformity with it and identify the elements which have been designed in accordance with the relevant provisions of the standards referred to in Article 6 (1), as well as the components of those standards;

4.2. perform, or have performed, the appropriate examinations and necessary tests to check whether the solutions adopted by the manufacturer meet the essential requirements of the Directive which are specified in Article 4 (a) and (b);

4.3. perform, or have performed, the appropriate examinations and necessary tests to check that the type meets the relevant common technical regulations specified in Article 6 (2);

4.4. agree with the applicant on the location where the examinations and necessary tests are to be carried out.

5. Where the type meets the provisions of the Directive, the notified body shall issue an EC type-examination certificate to the applicant. The certificate shall contain the name and address of the manufacturer, conclusions of the examination, condition for its validity and the necessary data for identification of the approved type.

A list of the relevant parts of the technical documentation shall be annexed to the certificate and a copy kept by the notified body.

6. The applicant shall inform the notified body that holds the technical documentation concerning the EC type-examination certificate of all modifications to the approved product which must receive additional approval where such changes may affect the conformity with the essential requirements or the prescribed conditions for use of the product. This additional approval is given in the form of an addition to the original EC type-examination certificate.

7. Each notified body shall communicate to the other notified bodies the relevant information concerning the EC type-examination certificates and additions issued and withdrawn.

8. The other notified bodies may request copies of the EC type-examination certificates and/or their additions. The Annexes to the certificate shall be kept at the disposal of the other notified bodies.

9. The manufacturer or his authorized representative shall keep with the technical documentation copies of EC type-examination certificates and their additions for a period ending at least 10 years after the last product has been manufactured.

Where neither the manufacturer nor his authorized representative is established within the Community, the obligation to keep the technical documentation available shall be the responsibility of the person who places the product on the Community market.

ANNEX II

CONFORMITY TO TYPE

1. Conformity to type is that part of the procedure whereby the manufacturer or his authorized representative established within the Community ensures and declares that the products con-

cerned are in conformity with the type as described in the EC type-examination certificate and satisfy the requirements of the Directive that applies to them. The manufacturer shall affix the marks referred to in Article 11 (1) to each product and draw up a written declaration of conformity to type.

2. The manufacturer shall take all measures necessary to ensure that the manufacturing process assures compliance of the manufactured products with the type as described in the EC type-examination certificate and with the requirements of the Directive that apply to them.

3. The manufacturer or his authorized representative shall keep a copy of the declaration of conformity for a period ending at least 10 years after the last product has been manufactured.

Where neither the manufacturer nor his authorized representative is established within the Community, the obligation to keep the declaration of conformity to type available shall be the responsibility of the person who places the product on the Community market.

4. A notified body chosen by the manufacturer shall carry out, or have carried out, product checks at random intervals. An adequate sample of the final products, which may be taken on site by the notified body or on its behalf, shall be examined and appropriate tests shall be carried out to check the conformity of products with the relevant requirements of the Directive. In those cases where one or more of the products checked do not conform, the notified body shall take appropriate measures.

ANNEX III

PRODUCTION QUALITY ASSURANCE

1. Production quality assurance is the procedure whereby the manufacturer who satisfies the obligations of point 2 ensures and declares that the products concerned are in conformity with the type as described in the EC type-examination certificate and satisfy the requirements of the Directive that apply to them. The manufacturer shall affix the marks referred to in Article 11 (1) to each product and draw up a written declaration of conformity to type.

2. The manufacturer shall operate an approved quality system for production, final product inspection and testing as specified in point 3 and shall be subject to monitoring as specified in point 4.

3. Quality system

3.1. The manufacturer shall lodge an application for assessment of his quality system with a notified body of his choice, for the products concerned.

The application shall include:

— all relevant information for the product category envisaged,
— the documentation concerning the quality system,
— if applicable, the technical documentation of the approved type and a copy of the EC type-examination certificate.

3.2. The quality system shall ensure compliance of the products with the type as described in the EC type-examination certificate and with the requirements of the Directive that apply to them.

All the element, requirements and provisions adopted by the manufacturer shall be documented in a systematic and orderly manner in the form of written policies, procedures and instructions. The quality system documentation must permit a consistent interpretation of the quality programmes, plan, manuals and records.

It shall contain in particular an adequate description of:

— the quality objectives and the organizational structure, responsibilities and powers of the management with regard to product quality,
— the manufacturing, quality control and quality assurance techniques, processes and systematic actions that will be used,
— the examinations and tests will be carried out before, during and after manufacture, and the frequency with which they will be carried out,
— the quality records, such as inspection reports and test data, calibration data, qualification reports of the personnel concerned, etc.
— the means to monitor the achievement of the required product quality and the effective operation of the quality system.

3.3. The notified body shall assess the quality system to determine whether it satisfies the requirements referred to in point 3.2. It shall presume conformity with these requirements in respect of quality systems that implement the relevant harmonized standard[13].

The auditing team shall have at least one member with experience of evaluation in the product technology concerned. The evaluation procedure shall include an inspection visit to the manufacturer's premises.

The decision shall be notified to the manufacturer. The notification shall contain the conclusions of the examination and the reasoned assessment decision.

3.4. The manufacturer shall undertake to fulfil the obligations arising out of the quality system as approved and to uphold it so that it remains adequate and efficient.

The manufacturer or his authorized representative shall keep the notified body that has approved the quality system informed of any intended updating of the quality system.

The notified body shall evaluate the modifications proposed and decide whether the amended quality system will still satisfy the requirements referred to in point 3.2. or whether a re-assessment is required.

It shall notify its decision to the manufacturer. The notification shall contain the conclusions of the examination and the reasoned assessment decision.

4.   Surveillance under the responsibility of the notified body

4.1. The purpose of surveillance is to make sure that the manufacturer duly fulfils the obligations arising out of the approved quality system.

4.2. The manufacturer shall allow the notified body access for inspection purpose to the location of manufacture, inspection and testing, and storage and shall provide it with all necessary information, in particular:

— the quality system documentation,
— the quality records, such as inspection reports and test data, calibration data, qualification reports of the personnel concerned, etc.

4.3. The notified body shall carry out audits at reasonable intervals to make sure that the manufacturer maintains and applies the quality system and shall provide an audit report to the manufacturer.

4.4. Additionally, the notified body may pay unexpected visits to the manufacturer. During such visits the notified body may carry out, or cause to be carried out, tests to verify that the quality system is functioning correctly, if necessary. The notified body shall provide the manufacturer with a visit report and, if a test has taken place, with a report.

---

[13] The harmonized standard will be EN 29002, supplemented, if necessary, to take into account the specific nature of the procedure for which it is implemented.

5. The manufacturer shall, for a period ending at least 10 years after the last product has been manufactured, keep at the disposal of the national authorities:
    — the documentation referred to in the second indent of point 3.1.,
    — the updating referred to in the second paragraph of point 3.4.,
    — the decisions and reports from the notified body which are referred to in the final paragraph of points 3.4., 4.3. and 4.4.

6. Each notified body referred to in Article 10 (1) shall make available to the other notified bodies referred to in that Article the relevant information concerning the quality system approvals issued and withdrawn.

ANNEX IV

FULL QUALITY ASSURANCE

1. Full quality assurance is the procedure whereby the manufacturer who satisfies the obligations of point 2 ensures and declares that the products concerned satisfy the requirements of the Directive that apply to them. The manufacturer shall affix the marks referred to in Article 11 (1) to each product and draw up a written declaration of conformity.

2. The manufacturer shall operate an approved quality system for design, manufacture and final product inspection and testing as specified in point 3 and shall be subject to surveillance as specified in point 4.

3. **Quality system**

3.1. The manufacturer shall lodge an application for assessment of his quality system with a notified body.

    The application shall include:

    — all relevant information for the products envisaged,
    — the quality system's documentation.

3.2. The quality system shall ensure compliance of the products with the requirements of the Directive that apply to them.

    All the elements, requirements and provisions adopted by the manufacturer shall be documented in a systematic and orderly manner in the form of written policies, procedures and instructions. This quality system documentation shall ensure a common understanding of the quality policies and procedures such as a quality programme, plans, manuals and records.

    It shall contain in particular an adequate description of:

    — the quality objectives and the organizational structure, responsibilities and powers of the management with regard to design and product quality,
    — the technical specifications, including the harmonized standards and technical regulations as well as relevant test specifications that will be applied and, where the standards referred to in Article 6 (1) will not be applied in full, the means will be used to ensure that the essential requirements of the Directive that apply to the products will be met,
    — the design control and design verification techniques, processes and systematic actions that will be used when designing the products pertaining to the product category covered,
    — the corresponding manufacturing, quality control and quality assurance techniques, processes and systematic actions that will be used,
    — the examinations and tests will be carried out before, during and after manufacture, and the frequency with which they will be carried out; as well as the results of the tests carried out before manufacture where appropriate,

— the means by which it is ensured that the test and examination facilities respect the appropriate requirements for the performance of the necessary test,
— the quality records, such as inspection reports and test data, calibration data, qualification reports of the personnel concerned, etc.,
— the means to monitor the achievement of the required design and product quality and the effective operation of the quality system.

3.3. The notified body shall assess the quality system to determine whether it satisfies the requirements referred to in point 3.2. It shall presume compliance with these requirements in respect of quality systems that implement the relevant harmonized standard[14].

The notified body shall assess in particular whether the quality control system ensures conformity of the products with the requirements of the Directive in the light of the relevant documentation supplied in respect of points 3.1. and 3.2. including, where relevant, test results supplied by the manufacturer.

The auditing team shall have at least one member experienced as an assessor in the product technology concerned. The evaluation procedure shall include an assessment visit tot he manufacturer's premises.

The decision shall be notified to the manufacturer. The notification shall contain the conclusions of the examination and the reasoned assessment decision.

3.4. The manufacturer shall undertake to fulfil the obligations arising out of the quality system as approved and to uphold it so that it remains adequate and efficient.

The manufacturer or his authorized representative shall keep the notified body that has approved the quality system informed of any intended updating of the quality system.

The notified body shall evaluate the modifications proposed and decide whether the amended quality system will still satisfy the requirements referred to in point 3.2. or whether a re-assessment is required.

It shall notify its decision to the manufacturer. The notification shall contain the conclusions of the examination and the reasoned assessment decision.

4. **EC surveillance under the responsibility of the notified body**

4.1. The purpose of surveillance is to make sure that the manufacturer duly fulfils the obligations arising out of the approved quality system.

4.2. The manufacturer shall allow the notified body access for inspection purposes to the location of design, manufacture, inspection and testing, and storage and shall provide it with all necessary information, in particular:

— the quality system documentation,
— the quality records as foreseen by the design part of the quality system, such as results of analyses, calculations, tests, etc.
— the quality records as foreseen by the manufacturing part of the quality system, such as inspection reports and test data, calibration data, qualification reports of the personnel concerned, etc.

4.3. The notified body shall carry out audits at reasonable intervals to make sure that the manufacturer maintains and applies the quality system and shall provide an audit report to the manufacturer.

4.4. Additionally, the notified body may pay unexpected visits to the manufacturer. At the time of such visits, the notified body may carry out tests or have them carried out in order to

---

[14] The harmonized standard shall be EN 29001, supplemented, if necessary, to take into account the specific nature of the products for which it is implemented.

check the proper functioning of the quality system where necessary; it shall provide the manufacturer with a visit report and, if a test has been carried out, with a test report.

5. The manufacturer shall, for a period ending at least 10 years after the last product has been manufactured, keep at the disposal of the national authorities:

    — the documentation referred to in the second indent of point 3.1.,
    — the updating referred to in the second paragraph of point 3.4.,
    — the decisions and reports from the modified body which are referred to in the final paragraph of points 3.4., 4.3. and 4.4.

6. Each notified body referred to in Article 10 (1) shall make available to the other notified bodies referred to in that Article the relevant information concerning quality system approvals including references to the product(s) concerned, issued and withdrawn.

ANNEX V

MINIMUM CRITERIA TO BE TAKEN INTO ACCOUNT BY MEMBER STATES WHEN DESIGNATING NOTIFIED BODIES IN ACCORDANCE WITH ARTICLE 10 (1)

1. The notified body, its director and the staff responsible for carrying out the tasks for which the notified body has been designated shall not be a designer, manufacturer, supplier or installer of terminal equipment, or a network operator or a service provider, nor the authorized representative of any of such parties. They shall not become directly involved in the design, construction, marketing or maintenance of terminal equipment, nor represent the parties engaged in these activities. This does not preclude the possibility of exchanges of technical information between the manufacturer an the notified body.

2. The notified body and its staff must carry out the tasks for which the notified body has been designated with the highest degree of professional integrity and technical competence and must be free from all pressures and inducements, particularly financial, which might influence their judgment or the results of any inspection, especially from persons or groups of persons with an interest in such results.

3. The notified body must have at its disposal the necessary staff and facilities to enable it to perform properly the administrative and technical work associated with the tasks for which it has been designated.

4. The staff responsible for inspections must have:

    — sound technical and professional training,
    — satisfactory knowledge of the requirements of the tests or inspections that are carried out and adequate experience of such tests or inspections,
    — the ability to draw up the certificates, records and reports required to authenticate the performance of the inspections.

5. The impartiality of inspection staff must be guaranteed. Their remuneration must not depend on the number of tests or inspections carried out nor on the results of such inspections.

6. The notified body must take out liability insurance unless its liability is assumed by the State in accordance with national law, or the Member State itself is directly responsible.

7. The staff of the notified body is bound to observe professional secrecy with regard to all information gained in carrying out its tasks (except *vis-à-vis* the competent administrative authorities of the State in which its activities are carried out) under this Directive or any provision of national law giving effect thereto.

ANNEX VI

MARKING FOR TERMINAL EQUIPMENT REFERRED TO IN ARTICLE 11 (1)

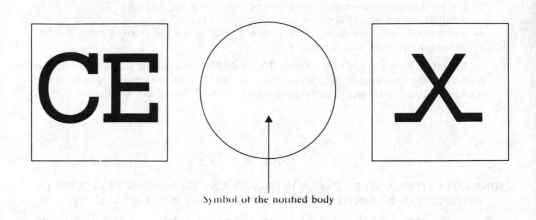

Symbol of the notified body

ANNEX VII

MARKING FOR EQUIPMENT REFERRED TO IN ARTICLE 11 (4)

ANNEX VIII

MODEL OF A DECLARATION REFERRED TO IN ARTICLE 2 (1)

The manufacturer/supplier[15] . . . .

. . . .

. . . .

Declares that[16] . . . .

. . . .

is not intended to be connected to a public telecommunications network.

The connection of such equipment to a public telecommunications network in the Community Member State will be in violation of the national law implementing Directive 91/263/EEC on the approximation of the laws of the Member States concerning telecommunication terminal equipment, including the mutual recognition of their conformity.

DATE, PLACE AND SIGNATURE

---

[15] Name and address.
[16] Equipment identification.

APPENDIX 17

Council Directive of 3 June 1991 on the frequency band to be designated for the coordinated introduction of digital European cordless telecommunications (DECT) into the Community

(91/287/EEC)

THE COUNCIL OF THE EUROPEAN COMMUNITIES,

Having regard to the Treaty establishing the European Economic Community, and in particular Article 100a thereof,

Having regard to the proposal from the Commission[1],

In cooperation with the European Parliament[2],

Having regard to the opinion of the Economic and Social Committee[3],

Whereas recommendation 84/549/EEC[4] calls for the introduction of services on the basis of a common harmonized approach in the field of telecommunications;

Whereas the Council in its resolution of 30 June 1988[5] on the development of the common market for telecommunications services and equipment calls for the promotion of Europe-wide services according to market requirements;

Whereas the resources offered by modern telecommunications networks should be utilized to the full for the economic development of the Community;

Whereas Council Directive 89/336/EEC of 3 May 1989 on the approximation of the laws of Member States relating to electromagnetic compatibility[6] is applicable, and particular attention should be taken to avoid harmful electromagnetic interference;

Whereas current cordless telephone systems in use in the Community, and the frequency bands they operate in, vary widely and may not allow the benefits of Europe-wide services or benefit from the economies of scale associated with a truly European market;

Whereas the European Telecommunications Standard Institute (ETSI) is currently developing the European Telecommunications Standard (ETS) or digital European cordless telecommunications (DECT);

Whereas the development of the European Telecommunications Standard (ETS) must take account of the safety of users, and the need for Europe-wide interoperability and enable users provided with a service based on DECT technology in one Member State to gain access to the service in any other Member State, where appropriate;

Whereas the European implementation of DECT will provide an important opportunity to establish truly European digital cordless telephone facilities;

Whereas ETSI has estimated that DECT will require 20 MHz in high density areas;

Whereas the European Conference of Postal and Telecommunications Administrations (CEPT) has recommended the common European frequency band 1880-1900 MHz for DECT, recognizing that, subject to the system, development of DECT additional frequency spectrum may be required;

---

[1] OJ No C 187, 27. 7. 1990, p. 5.
[2] OJ No C 19, 28. 1. 1991, p. 97 and OJ No C 106, 22. 4. 1991, p. 78.
[3] OJ No C 332, 31. 12. 1990, p. 172.
[4] OJ No L 298, 16. 11. 1984, p. 49.
[5] OJ No C 257, 4. 10. 1988, p. 1.
[6] OJ No L 139, 23. 5. 1989, p. 19.

Whereas this should be taken into account in the preparation for the 1992 World Administrative Radio Conference (WARC);

Whereas after the date of designation of the frequency band for DECT, existing services may continue in the band, providing that they do not interfere with DECT systems that may be established according to commercial demand;

Whereas the implementation of Council recommendation 91/288/EEC of 3 June 1991 on the coordinated introduction of DECT into the Community[7], will ensure the implementation of DECT by 31 December 1992 at the latest;

Whereas Council Directive 91/263/EEC of 29 April 1991 on the approximation of the laws of the Member States concerning telecommunications terminal equipment, including the mutual recognition of their conformity[8] will allow the rapid establishment of common conformity specifications for DECT;

Whereas the establishment of DECT depends on the allocation and availability of a frequency band in order to transmit and receive between fixed-base stations and mobile stations;

Whereas some flexibility will be needed in order to take account of different frequency requirements in different Member States; it will be necessary to ensure that such flexibility does not slow down the implementation of DECT technology according to commercial demand across the Community;

Whereas the progressive availability of the full range of the frequency band set out above will be indispensable for the establishment of DECT on a Europe-wide basis,

HAS ADOPTED THIS DIRECTIVE:

Article 1

For the purposes of this Directive, the digital European cordless telecommunications (DECT) system shall mean technology conforming to the European Telecommunications Standard (ETS) for digital cordless telecommunications referred to in recommendation 91/288/EEC, and the telecommunications systems, both public and private, which directly utilize such technology.

Article 2

Member States shall, in accordance with CEPT Recommendation T/R 22-02 of the European Conference of Postal and Telecommunications Administration designate the frequency band 1880–1900 MHz for digital European cordless telecommunications (DECT) by 1 January 1992.

In accordance with the CEPT Recommendation, DECT shall have priority over other services in the same band, and be protected in the designated band.

Article 3

1. Member States shall bring into force the laws, regulations and administrative provisions necessary to comply with this Directive by 31 December 1991. They shall forthwith inform the Commission thereof.

2. When Member States adopt these measures, they shall contain a reference to this Directive or shall be accompanied by such reference on the occasion of their official publication. The methods of making such a reference shall be laid down by the Member States.

Article 4

The Commission shall report to the Council on the implementation of this Directive not later than the end of 1995.

---

[7] See page 47 of this Official Journal.
[8] OJ No L 128, 23. 5. 1991, p. 1.

Article 5

This Directive is addressed to the Member States.

Done at Luxembourg, 3 June 1991.

For the Council
The President
A. BODRY

APPENDIX 18

Council Recommendation of 3 June 1991 on the coordinated introduction of digital European cordless telecommunications (DECT) into the Community

(91/288/EEC)

THE COUNCIL OF THE EUROPEAN COMMUNITIES,

Having regard to the Treaty establishing the European Economic Community, in particular Article 235 thereof,

Having regard to the proposal from the Commission[1],

Having regard to the opinion of the European Parliament[2],

Having regard to the opinion of the Economic and Social Committee[3],

Whereas recommendation 84/549/EEC[4] calls for the introduction of services on the basis of a common harmonized approach in the field of telecommunications;

Whereas the Council in its resolution of 30 June 1988[5] on the development of the common market for telecommunication services and equipment up to 1992 calls for the promotion of Europe-wide services according to market requirements;

Whereas the resources offered by modern telecommunications networks should be utilized to the full for the economic development of the Community;

Whereas the potential for cordless telecommunications in the Community has been demonstrated by recent developments such as recent agreements on public telepoint services; whereas the European Telecommunications Standard (ETS) for digital European cordless telecommunications (DECT) currently being developed by the European Telecommunications Standards Institute (ETSI) will greatly enhance the possibilities of cordless telecommunications;

Whereas the development of the ETS must take account of the safety of users, and the need for Europe-wide interoperability, enable users provided with a service based on DECT technology in one Member State to gain access to the service in any other Member State, where appropriate;

Whereas the European implementation of DECT technology will provide an important opportunity to establish truly European digital cordless telephone facilities;

Whereas a coordinated policy for the introduction of common standards for cordless telephones will make possible the establishment of a European market in mobile handsets which will be capable of creating, by virtue of their size, service features, and costs, the necessary development conditions to establish a lead in worldwide markets;

Whereas such a future system, offering both voice and data services, is to be based on digital techniques, thereby facilitating compatibility with the general digital environment and the Integrated Services Digital Network (ISDN) in the Community in accordance with recommendation 86/659/EEC[6];

---

[1] OJ No C 24, 1. 2. 1990, p. 20 and OJ No C 9, 15. 1. 1991, p. 3.
[2] OJ No C 19, 28. 1. 1991, p. 96.
[3] OJ No C 332, 31. 12. 1990, p. 172.
[4] OJ No L 298, 16. 11. 1984, p. 49.
[5] OJ No C 257, 4. 10. 1988, p. 1.
[6] OJ No L 382, 31. 12. 1986, p. 36.

Whereas the future Council Directive on the approximation of the laws of the Member States concerning telecommunications terminal equipment, including the mutual recognition of their conformity will allow the rapid establishment of common conformity specifications for DECT;

Whereas consideration shall be given to Council Directive 83/189/EEC of 28 March 1983 laying down a procedure for the provision of information in the field of technical standards and regulations[7], as last amended by Directive 90/230/EEC[8];

Whereas consideration should be given to Council Decision 87/95/EEC of 22 December 1986 on standardization in the field of information technology and telecommunications[9];

Whereas Council Directive 89/336/EEC of 3 May 1989 on the approximation of the laws of Member States relating to electromagnetic compatibility[10] is applicable, and particular attention should be taken to avoid harmful electromagnetic interference;

Whereas it is advantageous to facilitate access to cordless communications and necessary to allow free circulation of DECT equipment throughout the Community;

Whereas it is appropriate to make full use of the potential of the Community's allocated financial instruments in order to promote the development of the Community's telecommunications infrastructure in the Community;

Whereas consideration should be given to recommendation 87/371/EEC[11] which points out that special attention should be paid to the urgent requirement of certain users for pan-European land-based communications; whereas the Commission could in future submit other proposals in the field of mobile communications;

Whereas the implementation of such a policy will lead to closer cooperation within Europe between the public telecommunications administrations, the recognized public and private operating agencies and other authorized agencies offering public mobile telecommunications service, herein referred to as 'telecommunications organizations';

Whereas favourable opinions on this recommendation has been delivered by the telecommunications organizations by the European Conference of Postal and Telecommunications Administrations (CEPT) and by the telecommunications equipment manufacturers in the Member States;

Whereas these measures will allow the economic benefit and rapidly increasing market potential of cordless telephones to be fully realized in the Community;

Whereas the Treaty does not provide, for this recommendation, powers other than those of Article 235,

HEREBY RECOMMENDS:

1. that Member States and/or the telecommunications organizations, as appropriate, create the conditions for the coordinated introduction into the Community of digital European cordless telecommunications according to the technical requirements described in the Annex. For the purposes of this recommendation, digital European cordless telecommunications shall mean technology conforming to the European Telecommunications Standard for digital cordless telecommunications known as DECT.

2. that the telecommunications organizations continue the cooperation within the CEPT and/or ETSI, for the completion of the specifications and the introduction and exploitation of DECT technology;

---

[7] OJ No L 109, 26. 4. 1983, p. 8.
[8] OJ No L 128, 18. 5. 1990, p. 15.
[9] OJ No L 36, 7. 2. 1987, p. 11.
[10] OJ No L 139, 23. 5. 1989, p. 19.
[11] OJ No L 196, 17. 7. 1987, p. 81.

3. that the Commission takes appropriate initiatives, within the application of existing Directives, to encourage the completion of the specifications and the introduction and exploitation of DECT technology;

4. that the Commission prepares a long-term strategy in collaboration and consultation with interested parties, for the evolution of the soon to be introduced pan-European digital cellular and paging systems, and digital cordless systems, taking account of the general development towards a future universal personal communications system, and recent studies and the ETSI work programme;

5. that the Community's allocated financial instruments take this recommendation into account within the framework of their interventions, particularly regarding capital investments required for the implementation of the infrastructure for the DECT system;

6. that efforts are encouraged to develop the appropriate infrastructure to allow the use of DECT equipment also in a public environment and to work towards the coordinated introduction of DECT technology in such an environment, maintaining in particular those features necessary to allow European-wide interoperability;

7. that Member States inform the Commission at the end of each year, from the end of 1992 onwards, of the measures taken and the problems encountered in the course of implementing this recommendation; that measures be taken to consult telecommunications organizations, users, consumers, manufacturers, persons providing services, employer organizations and trade unions; that the progress of work be examined by the Commission and Senior Officials Group on Telecommunications (SOG-T) which was set up by the Council on 4 November 1983; and that the European Parliament be regularly informed, at least once a year.

Done at Luxembourg, 3 June 1991.

For the Council
The President
A. BODRY

ANNEX

DETAILED REQUIREMENTS ON THE COORDINATED INTRODUCTION OF DIGITAL EUROPEAN CORDLESS TELECOMMUNICATIONS (DECT) INTO THE COMMUNITY

Table of contents

1. General requirements
2. Choice of transmission system
3. Network architecture
4. System specification and implementation
5. System features
6. Tariff considerations
7. Time scale

1. **General requirements**

The future DECT systems should be developed in accordance with the ETS being developed by ETSI and should comply with the following general requirements:

— be suitable for operation over the frequency band 1880-1900 MHz to be made available for DECT in the Community in conformity with Directive 91/287/EEC,

— provide a means, using cordless technology, for meeting user requirements in respect of the following applications:

— a residential application that will interconnect to ISDN/PSTN,
— a business cordless telecommunications application that combines the features of a PABX with the mobility of cordless telecommunications for both voice and non-voice application,
— an application that offers public network access to a handset through a public, or privately owned, base station,
— an application that provides a radio means of extending public and private networks into customer user premises,

— permit simultaneous operation of two or more independent systems in the same geographical area.

2. Choice of transmission system

The detailed specification of the DECT transmission characteristics should be completed by October 1991 and should take account of the relevant international guidelines on limiting exposure to electromagnetic fields, and the Directive 89/336/EEC. The technology must be able to support geographically co-located DECT systems.

3. Network architecture

The standard for the network structure and the definition and allocation of functions between the various system components should be completely specified for all the applicable OSI layers, by October 1991.

4. DECT specification and implementation

The implementation of the system should be able to support full intersystem roaming where required. Roaming in the context of this recommendation is the ability to use handsets based on DECT technology to access the public network in any Member State.

5. System features

The system specification should provide a minimum number of generic capabilities and facilities as follows:

— satisfy the general requirements of section 1 above,
— provision of emergency services,
— provision for dialling and calling security,
— compatibility between residential, business and public access applications.

The provision of an additional service or facility beyond generic capability on any system should not impact the provision of the minimum service on other systems.

6. Tariff considerations

Agreement on such matters as the charging for the Community service and accounting between operators should be identified in a timely manner where required.

7. Time scale

Facilities for applications based on DECT technology should progressively be available from the end of 1992.

APPENDIX 19

Council Decision of 7 June 1991 adopting a specific research and technological development programme in the field of communication technologies (1990 to 1994)

(91/352/EEC)

THE COUNCIL OF THE EUROPEAN COMMUNITIES,

Having regard to the Treaty establishing the European Economic Community, and in particular Article 130q (2) thereof,

Having regard to the proposal from the Commission[1],

In cooperation with the European Parliament[2],

Having regard to the opinion of the Economic and Social Committee[3],

Whereas, by Decision 90/221/Euratom, EEC[4], the Council adopted a third framework programme for Community activities in the field of research and technological development (1990 to 1994), specifying *inter alia* the activities to be pursued in the field of communication technologies; whereas this Decision should be taken in the light of the grounds set out in the preamble to that Decision;

Whereas Article 130k of the Treaty stipulates that the framework programme shall be implemented through specific programmes developed within each activity;

Whereas in addition to the specific programme concerning human resources and mobility, it might be necessary to encourage the training of research workers in the context of this programme;

Whereas, pursuant to Article 4 of and Annex I to Decision 90/221/Euratom, EEC, the amount deemed necessary for the whole framework programme includes an amount of ECU 57 million for the centralized dissemination of knowledge and exploitation of results of the programmes, to be divided up in proportion to the amount envisaged for each specific programme;

Whereas, in the context of this programme, an assessment should be made of economic and social impact as well as of any technological risks;

Whereas Decision 90/221/Euratom, EEC provides that a particular aim of Community research must be to strengthen the scientific and technological basis of European industry, particularly in strategic sectors of advanced technology, and to encourage it to become more competitive at the international level; whereas it also provides that Community action is justified where research contributes, *inter alia*, to the strengthening of the economic and social cohesion of the Community and to the promotion of its harmonious development, while being consistent with the pursuit of scientific and technical excellence; whereas this should contribute to the achievement of these objectives;

Whereas small and medium-sized enterprises should be involved to the maximum extent possible in this programme; whereas account should be taken of their special requirements without prejudice to the scientific and technical quality of this programme;

Whereas the constitution or consolidation of a specifically European industrial potential in the technologies concerned is an urgent necessity; whereas its beneficiaries must be network operators, research establishments, undertakings, including small and medium-sized undertakings and other bodies established in the Community which are best suited to attain these objectives;

---

[1] OJ No C 174, 16. 7. 1990, p. 9.
[2] OJ No C 19, 28. 1. 1991, p. 139; and OJ No C 158, 17. 6. 1991.
[3] OJ No C 41, 18. 2. 1991, p. 12.
[4] OJ No L 117, 8. 5. 1990, p. 28.

Whereas priorities include integrated broadband communication system functions, intelligence in networks, mobile and personal communication, image and data communications, integrated services technologies, advanced communications experiments, information security technologies and test infrastructures; whereas the work includes R&D on systems engineering, advanced communications technology and validation of standards and common functional specifications;

Whereas basic research must be encouraged as far as is necessary throughout the Community;

Whereas the Scientific and Technical Research Committee (Crest) has been consulted,

HAS ADOPTED THIS DECISION:

Article 1

A specific research and technological development programme for the European Economic Community in the field of communication technologies, as defined in Annex I, is hereby adopted for a period beginning on 7 June 1991 and ending on 31 December 1994.

Article 2

1. The funds estimated as necessary for the execution of the programme amount to ECU 484,1 million, including expenditure on staff and administration amounting to ECU 41 million.

2. An indicative breakdown of funds is set out in Annex II.

3. Should the Council take a decision pursuant to Article 1 (4) of Decision 90/221/Euratom, EEC, this Decision shall be adapted accordingly,

Article 3

Detailed rules for the implementation of the programme and the amount of the Community's financial contribution are set out in Annex III.

Article 4

1. In the second year of implementation of the programme, the Commission shall review it and send a report on the results of its review to the European Parliament and the Council; the report shall be accompanied, where necessary, by proposals for amendment of the programme.

2. At the end of the programme, an evaluation of the results achieved shall be conducted for the Commission by a group of independent experts. This group's report, together with its comments, shall be submitted to the European Parliament and the Council.

3. The reports referred to in paragraphs 1 and 2 shall be established having regard to the objectives set out in Annex I to this Decision and in accordance with Article 2 (4) of Decision 90/221/Euratom, EEC.

Article 5

1. The Commission shall be responsible for the implementation of the programme.

2. Contracts concluded by the Commission shall govern the rights and obligations of each party, in particular the arrangements for the dissemination, protection and exploitation of research results, in accordance with the provisions adopted pursuant to the second paragraph of Article 130k of the Treaty.

3. A work programme shall be drawn up in accordance with the objectives defined in Annex I and updated where necessary. It shall set out the detailed objectives and types of projects to be undertaken, and the financial arrangements to be made for them. The Commission shall draw up calls for proposals for projects on the basis of the work programme.

Article 6

1. The Commission shall be assisted by a committee composed of representatives of the Member States and chaired by the representative of the Commission.

2. The representative of the Commission shall submit to the committee a draft of the measures to be taken. The committee shall deliver its opinion on the draft within a time limit which the chairman may lay down according to the urgency of the matter. The opinion shall be delivered by the majority laid down in Article 148 (2) of the Treaty in the case of decisions which the Council is required to adopt on a proposal from the Commission. The votes of the representatives of the Member States within the committee shall be weighted in the manner set out in that Article. The chairman shall not vote.

3. The Commission shall adopt the measures envisaged if they are in accordance with the opinion of the committee.

4. If the measures envisaged are not in accordance with the opinion of the committee, or if no opinion is delivered, the Commission shall without delay submit to the Council a proposal relating to the measures to be taken. The Council shall act by a qualified majority.

5. If, on the expiry of a period of three months from referral of the matter to the Council, the latter has not acted, the proposed measures shall be:

— adopted by the Commission, in the case of matters covered by the second, third, fourth, fifth, sixth, seventh and eighth indents of Article 7.
— adopted by the Commission, save where the Council has decided against the said measures by a simple majority, in the case of matters covered by the first indent of Article 7.

Article 7

1. The procedure laid down in Article 6 shall apply to:

— the preparation and updating of the work programme referred to in Article 5 (3),
— the assessment of the projects provided for in Annex III and the estimated amount of the Community's contribution to them where that amount exceeds ECU 2 million,
— the contents of the calls for proposals,
— any adaptation of the indicative breakdown of the amount set out in Annex II,
— the measures to be undertaken to evaluate the programme,
— arrangements for the dissemination, protection and exploitation of the results of research carried out under the programme,
— departures from the general rules set out in Annex III,
— the participation in any project by non-Community organizations and enterprises referred to in Article 8 (1) and (2).

2. Where, pursuant to the second indent of paragraph 1, the amount of the Community contribution is less than or equal to ECU 2 million, the Commission shall inform the Committee of the projects and of the outcome of their assessment.

The Commission shall also inform the Committee of the implementation of the accompanying measures and the concerted action projects referred to in Annex III.

Article 8

1. The Commission is authorized to negotiate, in accordance with Article 130n of the Treaty, international agreements with third countries which are members of COST, particularly the member countries of EFTA and the countries of Central and Eastern Europe, with a view to associating them with the whole programme or a part of it.

2. Where framework agreements for scientific and technical cooperation have been concluded between the Community and European non-member States, bodies and enterprises established in those countries may, in accordance with the procedure laid down in Article 6 and on the basis of the criterion of mutual benefit, be allowed to become partners in a project undertaken within the programme.

No contracting body based outside the Community and participating as a partner in a project undertaken under the programme may benefit from Community financing for this programme. The body concerned shall contribute to the general administrative costs.

Article 9

This Decision is addressed to the Member States.

Done at Luxembourg, 7 June 1991.

For the Council
The President
R. STEICHEN

ANNEX I

SCIENTIFIC AND TECHNICAL OBJECTIVES AND CONTENT OF THE PROGRAMME

The guidelines, scientific and technical objectives and underlying purposes of the third framework programme form an integral part of this specific programme.

Paragraph I.1.B of Annex II to the said framework programme forms an integral part of this specific programme.

On the basis and in the light of the above, there follows an analytical description of the contents of this specific programme.

This specific programme focuses on eight priority areas (including the provision of verification techniques and facilities) in which European collaboration between two or more telecommunications sector organizations is in the common interest. The priority areas are:

AREA 1: IBC (integrated broadband communications) R&D

AREA 2: Intelligence in networks/Flexible communications resource management

AREA 3: Mobile and personal communications

AREA 4: Image and data communications

AREA 5: Integrated services technologies

AREA 6: Information security technologies

AREA 7: Advanced communications experiments

AREA 8: Test infrastructures and interworking (horizontal R&D area supporting the other primary areas).

Work carried out on each of these areas will be of three types; the work will cover: development of implementation strategies for IBC systems, services and applications; advanced communication technologies, and validation of standards and common functional specifications for IBC. It will involve the use of experimental equipment and services to address generic applications.

AREA 1: IBC (integrated broadband communications) R&D

Integrated broadband communications technology forms the backbone for advanced services and largely determines their costs. Key technologies, systems, services and applications are being addressed under this IBC R&D heading using a systems approach. This area builds on and extends the work of the RACE I programme and in so doing focuses on the following subjects:

IBC systems design, architecture and operation

This work, based on a set of 'open' standards allowing universal access to integrated services, will enable integrated broadband communications to accomodate emerging new services. In order for the various organizations concerned to define their requirements clearly, reference models and common functional specifications will be systematically developed. Special emphasis will be given to examining the combination and interaction of different technical options, evaluating the demand for basic and enhanced services and addressing the impact of regulations.

IBC transition strategies

The transition leading to IBC services from current services requires the improvement of inter-operability between public and private networks with regard to new services. This work is essential for user acceptance of these new services and the optimum use of communication resources.

Research under this heading will include further development of common functional specifications and reference configurations, with close attention to recent developments. Particular attention will be given to the increased role of optical communications (taking into account the growing interest in 'fibre-to-the-home'), the emergence of synchronous/asynchronous transport switching techniques, the integration of mobile communication sub-systems (especially in rural areas) and the develop-ment of intelligence in the networks. Work will also be carried out on the definition of new value-added services adapted to evolving needs and their consequences on the management of local area networks. Specific tasks to be addressed will cover image communications and its integration in services; and the interworking between private networks, local and metropolitan area networks.

Common operational environment

This work aims at supporting standardization efforts, particularly those of the European Tele-communications Standards Institute (ETSI). It will include the dissemination of results, the seeking of outside information, and liaison with similar activities conducted in other fora. Common analytical tools will be developed and used for the transition and implementation scenarios for the IBC network.

Techniques for basic IBC system functions

This work will cover switching systems, integrated optical systems and networks, IBC customer systems and IBC software infrastructures.

Switching systems: The technology base of asynchronous transfer mode (ATM) will be broadened and interworking techniques between ATM networks and pre-existing networks will be developed. The work will enable ATM switching technology to support connectionless services and the inter-connection of local area networks (LANs) and metropolitan area networks (MANs). This develop-ment of ATM does not exclude basic research on new switching technologies or designs.

Integrated optical systems and networks: The work will provide the basis for low-cost broadband access networks and contribute to the introduction and evolution of integrated optical networks and photonic switching.

IBC terminals: In the study on access of business IBC subscribers, data processing requirements will be examined; for domestic access, communication protocols will be of most interest.

IBC software infrastructure: The research will support the cost-effective development of reliable telecommunications software and its full life-cycle support. Parameters such as software quality assurance and artificial intelligence will be taken into account. The research will also cover investigations of knowledge-based systems for life-cycle support.

Integration of IBC demonstrators

Interoperability characteristics and integration possibilities of 'technology demonstrators' will be verified for residential or business use and, where applicable, in both urban and rural areas. The research will validate the application feasibility of new technology, support standardization and provide the basis for the evaluation of the performance level of systems and services. It will cover the integration of access, transport and switching functions as well as control, management and signalling functions. Demonstrators of IBC terminals, as well as terminals developed elsewhere, will be connected in order to illustrate the large variety of terminals and services that can be supported.

Verification tools

Work in this area will involve the development of the necessary tools to verify functional specifications and compatibility of equipment. The tools will consist, in addition to the necessary facilities for physical verification, of the procedures and descriptions used to carry out such verification.

AREA 2: INTELLIGENCE IN NETWORKS/FLEXIBLE COMMUNICATIONS RESOURCE MANAGEMENT

This research will be related to the use of new techniques of information transfer, optical communications, and possibly artificial intelligence, for enhancing flexibility, both in the provision of new network services and network management.

The objective of this work will be to enable second generation systems to be developed and to contribute to standardization and definition of interconnection protocols.

This research will be related to the development and demonstration of techniques needed for the introduction of programmable networks and will cover the aspects of provision of new services, operations support systems (OSS) and telecommunications management networks (TMN).

AREA 3: MOBILE AND PERSONAL COMMUNICATIONS

Research in this area will contribute to the development of third generation integrated mobile communication systems. The aim will be to provide universal personal communications using audio, data and image. For cost-efficient implementation third generation systems will require a common radio-interface. They will exploit the microwave frequency ranges of 2 GHz, but certain mobile broadband services will require exploitation of the 60 GHz range. This work will focus on defining the functional specifications for IBC and radio networks (e.g. interconnection standards and mobility management). Interest will also be shown in the miniaturization of terminals. The terminals should be cost-effective for business and domestic use, with particular emphasis on low power consumption and efficient use of frequencies. Close attention will be given to the needs of different kinds of users and especially the requirements of pan-European access, necessitating truly compatible services and protocols.

AREA 4: IMAGE AND DATA COMMUNICATIONS

The research will involve the development of the technologies needed for the introduction and exploitation of advanced, low-cost and flexible image and data communication services, for both business and domestic needs. It will build on the foundations established by RACE, addressing in particular the impact of new transfer modes (such as ATM) on high-resolution visual services and fast packet data transmission at megabit rates. The work will concentrate on digital HDTV and will include coding and presentation techniques for still, moving and three-dimensional images. It will cover the interworking between the IBC system and the other networks with which it will co-exist.

AREA 5: INTEGRATED SERVICES TECHNOLOGIES

The development of demand in the field of services requires that the communications systems must be able to develop dynamically responding to end-user wishes. This field of study is defined below.

The object of this research is to contribute to the definition of common functional specifications for new communication services and multimedia-systems. Notably, work will have to be done on specifications for use and more generally on services design and on their links with networks.

IBC/Modular standardization

This work will contribute to the harmonization of architectures and specifications for the flexible integration of telematic services under user control. Due account will be taken of the trans-national scale of communication needs and the heterogeneous technical environment.

Service engineering will focus on modular standardization in the areas of architectures, service-user components, service-provider components and service-creator components. It will also cover service harmonization and usage modelling.

It will address the functional architecture of an integrated-services environment and the specification of the components and primitives for end-user applications. Research into usability will focus on the human-service interface and include the design of generic metaphors for integrated services access. The work on service-provider components will cover specifications for service management: the work on service-creator components will develop definitions of specifications of common tools for service creation. The harmonization efforts will be directed in particular towards a definition of specifications for usability and the definition of quality of service parameters. Specifications for mobile communication and for security requirements will also be studied. Usage modelling will enable problems linked to such use to be studied and in particular the factors concerning the acceptance of a service by users.

Integrated service technologies

This research will build on system engineering activities, and the results will contribute to the specification and harmonization work. It will address techniques for architecture realization, user components technologies, metaphors and user interface technologies, and service management systems.

Service technology verification

The research will involve the development of prototype facilities for flexible integration of services responding to the requirements of operators, service providers and users.

AREA 6: INFORMATION SECURITY TECHNOLOGIES

The accuracy, security and overall 'trustworthiness' of electronically-communicated information are evidently of great importance to private individual, commercial undertakings and industry and public administrations. Work in this area will ensure that considerations of quality, security and reliability of service are included in their development and implementation strategies for advanced communications. It will provide validated specifications, guidelines and technology for practical and effective information security at a pan-European level consistent with actions which are carried out in the other specific programmes. The priority in this area is to develop technologies for information security, consistent with actions related to information systems security undertaken by the Commission under various programmes for which it is responsible.

Service quality, security and reliability

The research will cover risk management, coherent security solutions and the creation of a favourable environment for secure information management.

Risk management: A common strategy will be developed to allow the rational management of risks. It will provide the scientific basis for legal measures to reduce risks.

Coherent security solutions: Coordinated strategies will be developed to guarantee the interworking of separate security mechanisms/procedures. They will allow shared scenarios for transition to be developed, especially in public security infrastructures. The work will provide the basis for collaboration between organizations on the security of information exchanged between them.

Creation of a favourable environment: Options for the diffusion of information security techniques and related measures will be identified. The actual diffusion of solutions amongst end users is outside the scope of this programme.

Information security technologies

Technologies for security mechanisms and technologies for the integration of secure systems will be investigated, especially for distributed systems. They will be addressed under the following major headings:

Systems technologies for information security: addressing usability, auditability, applications software, hardware and operating systems.

Network technologies for information security: covering both transmission and switching.

Tools for the administration of information security: involving the development of software tools incorporating methods for the administration of information security. The research will address the analysis of risks, the formulation and implementation of information security policies, and the ongoing administration of routines and quality-assurance of security systems.

Information security verification

The architectures, specifications and the technologies developed under this specific programme will be verified by building a series of demonstrators. This is essential in order to obtain genuine information security since the security of any system can only be as good as its weakest link and the systems studied in this context are complex. The work will fall under the following major headings:

Integration of information security technologies: addressing the use of a mix of several technologies for achieving optimal information security (ranging from electronics to suppress unwanted radiation of signals to protocol designs). These technologies cover many functions and form the constituent elements of the overall systems.

Verification of common tools for information security: covering three classes of tools; risk analysis tools, assurance criteria tools and tools for assessment of security.

Establishment of common infrastructure for information security: covering four areas: certification services for security products; accreditation services for secure systems; gateways for secure international traffic; and third-party security services. In all areas, the work will involve pilot schemes. These will be adapted to the needs of different branches of the economy, including public administrations, and directly supported by those who have developed the technologies within the R&D projects, in this programme or outside.

AREA 7: ADVANCED COMMUNICATION EXPERIMENTS

This pre-competitive and pre-standardization work is designed to prepare the ground for, and minimize the risks of investments in, advanced communications. It will identify generic service functions which are reusable and will permit the matching of different user needs while maintaining universal access and interoperability. The research will make it easier for user organizations to take up new technologies more rapidly and exploit the opportunities they present. By contributing to the creation of demand for advanced communications, work in this area is also in the interest of telecommunications operators and equipment manufacturers. The work focuses on the following subjects:

Study of generic functions

The research will focus on the identification of 'trigger' applications of advanced communications and of the generic applications which will be the basis for a spectrum of future universal services. It will cover the development of a usage reference model, development of consensus-based operational and functional specifications for services, consolidation of network and technology aspects and the identification of criteria and guidelines for the successful introduction and use of advanced communications. The work on the usage reference model will build on the pre-existing concepts, but with a new focus on entry strategies, generic applications and the relation between applications (the user/demand viewpoint) and services (the provider/supplier viewpoint). Consensus-based operational specifications, with user participation and common functional specifications for services will be developed where they are 'market enabling'. The identification of criteria and guidelines for the successful introduction and use of advanced communications will build on application experiments, relating to applications with a strong socio-economic impact. Some generic applications have already been identified: examples are distributed case handling, interpersonal communications and remote delivery of expertise.

Technology and techniques for advanced communications experiments

The technology and techniques necessary for experimentation with advanced applications will be addressed under this heading. Three themes have been identified: development and identification of technologies to support the development of the service infrastructures; development of techniques to support the elicitation of user requirements and responses to be made to satisfy these requirements. The work will include the identification of server modules required for applications such as translation/interpretation, integrity, multimedia conferences, multimedia databases and distribution. The modelling of user requirements will cover service and product elements, network capabilities (transport, switching and management) and terminal facilities, implemented in hardware and software. The development of techniques enabling the exploitation of responses to such requirements will concern in particular support for the demand reference process. Large-scale field experiments will be complemented by simulation techniques. Presentation techniques, including animation and graphics, will be used to complement detailed technical reporting.

Application experiments

The technical and economic future of subsequent feasibility applications of broadband communications will be verified by experiments. The experiences will enable one to identify, describe, model and define generic applications of advanced communications that cross business sectors and functions for all regions of the Community. Network operators and users will be able to draw on the results of these experiments to put together marketing and exploitation plans. A certain amount of equipment (including service and product elements) will be developed for generic applications, allowing sector-specific application experiments to be undertaken.

The work will take account of the future needs of users, confirm the existence of these generic applications and clarify their characteristics in field experimentation. The resulting knowledge will form a basis for the relevant telecommunications sector organizations in planning the standardization, implementation and operation of future communications networks.

AREA 8: TEST INFRASTRUCTURE AND INTERWORKING

The successful introduction of IBC services in Europe needs to be preceded by experimentation and trials. A test infrastructure is therefore necessary, connecting those involved. It is needed to validate standards and functional specifications. Under conditions to be agreed on by the partners the provision and operation of the test infrastructure is expected to be ensured by the operators and national test-beds, in collaboration and cooperation between them when necessary for interconnection and interworking. These national test-beds working in cooperation would provide the basis for the communications experiments. Correspondingly this area supports work required to establish interworking.

ANNEX II

INDICATIVE BREAKDOWN OF THE AMOUNT DEEMED NECESSARY

(in million ecus)

Area	Breakdown
1. IBC (integrated broadband communications) R&D	111
2. Intelligence in networks Flexible communications resource management	43
3. Mobile and personal communications	53
4. Image and data communications	68,11
5. Integrated services technologies	39
6. Information security technologies	29
7. Advanced communications experiments	121
8. Test infrastructures and interworking (horizontal R&D area supporting the other priority areas)	20
Total	484,11[1] [2]

[1] Including expenditure on staff which amounts to ECU 19,36 million and administrative expenditure amounting to ECU 21,64 million.
[2] An amount of ECU 4,89 million, not included in the ECU 484,11 million, will be earmarked as the contribution from this specific programme to the centralized scheme for the dissemination and exploitation of results.

The breakdown between different headings does not exclude the possibility that projects could come under several headings.

ANNEX III

RULES FOR IMPLEMENTING THE PROGRAMME

1. The Commission will implement the programme on the basis of the objectives and the scientific and technical content described in Annex I.

2. The rules for implementing this programme, referred to in Article 3, comprise research and technological development projects, accompanying measures and concerted action projects. Selection of projects must take account of the criteria listed in Annex III to Decision 90/221/ Euratom, EEC and of the objectives defined in Annex I to this Decision.

— Research projects

   The projects will be the subject of shared-cost research and technological development contracts, with Community financial participation not normally exceeding 50%. Universities and other research centres participating in shared-cost projects will have the option of requesting, for each project, either 50% funding of total expenditure or 100% funding of the additional marginal costs.

   Shared-cost research projects must, as a general rule, be carried out by participants established within the Community. Projects in which, for example, universities, research organizations and industrial firms, including small and medium-sized enterprises, may take part must provide, as a general rule, for the participation of at least two partners, independent of each other and established in different Member States. Contracts relating to shared-cost research projects must as a general rule be concluded following a selection procedure based on calls for proposals published in the *Official Journal of the European Communities*.

— Accompanying measures

The accompanying measures referred to in Article 7 of this Decision will consist of:

— the organization of seminars, workshops and scientific conferences,
— internal coordination through the creation of integrating groups,
— advanced technology training programmes, with emphasis being placed on multi-disciplinary,
— promotion of the exploitation of results,
— independent scientific and strategic evaluation of the operation of the projects and the programme.

— Concerted action projects

Concerted action projects consist of action by the Community to coordinate the individual research activities carried out in the Member States. They may benefit from funding of up to 100% of coordination expenditure.

3. The knowledge acquired in the course of the projects will be disseminated both within the specific programme and by means of a centralized activity, pursuant to the Decision referred to in the third subparagraph of Article 4 of Decision 90/221/Euratom, EEC.

APPENDIX 20

Council Decision of 7 June 1991 adopting a specific programme of research and technological development in the field of telematic systems in areas of general interest (1990 to 1994)

(91/353/EEC)

THE COUNCIL OF THE EUROPEAN COMMUNITIES,

Having regard to the Treaty establishing the European Economic Community, and in particular Article 130a (2) thereof,

Having regard to the proposal from the Commission[1],

In cooperation with the European Parliament[2],

Having regard to the opinion of the Economic and Social Committee[3],

Whereas, by Decision 90/221/Euratom, EEC[4], the Council adopted a third framework programme for Community activities in the field of research and technological development (1990 to 1994), specifying *inter alia* the activities to be pursued for developing the scientific knowledge and technical know-how needed by the Community, in particular to carry out its role in the field of telematic systems in areas of general interest; whereas this Decision should be taken in the light of the grounds set out in the preamble to that Decision;

Whereas Article 130k of the Treaty stipulates that the framework programme shall be implemented through specific programmes developed within each activity;

Whereas basic research must be encouraged as far as is necessary throughout the Community in each strategic sector of research in the framework programme;

Whereas in addition to the specific programme concerning human resources and mobility, it might be necessary to encourage the training of research workers in the context of this programme;

Whereas, in the context of this programme, an assessment should be made of economic and social impact as well as of any technological risks;

Whereas, pursuant to Article 4 of and Annex I to Directive 90/221/Euratom, EEC, the amount deemed necessary for the whole framework programme includes an amount of ECU 57 million for the centralized dissemination and exploitation of results, to be divided up in proportion to the amount envisaged for each specific programme;

Whereas Decision 90/221/Euratom, EEC provides that a particular aim of Community research must be to strengthen the scientific and technological basis of European industry, particularly in strategic sectors of advanced technology, and to encourage it to become more competitive at the international level; whereas it also provides that Community action is justified where research contributes, *inter alia*, to the strengthening of the economic and social cohesion of the Community and to the promotion of its overall harmonious development, while being consistent with the pursuit of scientific and technical excellence; whereas the programme of research in the field of telematic systems should contribute to the achievement of these objectives;

Whereas small and medium-sized enterprises should be involved to the maximum extent possible in this programme; whereas account should be taken of their special requirements without prejudice to the scientific and technical quality of the programme;

---

[1] OJ No C 174, 16. 7. 1990, p. 19.
[2] OJ No C 324, 24. 12. 1990, p. 271; and OJ No C 158, 17. 6. 1991.
[3] OJ No C 41, 18. 2. 1991, p. 6.
[4] OJ No L 117, 8. 5. 1990, p. 28.

Whereas research/development in the field of telematic systems in areas of general interest will contribute to the successful completion of the internal market and at the same time improve the performance of large public services facing, throughout the Community, the new technological, social and economic challenges which are implied by European integration;

Whereas it is important, when projects are selected, to ensure that data are protected and confidentiality maintained;

Whereas the Scientific and Technical Research Committee (Crest) has been consulted,

HAS ADOPTED THIS DECISION:

Article 1

A specific research and technological development programme for the European Economic Community in the field of telematic systems in areas of general interest, as defined in Annex I, is hereby adopted for a period beginning on 7 June 1991 and ending on 31 December 1994.

Article 2

1. The funds estimated as necessary for the execution of the programme amount to ECU 376,2 million, including expenditure on staff and administration amounting to ECU 41 million.

2. An indicative allocation of funds is set out in Annex II.

3. Should the Council take a decision in implementation of Article 1 (4) of Decision 90/221/ Euratom, EEC, this Decision shall be adapted accordingly.

Article 3

Detailed rules for the implementation of the programme and the amount of the Community's financial contribution are set out in Annex III.

Article 4

1. In the second year of implementation of the programme, the Commission shall review it and send a report on the results of its review to the European Parliament and the Council; the report shall be accompanied, where necessary, by proposals for amendment of the programme.

2. At the end of the programme, an evaluation of the results achieved shall be conducted for the Commission by a group of independent experts. This group's report, together with any comments by the Commission, shall be submitted to the European Parliament and the Council.

3. The reports referred to in paragraphs 1 and 2 shall be established having regard to the objectives set out in Annex I to this Decision and in accordance with Article 2 (4) of Decision 90/ 221/Euratom, EEC.

Article 5

1. The Commission shall be responsible for the implementation of the programme.

2. Contracts concluded by the Commission shall govern the rights and obligations of each party, in particular the arrangements for the dissemination, protection and exploitation of research results, in accordance with the provisions adopted pursuant to the second paragraph of Article 130k of the Treaty.

3. A work programme shall be drawn up in accordance with the aims set out in Annex I and updated where necessary. It shall set out the detailed objectives and types of projects to be undertaken, and the financial arrangements to be made for them. The Commission shall make calls for proposals for projects on the basis of the work programme.

Article 6

1. The Commission shall be assisted by a committee composed of representatives of the Member States and chaired by the representative of the Commission.

2. The representative of the Commission shall submit to the committee a draft of the measures to be taken. The committee shall deliver its opinion within a time limit which the chairman may lay down according to the urgency of the matter. The opinion shall be delivered by the majority provided for in Article 148 (2) of the EEC Treaty as regards adoption of decisions which the Council is required to adopt on a proposal from the Commission. When the committee votes, the votes of the representatives of the Member States shall be weighted as laid down in the above-mentioned Article. The chairman shall not vote.

3. The Commission shall adopt the proposed measures when they are in accordance with the committee's opinion.

4. When the proposed measures are not in accordance with the committee's opinion, or where no opinion is delivered, the Commission shall submit to the Council without delay a proposal concerning the measures to be taken. The Council shall act by a qualified majority.

5. If, on the expiry of a period of three months from referral of the matter to the Council, the latter has not acted, the proposed measures shall be adopted by the Commission.

Article 7

1. The procedure laid down in Article 6 shall apply to:

— the preparation and updating of the work programme referred to in Article 5 (3),
— the contents of the calls for proposals,
— the assessment of the projects provided for in Annex III and the estimated amount of the Community's contribution to them where this amount exceeds 1% of the amount deemed necessary for each field referred to in Annex II,
— departures from the general rules set out in Annex III,
— the participation in any project by non-Community organizations and enterprises referred to in Article 8 (1) and (2),
— any adaptation of the indicative allocation of the amount set out in Annex II,
— the measures to be undertaken to evaluate the programme,
— arrangements for the dissemination, protection and exploitation of the results of research carried out under the programme.

2. Where, pursuant to the third indent of paragraph one, the amount of the Community contribution is less than or equal to 1% of the amount deemed necessary for the projects, the Commission shall inform the committee of the projects and of the outcome of their assessment.

The Commission shall also inform the committee of the implementation of the accompanying measures and the concerted actions referred to in Annex III.

Article 8

1. The Commission is authorized to negotiate, in accordance with Article 130n of the Treaty, international agreements with third countries which are members of COST, particularly the member countries of EFTA and the countries of Central and Eastern Europe, with a view to associating them with the whole programme or a part of it.

2. Where framework agreements for scientific and technical cooperation have been concluded between the Community and European non-member States, bodies and enterprises established in those countries may, in accordance with the procedure laid down in Article 6 and on the basis of the criterion of mutual benefit, be allowed to become partners in a project undertaken within the programme.

No contracting body based outside the Community and participating as a partner in a project undertaken under the programme may benefit from Community financing for this programme. The body concerned shall contribute to the general administrative costs.

Article 9

This Decision is addressed to the Member States.

Done at Luxembourg, 7 June 1991.

For the Council
The President
R. STEICHEN

ANNEX I

OBJECTIVES AND SCIENTIFIC AND TECHNICAL CONTENT

The guidelines, scientific and technical objectives and underlying purposes of the third framework programme form an integral part of this specific programme.

Paragraph I.1.C of Annex II to the framework programme forms an integral part of this specific programme.

On this basis and in the light of the above, there follows an analytical description of the contents of this specific programme.

Introduction

In pursuit of the objectives outlined in the technical Annex to the framework programme, special account will be taken of the needs for management and transmission of electronic information as a consequence of completion of the single European market. These needs will be identified in collaboration with users: public authorities, businesses in manufacturing or service industries, academic institutions and individuals.

The activities will be pre-competitive and pre-normative and will concentrate on providing opportunities for interoperability between national systems, for defining standards, architectures and functional specifications. The activities will address such issues as user acceptance, security and privacy.

Pilot projects and demonstrators will be included when it can be shown there is a need to verify technology, to demonstrate interoperation standards and where there is broad interest to all Member States.

Close coordination will take place between these activities and those within lines 1.A and 1.B of the third framework programme as well as those outside the framework programme such as Eureka projects.

AREA 1: SUPPORT FOR THE ESTABLISHMENT OF TRANSEUROPEAN NETWORKS BETWEEN ADMINISTRATIONS

The objective of this area is to define common requirements for electronic information exchange and to examine the need for interoperability between electronic information networks within Member States; to carry out studies and pre-normative research for the definition and subsequent establishment of the trans-European telematic services networks essential to national administrations for the completion of the single market, for the provision of the services necessary to the free movement of persons, goods, services and capital and for increasing economic and social cohesion in the Community.

The priority subareas are those most closely linked to the completion of the internal market. In the first instance, work may concern such areas as customs, social services, emergency services and statistics. Several examples are given below.

With the elimination of frontiers within the Community as a result of the completion of the internal market, it will no longer be possible to monitor goods in transit at national frontier posts. Monitoring of goods in transit will require information to be exchanged between the customs of the country in which the goods enter or leave Community territory and the country of destination or origin of the goods. Consideration should therefore be given to whether, and how far, this will create a new need which new IT and telecommunication tools can help to satisfy.

Free movement of goods within the Community requires means of controlling their movements. Furthermore, the problems due to the incompatibility of existing national systems and to relations with non-Community countries, legal constraints and differing procedures and methods must be surmounted. Freedom of movement for persons cannot be achieved without a sustained, two-way flow of information between the various administrative establishments with responsibility for social services. Telecommunications interconnection between these administrations should help to provide social services for people. The setting-up of trans-European telematic services could help to do this, by ensuring rapid and secure information exchange, guaranteeing the compatibility of operational procedures while respecting citizens' rights, and promoting international coordination.

The interconnection and interoperability of existing statistical tools will allow the implementation of a European system of statistical information.

Identification of needs and implementation strategies

Selected areas closely linked to the completion of the single market will be examined in an exploratory action. This will comprise an assessment of the exchange of electronic information brought about by the completion of the single European market, an assessment of the needs of the users of this information to accommodate these changes and an assessment of the role of research and development in meeting these needs. The results of this work will enable the relevant administration of the Member States and the Commission, with the help of hardware and software products, telecommunications operators, and possibly service providers, to seek a consensus on the functional and technical specifications of the services required and strategies for setting up the transeuropean networks to provide these services.

The comparison of these descriptions with needs should enable the work remaining to be done to be identified by mutual agreement; this may involve some or all of the following tasks: description of the information desired, precise description of the types of messages required (free text, statistical tables or highly structured administrative messages), their format, the functional specifications and standards to be used, adapted or developed, as appropriate, and the protocols to be developed or converted.

Preference will be given to systems which are designed to intercommunicate using key elements, particularly those which have been standardized at European or world level. The standards relating to database access, storage and access protocols, languages, etc., will be identified and adapted where necessary. Arrangements must be made to ensure secure services.

Development of the technologies relating to telematic services and validation of common functional specifications

In order to take account of the complexity of these networks of services, the number of parties involved, the variety of information, real-time or batch processing, and capacity requirements, the architectures and the management of these trans-European networks will have to be thoroughly studied and researched in order to achieve the performance and reliability required to satisfy the specific needs of each administration. These studies and research will have to be carried out jointly by users of specialized networks, manufacturers of information and communications equipment, telecommunications operators and possibly service providers.

The work will concentrate initially on interoperability, common standards, architectures and functional specifications, user acceptability, data integrity and confidentiality. As a result of this work, a common reference model should be developed for the implementation or the adaptation of the telematic systems which are proposed. The results of the exploratory activities in a few subareas will be taken into account as work in this area is subsequently broadened.

This work will complement that conducted in the specific programmes on IT and communications.

To obtain the interoperability of computerized service networks, used by the administrations and end-users, it is important to verify common functional specifications. Special attention will be paid to the quality, reliability, security and ease of use of these services. To this end, a limited number of pilot projects will be carried out where there is a need to verify functional specifications and technology, where there is a general interest to all Member States and where this is in keeping with rules on personal data protection.

Where appropriate these experimental development activities will be carried out in cooperation with the work carried out under the Insis, Caddia and Tedis programmes and certain parts of the Esprit and RACE programmes.

AREA 2: TRANSPORT SERVICES

The activities aim to contribute to the development, in the field of transport, of integrated trans-European services using advanced IT and communications to improve the performance (safety and efficiency) of passenger and goods transport services, and at the same time the impact of transport on the environment. (See under 'road transport'.)

Account will have to be taken of the peculiarities and specific needs of the various parties involved, notably private and business users and administrations. Safety and ease of access for all users will be given special attention.

Road transport (Drive)

The objective is to contribute to development of a framework in which advanced IT and communications can be harnessed to improve the efficiency and safety of passenger and goods transport and reduce their impact on the environment. The work will build on the exploratory research in Drive under the second framework programme. There will be close liaison with relevant Eureka projects.

Work in this area should cover the interface between road and rail transport as well as that between road and sea transport.

The work will concentrate on the needs of users, those concerned with safety, provision and maintenance of infrastructure and provision of transport services.

The activities will be divided into three interactive parts: the definition of functional specifications in the context of a strategy for the use of technology and telematic systems for communication and traffic control, the development of new technologies and experimental systems, and validation work.

Strategies for the use of technologies, telematic services and systems and contribution to the definition of common functional specifications

The results of the work carried out so far under the Drive and relevant Eureka projects have enabled the needs specific to road transport and the technologies and systems available for communications and traffic control to be identified and evaluated. On the basis of these results, a strategy for using these technologies and systems will be sought in cooperation with transport users, business, providers of transport-related services and the administrations concerned.

Systems engineering work will continue on an integrated transport environment, addressing development and implementation strategies. It will help to draw up the functional specifications in terms of equipment, services and operating procedures, and to make recommendations to standard setting authorities such as CEN/Cenelec and ETSI for traffic control, transport management, driver support, road safety.

Technologies and experimental development of systems

The work will take account of the technologies emerging within information and communications, the results of research carried out under Drive and in other activities both in the Community and Member States.

Technologies and experimental systems for managing transport and controlling road traffic will be developed and evaluated for both passenger and goods transport.

Safety and communications systems will concentrate on helping drivers on long journeys. The research will focus on on-board safety systems and equipment able to detect warnings and incidents and communicate with the new fixed infrastructure equipment.

Research and technological development work specific to goods transport, including dangerous goods transport, will also be undertaken. It will cover the software, hardware and telematic systems needed to improve goods traffic management. This work will concern real-time monitoring of the various forms related to transactions, the goods themselves and vehicles; management systems for all kinds of vehicle fleets will also be developed.

In the field of public transport, work on monitoring and control will continue, to evaluate the cost-effectiveness of opportunities for on-line monitoring, scheduling and control for users and providers of services and to establish the necessary functional specifications.

The technological solutions will have to ensure that the telecommunications equipment to be introduced is suited, in terms of size, cost and performance, to the intended specific uses and the needs identified.

Special attention will be given to existing and emerging systems namely those related with satellites and digital cellular communication networks. Of particular importance is the potential of new systems to provide incident detection and provide usable information to network managers and road users through effective road-vehicle communications.

Validation and pilot projects

In order for the new systems and devices to be accepted by both the general public and the relevant authorities, they must be of proven performance and reliability and their potential impact on the environment must be assessed. This will require full-scale pilot experimentation to establish whether technologies serve market needs, contribute significant gains in efficiency (with existing and new infrastructure) safety and environmental benefits are cost effective and provide satisfactory system security and interoperability. These will be oriented towards the integration of multiple subsystems, functions and services which requires strong pre-standardization efforts. The sector actors should be closely associated with the work.

These experiments will cover areas including integrated urban traffic control; monitoring of air pollution; integrated motorway traffic control; vehicle roadside communications; driver information; transport demand management; public transport; freight transport and trip planning.

The need for rigorous evaluation should be a prime requirement in selection and design of pilot projects which may mean that pilot projects are established on an incremental basis. Projects should also evaluate technologies and systems of wide applicability.

AREA 3: HEALTH CARE (AIM)

The objective of this area is that of stimulating the development of harmonized applications of information and communication technologies in health care and the development of an European health-care information infrastructure taking into account the needs of users and technological opportunities.

The activities will depend on the needs of users and on the requirements of transnational exchange of electronic information. They will concentrate on interoperability of national systems, the establishment of standards, user acceptability, data integrity and confidentiality. The selection of activities will depend on strategic options within both the European health-care sector and European telematics sector.

Work in this area will be carried out along three main lines, making use of the exploratory work of the AIM programme (advanced informatics in medicine) and in close cooperation with other Community programmes.

Strategies for the use of technologies, telematic systems and services and contribution to the definition of common functional specifications

The nature of research and technological development activities will depend to a large extent on user needs and the general constraints associated with the transnational nature of the information infrastructure required. This transnational aspect requires compliance with three principles: integration (notably the emergence of standards); modularity, to facilitate adaptation to different types of needs, and data security. The research and technological development activities will depend on the assessment of technological needs in the light of the main factors affecting the development of health care. They will also depend on the strategic options for European telematic services in the sector. Essential problems such as confidentiality and data protection will be given high priority.

Development of telematic technology applied to medicine

Activities are expected to fall into one or more of the following domains:

— alphanumeric data and text coding standards,
— images and biosignals with coding standards,
— integrated medical instrumentation and devices,
— knowledge based on decision support systems,
— medical use of multi-media workstations,
— health-care communication systems,
— telemedical systems and archiving systems,
— modularity and integration of medical and health information systems,
— regulatory tools and incentives (medical, legal, ethical, economic and social),
— technologies and services for the handicapped and elderly,
— inter-hospital telematics for increased security in distance care and improved management of staff and specialized equipment.

Validation and integration

Pilot applications will be set up to demonstrate and evaluate the innovative nature of using IT and communications in this area. Tests of the applicability of the research and development results and the interoperability of telemedicine services will be conducted.

AREA 4: FLEXIBLE AND DISTANCE LEARNING (Delta)

On the basis of the exploratory work of the Delta programme and in close cooperation with other Community activities such as Comett and Eurotecnet, the work in this area will be carried out in three interdependent parts: drawing-up of implementation strategies, development of technologies and systems, and validation and integration of services.

Strategies for the use of technologies, telematic systems and services and contribution to the definition of common functional specifications

In the light of the interests of the various categories of users and taking account of the technological potentials, the various possible options to satisfy these needs will be identified. The measures needed to overcome the difficulties of implementing educational technologies will be determined.

Systems engineering work will be carried out: it will consist of identifying user needs and then reaching a consensus on specifications and functional standards which satisfy the needs of the various categories of users, producers of educational materials and providers of flexible and distance learning services.

The work will centre on the development of production methods for multimedia educational materials which are portable and transferable between various systems with the prospect of transnational use, including remote assistance and help procedures for the various categories of users.

Development of systems and technologies

The work will relate to the technologies required to obtain a telematic service for local and distance learning which is flexible, effective, modular and interoperable.

It will be necessary to integrate and adapt the information and communications technologies, hardware configurations and protocols for educational and training applications and ensure compatibility and portability of the various systems developed for the potential users, whether they be students, authors, tutors, producers or simply people requesting information on education services.

Experiments on the validation and integration of services

The performance of the various possible services and technical configurations must be evaluated. Experiments in the real environment will allow testing of the value added by interconnecting the various systems using new technologies for education, information and user assistance. The experiments will establish the comparative advantages and the performance, in relation to their cost, of these various configurations of flexible distance learning systems for different categories of users.

AREA 5: LIBRARIES

The objective is to facilitate user access, by optimum use and development of equipment and telematic systems, to the wealth of knowledge held in libraries while reducing the handicaps caused by the present disparate infrastructures in the Community.

To this end, the work will have to help develop modern library services all over the Community by promoting faster, but orderly and cost-effective penetration of new technologies into libraries.

Initial Community activity in this area must be selective, concentrating on urgent problems which can catalyse change in a concrete and practical way. Applied research and development will therefore be used to support the development of appropriate tools, methods and resources which will be able to stimulate modernization of the operational infrastructure and services provided, and facilitate cooperation and resource sharing at national and European levels.

This activity will consist of setting up computerized bibliographies where these are lacking, and helping to improve computerized bibliographies or collective catalogues. Support will also be given to retrospective conversion of catalogues of important collections at international level, by developing the necessary tools and methods.

Projects will be set up to facilitate the international interconnection of the systems managing these basic data for particular functions (shared cataloguing, inter-library loans, etc.) and thus help to prepare and apply a range of international or European standards.

The provision of new library services using IT and communications in small units will be stimulated. Initial support will be given to the creation of a range of innovative experimental services for library users, taking account of the different levels of development of library services in the Member States.

Finally, projects will be set up to encourage the development of a European market in telematic products and services specific to libraries. Interaction between libraries and IT industries will be stimulated by improving the definition of libraries' needs which new IT and communications can satisfy. Limited initial support will be given to experimental demonstrations of products (such as software) and services.

AREA 6: LINGUISTIC RESEARCH AND ENGINEERING

The aim of this area is to develop a basic linguistic technology which can be incorporated into a large number of computer applications where natural language is an essential ingredient, with a view to accommodating or overcoming limitations and inefficiencies within the Community brought about by different natural languages. This requires the creation of linguistic resources (grammars, dictionaries, terminology collections and corpora of text) for the nine official Community languages, and the definition of standards for these data. A number of pilot applications and demonstration projects will be undertaken to show how the technology will be used and demonstrate the technical and economic feasibility of the solutions adopted.

The area is divided into three parts: research, development of resources and pilot applications. It is based on the results and experience drawn from Eurotra and certain specific projects conducted under Esprit and national research programmes.

The research work will concentrate on the development of a common computer-based linguistic model for text representation in different languages and on the pursuit of automated techniques for reducing the number of possible interpretations of a given text. The development of advanced computational technologies will encourage the application, for linguistics, of progress made in the field of advanced expert systems, database technologies, speech processing and computer architectures. It is also intended to create methods, tools and linguistic resources, especially portable software tools, grammars, dictionaries, domain specific terminological collections, as well as large, high/quality corpora and the stimulation of standards work. Pilot applications and demonstration projects will help to test the progress of research work and to demonstrate the technical and economic feasibility of tools, methods and resources in an operational environment.

AREA 7: TELEMATICS SYSTEMS FOR RURAL AREAS

Half the European population still lives outside major cities and towns, and rural areas need comparable telematic service infrastructures to those in urban centres if they are to develop more balanced economic activities with a greater diversity of employment. The introduction of such services in rural areas will be a gradual process, the investments required will be large, and the infrastructures installed will have a lifetime of some decades. It is therefore essential that the right choices are made on technologies and system configurations. There is a need for pre-normative actions to harmonize the Community markets for equipment and services adapted to the needs of rural areas; for development and stimulation of specialized services and for the impacts of telematics in rural areas to be consistently assessed.

Community action in this area will contribute to completion of the single market, to strengthening the socio-economic cohesion of Europe, to improvements in the quality of life in rural areas, to industrial innovation (in particular for small and medium-sized enterprises) and to rural development. The actions will be part of a wider programme of actions strengthening rural development in the Community.

The goal is to create the conditions for geographically dispersed small businesses to provide more diverse employment opportunities and a more balanced economic activity in rural areas; to establish a basis for provision of improved services to dispersed and isolated populations, to raise the level of awareness of the potential of information and communication technologies in rural areas; to encourage manufacturers and service providers to make equipment and services easier to use by rural communities, and to ensure that applications of information and communication technologies in rural areas do not contribute to a further centralization of business and administrative activities and a loss of the cultural and economic diversity of rural areas in Europe.

The specific objectives are to develop a better understanding of the common needs and opportunities for telematic services and of the impacts of such services on rural life; to establish a common understanding of network configuration requirements and options and a common understanding of service requirements for telematic services, and to prepare the way for the harmonized planning and introduction of telematic service infrastructures in rural areas.

In order to achieve these objectives, the actions will involve consensus development with industry and rural development agencies; identification of needs and opportunities for telematics services and assessment of their impacts; specification of service and technology requirements; development of telematic systems, some pilot applications and research on infrastructure planning and implementation strategies.

ANNEX II

INDICATIVE BREAKDOWN OF THE AMOUNT DEEMED NECESSARY

(in million ecus)

Area	Breakdown
1. Administrations	41,3
2. Transport	124,4
3. Health care (including the handicapped and elderly)	97
4. Flexible and distance learning	54,5
5. Libraries	22,5
6. Linguistics	22,5
7. Rural areas	14
Total	376,2[1] [2]

[1] Including expenditure on staff which comes to ECU 30 million and administrative expenditure totalling ECU 11 million.
[2] An amount of ECU 3,8 million, not included in the ECU 376,2 million will be earmarked as the contribution from the specific programme in the field of telematic systems in areas of general interest to the centralized scheme for the dissemination and exploitation of results.

The breakdown between different headings does not exclude the possibility that projects could come under several headings.

ANNEX III

RULES FOR IMPLEMENTING THE PROGRAMME

1. The Commission will implement the programme on the basis of the scientific and technical content described in Annex I.

2. The rules for implementing the programme, referred to in Article 3, comprise research and technological development projects, accompanying measures and concerted actions:

— Research projects

The projects will be the subject of shared-cost research and technological development contracts. Selection of projects must take account of the criteria listed in Annex III to Decision 90/221/Euratom, EEC and of the objectives set out in Annex I to this programme.

For shared-cost projects Community financial participation will not normally be more than 50%. Universities and other research centres participating in shared-cost projects will have the opinion of requesting, for each project, either 50% funding of total expenditure or 100% funding of the additional marginal costs.

Shared-cost research projects must, as a general rule, be carried out by participants established within the Community. Projects in which, for example, universities, research organizations and industrial firms, including small and medium-sized enterprises, may take part must provide, as a general rule, for the participation of at least two partners, independent of each other and established in different Member States. Contracts relating to shared-cost research projects must as a general rule be concluded following a selection procedure based on calls for proposals published in the *Official Journal of the European Communities*.

The Commission will publish a vade-mecum setting out all the rules applying to the selection of projects, in order to guarantee full transparency.

— Accompanying measures

the accompanying measures referred to in Article 7 will consist of:

— the organization of seminars, workshops and scientific conferences,
— internal coordination through the creation of integrating groups,
— advanced technology training programmes, with emphasis being placed on multi-disciplinary,
— promotion of the exploitation of results,
— independent scientific and strategic evaluation of the operation of the projects and the programme.

— Concerted actions

Concerted actions consist of action by the Community to coordinate the individual research activities carried out in the Member States. They may benefit from funding of up to 100% of coordinating expenditure.

3. The knowledge acquired in the course of the projects will be disseminated both within the specific programme and by means of a centralized activity, pursuant to the Decision referred to in the third subparagraph of Article 4 of Decision 90/221/Euratom, EEC.

APPENDIX 21

Council Decision of 22 July 1991 establishing the second phase of the Tedis programme (Trade electronic data interchange systems)

(91/385/EEC)

THE COUNCIL OF THE EUROPEAN COMMUNITIES,

Having regard to the Treaty establishing the European Economic Community, and in particular Article 235 thereof,

Having regard to the proposal from the Commission[1],

Having regard to the opinion of the European Parliament[2],

Having regard to the opinion of the Economic and Social Committee[3],

Whereas one of the Community's tasks is, by establishing a common market and gradually reducing the gap between the economic policies of the Member States, to promote the harmonious development of economic activities throughout the Community and closer relations between its constituent States;

Whereas the Commission White Paper on the completion of the internal market stresses the importance of the future development of new transfrontier services and the contribution made by telecommunications networks based on common standards towards the creation of a market free of barriers at Community level;

Whereas the exchange of computerized data (EDI) can contribute increasingly towards the competitiveness of European undertakings in the production and services sectors;

Whereas there is rapid growth at present in public and private initiatives for putting into service within a company or group of companies or sector of activity, at national and international level, electronic data interchange systems which are not compatible;

Whereas, as regards electronic data interchange, the diversity and fragmentation of initiatives taken at national level or more generally by a company, group of companies or sector of activity may lead to the creation of incompatible and non-communicating systems and to preventing suppliers of equipment and services, and users, from deriving maximum benefit from the advantags created by the growth in electronic data interchange;

Whereas, in line with the Council Resolution of 22 January 1990 on trans-European networks[4] and the conclusions of the Strasbourg and Dublin European Councils, the smooth running of the internal market depends on undertakings and authorities involved in it being able to exchange data as part of their activities by making use of compatible systems which enable genuine pan-European data interchange networks to be developed;

Whereas Tedis needs in particular to be dovetailed with the specific programme of research and technological development in communications technology (1990 to 1994), the specific programme of research and technological development in the field of telematics systems of general interest (1990 to 1994) and the specific programme for information technology (1990 to 1994) which are part of the Community's third framework research programme;

---

[1] OJ No C 311, 12. 12. 1990, p. 6.
[2] OJ No C 106, 22. 4. 1991, p. 167.
[3] OJ No C 102, 18. 4. 1991, p. 13.
[4] OJ No C 27, 6. 2. 1990, p. 8.

Whereas the work already initiated in the field of electronic data interchange (EDI) during the first phase of the Tedis programme (1988 to 1989) established by Decision 87/499/EEC[5] makes it possible to envisage the establishment of such pan-European networks, provided that this work is continued and expanded by instituting a second phase to the programme;

Whereas a programme lasting three years is called for;

Whereas an amount of ECU 25 million is estimated as necessary to implement this multi-annual programme; whereas, for the period 1991 to 1992, in the framework of the current financial perspective, the funds estimated as necessary are ECU 10 million;

Whereas the amounts to be committed for the financing of the programme for the period after the budget year 1992 will have to fall within the Community financial framework in force;

Whereas, by Decision 89/241/EEC[6], the Council amended the initial Decision on the Tedis programme to allow non-member countries, in particular Member States of the European Free Trade Association (EFTA), to be associated with the Tedis programme and, in accordance with Article 228 of the Treaty, authorized the Commission to negotiate agreements with the EFTA Member States;

Whereas, by Decision 89/689/EEC[7], 89/690/EEC[8], 89/691/EEC[9], 89/692/EEC[10], 89/693/EEC[11] and 89/694/EEC[12], the Council approved the agreements on systems for the electronic transfer of data for commercial use concluded between the European Economic Community and, respectively, Austria, Finland, Iceland, Norway, Sweden and Switzerland;

Whereas the Treaty does not provide, for the adoption of this Decision, powers of action other than those of Article 235,

HAS DECIDED AS FOLLOWS:

Article 1

1. A second phase of the Tedis (Trade electronic data interchange systems) Community programme concerning the exchange of electronic data (EDI) in trade, industry and administration, hereinafter called the 'programme', is hereby set up.

The programme shall last three years.

2. The Community financial resources estimated as necessary for its implementation amount to ECU 25 million of which ECU 10 million is for the period 1991 to 1992 in the framework of the 1988 to 1992 financial perspective.

For the subsequent period of implementation of the programme, the amount shall fall within the Community financial framework in force.

3. The budget authority shall determine the appropriations available for each financial year, taking into account the principles of sound management referred to in Article 2 of the Financial Regulation applicable to the general budget of the European Communities.

Article 2

The objectives of the programme are to ensure that electronic data interchange systems are established to the best effect, in view of the socio-economic importance of such systems, and to mobilize the necessary resources to achieve this end at Community level.

---

[5] OJ No L 285, 8. 10. 1987, p. 35.
[6] OJ No L 97, 11. 4. 1989, p. 46.
[7] OJ No L 400, 30. 12. 1989, p. 1.
[8] OJ No L 400, 30. 12. 1989, p. 6.
[9] OJ No L 400, 30. 12. 1989, p. 11.
[10] OJ No L 400, 30. 12. 1989, p. 16.
[11] OJ No L 400, 30. 12. 1989, p. 21.
[12] OJ No L 400, 30. 12. 1989, p. 26.

Article 3

In order to achieve the objectives defined in Article 2, measures will be taken and continued in the following areas:

— standardization of EDI messages,
— specific EDI needs as regards telecommunications,
— legal aspects of EDI,
— security of EDI messages,
— multi-sector and Europe-wide projects,
— analysis of the impact of EDI on company management,
— information campaigns.

A list of the proposed measures is given in Annex I. These measures shall be implemented under the procedures provided for in Articles 6 and 7.

Article 4

The implementation of the programme shall be coordinated with existing or planned Community policies and activities concerning telecommunications particularly in respect, where necessary, of initiatives under the Open Network Provision Framework Directive (90/387/EEC)[13], the information market (Impact programme), security of information systems and standardization, and in particular with the Caddia programme and the CD project, so as to ensure the necessary interaction with the specific requirements of the exchange of electronic data.

Article 5

Contracts arising from the programme shall be concluded with undertakings, including small and medium-sized enterprises, research establishments, national administrations and other bodies established in the Community, in the member countries of the European Free Trade Association or in a third country with which the Community has concluded an agreement associating that country with the programme.

Article 6

1. The Commission shall be responsible for implementing the programme. The Commission shall be assisted by a Committee of an advisory nature composed of the representatives of the Member States and chaired by the representative of the Commission.

2. The representative of the Commission shall submit to the Committee a draft of the measures to be taken. The Committee shall deliver its opinion on the draft, within a time limit which the Chairman may lay down according to the urgency of the matter, if necessary by taking a vote.

3. The opinion shall be recorded in the minutes; in addition, each Member State shall have the right to ask to have its position recorded in the minutes.

4. The Commission shall take the utmost account of the opinion delivered by the Committee. It shall inform the Committee of the manner in which its opinion has been taken into account.

Article 7

1. Notwithstanding the provisions of Article 6, the following procedure shall apply in drawing up the work programme as set out in Annex I, the breakdown of the relevant budgetary expenditure and the assessment of projects and actions provided for in that Annex of a total value of above ECU 200 000, and the estimated amount of the Community's contribution to them.

2. The representative of the Commission shall submit to the Committee a draft of the measures to be taken. The Committee shall deliver its opinion on the draft within a time limit which the Chairman may lay down according to the urgency of the matter. The opinion shall be delivered by

---

[13] OJ No L 192, 24. 7. 1990, p. 1.

the majority laid down in Article 148 (2) of the Treaty in the case of decisions which the Council is required to adopt on a proposal from the Commission. The votes of the representatives of the Member States within the Committee shall be weighted in the manner set out in that Article. The Chairman shall not vote.

3. The Commission shall adopt measures which shall apply immediately. However, if these measures are not in accordance with the opinion of the Committee, they shall be communicated by the Commission to the Council forthwith.

4. In that event, the Commission shall defer application of the measures which it has decided for a period of three months from the date of communication,

The Council, acting by a qualified majority, may take a different decision within the time limit referred to in the foregoing subparagraph.

Article 8

At the end of the Tedis programme, the Commission shall present to the European Parliament, the Council and the Economic and Social Committee a final report containing an assessment by independent experts of the progress made towards each of the objectives set under the programme on the basis of the criteria and indicators as set out in Annex II to this Decision.

Article 9

This Decision shall take effect on 1 July 1991.

Done at Brussels, 22 July 1991.

For the Council
The President
P. DANKERT

ANNEX I

1. **Standardization of EDI messages:**
   — support the development work of the international Edifact standard and in particular the work of the Edifact Board for Western Europe; coordinate work regarding elaboration of Edifact messages and provide the necessary technical assistance,
   — supply the appropriate means to ensure conformity to Edifact of, on the one hand, EDI messages and, on the other hand, of conversion software,
   — adapt, if necessary, the Edifact standard to take account of the new developments in EDI, such as graphical EDI, technical EDI and interactive EDI,
   — support 'migration' towards the use of international standards and particularly towards the use of Edifact,
   — seek compatibility between the American standard ANSI X12 and the international Edifact standard.

2. **Specific EDI needs as regards telecommunications:**
   — to make proposals for improving technical interconnectivity between EDI users in Europe, ensuring close liaison with existing Community activities in this area and in particular ONP, namely:
      (a) encouraging the use of standardized communication protocols suitable for EDI in underlying services, especially P-edi, X.400 (1988) or X.500, coordinating where necessary with the ONP plans to harmonize for instance standards for packet switched data services and leased lines;
      (b) encouraging the existence of gateways between existing EDI services;

(c) helping to establish a system of registration authorities, to ensure the solution of the problem of identifying the names and addresses of EDI users in a multisectorial and trans-European context,
— to encourage the increased use of integrated services digital networks for EDI,
— to favour the gathering of the EDI interest groups dealing with telecommunications aspects,
— to encourage the practice of 'one-stop shopping/billing' concepts in EDI.

3. Legal aspects of EDI:
— finalize the draft European EDI agreement,
— set up and investigate thoroughly the constraints and needs of a legal nature in specific areas,
— undertake the thorough legal analysis of media and means of storage and of the electronic signatures for EDI messages,
— prepare a discussion document on the adaptation and harmonization of European legislations in order to integrate into the legal regimes the necessary provisions for the use of EDI; define the proposal of adaptation and harmonization required,
— ensure, from a legal aspect, that functions accomplished by EDI messages are also valid in order to carry out functions of a legal and reglementary nature,
— analyse the impact of EDI messages on the traditional functions of negotiability,
— follow the issues of data protection and confidential data in order to take account of the specific needs which could arise with the development of EDI,
— ensure the coordination between Member States on legal matters in connection with EDI and participate in the international coordination.

4. Security of EDI messages:
— create an informal expert group in this specific area,
— organize each year workshops which will treat different themes related to the security of EDI messages,
— increase the awareness of EDI users and of other appropriate groups to EDI message security,
-- facilitate the development of procedures, methods, services and standards related to EDI security,
— examine the user environment; identify the constraints, quantify the risks and investigate, if possible, an appropriate model to ensure EDI security,
— examine the security requirements related to new forms of EDI and the impact of new technologies,
— evaluate the services and products available to ensure the security of EDI messages, and if necessary examine the question of certification,
— examine from the EDI security viewpoint open multi-service environments.

5. Multi-sector and Europe-wide projects:
— establish and keep up-to-date a permanent inventory of existing or potential EDI projects in Europe,
— ensure the coordination of sectoral projects to meet industry and user needs,
— support of development of an intersectoral forum for EDI measures,
— encourage the launch of intersectoral projects to meet industry and user needs,
— encourage the participation of national administrations and Community institutions in the intersectoral projects,
— support the promotion of EDI systems to ensure wider use of EDI in Europe,
— identify long-term actions liable to progressively stimulate and interface EDI systems in countries of the Mediterranean, in Central and Eastern Europe.

6. Analysis of the impact of EDI on company management:
— identify and analyse changes in the methods of management and organization brought about by the introduction of EDI; small and medium-sized enterprises (SMEs) should particularly be taken into account,

— examine the economic and social effects of EDI,

— measure up the cost benefit of introducing EDI in private or public sectors,

— elaboration of a general implantation model of EDI in administrations, private and public enterprises,

— study the opportuneness of setting up a mechanism of coordination on a European level with regard to intercompany relations based on EDI.

7. **Information campaigns:**

— conduct regular surveys on the development of EDI in Europe and of available EDI products and services,

— undertake detailed studies more particularly of certain countries, regions or industrial sectors,

— publish the studies, analyses and other results of actions undertaken within the framework of the programme,

— support the setting up of national and/or regional awareness centres. Ensure the coordination, the provision of material support and contribution of their awareness activities,

— encourage in particular actions designed to make SMEs more aware of EDI.

ANNEX II

Guidelines for assessing progress made towards the objectives of the Tedis programme

In order to achieve the objectives defined in Article 2, several measures, referred to in Article 3, will be taken and continued. The progress thereby achieved will then be assessed.

1. For *standardization*, this will mean assessing the influence of the Tedis programme on:

    (a) the development and use of the Edifact standard in Western Europe;

    (b) the availability and use of conversion software and its conformity to the international Edifact standard.

2. *Interconnection of EDI services:* assessment of the Tedis programme's impact on the capacity of data networks to operate together and the availability of Europe-wide EDI services.

3. *Legal aspects:* examination of how the measures taken under the Tedis programme have helped ensure the legal validity of EDI data interchange in each Member State and how they have encouraged the introduction of 'paperless' trading.

4. *Security of messages:* examination of how the Tedis programme has helped protect the EDI message itself and the security of EDI messages in an interlinked business environment.

5. *Multi-sector and Europe-wide projects:* measuring how far support for the launching of multi-sectoral pilot projects has contributed towards the sectoral and geographical integration of EDI projects.

6. *Management:* assessment of the value of studies and analyses – in particular concerning SMEs – carried out under the Tedis programme to assess the impact of EDI on company management and its economic and social impact.

7. *Information campaigns:* assessment of the impact of measures – in particular concerning SMEs – taken under the Tedis programme on the use of EDI in Western Europe.

APPENDIX 22

Council Decision of 29 July 1991 on the introduction of a single European emergency call number

(91/396/EEC)

THE COUNCIL OF THE EUROPEAN COMMUNITIES,

Having regard to the Treaty establishing the European Economic Community, and in particular Article 235 thereof,

Having regard to the proposal from the Commission[1],

Having regard to the opinion of the European Parliament[2],

Having regard to the opinion of the Economic and Social Committee[3],

Whereas the telephone is the best means of access to emergency services of all kinds; whereas at present various telephone numbers are used for this purpose in the Member States;

Whereas the effect of such differences is to create problems in contacting the responsible services for citizens facing emergency situations in other Member States;

Whereas the substantial increase in both private and business travel within the Community has created a demand for the introduction of a single European emergency call number;

Whereas the introduction of new technologies in public telephone networks and the coordinated introduction of advanced telecommunications infrastructures present a unique opportunity for the implementation of a single European emergency call number, in parallel to the existing national emergency numbers, where appropriate;

Whereas the Council, in its resolution of 13 February 1989 on the new developments in Community cooperation on civil protection[4], stressed the desirability of a Community-wide single additional emergency telephone number which will in particular enable citizens in an emergency or disaster to call the relevant national emergency services;

Whereas the European Parliament has repeatedly emphasized the importance of the introduction of such a number, in particular in its resolutions of 12 December 1988 on telecommunications[5];

Whereas the European Conference of Post and Telecommunications (CEPT) recommended in its recommendation T/SF1 of 1976 the use of the number 112 as the single European emergency call number;

Whereas this recommendation has only been followed by a very small number of Member States;

Whereas it will be possible in all Member States to devise a plan to make the number 112 available;

Whereas several Member States could introduce the number 112 by 1992; whereas however, for some Member States this would cause problems since they would need to make unplanned changes or to change plans already made;

Whereas, therefore, flexibility is needed in the time schedule for introducing the emergency call number in these Member States;

---

[1] OJ No C 275, 1. 11. 1990, p. 4.
[2] OJ No C 231, 17. 9. 1990, p. 84 and OJ No C 183, 15. 7. 1991.
[3] OJ No C 62, 12. 3. 1990, p. 1.
[4] OJ No C 44, 23. 2. 1989, p. 1.
[5] OJ No C 12, 16. 1. 1989, p. 66.

Whereas the introduction of the number 112 will be possible by 1996, even in the Member States where difficulties exist;

Whereas, in addition to the technical, financial, operational and commercial implications of introducing the chosen number within public telecommunications networks, Member States will have to make the necessary organizational arrangements best suited to the national organization of the emergency systems, in order to ensure that calls to this number are adequately answered and handled; whereas it would be desirable to devote efforts to easing difficulties of comprehension which may arise from different language capabilities, taking account of the possibilities of the various national systems; whereas the single European emergency call number could therefore be used in parallel with any other existing national arrangements, where appropriate;

Whereas the provision of emergency call numbers is prescribed in all Member States by law, regulation, or administrative action, and divergent developments in this area must be avoided;

Whereas the Treaty does not provide, for the adoption of this Decision, powers other than those of Article 235,

HAS ADOPTED THIS DECISION:

Article 1

1. Member States shall ensure that the number 112 is introduced in public telephone networks as well as in future integrated services digital networks and public mobile services, as the single European emergency call number.

2. The single European emergency call number shall be introduced in parallel with any other existing national emergency call numbers, where this seems appropriate.

Article 2

The single European emergency call number shall be introduced by 31 December 1992 at the latest, except where Article 3 applies.

Article 3

1. Where particular technical, financial, geographical or organizational difficulties in a Member State make the full introduction of the single European emergency call number by the date provided for in Article 2 impossible or too costly, the Member State concerned shall inform the Commission of these difficulties.

2. In the case referred to in paragraph 1, the Member State concerned shall communicate to the Commission, with adequate explanations and justifications, a new date for the full introduction of the single European emergency call number which, however, must be no later than 31 December 1966.

Article 4

Member States shall take the necessary measures to ensure that calls to the single European emergency call number are appropriately answered and handled, in a manner best suited to the national organization of emergency systems and within the technological possibilities of the networks.

Article 5

This Decision is addressed to the Member States.

Done at Brussels, 29 July 1991.

For the Council
The President
H. VAN DEN BROEK

APPENDIX 23

Guidelines on the Application of EEC Competition Rules in the Telecommunications Sector

(91/C 233/02)

PREFACE

These guidelines aim at clarifying the application of Community competition rules to the market participants in the telecommunications sector. They must be viewed in the context of the special conditions of the telecommunications sector, and the overall Community telecommunications policy will be taken into account in their application. In particular, account will have to be taken of the actions the Commission will be in a position to propose for the telecommunications industry as a whole, actions deriving from the assessment of the state of play and issues at stake for this industry, as has already been the case for the European electronics and information technology industry in the communication of the Commission of 3 April 1991[1].

A major political aim, as emphasized by the Commission, the Council, and the European Parliament, must be the development of efficient Europe-wide networks and services, at the lowest cost and of the highest quality, to provide the European user in the single market of 1992 with a basic infrastructure for efficient operation.

The Commission has made it clear in the past that in this context it is considered that liberalization and harmonization in the sector must go hand in hand.

Given the competition context in the telecommunications sector, the telecommunications operators should be allowed, and encouraged, to establish the necessary cooperation mechanisms, in order to create – or ensure – Community-wide full interconnectivity between public networks, and where required between services to enable European users to benefit from a wider range of better and cheaper telecommunications services.

This can and has to be done in compliance with, and respect of, EEC competition rules in order to avoid the diseconomies which otherwise could result. For the same reasons, operators and other firms that may be in a dominant market position should be made aware of the prohibition of abuse of such positions.

The guidelines should be read in the light of this objective. They set out to clarify, *inter alia*, which forms of cooperation amount to undesirable collusion, and in this sense they list what is *not* acceptable. They should therefore be seen as one aspect of an overall Community policy towards telecommunications, and notably of policies and actions to encourage and stimulate those forms of cooperation which promote the development and availability of advanced communications for Europe.

The full application of competition rules forms a major part of the Community's overall approach to telecommunications. These guidelines should help market participants to shape their strategies and arrangements for Europe-wide networks and services from the outset in a manner which allows them to be fully in line with these rules. In the event of significant changes in the conditions which prevailed when the guidelines were drawn up, the Commission may find it appropriate to adapt the guidelines to the evolution of the situation in the telecommunications sector.

I. SUMMARY

1. The Commission of the European Communities in its Green Paper on the development of the common market for telecommunications services and equipment (COM(87)290) dated 30 June

---

[1] The European electronics and information technology industry: state of play, issues at stake and proposals for action, SEC(91) 565, 3 April 1991.

1987 proposed a number of Community positions. Amongst these, positions (H) and (I) are as follows:

'(H) strict continuous review of operational (commercial) activities of telecommunications administrations according to Articles 85, 86 and 90 of the EEC Treaty. This applies in particular to practices of cross-subsidization of activities in the competitive services sector and of activities in manufacturing;

'(J) strict continuous review of all private providers in the newly opened sectors according to Articles 85 and 86, in order to avoid the abuse of dominant positions;'.

2. These positions were restated in the Commission's document of 9 February 1988 'Implementing the Green Paper on the development of the common market for telecommunications services and equipment/state of discussions and proposals by the Commission' (COM(88)48). Among the areas where the development of concrete policy actions is now possible, the Commission indicated the following:

'Ensuring fair conditions of competition:

Ensuring an open competitive market makes continuous review of the telecommunications sector necessary.

The Commission intends to issue guidelines regarding the application of competition rules to the telecommunications sector and on the way that the review should be carried out.'

This is the objective of this communication.

The telecommunications sector in many cases requires cooperation agreements, *inter alia*, between telecommunications organizations (TOs) in order to ensure network and services interconnectivity, one-stop shopping and one-stop billing which are necessary to provide for Europe-wide services and to offer optimum service to users. These objectives can be achieved, *inter alia*, by TOs cooperating – for example, in those areas where exclusive or special rights for provision may continue in accordance with Community law, including competition law, as well as in areas where optimum service will require certain features of cooperation. On the other hand the overriding objective to develop the conditions for the market to provide European users with a greater variety of telecommunications services, of better quality and at lower cost requires the introduction and safeguarding of a strong competitive structure. Competition plays a central role for the Community, especially in view of the completion of the single market for 1992. This role has already been emphasized in the Green Paper.

The single market will represent a new dimension for telecoms operators and users. Competition will give them the opportunity to make full use of technological development and to accelerate it, and encouraging them to restructure and reach the necessary economies of scale to become competitive not only on the Community market, but worldwide.

With this in mind, these guidelines recall the main principles which the Commission, according to its mandate under the Treaty's competition rules, has applied and will apply in the sector without prejudging the outcome of any specific case which will have to be considered on the facts.

The objective is, *inter alia*, to contribute to more certainty of conditions for investment in the sector and the development of Europe-wide services.

The mechanisms for creating certainty for individual cases (apart from complaints and ex-officio investigations) are provided for by the notification and negative clearance procedures provided under Regulation No 17, which give a formal procedure for clearing cooperation agreements in this area whenever a formal clearance is requested. This is set out in further detail in this communication.

II. INTRODUCTION

3. The fundamental technological development worldwide in the telecommunications sector[2] has caused considerable changes in the competition conditions. The traditional monopolistic administrations cannot alone take up the challenge of the technological revolution. New economic forces have appeared on the telecoms scene which are capable of offering users the numerous enhanced services generated by the new technologies. This has given rise to and stimulated a wide deregulation process propagated in the Community with various degrees of intensity.

This move is progressively changing the face of the European market structure. New private suppliers have penetrated the market with more and more transnational value-added services and equipment. The telecommunications administrations, although keeping a central role as public services providers, have acquired a business-like way of thinking. They have started competing dynamically with private operators in services and equipment. Wide restructuring, through mergers and joint ventures, is taking place in order to compete more effectively on the deregulated market through economies of scale and rationalization. All these events have a multiplier effect on technological progress.

4. In the light of this, the central role of competition for the Community appears clear, especially in view of the completion of the single market for 1992. This role has already been emphasized in the Green Paper.

5. In the application of competition rules the Commission endeavours to avoid the adopting of State measures or undertakings erecting or maintaining artificial barriers incompatible with the single market. But it also favours all forms of cooperation which foster innovation and economic progress, as contemplated by competition law. Pursuing effective competition in telecoms is not a matter of political choice. The choice of a free market and a competition-oriented economy was already envisaged in the EEC Treaty, and the competition rules of the Treaty are directly applicable within the Community. The abovementioned fundamental changes make necessary the full application of competition law.

6. There is a need for more certainty as to the application of competition rules. The telecommunication administrations together with keeping their duties of public interest, are now confronted with the application of these rules practically without transition from a long tradition of legal protection. Their scope and actual implications are often not easily perceivable. As the technology is fast-moving and huge investments are necessary, in order to benefit from the new possibilities on the market-place, all the operators, public or private, have to take quick decisions, taking into account the competition regulatory framework.

7. This need for more certainty regarding the application of competition rules is already met by assessments made in several individual cases. However, assessments of individual cases so far have enabled a response to only some of the numerous competition questions which arise in telecommunications. Future cases will further develop the Commission's practice in this sector.

Purpose of these guidelines

8. These guidelines are intended to advise public telecommunications operators, other telecommunications service and equipment suppliers and users, the legal profession and the interested members of the public about the general legal and economic principles which have been and are being followed by the Commission in the application of competition rules to undertakings in the telecommunications sector, based on experience gained from individual cases in compliance with the rulings of the Court of Justice of the European Communities.

9. The Commission will apply these principles also to future individual cases in a flexible way, and taking the particular context of each case into account. These guidelines do not cover all the general principles governing the application of competition rules, but only those which are of specific

---

[2] Telecommunications embraces any transmission, emission or reception of signs, signals, writing, images and sounds or intelligence of any nature by wire, radio, optical and other electromagnetic systems (Article 2 of WATTC Regulation of 9 December 1988).

relevance to telecommunication issues. The general principles of competition rules not specifically connected with telecommunications but entirely applicable to these can be found, *inter alia*, in the regulatory acts, the Court judgments and the Commission decisions dealing with the individual cases, the Commission's yearly reports on competition policy, press releases and other public information originating from the Commission.

10. These guidelines do not create enforceable rights. Moreover, they do not prejudice the application of EEC competition rules by the Court of Justice of the European Communities and by national authorities (as these rules may be directly applied to each Member State, by the national authorities, administrative or judicial).

11. A change in the economic and legal situation will not automatically bring about a simultaneous amendment to the guidelines. The Commission, however, reserves the possibility to make such an amendment when it considers that these guidelines no longer satisfy their purpose, because of fundamental and/or repeated changes in legal precedents, methods of applying competition rules, and the regulatory, economic and technical context.

12. These guidelines essentially concern the direct application of competition rules to undertakings, i.e. Articles 85 and 86 of the EEC Treaty. They do not concern those applicable to the Member States, in particular Articles 5 and 90 (1) and (3). Principles ruling the application of Article 90 in telecommunications are expressed in Commission Directives adopted under Article 90 (3) for the implementation of the Green Paper[3].

Relationship between competition rules applicable to undertakings and those applicable to Member States

13. The Court of Justice of the European Communities[4] has ruled that while it is true that Articles 85 and 86 of the Treaty concern the conduct of undertakings and not the laws or regulations of the Member States, by virtue of Article 5 (2) of the EEC Treaty, Member States must not adopt or maintain in force any measure which could deprive those provisions of their effectiveness. The Court has stated that such would be the case, in particular, if a Member State were to require or favour prohibited cartels or reinforce the effects thereof or to encourage abuses by dominant undertakings.

If those measures are adopted or maintained in force *vis-à-vis* public undertakings or undertakings to which a Member State grants special or exclusive rights, Article 90 might also apply.

14. When the conduct of a public undertaking or an undertaking to which a Member State grants special or exclusive rights arises entirely as a result of the exercise of the undertaking's autonomous behaviour, it can only be caught by Articles 85 and 86.

When this behaviour is imposed by a mandatory State measure (regulative or administrative), leaving no discretionary choice to the undertakings concerned. Article 90 may apply to the State involved in association with Articles 85 and 86. In this case Articles 85 and 86 apply to the undertakings' behaviour taking into account the constraints to which the undertakings are submitted by the mandatory State measure.

Ultimately, when the behaviour arises from the free choice of the undertakings involved, but the State has taken a measure which encourages the behaviour or strengthens its effects. Articles 85 and/or 86 apply to the undertakings' behaviour and Article 90 may apply to the State measure.

---

[3] Commission Directive 88/301/EEC of 16 May 1988 on competition in the markets in telecommunications terminal equipment (OJ No L 131, 27.5. 1988, p. 73).
Commission Directive 90/388/EEC of 28 June 1990 on competition in the markets for telecommunications services (OJ No L 192, 24.7. 1990, p. 10).

[4] Judgment of 10. 1. 1985 in Case 229/83, Leclerc/gasoline [1985] ECR 17; Judgment of 11. 7. 1985 in Case 299/83, Leclerc/books [1985] ECR 2517; Judgment of 30. 4. 1986 in Cases from 209 to 213/84, Ministère public v. Asjes [1986] ECR 1425; Judgment of 1. 10. 1987 in Case 311/85, Vereniging van Vlaamse Reisbureaus v. Sociale Dienst van de Plaatselijke en Gewestelijke Overheidsdiensten [1987] ECR 3801.

This could be the case, *inter alia*, when the State has approved and/or legally endorsed the result of the undertakings' behaviour (for instance tarifs).

These guidelines and the Article 90 Directives complement each other to a certain extent in that they cover the principles governing the application of the competition rules: Articles 85 and 86 on the one hand, Article 90 on the other.

Application of competition rules and other Community law, including open network provision (ONP) rules

15. Articles 85 and 86 and Regulations implementing those Articles in application of Article 87 of the EEC Treaty constitute law in force and enforceable throughout the Community. Conflicts should not arise with other Community rules because Community law forms a coherent regulatory framework. Other Community rules, and in particular those specifically governing the telecommunications sector, cannot be considered as provisions implementing Articles 85 an 86 in this sector. However it is obvious that Community acts adopted in the telecommunications sector are to be interpreted in a way consistent with competition rules, so to ensure the best possible implementation of all aspects of the Community telecommunications policy.

16. This applies, *inter alia*, to the relationship between competition rules applicable to undertakings and the ONP rules. According to the Council Resolution of 30 June 1988 on the development of the common market for telecommunications services and equipment up to 1992[5], ONP comprises the 'rapid definition, by Council Directives, of technical conditions, usage conditions, and tariff principles for open network provision, starting with harmonized conditions for the use of leased lines'. The details of the ONP procedures have been fixed by Directive 90/387/EEC[6] on the establishment of the internal market for telecommunications services through the implementation of open network provision, adopted by Council on 28 June 1990 under Article 100a of the EEC Treaty.

17. ONP has a fundamental role in providing European-wide access to Community-wide interconnected public networks. When ONP harmonization is implemented, a network user will be offered harmonized access conditions throughout the EEC, whichever country they address. Harmonized access will be ensured in compliance with the competition rules as mentioned above, as the ONP rules specifically provide.

ONP rules cannot be considered as competition rules which apply to States and/or to undertakings' behaviour. ONP and competition rules therefore constitute two different but coherent sets of rules. Hence, the competition rules have full application, even when all ONP rules have been adopted.

18. Competition rules are and will be applied in a coherent manner with Community trade rules in force. However, competition rules apply in a non-discriminatory manner to EEC undertakings and to non-EEC ones which have access to the EEC market.

III. COMMON PRINCIPLES OF APPLICATION OF ARTICLES 85 AND 86

Equal application of Articles 85 and 86

19. Articles 85 and 86 apply directly and throughout the Community to all undertakings, whether public or private, on equal terms and to the same extent, apart from the exception provided in Article 90 (2)[7]. The Commission and national administrative and judicial authorities are competent to apply these rules under the conditions set out in Council Regulation No 17[8].

---

[5] OJ No C 257, 4. 10. 1988, p. 1.

[6] OJ No L 192, 24.7. 1990. p. 1.

[7] Article 90 (2) states: 'Undertakings entrusted with the operation of services of general economic interest or having the character of a revenue-producing monopoly shall be subject to the rules contained in this Treaty, in particular to the rules on competition, in so far as the application of such rules does not obstruct the performance, in law or in fact, of the particular tasks assigned to them. The development of trade must not be affected to such an extent as would be contrary to the interests of the Community'.

[8] OJ No 13, 21. 2. 1962, p. 204/62 (Special Edition 1959–62, p. 87).

20. Therefore, Articles 85 and 86 apply both to private enterprises and public telecommunications operators embracing telecommunications administrations and recognized private operating agencies, hereinafter called 'telecommunications organizations' (TOs).

TOs are undertakings within the meaning of Articles 85 and 86 to the extent that they exert an economic activity, for the manufacturing and/or sale of telecommunications equipment and/or for the provision of telecommunications services, regardless of other facts such as, for example, whether their nature is economic or not and whether they are legally distinct entities or form part of the State organization[9]. Associations of TOs are associations of undertakings within the meaning of Article 85, even though TOs participate as undertakings in organizations in which governmental authorities are also represented.

Articles 85 and 86 apply also to undertakings located outside the EEC when restrictive agreements are implemented or intended to be implemented or abuses are committed by those undertakings within the common market to the extent that trade between Member States is affected[10].

Competition restrictions justified under Article 90 (2) or by essential requirements

21. The exception provided in Article 90 (2) may apply both to State measures and to practices by undertakings. The Services Directive 90/388/EEC, in particular in Article 3, makes provision for a Member State to impose specified restrictions in the licences which it can grant for the provision of certain telecommunications services. These restrictions may be imposed under Article 90 (2) or in order to ensure the compliance with State essential requirements specified in the Directive.

22. As far as Article 90 (2) is concerned, the benefit of the exception provided by this provision may still be invoked for a TO's behaviour when it brings about competition restrictions which its Member State did not impose in application of the Services Directive. However, the fact should be taken into account that in this case the State whose function is to protect the public and the general economic interest, did not deem it necessary to impose the said restrictions. This makes particularly hard the burden of proving that the Article 90 (2) exception still applies to an undertakings's behaviour involving these restrictions.

23. The Commission infers from the case law of the Court of Justice[11] that it has exclusive competence, under the control of the Court, to decide that the exception of Article 90 (2) applies. The national authorities including judicial authorities can assess that this exception does not apply, when they find that the competition rules clearly do not obstruct the performance of the task of general economic interest assigned to undertakings. When those authorities cannot make a clear assessment in this sense they should suspend their decision in order to enable the Commission to find that the conditions for the application of that provision are fulfilled.

24. As to measures aiming at the compliance with 'essential requirements' within the meaning of the Services Directive, under Article 1 of the latter[12], they can only be taken by Member States and not by undertakings.

The relevant market

25. In order to assess the effects of an agreement on competition for the purposes of Article 85 and whether there is a dominant position on the market for the purposes of Article 86, it is necessary to define the relevant market(s), product or service market(s) and geographic market(s), within the domain of telecommunications. In a context of fast-moving technology the relevant market definition is dynamic and variable.

---

[9] See Judgment of the Court 16. 6. 1987 in Case 118/85, Commission v. Italy – Transparency of Financial Relations between Member States and Public Undertakings [1987] ECR 2599.

[10] See Judgment of the Court of 27. 9. 1988 in Joined Cases 89, 104, 114, 116, 117, 125, 126, 127, 129/85, Ålström & others v. Commission ('Woodpulp'), [1988] ECR 5193.

[11] Case 10/71, Mueller-Hein [1971] ECR 723; Judgment of 11. 4. 1989 in Case 66/86, Ahmed Saeed [1989] ECR 803.

[12] '. . . the non-economic reasons in the general interest which may cause a Member State to restrict access to the public telecommunications network or public telecommunications services.'

(a) The product market

26. A product market comprises the totality of the products which, with respect to their characteristics, are particularly suitable for satisfying constant needs and are only to a limited extent interchangeable with other products in terms of price, usage and consumer preference. An examination limited to the objective characteristics only of the relevant products cannot be sufficient: the competitive conditions and the structure of supply and demand on the market must also be taken into consideration[13].

The Commission can precisely define these markets only within the framework of individual cases.

27. For the guidelines' purpose it can only be indicated that distinct service markets could exist at least for terrestrial network provision, voice communication, data communication and satellites. With regard to the equipment market, the following areas could all be taken into account for the purposes of market definition: public switches, private switches, transmission systems and more particularly, in the field of terminals, telephone sets, modems, telex terminals, data transmission terminals and mobile telephones. The above indications are without prejudice to the definition of further narrower distinct markets. As to other services – such as value-added ones – as well as terminal and network equipment, it cannot be specified here whether there is a market for each of them or for an aggregate of them, or for both, depending upon the interchangeability existing in different geographic markets. This is mainly determined by the supply and the requirements in those markets.

28. Since the various national public networks compete for the installation of the telecommunication hubs of large users, market definition may accordingly vary. Indeed, large telecommunications users, whether or not they are service providers, locate their premises depending, *inter alia*, upon the features of the telecommunications services supplied by each TO. Therefore, they compare national public networks and other services provided by the TOs in terms of characteristics and prices.

29. As to satellite provision, the question is whether or not it is substantially interchangeable with terrestrial network provision.

(a) communication by satellite can be of various kinds: fixed service (point to point communication), multipoint (point to multipoint and multipoint to multipoint), one-way or two-way;

(b) satellites' main characteristics are: coverage of a wide geographic area not limited by national borders, insensitivity of costs to distance, flexibility and ease of networks deployment, in particular in the very small aperture terminals (VSAT) systems;

(c) satellites' uses can be broken down into the following categories: public switched voice and data transmission, business value-added services and broadcasting;

(d) a satellite provision presents a broad interchangeability with the terrestrial transmission link for the basic voice and data transmission on long distance. Conversely, because of its characteristics it is not substantially interchangeable but rather complementary to terrestrial transmission links for several specific voice and data transmission uses. These uses are: services to peripheral or less-developed regions, links between non-contiguous countries, reconfiguration of capacity and provision of routing for traffic restoration. Moreover, satellites are not currently substantially interchangeable for direct broadcasting and multipoint private networks for value-added business services. Therefore, for all those uses satellites should constitute distinct product markets. Within satellites, there may be distinct markets.

30. In mobile communications distinct services seem to exist such as cellular telephone, paging, telepoint, cordless voice and cordless data communication. Technical development permits providing each of these systems with more and more enhanced features. A consequence of this is that

---

[13] Case 322/81, Michelin v. Commission, 9 November 1983 [1983] ECR 3529, Ground 37.

the differences between all these systems are progressively blurring and their interchangeability increasing. Therefore, it cannot be excluded that in future for certain uses several of those systems be embraced by a single product market. By the same token, it is likely that, for certain uses, mobile systems will be comprised in a single market with certain services offered on the public switched network.

(b) The geographic market

31. A geographic market is an area:
— where undertakings enter into competition with each other, and
— where the objective conditions of competition applying to the product or service in question are similar for all traders[14].

32. Without prejudice to the definition of the geographic market in individual cases, each national territory within the EEC seems still to be a distinct geographic market as regards those relevant services or products, where:

— the customer's needs cannot be satisfied by using a non-domestic service,
— there are different regulatory conditions of access to services, in particular special or exclusive rights which are apt to isolate national territories,
— as to equipment and network, there are no Community-common standards, whether mandatory or voluntary, whose absence could also isolate the national markets. The absence of voluntary Community-wide standards shows different national customers' requirements.

However, it is expected that the geographic market will progressively extend to the EEC territory at the place of the progressive realization of a single EEC market.

33. It has also to be ascertained whether each national market or a part thereof is a substantial part of the common market. This is the case where the services of the product involved represent a substantial percentage of volume within the EEC. This applies to all services and products involved.

34. As to satellite uplinks, for cross-border communication by satellite the uplink could be provided from any of several countries. In this case, the geographic market is wider than the national territory and may cover the whole EEC.

As to space segment capacity, the extension of the geographic market will depend on the power of the satellite and its ability to compete with other satellites for transmission to a given area, in other words on its range. This can be assessed only case by case.

35. As to services in general as well as terminal and network equipment, the Commission assesses the market power of the undertakings concerned and the result for EEC competition of the undertakings' conduct, taking into account their interrelated activities and interaction between the EEC and world markets. This is even more necessary to the extent that the EEC market is progressively being opened. This could have a considerable effect on the structure of the markets in the EEC, on the overall competitivity of the undertakings operating in those markets, and in the long run, on their capacity to remain independent operators.

IV. APPLICATION OF ARTICLE 85

36. The Commission recalls that a major policy target of the Council Resolution of 30 June 1988 on the development of the common market for telecommunications services and equipment up to 1992 was that of:

'. . . . . stimulating European cooperation at all levels, as far as compatible with Community competition rules, and particularly in the field of research and development, in order to secure a strong European presence on the telecommunications markets and to ensure the full participation of all Member States'.

---

[14] Judgment of 14. 2. 1978 in Case 27/76, United Brands v. Commission [1978] ECR 207, Ground 44. In the telecommunications sector: Judgment of 5. 10. 1988 in Case 247/86, Alsatel-Novasam [1988] ECR 5987.

In many cases Europe-wide services can be achieved by TOs' cooperation – for example, by ensuring interconnectivity and interoperability

(i) in those areas where exclusive or special rights for provision may continue in accordance with Community law and in particular with the Services Directive 90/388/EEC; and

(ii) in areas where optimum service will require certain features of cooperation, such as so-called 'one-stop shopping' arrangements, i.e. the possibility of acquiring Europe-wide services at a single sales point.

The Council is giving guidance, by Directives, Decisions, recommendations and resolutions on those areas where Europe-wide services are most urgently needed; such as by recommendation 86/659/EEC on the coordinated introduction of the integrated services digital network (ISDN) in the European Community[15] and by recommendation 87/371/EEC on the coordinated introduction of public pan-European cellular digital land-based mobile communications in the Community[16].

The Commission welcomes and fully supports the necessity of cooperation particularly in order to promote the development of trans-European services and strengthen the competitivity of the EEC industry throughout the Community and in the world markets. However, this cooperation can only attain that objective if it complies with Community competition rules. Regulation No 17 provides well-defined clearing procedures for such cooperation agreements. The procedures foreseen by Regulation No 17 are:

(i) the application for negative clearance, by which the Commission certifies that the agreements are not caught by Article 85, because they do not restrict competition and/or do not affect trade between Member States; and

(ii) the notification of agreements caught by Article 85 in order to obtain an exemption under Article 85 (3). Although if a particular agreement is caught by Article 85, an exemption can be granted by the Commission under Article 85 (3), this is only so when the agreement brings about economic benefits – assessed on the basis of the criteria in the said paragraph 3 – which outweigh its restrictions on competition. In any event competition may not be eliminated for a substantial part of the products in question. Notification is not an obligation; but if, for reasons of legal certainty, the parties decide to request an exemption pursuant to Article 4 of Regulation No 17 the agreements may not be exempted until they have been notified to the Commission.

37. Cooperation agreements may be covered by one of the Commission block exemption Regulations or Notices[17]. In the first case the agreement is automatically exempted under Article 85 (3). In the latter case, in the Commission's view, the agreement does not appreciably restrict competition and trade between Member States and therefore does not justify a Commission action. In either case, the agreement does not need to be notified; but it may be notified in case of doubt. If the Commission receives a multitude of notifications of similar cooperation agreements in the telecommunications sector, it may consider whether a specific block exemption regulation for such agreement would be appropriate.

38. The categories of agreements[18] which seem to be typical in telecommunications and may be caught by Article 85 are listed below. This list provides examples only and is, therefore, not exhaustive. The Commission is thereby indicating possible competition restrictions which could be caught by Article 85 and cases where there may be the possibility of an exemption.

39. These agreements may affect trade between Member States for the following reasons:

(i) services other than services reserved to TOs, equipment and spatial segment facilities are traded throughout the EEC; agreements on these services and equipment are therefore

---

[15] OJ No L 382, 31. 12. 1986, p. 36.

[16] OJ No L 196, 17. 7. 1987, p. 81.

[17] Reported in 'Competition Law in the European Communities' Volume I (situation at 31. 12. 1989) published by the Commission.

[18] For simplification's sake this term stands also for 'decisions by associations' and 'concerted practices' within the meaning of Article 85.

likely to affect trade. Although at present cross-frontier trade is limited, there is potentially no reason to suppose that suppliers of such facilities will in future confine themselves to their national market;

(ii) as to reserved network services, one can consider that they also are traded throughout the Community. These services could be provided by an operator located in one Member State to customers located in other Member States, which decide to move their telecommunications hub into the first one because it is economically or qualitatively advantageous. Moreover, agreements on these matters are likely to affect EEC trade at least to the extent they influence the conditions under which the other services and equipment are supplied throughout the EEC.

40. Finally, to the extent that the TOs hold dominant positions in facilities, services and equipment markets, their behaviour leading to – and including the conclusion of – the agreements in question could also give rise to a violation of Article 86, if agreements have or are likely to have as their effect hindering the maintenance of the degree of competition still existing in the market or the growth of that competition, or causing the TOs to reap trading benefits which they would not have reaped if there had been normal and sufficiently effective competition.

A. *Horizontal agreements concerning the provision of terrestrial facilities and reserved services*

41. Agreements concerning terrestrial facilities (public switched network or leased circuits) or services (e.g. voice telephony for the general public) can currently only be concluded between TOs because of this legal regime providing for exclusive or special rights. The fact that the Services Directive recognizes the possibility for a Member State to reserve this provision to certain operators does not exempt those operators from complying with the competition rules in providing these facilities or services. These agreements may restrict competition within a Member State only where such exclusive rights are granted to more than one provider.

42. These agreements may restrict the competition between TOs for retaining or attracting large telecommunications users for their telecommunications centres. Such 'hub competition' is substantially based upon favourable rates and other conditions, as well as the quality of the services. Member States are not allowed to prevent such competition since the Directive allows only the granting of exclusive and special rights by each Member State in its own territory.

43. Finally, these agreements may restrict competition in non-reserved services from third party undertakings, which are supported by the facilities in question, for example if they impose discriminatory or inequitable trading conditions on certain users.

44. (aa) *Price agreements:* all TOs' agreements on prices, discounting or collection charges for international services, are apt to restrict the hub competition to an appreciable extent. Coordination on or prohibition of discounting could cause particularly serious restrictions. In situations of public knowledge such as exists in respect of the tariff level, discounting could remain the only possibility of effective price competition.

45. In several cases the Court of Justice and the Commission have considered price agreements among the most serious infringements of Article 85[19]. While harmonization of tariff structures may be a major element for the provision of Community-wide services, this goal should be pursued as far as compatible with Community competition rules and should include definition of efficient pricing principles throughout the Community. Price competition is a crucial, if not the principal, element of customer choice and is apt to stimulate technical progress. Without prejudice to any application for individual exemption that may be made, the justification of any price agreement in terms of Article 85 (3) would be the subject of very rigorous examination by the Commission.

46. Conversely, where the agreements concern only the setting up of common tariff structures or principles, the Commission may consider whether this would not constitute one of the economic

---

[19] PVC, Commission Decision 89/190/EEC, OJ No L 74, 17. 3. 1989, p. 1; Case 123/85, BNIC v. Clair [1985] ECR 391; Case 8/72, Cementhandelaren v. Commission (1972) ECR 977; Polypropylene, Commission Decision 86/398/EEC (OJ No L 230/1, 18. 8. 1986, p. 1) on appeal Case 179/86.

benefits under Article 85 (3) which outweigh the competition restriction. Indeed, this could provide the necessary transparency on tariff calculations and facilitate users' decisions about traffic flow or the location of headquarters or premises. Such agreements could also contribute to achieving one of the Green Paper's economic objectives – more cost-orientated tariffs.

In this connection, following the intervention of the Commission, the CEPT has decided to abolish recommendation PGT/10 on the general principles for the lease of international telecommunications circuits and the establishment of private international networks. This recommendation recommended, *inter alia*, the imposition of a 30% surcharge or an access charge where third-party traffic was carried on an international telecommunications leased circuit, or if such a circuit was interconnected to the public telecommunications network. It also recommended the application of uniform tariff coefficients in order to determine the relative price level of international telecommunications leased circuits. Thanks to the CEPT's cooperation with the Commission leading to the abolition of the recommendation, competition between telecoms operators for the supply of international leased circuits is re-established, to the benefit of users, especially suppliers of non-reserved services. The Commission has found that the recommendation amounted to a price agreement between undertakings under Article 85 of the Treaty which substantially restricted competition within the European Community[20].

47. (ab) *Agreements on other conditions for the provision of facilities*

These agreements may limit hub competition between the partners. Moreover, they may limit the access of users to the network, and thus restrict third undertakings' competition as to non-reserved services. This applies especially to the use of leased circuits. The abolished CEPT recommendation PGT/10 on tariffs had also recommended restrictions on conditions of sale which the Commission objected to. These restrictions were mainly:

— making the use of leased circuits between the customer and third parties subject to the condition that the communication concern exclusively the activity for which the circuit has been granted,
— a ban on subleasing,
— authorization of private networks only for customers tied to each other by economic links and which carry out the same activity,
— prior consultation between the TOs for any approval of a private network and of any modification of the use of the network, and for any interconnection of private networks.

For the purpose of an exemption under Article 85 (3), the granting of special conditions for a particular facility in order to promote its development could be taken into account among other elements. This could foster technologies which reduce the costs of services and contribute to increasing competitiveness of European industry structures. Naturally, the other Article 85 (3) requirements should also be met,

48. (ac) *Agreements on the choice of telecommunication routes.*

These may have the following restrictive effects:

(i) to the extent that they coordinate the TOs' choice of the routes to be set up in international services, they may limit competition between TOs as suppliers to users' communications hubs, in terms of investments and production, with a possible effect on tariffs. It should be determined whether this restriction of their business autonomy is sufficiently appreciable to be caught by Article 85. In any event, an argument for an exemption under Article 85 (3) could be more easily sustained if common routes designation were necessary to enable interconnections and, therefore, the use of a Europe-wide network;

(ii) to the extent that they reserve the choice of routes already set up to the TOs, and this choice concerns one determined facility, they could limit the use of other facilities and thus services provision possibly to the detriment of technological progress. By contrast, the

---

[20] See Commission press release IP(90) 188 of 6 March 1990.

choice of routes does not seem restrictive in principle to the extent that it constitutes a technical requirement.

49. (ad) *Agreements on the imposition of technical and quality standards on the services provided on the public network*

Standardization brings substantial economic benefits which can be relevant under Article 85 (3). It facilitates *inter alia* the provision of pan-European telecommunications services. As set out in the framework of the Community's approach to standardization, products and services complying with standards may be used Community-wide. In the context of this approach, European standards institutions have developed in this field (ETSI and CEN-Cenelec). National markets in the EC would be opened up and form a Community market. Service and equipment markets would be enlarged, hence favouring economies of scale. Cheaper products and services are thus available to users. Standardization may also offer an alternative to specifications controlled by undertakings dominant in the network architecture and in non-reserved services. Standardization agreements may, therefore, lessen the risk of abuses by these undertakings which could block the access to the markets for non-reserved services and for equipment. However, certain standardization agreements can have restrictive effects on competition: hindering innovation, freezing a particular stage of technical development, blocking the network access of some users/service providers. This restriction could be appreciable, for example when deciding to what extent intelligence will in future be located in the network or continue to be permitted in customers' equipment. The imposition of specifications other than those provided for by Community law could have restrictive effects on competition. Agreements having these effects are, therefore, caught by Article 85.

The balance between economic benefits and competition restrictions is complex. In principle, an exemption could be granted if an agreement brings more openness and facilitates access to the market, and these benefits outweigh the restrictions caused by it.

50. Standards jointly developed and/or published in accordance with the ONP procedures carry with them the presumption that the cooperating TOs which comply with those standards fulfil the requirement of open and efficient access (see the ONP Directive mentioned in paragraph 16). This presumption can be rebutted, *inter alia*, if the agreement contains restrictions which are not foreseen by Community law and are not indispensable for the standardization sought.

51. One important Article 85 (3) requirement is that users must also be allowed a fair share of the resulting benefit. This is more likely to happen when users are directly involved in the standardization process in order to contribute to deciding what products or services will meet their needs. Also, the involvement of manufacturers or service providers other than TOs seems a positive element for Article 85 (3) purposes. However, this involvement must be open and widely representative in order to avoid competition restrictions to the detriment of excluded manufacturers or service providers. Licensing other manufacturers may be deemed necessary, for the purpose of granting an exemption to these agreements under Article 85 (3).

52. (ae) *Agreements foreseeing special treatment for TOs' terminal equipment or other companies' equipment for the interconnection or interoperation of terminal equipment with reserved services and facilities*

53. (af) *Agreements on the exchange of information*

A general exchange of information could indeed be necessary for the good functioning of international telecommunications services, and for cooperation aimed at ensuring interconnectivity or one-stop shopping and billing. It should not be extended to competition-sensitive information, such as certain tariff information which constitutes business secrets, discounting, customers and commercial strategy, including that concerning new products. The exchange of this information would affect the autonomy of each TO's commercial policy and it is not necessary to attain the said objectives.

B. *Agreements concerning the provision of non-reserved services and terminal equipment*

54. Unlike facilities markets, where only the TOs are the providers, in the services markets the actual or potential competitors are numerous and include, besides the TOs, international private

companies, computer companies, publishers and others. Agreements on services and terminal equipment could therefore be concluded between TOs, between TOs and private companies, and between private companies.

55. The liberalizing process has led mostly to strategic agreements between (i) TOs, and (ii) TOs and other companies. These agreements usually take the form of joint ventures.

56. (ba) *Agreements between TOs*

The scope of these agreements, in general, is the provision by each partner of a value-added service including the management of the service. Those agreements are mostly based on the 'one-stop shopping' principle, i.e. each partner offers to the customer the entire package of services which he needs. These managed services are called managed data network services (MDNS). An MDNS essentially consists of a broad package of services including facilities, value-added services and management. The agreements may also concern such basic services as satellite uplink.

57. These agreements could restrict competition in the MDNS market and also in the markets for a service or a group of services included in the MDNS:

(i) between the participating TOs themselves; and
(ii) *vis-à-vis* other actual or potential third-party providers.

58. (i) *Restrictions of competition between TOs*

Cooperation between TOs could limit the number of potential individual MDNS offered by each participating TO.

The agreements may affect competition at least in certain aspects which are contemplated as specific examples of prohibited practices under Article 85 (1) (a) to (c), in the event that:

— they fix or recommend, or at least lead (through the exchange of price information) to coordination of prices charged by each participant to customers,
— they provide for joint specification of MDNS products, quotas, joint delivery, specification of customers' systems; all this would amount to controlling production, markets, technical development and investments,
— they contemplate joint purchase of MDNS hardware and/or software, which would amount to sharing markets or sources of supply.

59. (ii) *Restrictive effects on third party undertakings*

Third parties' market entry could be precluded or hampered if the participating TOs:

— refuse to provide facilities to third party suppliers of services,
— apply usage restrictions only to third parties and not to themselves (e.g. a private provider is precluded from placing multiple customers on a leased line facility to obtain lower unit costs),
— favour their MDNS offerings over those of private suppliers with respect to access, availability, quality and price of leased circuits, maintenance and other services,
— apply especially low rates to their MDNS offerings, cross-subsidizing them with higher rates for monopoly services.

Examples of this could be the restrictions imposed by the TOs on private network operators as to the qualifications of the users, the nature of the messages to be exchanged over the network or the use of international private leased circuits.

60. Finally, as the participating TOs hold, individually or collectively, a dominant position for the creation and the exploitation of the network in each national market, any restrictive behaviour described in paragraph 59 could amount to an abuse of a dominant position under Article 86 (see V below).

61. On the other hand, agreements between TOs may bring economic benefits which could be taken into account for the possible granting of an exemption under Article 85 (3). *Inter alia*, the possible benefits could be as follows:

— a European-wide service and 'one-stop shopping' could favour business in Europe. Large multinational undertakings are provided with a European communication service using only a single point of contact,
— the cooperation could lead to a certain amount of European-wide standardization even before further EEC legislation on this matter is adopted,
— the cooperation could bring a cost reduction and consequently cheaper offerings to the advantage of consumers,
— a general improvement of public infrastructure could arise from a joint service provision.

62. Only by notification of the cases in question, in accordance with the appropriate procedures under Regulation No 17, will the Commission be able, where requested, to ascertain, on the merits, whether these benefits outweigh the competition restrictions. But in any event, restrictions on access for third parties seem likely to be considered as not indispensable and to lead to the elimination of competition for a substantial part of the products and services concerned within the meaning of Article 85 (3), thus excluding the possibility of an exemption. Moreover, if an MDNS agreement strengthens appreciably a dominant position which a participating TO holds in the market for a service included in the MDNS, this is also likely to lead to a rejection of the exemption.

63. The Commission has outlined the conditions for exempting such forms of cooperation in a case concerning a proposed joint venture between 22 TOs for the provision of a Europe-wide MDNS, later abandoned for commercial reasons[21], The Commission considered that the MDNS project presented the risks of restriction of competition between the operators themselves and private service suppliers but it accepted that the project also offered economic benefits to tele-communications users such as access to Europe-wide services through a single operator. Such cooperation could also have accelerated European standardization, reduced costs and increased the quality of the services. The Commission had informed the participants that approval of the project would have to be subject to guarantees designed to prevent undue restriction of competition in the telecommunications services markets, such as discrimination against private services suppliers and cross-subsidization. Such guarantees would be essential conditions for the granting of an exemption under the competition rules to cooperation agreements involving TOs. The requirement for an appropriate guarantee of non-discrimination and non-cross-subsidization will be specified in individual cases according to the examples of discrimination indicated in Section V below con-cerning the application of Article 86.

64. (bb) *Agreements between TOs and other service providers*

Cooperation between TOs and other operators is increasing in telecommunications services. It frequently takes the form of a joint venture. The Commission recognizes that it may have beneficial effects. However, this cooperation may also adversely affect competition and the opening up of services markets. Beneficial and harmful effects must therefore be carefully weighed.

65. Such agreements may restrict competition for the provision of telecommunications services:

(i) between the partners; and
(ii) from third parties.

66. (i) Competition between the partners may be restricted when these are actual or potential competitors for the relevant telecommunications service. This is generally the case, even when only the other partners and not the TOs are already providing the service. Indeed, TOs may have the required financial capacity, technical and commercial skills to enter the market for non-reserved services and could reasonably bear the technical and financial risk of doing it. This is also generally the case as far as private operators are concerned, when they do not yet provide the service in the

---

[21] Commission press release IP(89) 948 of 14. 12. 1989.

geographical market covered by the cooperation, but do provide this service elsewhere. They may therefore be potential competitors in this geographic market.

67. (ii) The cooperation may restrict competition from third parties because:

— there is an appreciable risk that the participant TO, i.e. the dominant network provider, will give more favourable network access to its cooperation partners than to other service providers in competition with the partners,

— potential competitors may refrain from entering the market because of this objective risk or, in any event, because of the presence on the market-place of a cooperation involving the monopolist for the network provision. This is especially the case when market entry barriers are high: the market structure allows only few suppliers and the size and the market power of the partners are considerable.

68. On the other hand, the cooperation may bring economic benefits which outweigh its harmful effect and therefore justify the granting of an exemption under Article 85 (3). The economic benefits can consist, *inter alia*, of the rationalization of the production and distribution of telecommunication services, in improvements in existing services or development of new services, or transfer of technology which improves the efficiency and the competitiveness of the European industrial structures.

69. In the absence of such economic benefits a complementarity between partners, i.e. between the provision of a reserved activity and that of a service under competition, is not a benefit as such. Considering it as a benefit, would be equal to justifying an involvement through restrictive agreements of TOs in any non-reserved service provision. This would be to hinder a competitive structure in this market.

In certain cases, the cooperation could consolidate or extend the dominant position of the TOs concerned to a non-reserved services market, in violation of Article 86.

70. The imposition or the proposal of cooperation with the service provider as a condition for the provision of the network may be deemed abusive (see paragraph 98 (vi)).

71. (bc) *Agreements between service providers other than TOs*

The Commission will apply the same principles indicated in (ba) and (bb) above also to agreements between private service providers, *inter alia*, agreements providing quotas, price fixing, market and/or customer allocation. In principle, they are unlikely to qualify for an exemption. The Commission will be particularly vigilant in order to avoid cooperation on services leading to a strengthening of dominant positions of the partners or restricting competition from third parties. There is a danger of this occurring for example when an undertaking is dominant with regard to the network architecture and its proprietary standard is adopted to support the service contemplated by the cooperation. This architecture enabling interconnection between computer systems of the partners could attract some partners to the dominant partner. The dominant position for the network architecture will be strengthened and Article 86 may apply.

72. In any exemption of agreements between TOs and other services and/or equipment providers, or between these providers, the Commission will require from the partners appropriate guarantees of non-cross-subsidization and non-discrimination. The risk of cross-subsidization and discrimination is higher when the TOs or the other partners provide both services and equipment, whether within or outside the Community.

C. *Agreements on research and development (R&D)*

73. As in other high technology based sectors, R&D in telecommunications is essential for keeping pace with technological progress and being competitive on the market-place to the benefit of users. R&D requires more and more important financial, technical and human resources which only few undertakings can generate individually. Cooperation is therefore crucial for attaining the above objectives.

74. The Commission has adopted a Regulation for the block exemption under Article 85 (3) of R&D agreements in all sectors, including telecommunications[22].

75. Agreements which are not covered by this Regulation (or the other Commission block exemption Regulations) could still obtain an individual exemption from the Commission if Article 85 (3) requirements are met individually. However, not in all cases do the economic benefits of an R&D agreement outweigh its competition restrictions. In telecommunications, one major asset, enabling access to new markets, is the launch of new products or services. Competition is based not only on price, but also on technology. R&D agreements could constitute the means for powerful undertakings with high market shares to avoid or limit competition from more innovative rivals. The risk of excessive restrictions of competition increases when the cooperation is extended from R&D to manufacturing and even more to distribution.

76. The importance which the Commission attaches to R&D and innovation is demonstrated by the fact that it has launched several programmes for this purpose. The joint companies' activities which may result from these programmes are not automatically cleared or exempted as such in all aspects from the application of the competition rules. However, most of those joint activities may be covered by the Commission's block exemption Regulations. If not, the joint activities in question may be exempted, where required, in accordance with the appropriate criteria and procedures.

77. In the Commission's experience joint distribution linked to joint R&D which is not covered by the Regulation on R&D does not play the crucial role in the exploitation of the results of R&D. Nevertheless, in individual cases, provided that a competitive environment is maintained, the Commission is prepared to consider full-range cooperation even between large firms. This should lead to improving the structure of European industry and thus enable it to meet strong competition in the world market place.

V. APPLICATION OF ARTICLE 86

78. Article 86 applies when:

    (i)   the undertaking concerned holds an individual or a joint dominant position;
    (ii) it commits an abuse of that dominant position; and
    (iii) the abuse may affect trade between Member States.

Dominant position

79. In each national market the TOs hold individually or collectively a dominant position for the creation and the exploitation of the network, since they are protected by exclusive or special rights granted by the State. Moreover, the TOs hold a dominant position for some telecommunications services, in so far as they hold exclusive or special rights with respect to those services[23].

80. The TOs may also hold dominant positions on the markets for certain equipment or services, even though they no longer hold any exclusive rights on those markets. After the elimination of these rights, they may have kept very important market shares in this sector. When the market share in itself does not suffice to give the TOs a dominant position, it could do it in combination with the other factors such as the monopoly for the network or other related services and a powerful and wide distribution network. As to the equipment, for example terminal equipment, even if the TOs are not involved in the equipment manufacturing or in the services provision, they may hold a dominant position in the market as distributors.

81. Also, firms other than TOs may hold individual or collective dominant positions in markets where there are no exclusive rights. This may be the case especially for certain non-reserved services because of either the market shares alone of those undertakings, or because of a combination of several factors. Among these factors, in addition to the market shares, two of particular importance

---

[22] Regulation (EEC) No 418/85, OJ No L 53, 22. 2. 1985, p. 5.
[23] Commission Decision 82/861/EEC in the 'British Telecommunications' case, point 26, OJ No L 360, 21. 12. 1982, p. 36, confirmed in the Judgment of 20. 3. 1985 in Case 41/83, Italian Republic v. Commission [1985] ECR 873, generally known as 'British Telecom'.

are the technological advance and the holding of the information concerning access protocols or interfaces necessary to ensure interoperability of software and hardware. When this information is covered by intellectual property rights this is a further factor of dominance.

82. Finally, the TOs hold, individually or collectively, dominant positions in the demand for some telecommunication equipment, works or software services. Being dominant for the network and other services provisions they may account for a purchaser's share high enough to give them dominance as to the demand, i.e. making suppliers dependent on them. Dependence could exist when the supplier cannot sell to other customers a substantial part of its production or change a production. In certain national markets, for example in large switching equipment, big purchasers such as the TOs face big suppliers. In this situation, it should be weighed up case by case whether the supplier or the customer position will prevail on the other to such an extent as to be considered dominant under Article 86.

With the liberalization of services and the expansion of new forces on the services markets, dominant positions of undertakings other than the TOs may arise for the purchasing of equipment.

Abuse

83. Commission's activity may concern mainly the following broad areas of abuses:

A. *TOs' abuses:* in particular, they may take advantage of their monopoly or at least dominant position to acquire a foothold or to extend their power in non-reserved neighbouring markets, to the detriment of competitors and customers.

B. *Abuses by undertaking other than TOs:* these may take advantage of the fundamental information they hold, whether or not covered by intellectual property rights, with the object and/or effect of restricting competition.

C. *Abuses of a dominant purchasing position:* for the time being this concerns mainly the TOs, especially to the extent that they hold a dominant position for reserved activities in the national market. However, it may also increasingly concern other undertakings which have entered the market.

A. *TOs' Abuses*

84. The Commission has recognized in the Green Paper the central role of the TOs, which justifies the maintenance of certain monopolies to enable them to perform their public task. This public task consists in the provision and exploitation of a universal network or, where appropriate, universal service, i.e. one having general coverage and available to all users (including service providers and the TOs themselves) upon request on reasonable and non-discriminatory conditions.

This fundamental obligation could justify the benefit of the exception provided in Article 90 (2) under certain circumstances, as laid down in the Services Directive.

85. In most cases, however, the competition rules, far from obstructing the fulfilment of this obligation, contribute to ensuring it. In particular, Article 86 can apply to behaviour of dominant undertakings resulting in a refusal to supply, discrimination, restrictive tying clauses, unfair prices or other inequitable conditions.

If one of these types of behaviour occurs in the provision of one of the monopoly services, the fundamental obligation indicated above is not performed. This could be the case when a TO tries to take advantage of its monopoly for certain services (for instance: network provision) in order to limit the competition they have to face in respect of non-reserved services, which in turn are supported by those monopoly services.

It is not necessary for the purpose of the application of Article 86 that competition be restricted as to a service which is supported by the monopoly provision in question. It would suffice that the behaviour results in an appreciable restriction of competition in whatever way. This means that an abuse may occur when the company affected by the behaviour is not a service provider but an end user who could himself be disadvantaged in competition in the course of his own business.

86. The Court of Justice has set out this fundamental principle of competition in tele-communications in one of its judgments[24]. An abuse within the meaning of Article 86 is committed where, without any objective necessity, an undertaking holding a dominant position on a particular market reserves to itself or to an undertaking belonging to the same group an ancillary activity which might be carried out by another undertaking as part of its activities on a neighbouring but separate market, with the possibility of eliminating all competition from such undertaking.

The Commission believes that this principle applies, not only when a dominant undertaking monopolizes other markets, but also when by anti-competitive means it extends its activity to other markets.

Hampering the provision of non-reserved services could limit production, markets and above all the technical progress which is a key factor of telecommunications. The Commission has already shown these adverse effects of usage restrictions on monopoly provision in its decision in the 'British Telecom' case[25]. In this Decision it was found that the restrictions imposed by British Telecom on telex and telephone networks usage, namely on the transmission of international messages on behalf of third parties:

(i) limited the activity of economic operators to the detriment of technological progress;

(ii) discriminated against these operators, thereby placing them at a competitive disadvantage *vis-à-vis* TOs not bound by these restrictions; and

(iii) made the conclusion of the contracts for the supply of telex circuits subject to acceptance by the other parties of supplementary obligations which had no connection with such contracts. These were considered abuses of a dominant position identified respectively in Article 86 (b), (c) and (d).

This could be done:

(a) as above, by refusing or restricting the usage of the service provided under monopoly so as to limit the provision of non-reserved services by third parties; or

(b) by predatory behaviour, as a result of cross-subsidization.

87. The separation of the TOs' regulatory power from their business activity is a crucial matter in the context of the application of Article 86. This separation is provided in the Article 90 Directives on terminals and on services mentioned in Note 2 above.

(a) Usage restrictions

88. Usage restrictions on provisions of reserved services are likely to correspond to the specific examples of abuses indicated in Article 86. In particular:

— they may limit the provision of telecommunications services in free competition, the investments and the technical progress, to the prejudice of telecommunications consumers (Article 86 (b)),
— to the extent that these usage restrictions are not applied to all users, including the TOs themselves as users, they may result in discrimination against certain users, placing them at a competitive disadvantage (Article 86 (c)),
— they may make the usage of the reserved services subject to the acceptance of obligations which have no connection wit this usage (Article 86 (d)).

89. The usage restrictions in question mainly concern public networks (public switched telephone network (PSTN) or public switched data networks (PSDN)) and especially leased circuits. They may also concern other provisions such as satellite uplink, and mobile communication networks. The most frequent types of behaviour are as follows:

---

[24] Case 311/84, Centre belge d'études de marché Télémarketing (CBEM) SA v. Compagnie luxembourgoise de télédiffusion SA and Information Publicité Benelux SA, 3 October 1985 [1985] ECR 3261, Grounds 26 and 27.
[25] See Note[22].

(i) *Prohibition imposed by TOs on third parties:*

(a) *to connect private leased circuits by means of concentrator, multiplexer or other equipment to the public switched network; and/or*

(b) *to use private leased circuits for providing services, to the extent that these services are not reserved, but under competition.*

90. To the extent that the user is granted a licence by State regulatory authorities under national law in compliance with EEC law, these prohibitions limit the user's freedom of access to the leased circuits, the provision of which is a public service. Moreover, it discriminates between users, depending upon the usage (Article 86 (c)). This is one of the most serious restrictions and could substantially hinder the development of international telecommunications services (Article 86 (b)).

91. When the usage restriction limits the provision of non-reserved service in competition with that provided by the TO itself the abuse is even more serious and the principles of the above-mentioned 'Teélémarketing' judgment (Note 24 *supra*) apply.

92. In individual cases, the Commission will assess whether the service provided on the leased circuit is reserved or not, on the basis of the Community regulatory acts interpreted in the technical and economic context of each case. Even though a service could be considered reserved according to the law, the fact that a TO actually prohibits the usage of the leased circuit only to some users and not to others could constitute a discrimination under Article 86 (c).

93. The Commission has taken action in respect of the Belgian Régie des télégraphes et téléphones after receiving a complaint concerning an alleged abuse of dominant position from a private supplier of value-added telecommunications services relating to the conditions under which tele-communications circuits were being leased. Following discussions with the Commission, the RTT authorized the private supplier concerned to use the leased telecommunications circuits subject to no restrictions other than that they should not be used for the simple transport of data.

Moreover, pending the possible adoption of new rules in Belgium, and without prejudice to any such rules, the RTT undertook that all its existing and potential clients for leased tele-communications circuits to which third parties may have access shall be governed by the same conditions as those which were agreed with the private sector supplier mentioned above[26].

(ii) *Refusal by TOs to provide reserved services (in particular the network and leased circuits) to third parties*

94. Refusal to supply has been considered an abuse by the Commission and the Court of Justice[27]. This behaviour would make it impossible or at least appreciably difficult for third parties to provide non-reserved services. This, in turn, would lead to a limitation of services and of technical development (Article 86 (b)) and, if applied only to some users, result in discrimination (Article 86 (c)).

(iii) *Imposition of extra charges or other special conditions for certain usages of reserved services*

95. An example would be the imposition of access charges to leased circuits when they are con-nected to the public switched network or other special prices and charges for service provision to third parties. Such access charges may discriminate between users of the same service (leased circuits provision) depending upon the usage and result in imposing unfair trading conditions. This will limit the usage of leased circuits and finally non-reserved service provision. Conversely, it does not constitute an abuse provided that it is shown, in each specific case, that the access charges correspond to costs which are entailed directly for the TOs for the access in question. In this case, access charges can be imposed only on an equal basis to all users, including TOs themselves.

96. Apart from these possible additional costs which should be covered by an extra charge, the interconnection of a leased circuit to the public switched network is already remunerated by the

---

[26] Commission Press release IP(90) 67 of 29. 1. 1990.
[27] Cases 6 and 7/73 Commercial Solvents v. Commission [1974] ECR 223; United Brands v. Commission (Note 13, above).

price related to the use of this network. Certainly, a leased circuit can represent a subjective value for a user depending on the profitability of the enhanced service to be provided on that leased circuit. However, this cannot be a criterion on which a dominant undertaking, and above all a public service provider, can base the price of this public service.

97. The Commission appreciates that the substantial difference between leased circuits and the public switched network causes a problem of obtaining the necessary revenues to cover the costs of the switched network. However, the remedy chosen must not be contrary to law, i.e. the EEC Treaty, as discriminatory pricing between customers would be.

(iv)   *Discriminatory price or quality of the service provided*

98. This behaviour may relate, *inter alia*, to tariffs or to restrictions or delays in connection to the public switched network or leased circuits provision, in installation, maintenance and repair, in effecting interconnection of systems or in providing information concerning network planning, signalling, protocols, technical standards and all other information necessary for an appropriate interconnection and interoperation with the reserved service and which may affect the interworking of competitive services or terminal equipment offerings.

(v)   *Tying the provision of the reserved service to the supply by the TOs or others of terminal equipment to be interconnected or interoperated, in particular through imposition, pressure, offer of special prices or other trading conditions for the reserved service linked to the equipment.*

(vi)   *Tying the provision of the reserved service to the agreement of the user to enter into cooperation with the reserved service provider himself as to the non-reserved service to be carried on the network*

(vii) *Reserving to itself for the purpose of non-reserved service provision or to other service providers information obtained in the exercise of a reserved service in particular information concerning users of a reserved services providers more favourable conditions for the supply of this information*

This latter information could be important for the provision of services under competition to the extent that it permits the targeting of customers of those services and the definition of business strategy. The behaviour indicated above could result in a discrimination against undertakings to which the use of this information is denied in violation of Article 86 (c). The information in question can only be disclosed with the agreement of the users concerned and in accordance with relevant data protection legislation (see the proposal for a Council Directive concerning the protection of personal data and privacy in the context of public digital telecommunications networks, in particular the integrated services digital network (ISDN) and public digital mobile networks[28].

(viii) *Imposition of unneeded reserved services by supplying reserved and/or non-reserved services when the former reserved services are reasonably separable from the others*

99. The practices under (v) (vi) (vii) and (viii) result in applying conditions which have no connection with the reserved service, contravening Article 86 (d).

100. Most of these practices were in fact identified in the Services Directive as restrictions on the provision of services within the meaning of Article 59 and Article 86 of the Treaty brought about the State measures. They are therefore covered by the broader concept of 'restrictions' which under Article 6 of the Directive have to be removed by Member States.

101. The Commission believes that the Directives on terminals and on services also clarify some principles of application of Articles 85 and 86 in the sector.

The Services Directive does not apply to important sectors such as mobile communications and satellites; however, competition rules apply fully to these sectors. Moreover, as to the services covered by the Directive it will depend very much on the degree of precision of the licences given by the regulatory body whether the TOs still have a discretionary margin for imposing conditions which should be scrutinized under competition rules. Not all the conditions can be regulated in licences: consequently, there could be room for discretionary action. The application of compe-

---

[28] Commission document COM(90) 314 of 13. 9. 1990.

tition rules to companies will therefore depend very much on a case-by-case examination of the licences. Nothing more than a class licence can be required for terminals.

(b) Cross-subsidization

102. Cross-subsidization means that an undertaking allocates all or part of the costs of its activity in one product or geographic market to its activity in another product or geographic market. Under certain circumstance, cross-subsidization in telecommunications could distort competition, i.e. lead to beating other competitors with offers which are made possible not by efficiency and performance but by artificial means such as subsidies. Avoiding cross-subsidization leading to unfair competition is crucial for the development of service provision and equipment supply.

103. Cross-subsidization does not lead to predatory pricing and does not restrict competition when it is the costs of reserved activities which are subsidized by the revenue generated by other reserved activities since there is no competition possible as to these activities. This form of subsidization is even necessary, as it enables the TOs holders of exclusive rights to perform their obligation to provide a public service universally and on the same conditions to everybody. For instance, telephone provision in unprofitable rural areas is subsidized through revenues from telephone provision and profitable urban areas or long-distance calls. The same could be said of subsidizing the provision of reserved services through revenues generated by activities under competition. The application of the general principle of cost-orientation should be the ultimate goal, in order, *inter alia*, to ensure that prices are not inequitable as between users.

104. Subsidizing activities under competition, whether concerning services or equipment, by allocating their costs to monopoly activities, however, is likely to distort competition in violation of Article 86. It could amount to an abuse by an undertaking holding a dominant position within the Community. Moreover, users of activities under monopoly have to bear unrelated costs for the provision of these activities. Cross-subsidization can also exist between monopoly provision and equipment manufacturing and sale. Cross-subsidization can be carried out through:

— funding the operation of the activities in question with capital remunerated substantially below the market rate;
— providing for those activities premises, equipment, experts and/or services with a remuneration substantially lower than the market price.

105. As to funding through monopoly revenues or making available monopoly material and intellectual means for the starting up of new activities under competition, this constitutes an investment whose costs should be allocated to the new activity. Offering the new product or service should normally include a reasonable remuneration of such investment in the long run. If it does not, the Commission will assess the case on the basis of the remuneration plans of the undertaking concerned and of the economic context.

106. Transparency in the TOs' accounting should enable the Commission to ascertain whether there is cross-subsidization in the cases in which this question arises. The ONP Directive provides in this respect for the definition of harmonized tariff principles which should lessen the number of these cases.

This transparency can be provided by an accounting system which ensures the fully proportionate distribution of all costs between reserved and non-reserved activities. Proper allocation of costs is more easily ensured in cases of structural separation, i.e. creating distinct entities for running each of these two categories of activities.

An appropriate accounting system approach should permit the identification and allocation of all costs between the activities which they support. In this system all products and services should bear proportionally all the relevant costs, including costs of research and development, facilities and overheads. It should enable the production of recorded figures which can be verified by accountants.

107. As indicated above (paragraph 59), in cases of cooperation agreements involving TOs a guarantee of no cross-subsidization is one of the conditions required by the Commission for

exemption under Article 85 (3). In order to monitor properly compliance with that guarantee, the Commission now envisages requesting the parties to ensure an appropriate accounting system as described above, the accounts being regularly submitted to the Committee. Where the accounting method is chosen, the Commission will reserve the possibility of submitting the accounts to independent audit, especially if any doubt arises as to the capability of the system to ensure the necessary transparency or to detect any cross-subsidization. It the guarantee cannot be properly monitored, the Commission may withdraw the exemption.

108. In all other cases, the Commission does not envisage requiring such transparency of the TOs. However, if in a specific case there are substantial elements converging in indicating the existence of an abusive cross-subsidization and/or predatory pricing, the Commission could establish a presumption of such cross-subsidization and predatory pricing. An appropriate separate accounting system could be important in order to counter this presumption.

109. Cross-subsidization of a reserved activity by a non-reserved one does not in principle restrict competition. However, the application of the exception provided in Article 90 (2) to this non-reserved activity could not as a rule be justified by the fact that the financial viability of the TO in question rests on the non-reserved activity. Its financial viability and the performance of its task of general economic interest can only be ensured by the State where appropriate by the granting of an exclusive or special right and by imposing restrictions on activities competing with the reserved ones.

110. Also cross-subsidization by a public or private operators outside the EEC may be deemed abusive in terms of Article 86 if that operator holds a dominant position for equipment or non-reserved services within the EEC. The existence of this dominant position, which allows the holder to behave to an appreciable extent independently of its competitors and customers and ultimately of consumers, will be assessed in the light of all elements in the EEC and outside.

B. *Abuses by undertakings other than the TOs*

111. Further to the liberalization of services, undertakings other than the TOs may increasingly extend their power to acquire dominant positions in non-reserved markets. They may already hold such a position in some services markets which had not been reserved. When they take advantage of their dominant position to restrict competition and to extend their power, Article 86 may also apply to them. The abuses in which they might indulge are broadly similar to most of those previously described in relation to the TOs.

112. Infringement of Article 86 may be committed by the abusive exercise of industrial property rights in relation with standards, which are of crucial importance for telecommunications. Standards may be either the results of international standardization, or *de facto* standards and the property of undertakings.

113. Producers of equipment or suppliers of services are dependent on proprietary standards to ensure the interconnectivity of their computer resources. An undertaking which owns a dominant network architecture may abuse its dominant position by refusing to provide the necessary information for the interconnection of other architecture resources to its architecture products. Other possible abuses – similar to those indicated as to the TOs – are, *inter alia*, delays in providing the information, discrimination in the quality of the information, discriminatory pricing or other trading conditions, and making the information provision subject to the acceptance by the producers, supplier or user of unfair trading conditions.

114. On 1 August 1984, the Commission accepted a unilateral undertaking from IBM to provide other manufacturers with the technical interface information needed to permit competitive products to be used with IBM's then most powerful range of computers, the System/370. The Commission thereupon suspended the proceedings under Article 86 which it had initiated against IBM in December 1980. The IBM Undertaking[29] also contains a commitment relating to SNA formats and protocols.

---

[29] Reproduced in full in EC Bulletin 10-1984 (point 3.4.1). As to its continued application, see Commission press release No IP(88) 814 of 15 December 1988.

115. The question how to reconcile copyrights on standards with the competition requirements is particularly difficult. In any event, copyright cannot be used unduly to restrict competition.

C. *Abuses of dominant purchasing position*

116. Article 86 also applies to behaviour of undertakings holding a dominant purchasing position. The examples of abuses indicated in that Article may therefore also concern that behaviour.

117. The Council Directive 90/531/EEC[30] based on Articles 57 (2), 66, 100a and 113 of the EEC Treaty on the procurement procedures of entities operating in *inter alia* the telecommunications sector regulates essentially:

    (i) procurement procedures in order to ensure on a reciprocal basis non-discrimination on the basis of nationality; and

    (ii) for products or services for use in reserved markets, not in competitive markets. That Directive, which is addressed to States, does not exclude the application of Article 86 to the purchasing of products within the scope of the Directive. The Commission will decide case by case how to ensure that these different sets of rules are applied in a coherent manner.

118. Furthermore, both in reserved and competitive markets, practices other than those covered by the Directive may be established in violation of Article 86. One example is taking advantage of a dominant purchasing position for imposing excessively favourable prices or other trading conditions, in comparison with other purchasers and suppliers (Article 86 (a)). This could result in discrimination under Article 86 (c). Also obtaining, whether or not through imposition, an exclusive distributorship for the purchased product by the dominant purchaser may constitute an abusive extension of its economic power to other markets (see 'Télémarketing' Court judgment (Note 24 *supra*)).

119. Another abusive practice could be that of making the purchase subject to licensing by the supplier of standards for the product to be purchased or for other products, to the purchaser itself, or to other suppliers (Article 86 (d)).

120. Moreover, even in competitive markets, discriminatory procedures on the basis of nationality may exist, because national pressures and traditional links of a non-economic nature do not always disappear quickly after the liberalization of the markets. In this case, a systematic exclusion or considerably unfavourable treatment of a supplier, without economic necessity, could be examined under Article 86, especially (b) (limitation of outlets) and (c) (discrimination). In assessing the case, the Commission will substantially examine whether the same criteria for awarding the contract have been followed by the dominant undertaking for all suppliers. The Commission will normally take into account criteria similar to those indicated in Article 27 (1) of the Directive[31]. The purchases in question being outside the scope of the Directive, the Commission will not require that transparent purchasing procedures be pursued.

D. *Effect on trade between Member States*

121. The same principle outlined regarding Article 85 applies here. Moreover, in certain circumstances, such as the case of the elimination of a competition by an undertaking holding a dominant position, although trade between Member States is not directly affected, for the purposes of Article 86 it is sufficient to show that there will be repercussions on the competitive structure of the common market.

---

[30] OJ No L 297, 29. 10. 1990, p. 1.

[31] (See Note 26) Article 27 (1) (a) and (b). The criteria on which the contracting entities shall base the award of the contracts shall be: (a) the most economically advantageous tender involving various criteria such as delivery date, period for completion, running costs, cost-effectiveness, quality, aesthetic and functional characteristics, technical merit, after-sales services and technical assistance, commitments with regard to spare parts, security of supplies and price; or (b) the lowest price only.

VI. APPLICATION OF ARTICLES 85 AND 86 IN THE FIELD OF SATELLITES

122. The development of this sector is addressed globally by the Commission in the 'Green Paper on a common approach in the field of satellite communications in the European Community' of 20 November 1990 (Doc. COM(90) 490 final). Due to the increasing importance of satellites and the particular uncertainty among undertakings as to the application of competition rules to individual cases in this sector, it is appropriate to address the sector in a distinct section in these guidelines.

123. State regulations on satellites are not covered by the Commission Directives under Article 90 of the EEC Treaty respectively on terminals and services mentioned above except in the Directive on terminals which contemplates receive-only satellite stations not connected to a public network. The Commission's position on the regulatory framework compatible with the Treaty competition rules is stated in the Commission Green Paper on satellites mentioned above.

124. In any event the Treaty competition rules fully apply to the satellites domain, *inter alia*, Articles 85 and 86 to undertakings. Below is indicated how the principles set out above, in particular in Sections IV and V, apply to satellites.

125. Agreements between European TOs in particular within international conventions may play an important role in providing European satellites systems and a harmonious development of satellite services throughout the Community. These benefits are taken into consideration under competition rules, provided that the agreements do not contain restrictions which are not indispensable for the attainment of these objectives.

126. Agreements between TOs concerning the operation of satellite systems in the broadest sense may be caught by Article 85. As to space segment capacity, the TOs are each other's competitors, whether actual or potential. In pooling together totally or partially their supplies of space segment capacity they may restrict competition between themselves. Moreover, they are likely to restrict competition *vis-à-vis* third parties to the extent that their agreements contain provisions with this object or effect: for instance provisions limiting their supplies in quality and/or quantity, or restricting their business autonomy by imposing directly and indirectly a coordination between these third parties and the parties to the agreements. It should be examined whether such agreements could qualify for an exemption under Article 85 (3) provided that they are notified. However, restrictions on third parties' ability to compete are likely to preclude such an exemption. It should also be examined whether such agreements strengthen any individual or collective dominant position of the parties, which also would exclude the granting of an exemption. This could be the case in particular if the agreement provides that the parties are exclusive distributors of the space segment capacity provided by the agreement.

127. Such agreements between TOs could also restrict competition as to the uplink with respect to which TOs are competitors. In certain cases the customer for satellite communication has the choice between providers in several countries, and his choice will be substantially determined by the quality, price and other sales conditions of each provider. This choice will be even ampler since uplink is being progressively liberalized and to the extent that the application of EEC rules to State legislations will open up the uplink markets. Community-wide agreements providing directly or indirectly for coordination as to the parties' uplink provision are therefore caught in Article 85.

128. Agreements between TOs and private operators on space segment capacity may be also caught by Article 85, as that provision applies, *inter alia*, to cooperation, and in particular joint venture agreements. These agreements could be exempted if they bring specific benefits such as technology transfer, improvements of the quality of the service or enabling better marketing, especially for a new capacity, outweighing the restrictions. In any event, imposing on customers the bundled uplink and space segment capacity provision is likely to exclude an exemption since it limits competition in uplink provision to the detriment of the customer's choice, and in the current market situation will almost certainly strengthen the TOs' dominant position in violation of Article 86. An exemption is unlikely to be granted also when the agreement has the effect of reducing substantially the supply in an oligopolistic market, and even more clearly when an effect of the agreement is to prevent the only potential competitor of a dominant provider in a given market

from offering its services independently. This could amount to a violation of Article 86. Direct or indirect imposition of any kind of agreement by a TO, for instance by making the uplink subject to the conclusion of an agreement with a third party, would constitute an infringement of Article 86.

VII. RESTRUCTURING IN TELECOMMUNICATIONS

129. Deregulation, the objective of a single market for 1992 and the fundamental changes in the telecommunications technology have caused wide strategic restructuring in Europe and throughout the world as well. They have mostly taken the form of mergers and joint ventures.

(a) Mergers

130. In assessing telecom mergers in the framework of Council Regulation (EEC) No 4064/89 on the control of concentrations between undertakings[32] the Commission will take into account, *inter alia*, the following elements.

131. Restructuring moves are in general beneficial to the European telecommunications industry. They may enable the companies to rationalize and to reach the critical mass necessary to obtain the economies of scale needed to make the important investments in research and development. These are necessary to develop new technologies and to remain competitive in the world market.

However, in certain cases they may also lead to the anti-competitive creation or strengthening of dominant positions.

132. The economic benefits resulting from critical mass must be demonstrated. The concentration operation could result in a mere aggregation of market shares, unaccompanied by restructuring measures or plans. This operation may create or strengthen Community or national dominant positions in a way which impedes competition.

133. When concentration operations have this sole effect, they can hardly be justified by the objective of increasing the competitivity of Community industry in the world market. This objective, strongly pursued by the Commission, rather requires competition in EEC domestic markets in order that the EEC undertakings acquire the competitive structure and attitude needed to operate in the world market.

134. In assessing concentration cases in telecommunications, the Commission will be particularly vigilant to avoid the strengthening of dominant positions through integration. If dominant service providers are allowed to integrate into the equipment market by way of mergers, access to this market by other equipment suppliers may be seriously hindered. A dominant service provider is likely to give preferential treatment to its own equipment subsidiary.

Moreover, the possibility of disclosure by the service provider to its subsidiary of sensitive information obtained from competing equipment manufacturers can put the latter at a competitive disadvantage.

The Commission will examine case by case whether vertical integration has such effects or rather is likely to reinforce the competitive structure of the Community.

135. The Commission has enforced principles on restructuring in a case concerning the GEC and Siemens joint bid for Plessey[33].

136. Article 85 (1) applies to the acquisition by an undertaking of a minority shareholding in a competitor where, *inter alia*, the arrangements involve the creation of a structure of cooperation between the investor and the other undertakings, which will influence these undertakings' competitive conduct[34].

---

[32] OJ No L 395, 30. 12. 1989, p. 1; Corrigendum OJ No L 257, 21. 9. 1990, p. 13.

[33] Commission Decision rejecting Plessey's complaint against the GEC-Siemens bid (Case IV/33.018 GEC-Siemens/ Plessey), OJ No C 239, 25. 9. 1990, p. 2.

[34] British American Tobacco Company Ltd and RJ Reynolds Industries Inc. v. Commission (Joined Cases 142 and 156/84) of 17. 11. 1987 (1987) ECR 4487.

(b) Joint ventures

137. A joint venture can be of a cooperative or a concentrative nature. It is of a cooperative nature when it has as its object or effect the coordination of the competitive behaviour of undertakings which remain independent. The principles governing cooperative joint ventures are to be set out in Commission guidelines to that effect. Concentrative joint ventures fall under Regulation (EEC) No 4064/89[35].

138. In some of the latest joint venture cases the Commission granted an exemption under Article 85 (3) on grounds which are particularly relevant to telecommunications. Precisely in a direction concerning telecommunications, the 'Optical Fibres' case[36], the Commission considered that the joint venture enabled European companies to produce a high technology product, promoted technical progress, and facilitated technology transfer. Therefore, the joint venture permits European companies to withstand competition from non-Community producers, especially in the USA and Japan, in an area of fast-moving technology characterized by international markets. The Commission confirmed this approach in the 'Canon-Olivetti' case[37].

VIII. IMPACT OF THE INTERNATIONAL CONVENTIONS ON THE APPLICATION OF EEC COMPETITION RULES TO TELECOMMUNICATIONS

139. International conventions (such as the Convention of International Telecommunication Union (ITU) or Conventions on Satellites) play a fundamental role in ensuring worldwide cooperation for the provision of international services. However, application of such international conventions on telecommunications by EEC Member States must not affect compliance with the EEC law, in particular with competition rules.

140. Article 234 of the EEC Treaty regulates this matter[38]. The relevant obligations provided in the various conventions or related Acts do not pre-date the entry into force of the Treaty. As to the ITU and World Administrative Telegraph and Telephone Conference (WATTC), whenever a revision or a new adoption of the ITU Convention or of the WATTC Regulations occurs, the ITU or WATTC members recover their freedom of action. The Satellites Conventions were adopted much later.

Moreover, as to all conventions, the application of EEC rules does not seem to affect the fulfilment of obligations of Member States *vis-à-vis* third countries. Article 234 does not protect obligations between EEC Member States entered into in international treaties. The purpose of Article 234 is to protect the right of third countries only and it is not intended to crystallize the acquired international treaty rights of Member States to the detriment of the EEC Treaty's objectives or of the Community interest. Finally, even if Article 234 (1) did apply, the Member States concerned would nevertheless be obliged to take all appropriate steps to eliminate incompatibility between their obligations *vis-à-vis* third countries and the EEC rules. This applies in particular where Member States acting collectively have the statutory possibility to modify the international convention in question as required, e.g. in the case of the Eutelsat Convention.

141. As to the WATTC Regulations, the relevant provisions of the Regulations in force from 9 December 1988 are flexible enough to give the parties the choice whether or not to implement them or how to implement them.

In any event, EEC Member States, by signing the Regulations, have made a joint declaration that they will apply them in accordance with their obligations under the EEC Treaty.

---

[35] OJ No C 203, 14. 8. 1990, p. 10.
[36] Decision 86/405/EEC, OJ No L 236, 22. 8. 86, p. 30.
[37] Decision 88/88/EEC, OJ No L 52, 26. 2. 1988, p. 51.
[38] 'The rights and obligations arising from agreements concluded before the entry into force of this Treaty between one or more Member States on the one hand and one or more third countries on the other, shall not be affected by the provisions of this Treaty. To the extent that such agreements are not compatible with this Treaty, the Member State or States concerned shall take all appropriate steps to eliminate the incompatibilities established. Member States shall, where necessary, assist each other to this end and shall, where appropriate, adopt a common attitude . . . .'

142. As to the International Telegraph and Telephone Consultative Committee (CCITT) recommendations, competition rules apply to them.

143. Members of the CCITT are, pursuant to Article 11 (2) of the International Telecommunications Convention, 'administrations' of the Members of the ITU and recognized private operating agencies ('RPOAs') which so request with the approval of the ITU members which have recognized them. Unlike the members of the ITU or the Administrative Conferences which are States, the members of the CCITT are telecommunications administrations and RPOAs. Telecommunications administrations are defined in Annex 2 to the International Telecommunications Conventions as 'tout service ou département gouvernemental responsable des mesures à prendre pour exécuter les obligations de la Convention Internationale des télécommunications et des règlements' [any government service or department responsible for the measures to be taken to fulfil the obligations laid down in the International Convention on Telecommunications and Regulations]. The CCITT meetings are in fact attended by TOs. Article 11 (2) of the International Telecommunications Convention clearly provides that telecommunications administrations and RPOAs are members of the CCITT by themselves. The fact that, because of the ongoing process of separation of the regulatory functions from the business activity, some national authorities participate in the CCITT is not in contradiction with the nature of undertakings of other members. Moreover, even if the CCITT membership became governmental as a result of the separation of regulatory and operational activities of the telecommunications administrations, Article 90 in association with Article 85 could still apply either against the State measures implementing the CCITT recommendations and the recommendations themselves on the basis of Article 90 (1), or if there is no such national implementing measure, directly against the telecommunications organizations which followed the recommendation[39].

144. In the Commission's view, the CCITT recommendations are adopted, *inter alia*, by undertakings. Such CCITT recommendations, although they are not legally binding, are agreements between undertakings or decisions by an association of undertakings. In any event, according to the case law of the Commission and the European Court of Justice[40] a statutory body entrusted with certain public functions and including some members appointed by the government of a Member State may be an 'association of undertakings' if it represents the trading interests of other members and takes decisions or makes agreements in pursuance of those interests.

The Commission draws attention to the fact that the application of certain provisions in the context of international conventions could result in infringements of the EEC competition rules:

— As to the WATTC Regulations, this is the case for the respective provisions for mutual agreement between TOs on the supply of international telecommunications services (Article 1 (5)), reserving the choice of telecommunications routes to the TOs (Article 3 (3) (3)), recommending practices equivalent to price agreements (Articles 6 (6) (1) (2)), and limiting the possibility of special arrangements to activities meeting needs within and/or between the territories of the Members concerned (Article 9) and only where existing arrangements cannot satisfactorily meet the relevant telecommunications needs (Opinion PL A).
— CCITT recommendations D1 and D2 as they stand at the date of the adoption of these guidelines could amount to a collective horizontal agreement on prices and other supply conditions of international leased lines to the extent that they lead to a coordination of sales policies between TOs and therefore limit competition between them. This was indicated by the Commission in a CCITT meeting on 23 May 1990. The Commission reserved the right to examine the compatibility of other recommendations with Article 85.
— The agreements between TOs concluded in the context of the Conventions on Satellites are likely to limit competition contrary to Article 85 and/or 86 on the grounds set out in paragraphs 126 to 128 above.

---

[39] See Commission Decision 87/3/EEC ENI/Montedison, OJ No L 5, 7. 1. 1987, p. 13.
[40] See Pabst & Richarz/BNIA, OJ No L 231, 21. 8. 1976, p. 24, AROW/BNIC, OJ No L 379, 31. 12. 1982, p. 1, and Case 123/83 BNIC v. Clair (1985) ECR 391.

APPENDIX 24

Council Directive 92/13/EEC of 25 February 1992 coordinating the laws, regulations and administrative provisions relating to the application of Community rules on the procurement procedures of entities operating in the water, energy, transport and telecommunications sectors

(92/13/EEC)

THE COUNCIL OF THE EUROPEAN COMMUNITIES,

Having regard to the Treaty establishing the European Economic Community, and in particular Article 100a thereof,

Having regard to the proposal from the Commission[1],

In cooperation with the European Parliament[2],

Having regard to the opinion of the Economic and Social Committee[3],

Whereas Council Directive 90/531/EEC of 17 September 1990 on the procurement procedures of entities operating in the water, energy, transport and telecommunications sectors[4] lays down rules for procurement procedures to ensure that potential suppliers and contractors have a fair opportunity to secure the award of contracts, but does not contain any specific provisions ensuring its effective application;

Whereas the existing arrangements at both national and Community levels for ensuring its application are not always adequate;

Whereas the absence of effective remedies or the inadequacy of existing remedies could deter Community undertakings from submitting tenders; whereas, therefore, the Member States must remedy this situation;

Whereas Council Directive 89/665/EEC of 21 December 1989 on the coordination of the laws, regulations and administrative provisions relating to the application of review procedures to the award of public supply and public works contracts[5] is limited to contract award procedures within the scope of Council Directive 71/305/EEC of 26 July 1971 concerning the coordination of procedures for the award of public works contracts[6], as last amended by Directive 90/531/EEC, and Council Directive 77/62/EEC of 21 December 1976 coordinating procedures for the award of public supply contracts[7], as last amended by Directive 90/531/EEC;

Whereas the opening-up of procurement in the sectors concerned to Community competition implies that provisions must be adopted to ensure that appropriate review procedures are made available to suppliers or contractors in the event of infringement of the relevant Community law or national rules implementing that law;

Whereas it is necessary to provide for a substantial increase in the guarantees of transparency and non-discrimination and whereas, for it to have tangible effects, effective and rapid remedies must be available;

---

[1] OJ No C 216, 31. 8. 1990, p. 8; and OJ No C 179, 10. 7. 1991, p. 18.
[2] OJ No C 106, 22. 4. 1991, p. 82; and OJ No C 39, 17. 2. 1992.
[3] OJ No C 60, 8. 3. 1991, p. 16.
[4] OJ No L 297, 29. 10. 1990, p. 1.
[5] OJ No L 395, 30. 12. 1989, p. 33.
[6] OJ No L 185, 16. 8. 1971, p. 5.
[7] OJ No L 13, 15. 1. 1977, p. 1.

Whereas account must be taken of the specific nature of certain legal orders by authorizing the Member States to choose between the introduction of different powers for the review bodies which have equivalent effects;

Whereas one of these options includes the power to intervene directly in the contracting entities' procurement procedures such as by suspending them, or by setting aside decisions or discriminatory clauses in documents or publications;

Whereas the other option provides for the power to exert effective indirect pressure on the contracting entities in order to make them correct any infringements or prevent them from committing infringements, and to prevent injury from occurring;

Whereas claims for damages must always be possible;

Whereas, where a claim is made for damages representing the costs of preparing a bid or of participating in an award procedure, the person making the claim is not be required, in order to obtain the reimbursement of his costs, to prove that the contract would have been awarded to him in the absence of such infringement;

Whereas the contracting entities which comply with the procurement rules may make this known through appropriate means; whereas this requires an examination, by independent persons, of procurement procedures and practices applied by those entities;

Whereas for this purpose an attestation system, allowing for a declaration on the correct application of the procurement rules, to be made in notices published in the *Official Journal of the European Communities*, is appropriate;

Whereas the contracting entities should have the opportunity of having recourse to the attestation system if they so wish; whereas the Member States must offer them the possibility of doing so; whereas they can do so either by setting up the system themselves or by allowing the contracting entities to have recourse to the attestation system established by another Member State; whereas they may confer the task of carrying out the examination under the attestation system to persons, professions or staff of institutions;

Whereas the necessary flexibility in the introduction of such a system is guaranteed by laying down the essential requirements for it in this Directive; whereas operational details should be provided in European Standards to which this Directive refers;

Whereas the Member States may need to determine operational details prior to, or in addition to, the rules contained in European Standards;

Whereas, when undertakings do not seek review, certain infringements may not be corrected unless a specific mechanism is put in place;

Whereas, accordingly, the Commission, when it considers that a clear and manifest infringement has been committed during a contract award procedure, should be able to bring it to the attention of the competent authorities of the Member State and of the contracting entity concerned so that appropriate steps are taken for the rapid correction of that infringement;

Whereas it is necessary to provide for the possibility of conciliation at Community level to enable disputes to be settled amicably;

Whereas the application in practicer of this Directive should be reviewed at the same time as that of Directive 90/531/EEC on the basis of information to be supplied by the Member States concerning the functioning of the national review procedures;

Whereas this Directive must be brought into effect at the same time as Directive 90/531/EEC;

Whereas it is appropriate that the Kingdom of Spain, the Hellenic Republic and the Portuguese Republic are granted adequate additional periods to transpose this Directive, taking account of the dates of application of Directive 90/531/EEC in those countries,

HAS ADOPTED THIS DIRECTIVE:

CHAPTER 1

Remedies at national level

Article 1

1. The Member States shall take the measures necessary to ensure that decisions taken by contracting entities may be reviewed effectively and, in particular, as rapidly as possible in accordance with the conditions set out in the following Articles and, in particular, Article 2 (8), on the grounds that such decisions have infringed Community law in the field or procurement or national rules implementing that law as regards:

(a) contract award procedures falling within the scope of Council Directive 90/531/EEC; and
(b) compliance with Article 3 (2) (a) of that Directive in the case of the contracting entities to which that provision applies.

2. Member States shall ensure that there is no discrimination between undertakings likely to make a claim for injury in the context of a procedure for the award of a contract as a result of the distinction made by this Directive between national rules implementing Community law and other national rules.

3. The Member States shall ensure that the review procedures are available, under detailed rules which the Member States may establish, at least to any person having or having had an interest in obtaining a particular contract and who has been or risks being harmed by an alleged infringement. In particular, the Member States may require that the person seeking the review must have previously notified the contracting entity of the alleged infringement and of his intention to seek review.

Article 2

1. The Member States shall ensure that the measures taken concerning the review procedures specified in Article 1 include provision for the powers:

either

(a) to take, at the earliest opportunity and by way of interlocutory procedure, interim measures with the aim of correcting the alleged infringement or preventing further injury to the interests concerned, including measures to suspend or to ensure the suspension of the procedure for the award of a contract or the implementation of any decision taken by the contracting entity; and
(b) to set aside or ensure the setting aside of decisions taken unlawfully, including the removal of discriminatory technical, economic or financial specifications in the notice of contract, the periodic indicative notice, the notice on the existence of a system of qualification, the invitation to tender, the contract documents or in any other document relating to the contract award procedure in question;

or:

(c) to take, at the earliest opportunity, if possible by way of interlocutory procedures and if necessary by a final procedure on the substance, measures other than those provided for in points (a) and (b) with the aim of correcting any identified infringement and preventing injury to the interests concerned; in particular, making an order for the payment of a particular sum, in cases where the infringement has not been corrected or prevented.

Member States may take this choice either for all contracting entities or for categories of entities defined on the basis of objective criteria, in any event preserving the effectiveness of the measures laid down in order to prevent injury being caused to the interests concerned;

(d) and, in both the above cases, to award damages to persons injured by the infringement.

Where damages are claimed on the grounds that a decision had been taken unlawfully, Member States may, where their system of internal law so requires and provides bodies having the necessary powers for that purpose, provide that the contested decision must first be set aside or declared illegal.

2. The powers referred to in paragraph 1 may be conferred on separate bodies responsible for different aspects of the review procedure.

3. Review procedures need not in themselves have an automatic suspensive effect on the contract award procedures to which they relate.

4. Member States may provide that, when considering whether to order interim measures, the body responsible may take into account the probable consequences of the measures for all interests likely to be harmed, as well as the public interest, and may decide not to grant such measures where their negative consequences could exceed their benefits. A decision not to grant interim measures shall not prejudice any other claim of the person seeking these measures.

5. The sum to be paid in accordance with paragraph 1 (c) must be set at a level high enough to dissuade the contracting entity from committing or persisting in an infringement. The payment of that sum may be made to depend upon a final decision that the infringement has in fact taken place.

6. The effects of the exercise of the powers referred to in paragraph 1 on a contract concluded subsequent to its award shall be determined by national law. Furthermore, except where a decision must be set aside prior to the award of damages, a Member State may provide that, after the conclusion of a contract following its award, the powers of the body responsible for the review procedures shall be limited to awarding damages to any person harmed by an infringement.

7. Where a claim is made for damages representing the costs of preparing a bid or of participating in an award procedure, the person making the claim shall be required only to prove an infringement of Community law in the field of procurement or national rules implementing that law and that he would have had a real chance of winning the contract and that, as a consequence of that infringement, that change was adversely affected.

8. The Member States shall ensure that decisions taken by bodies responsible for review procedures can be effectively enforced.

9. Whereas bodies responsible for review procedures are not judicial in character, written reasons for their decisions shall always be given. Furthermore, in such a case, provision must be made to guarantee procedures whereby any allegedly illegal measures taken by the review body or any alleged defect in the exercise of the powers conferred on it can be the subject of judicial review or review by another body which is a court or tribunal within the meaning of Article 177 of the Treaty and independent of both the contracting entity and the review body.

The members of the independent body referred to in the first paragraph shall be appointed and leave office under the same conditions as members of the judiciary as regards the authority responsible for their appointment, their period of office, and their removal. At least the President of this independent body shall have the same legal and professional qualifications as members of the judiciary. The independent body shall take its decisions following a procedure in which both sides are heard, and these decisions shall, by means determined by each Member State, be legally binding.

CHAPTER 2

Attestation

Article 3

The Member States shall give contracting entities the possibility of having recourse to an attestation system in accordance with Articles 4 to 7.

Article 4

Contracting entities may have their contract award procedures and practices which fall within the scope of Directive 90/531/EEC examined periodically with a view to obtaining an attestation that, at that time, those procedures and practices are in conformity with Community law concerning the award of contracts and the national rules implementing the law.

Article 5

1. Attestors shall report to the contracting entity, in writing, on the results of their examination. They shall satisfy themselves, before delivering to the contracting entity the attestation referred to in Article 4, that any irregularities identified in the contracting entity's award procedures and practices have been corrected and measures have been taken to ensure that those irregularities are not repeated.

2. Contracting entities having obtained that attestation may include the following statement in notice published in the *Official Journal of the European Communities* pursuant to Articles 16 to 18 of Directive 90/531/EEC:

> 'The contracting entity has obtained an attestation in accordance with Council Directive 92/13/ EEC that, on ...., its contract award procedures and practices were in conformity with Community law and the national rules implementing that law.'

Article 6

1. Attestors shall be independent of the contracting entities and must be completely objective in carrying out their duties. They shall offer appropriate guarantees of relevant professional qualifications and experience.

2. Member States may identify any persons, professions or institutions whose staff, called upon the act as attestors, they regard as fulfilling the requirements of paragraph 1. For these purposes, Member States may require professional qualifications, at least at the level of a higher education diploma within the meaning of Directive 89/48/EEC[8], which they regard as relevant, or provide that particular examinations of professional competence organized or recognized by the State offer such guarantees.

Article 7

The provisions of Articles 4, 5 and 6 shall be considered as essential requirements for the development of European standards on attestation.

CHAPTER 3

Corrective mechanism

Article 8

1. The Commission may invoke the procedures for which this Article provides when, prior to a contract being concluded, it considers that a clear and manifest infringement of Community provisions in the field of procurement has been committed during a contract award procedure falling within the scope of Directive 90/531/EEC or in relation to Article 3 (2) of that Directive in the case of the contracting entities to which that provision applies.

2. The Commission shall notify the Member States and the contracting entity concerned of the reasons which have led it to conclude that a clear and manifest infringement has been committed and request its correction by appropriate means.

3. Within 30 days of receipt of the notification referred to in paragraph 2, the Member States concerned shall communicate to the Commission:

---

[8] OJ No L 19, 24. 1. 1989, p. 16.

(a) its confirmation that the infringement has been corrected; or

(b) a reasoned submission as to why no correction has been made; or

(c) a notice to the effect that the contract award procedure has been supported either by the contracting entity on its own initiative or on the basis of the powers specified in Article 2 (1) (a).

4. A reasoned submission in accordance with paragraph 3 (b) may rely among other matters on the fact that the alleged infringement is already the subject of judicial review proceedings or of a review as referred to in Article 2 (9). In such a case, the Member State shall inform the Commission of the result of those proceedings as soon as it becomes known.

5. Where notice has been given that a contract award procedure has been suspended in accordance with paragraph 3 (c), the Member State concerned shall notify the Commission when the suspension is lifted or another contract procedure relating in whole or in part to the same subject matter is begun. That new notification shall confirm that the alleged infringement has been corrected or include a reasoned submission as to why no correction has been made.

CHAPTER 4

Conciliation

Article 9

1. Any person having or having had an interest in obtaining a particular contract falling within the scope of Directive 90/531/EEC and who, in relation to the procedure for the award of that contract, considers that he has been or risks being harmed by an alleged infringement of Community law in the field of procurement or national rules implementing that law may request the application of the conciliation procedure provided for in Articles 10 and 11.

2. The request referred to in paragraph 1 shall be addressed in writing to the Commission or to the national authorities listed in the Annex. These authorities shall forward requests to the Commission as quickly as possible.

Article 10

1. Where the Commission considers, on the basis of the request referred to in Article 9, that the dispute concerns the correct application of Community law, it shall ask the contracting entity to state whether it is willing to take part in the conciliation procedure. If the contracting entity declines to take part, the Commission shall inform the person who made the request that the procedure cannot be initiated. If the contracting entity agrees, paragraphs 2 to 7 shall apply.

2. The Commission shall propose, as quickly as possible, a conciliator drawn from a list of independent persons accredited for this purpose. This list shall be drawn up by the Commission, following consultation of the Advisory Committee for Public Contracts or, in the case of contracting entities the activities of which are defined in Article 2 (2) of Directive 90/531/EEC, following consultation of the Advisory Committee on Telecommunications Procurement.

Each party to the conciliation procedure shall declare whether it accepts the conciliator, and shall designate an additional conciliator. The conciliators may invite not more than two other persons as experts to advise them in their work. The parties to the conciliation procedure and the Commission may reject any expert invited by the conciliators.

3. The conciliators shall give the person requesting the application of the conciliation procedure, the contracting entity and any other candidate or tenderer participating in the relevant contract award procedure the opportunity to make representations on the matter either orally or in writing.

4. The conciliators shall endeavour as quickly as possible to reach an agreement between the parties which is in accordance with Community law.

5. The conciliators shall report to the Commission on their findings and on any result achieved.

6. The person requesting the application of the conciliation procedure and the contracting entity shall have the right to terminate the procedure at any time.

7. Unless the parties decide otherwise, the person requesting the application of the conciliation procedure and the contracting entity shall be responsible for their own costs. In addition, they shall each bear half of the costs of the procedure, excluding the costs of intervening parties.

Article 11

1. Where, in relation to a particular contract award procedure, an interested person within the meaning of Article 9, other than the person requesting the conciliation procedure, is pursuing judicial review proceedings or other proceedings for review within the meaning of this Directive, the contracting entity shall inform the conciliators. These shall inform that person that a request has been made to apply the conciliation procedure and shall invite that person to indicate within a given time limit whether he agrees to participate in that procedure. If that person refuses to participate, the conciliators may decide, acting if necessary by a majority, to terminate the conciliation procedure if they consider that the participation of this person is necessary to resolve the dispute. They shall notify their decision to the Committee and give the reasons for it.

2. Action taken pursuant to this Chapter shall be without prejudice to:

(a) any action that the Commission or any Member State might take pursuant to Articles 169 or 170 of the Treaty or pursuant to Chapter 3 of this Directive;
(b) the rights of the persons requesting the conciliation procedure, of the contracting entity or of any other person.

CHAPTER 5

Final provisions

Article 12

1. Not later than four years after the application of this Directive, the Commission, in consultation with the Advisory Committee for Public Contracts, shall review the manner in which the provisions of this Directive have been implemented and, in particular, the use of the European Standards and, if necessary, make proposals for amendments.

2. Before 1 March each year the Member States shall communicate to the Commission information on the operation of their national review procedures during the preceding calendar year. The nature of the information shall be determined by the Commission in consultation with the Advisory Committee for Public Contracts.

3. In the case of matters relating to contracting entities the activities of which are defined in Article 2 (2) (d) of Directive 90/531/EEC, the Commission shall also consult the Advisory Committee on Telecommunications Procurement.

Article 13

1. Member States shall take, before 1 January 1993, the measures necessary to comply with this Directive. The Kingdom of Spain shall take these measures not later than 30 June 1995. The Hellenic Republic and the Portuguese Republic shall take these measures not later than 30 June 1997. They shall forthwith inform the Commission thereof.

When Member States adopt these measures, they shall contain a reference to this Directive or shall be accompanied by such reference on the occasion of their official publication. The methods of making such a reference shall be laid down by the Member States.

2. Member States shall bring into force the measures referred to in paragraph 1 on the same dates as those (laid down in Directive 90/531/EEC).

3. Member States shall communicate to the Commission the texts of the main provisions of domestic law which they adopt in the field governed by this Directive.

Article 14

This Directive is addressed to the Member States.

Done at Brussels, 25 February 1992.

For the Council
The President
Vitor MARTINS

ANNEX

National authorities to which requests for application of the conciliation procedure referred to in Article 9 may be addressed

Belgium

Services du Premier Ministre
Diensten Van de Eerste Minister

Ministère des Affaires économiques
Ministerie van Economische Zaken

Denmark

Industri- og Handelsstyrelsen (supply contracts)
Boligsministeriet (works contracts)

Germany

Bundesministerium für Wirtschaft

Greece

Υπουργείο Βιομηχανίας, Ενεργείας και Τεχνολογίας
Υπουργείο Εμπορίου Υπουργείο Περιβαλλονρος Χωροταζίας και Δημοσίων 'Εργων

Spain

Ministerio de Economia y Hacienda

France

Commission centrale des marchés

Ireland

Department of Finance

Italy

Presidenza del Consiglio dei Ministri Politiche Comunitarie

Luxembourg

Ministère des travaux publics

Netherlands

Ministerie van Economische Zaken

Portugal

Conselho de mercados de obras publicas e particulares

United Kingdom

HM Treasury

APPENDIX 25

Council Directive 92/31/EEC of 28 April 1992 amending Directive 89/336/EEC on the approximation of the laws of the Member States relating to electromagnetic compatibility

(92/31/EEC)

THE COUNCIL OF THE EUROPEAN COMMUNITIES,

Having regard to the Treaty establishing the European Economic Community, and in particular Article 100a thereof,

Having regard to the proposal from the Commission[1],

In cooperation with the European Parliament[2],

Having regard to the opinion of the Economic and Social Committee[3],

Whereas Directive 89/336/EEC[4] provides for complete harmonization relating to electromagnetic compatibility;

Whereas a uniform application of that Directive requires the availability of harmonized standards; whereas these standards will not be available by the date of application of that Directive;

Whereas that Directive has not provided for an adequate transitional period during which it would be permitted to place on the market apparatus manufactured in accordance with national regulations applicable before the date of application of the said Directive;

Whereas manufacturers must have the time needed to allow apparatus in stock to be marketed;

Whereas Directive 89/336/EEC should accordingly be amended,

HAS ADOPTED THIS DIRECTIVE:

Article 1

Directive 89/336/EEC is hereby amended as follows:

1. Article 10 (3) shall be deleted.

2. Article 12 (1) shall be supplemented by the following paragraph:

'However, Member States shall, for the period up to 31 December 1995, authorize the placing on the market and/or the putting into service of apparatus referred to in this Directive conforming to the national regulations in force in their territory on 30 June 1992.'

Article 2

1. Member States shall adopt and publish the laws, regulations and administrative provisions necessary to comply with this Directive not later than three months after its adoption. They shall forthwith inform the Commission thereof.

When Member States adopt these measures, they shall contain a reference to this Directive or shall be accompanied by such reference on the occasion of their official publication. The methods of making such a reference shall be laid down by the Member States.

---

[1] OJ No C 126, 21. 6. 1991, p. 7.
[2] OJ No C 13, 20. 1. 1992, p. 506 and OJ No C 94, 13. 4. 1992.
[3] OJ No C 339, 31. 12. 1991, p. 1.
[4] OJ No L 139, 23. 5. 1989, p. 19. Directive amended by Directive 91/263/EEC (OJ No L 128, 23. 5. 1991, p. 1).

Member States shall apply these provisions not later than six months after the adoption of this Directive.

2.   Member States shall communicate to the Commission the texts of the main provisions of domestic law which they adopt in the field governed by this Directive.

Article 3

This Directive is addressed to the Member States.

Done at Luxembourg, 28 April 1992.

For the Council
The President
Arlindo MARQUES CUNHA

APPENDIX 26

Council Decision of 11 May 1992 on the introduction of a standard international telephone access code in the Community

(92/264/EEC)

THE COUNCIL OF THE EUROPEAN COMMUNITIES,

Having regard to the Treaty establishing the European Economic Community, and in particular Article 100a thereof,

Having regard to the proposal from the Commission[1],

In cooperation with the European Parliament[2],

Having regard to the opinion of the Economic and Social Committee[3],

Whereas the telephone service is the most important telecommunications means in the Community and easy access to international telephone services is vital for European citizens and European businesses;

Whereas at present different telephone access codes are required in the Member States for access to public international telephone services;

Whereas this situation complicates unduly use of these services in a professional or private capacity for citizens travelling in the Member State;

Whereas access to telephone services is provided for in all Member States by law, regulation, or administrative action; whereas continuing divergent developments in access to international telephone services due to different international telephone access codes must be avoided;

Whereas, therefore, the harmonization of the international telephone access code in the Community would promote the establishment and functioning of the internal market;

Whereas the European Conference of Postal and Telecommunications Administrations (CEPT) has advocated in its recommendation T/SF 1 of 1976 the use of the prefix 00 as the standard international telephone access code;

Whereas this recommendation has been followed by only six Member States;

Whereas all Member States will find it possible to devise a plan to make the 00 code available;

Whereas several Member States have already introduced 00 as the international telephone access code or could do so by the end of 1992;

Whereas the introduction of this code could cause serious difficulties for other Member States, since they would need to make unplanned changes or to advance plans already made; whereas, therefore, a certain measure of flexibility is needed in the time schedule to allow these Member States to carry out the necessary adjustments;

Whereas the introduction of the 00 code will, however, be possible by 1998, even in Member States where difficulties exist;

Whereas these Member States should, nevertheless, do their best to introduce the 00 code by a date which is as close as possible to 1992;

Whereas special arrangements for making calls between adjacent locations across borders between Member States may be established or continued.

---

[1] OJ No C 157, 15. 6. 1991, p. 6.
[2] OJ No C 326, 16. 11. 1991, p. 120 and OJ No C 94, 13. 4. 1992.
[3] OJ No C 269, 14. 10. 1991, p. 33.

HAS ADOPTED THIS DECISION:

Article 1

Member States shall ensure that the 00 code is introduced in public telephone networks as the standard international telephone access code.

Article 2

The standard international telephone access code shall be introduced by 31 December 1992 at the latest, except as provided for in Article 3.

Article 3

Should a telecommunications organization in a Member State experience particular technical, financial or organizational difficulties in introducing the standard international telephone access code by the date laid down in Article 2, the Member State in question shall inform the Commission accordingly.

The Member State concerned shall communicate to the Commission, within the three months following notification of this Decision, with adequate explanations and justification, a new date for the introduction of the standard international telephone access code which, however, shall not be later than 31 December 1998.

Article 4

1. Special arrangements for making calls between adjacent locations across borders between Member States may be established or continued.

2. The telephone subscribers in the locations concerned shall be fully informed of the arrangements referred to in paragraph 1.

Article 5

This Decision is addressed to the Member States.

Done at Brussels, 11 May 1992.

For the Council
The President
João PINHEIRO

APPENDIX 27

European Telecommunications Standards (NET) – Application of Directive 86/361/EEC

(92/C 143/03)

The publication of the following advice is made in compliance with Council Directive 86/361/EEC of 24 July 1986 on the initial stage of the mutual recognition of type approval for tele-communications terminal equipment[1], following the provisions of Article 6 (1).

For the application of this Directive, the published NET (Normes Européennes de Télé-communications) has to be regarded as the equivalent of common conformity specifications, used in the Community by the authority competent for testing the conformity of telecommunications equipment.

NET 10 (European 900 MHz Digital Cellular Mobile Telecommunications Network Access and Telephony Characteristics)

This NET specifies the technical characteristics (radio frequency, modulation, method of access and signalling, as well as logical and acoustic characteristics) to be offered by voice and non-voice terminal equipment to a European 900 MHz digital cellular mobile telecommunications network (Council Directive 87/372/EEC and Council Recommendation 87/371/EEC, both dated 25 June 1987, refer).

The precise scope and field of application of this NET have been established according to the procedures laid down in the Memorandum of Understanding referred to in Article 2 (15) of Directive 86/361/EEC.

In accordance with Article 6 (3) of Directive 86/361/EEC, this standard will have to be applied in all Member States, in particular by the competent authorities, for type approval of equipment.

This NET is applicable as from 22 April 1992.

The full text of the abovementioned NET can be obtained at the following address:

Office de liaison de la CEPT,
Case Postale,
CH-3001 Berne;

or at the national PTT Administrations.

---

[1] OJ No L 217, 5. 8. 1986, p. 21.

APPENDIX 28

Council Directive 92/44/EEC of 5 June 1992 on the application of open network provision to leased lines

(92/44/EEC)

THE COUNCIL OF THE EUROPEAN COMMUNITIES,

Having regard to the Treaty establishing the European Economic Community, and in particular Article 100a thereof,

Having regard to the proposal from the Commission[1],

In cooperation with the European Parliament[2],

Having regard to the opinion of the Economic and Social Committee[3],

(1) Whereas Council Directive 90/387/EEC of 28 June 1990 on the establishment of the internal market for telecommunications services through the implementation of open network provision[4], provides that the Council shall adopt specific open network provision conditions for leased lines;

(2) Whereas in this Directive the concept of leased lines covers the offer of transparent transmission capacity between network termination points as a separate service and does not include on-demand switching or offers which form part of a switched service offered to the public;

(3) Whereas, in accordance with Commission Directive 90/388/EEC of 28 June 1990 on competition in the markets for telecommunications services[5], Member States which maintain special or exclusive rights for the provision and operation of public telecommunications networks shall take the necessary measures to make the conditions governing access to and use of the network objective and non-discriminatory and publish them; whereas it is necessary to harmonize which specifications should be published and under which form, in order to facilitate the provision of competitive services using leased lines, within Member States and between Member States, and in particular the provision of services by companies, firms or natural persons established in a Member State other than that of the company, firm or natural person for whom the services are intended;

(4) Whereas, in application of the principle of non-discrimination, leased lines shall be offered and provided on request without discrimination to all users;

(5) Whereas the principle of non-discrimination as laid down in the Treaty applies to, *inter alia*, availability of technical access, tariffs, quality of service, provision time (delivery period), fair distribution of capacity in case of scarcity, repair time, availability of network information and customer proprietary information, subject to relevant regulatory provisions on data protection;

(6) Whereas a number of technical restrictions have been applied, in particular for the interconnection of leased lines among each other or for the interconnection of leased lines and public telecommunications networks; whereas such restrictions, which impede the use of leased lines for the provision of competitive services, are not justified, as they can be replaced by less restrictive regulatory measures;

---

[1] OJ No C 58, 7. 3. 1991, p. 10.
[2] OJ No C 305, 25. 11. 1991, p. 61 and Decision of 13 May 1992 (not yet published in the Official Journal).
[3] OJ No C 269, 14. 10. 1991, p. 30.
[4] OJ No L 192, 24. 7. 1990, p. 1.
[5] OJ No L 192, 24. 7. 1990, p. 10.

(7)   Whereas, in accordance with Community law, access to and use of leased lines may only be restricted in application of essential requirements as defined in this Directive and to safeguard exclusive or special rights; whereas those restrictions must be objectively justified, must follow the principle of proportionality and must not be excessive in relation to the aim pursued; whereas it is necessary to specify the application of these essential requirements in respect of leased lines;

(8)   Whereas, in accordance with Directive 90/388/EEC which does not apply to telex, mobile radiotelephony, paging and satellite services, Member States shall withdraw all special or exclusive rights for the supply of telecommunications services other than voice telephony; whereas this is the commercial provision for the public of the direct transport and switching of speech in real-time between public switched network termination points, enabling any user to use equipment connected to such a network termination point in order to communicate with another termination point;

(9)   Whereas Member States may, until the dates provided in Directive 90/388/EEC prohibit, as regards packet- or circuit-switched data services, economic operators from offering leased line capacity for simple resale to the public; whereas there should be no other restriction on the use of leased lines, in particular in respect of the transmission of signals which are not originated by the user who subscribed to the leased line offering, the transmission of signals which are not finally destined for the user who subscribed to the leased line offering, or the transmission of signals which are neither originated by nor finally destined for the user who subscribed to the leased line offering;

(10) Whereas, in accordance with Directive 90/387/EEC, the Community-wide definition of harmonized technical interfaces and access conditions must be based on the definition of common technical specifications based on international standards and specifications;

(11) Whereas, in accordance with Directive 90/388/EEC, Member States which maintain special or exclusive rights for the provision and operation of public telecommunications networks shall ensure that those who so request can obtain leased lines within a reasonable period;

(12) Whereas, in order to make leased lines available to a sufficient extent to users for their own use, for shared use or for the provision of services to third parties, it is necessary that Member States ensure that a harmonized set of leased lines with defined network termination points is made available in all Member States both for communications within a Member State and between Member States; whereas it is therefore necessary to determine which type of leased lines should be included in the harmonized set and within which time limit if they are not yet available; whereas given the dynamic technological development in this sector, it is necessary to establish a procedure for adjusting or enlarging such a set;

(13) Whereas other leased lines, in addition to the harmonized minimum set, will also be provided subject to market demand and the state of public telecommunications network; whereas the other provisions of this Directive apply to these leased lines; whereas however it should be ensured that the provision of these other leased lines does not impede the provision of the minimum set of leased lines;

(14) Whereas in conformity with the principle of separation of regulatory and operational functions and in application of the principle of subsidiarity, the national regulatory authority of each Member State will play an important role for the implementation of this Directive;

(15) Whereas common ordering procedures, as well as one-stop ordering and one-stop billing are needed in order to encourage the use of leased lines throughout the Community; whereas any cooperation of the telecommunications organizations in that respect is subject to compliance with Community competition law; whereas, in particular, such procedures should respect the principle of cost orientation and should not result in any price fixing or market sharing;

(16)   Whereas the implementation of one-stop ordering and one-stop billing procedures by telecommunications organizations must not prevent offers by service providers other than telecommunications organizations;

(17)   Whereas, in accordance with Directive 90/387/EEC, tariffs for leased lines must be based on the following principles; they must be based on objective criteria and must follow the principle of cost-orientation, taking into account a reasonable time needed for rebalancing; they must be transparent and properly published; they must be sufficiently unbundled in accordance with the competition rules of the Treaty and they must be non-discriminatory and guarantee equality of treatment; whereas tariffs for leased lines provided by one or more telecommunications organization must be based on the same principles; whereas a favourable prejudice is given to a tariff based on a flat-rate periodic rental, except where other types of tariffs are justified by cost;

(18)   Whereas any charge for access to and use of leased lines must comply with the principles set out above and with the competition rules of the Treaty and must also take into account the principle of fair sharing in the global cost of the resources used and the need for a reasonable level of return on investment which is required for the further development of the telecommunications infrastructure;

(19)   Whereas, in order to ensure the application of the tariff principles set out in the previous two recitals, telecommunications organizations shall use an appropriate transparent cost accounting system which can be verified by accounting experts ensuring the production of recorded figures; whereas such requirement can be fulfilled for example by the implementation of the principle of fully distributed costing;

(20)   Whereas to enable the Commission to monitor effectively the application of this Directive, it is necessary that Member States notify to the Commission which national regulatory authority will be responsible for its implementation and provide the relevant information requested by the Commission;

(21)   Whereas the Committee referred to in Articles 9 and 10 of Directive 90/387/EEC should play an important role for the application of this Directive;

(22)   Whereas disagreements between users and telecommunications organizations on the provision of leased lines will normally be solved between these parties involved; whereas it must be possible for parties to refer their case to a national regulatory authority and the Commission in cases where this is considered necessary; whereas this does not prejudice normal application of the procedures laid down in Articles 169 and 170 and the competition rules of the Treaty;

(23)   Whereas a specific procedure must be established in order to examine whether, in justified cases, the time limit set out in this Directive for the provision of a minimum set of leased lines and for the implementation of an appropriate cost accounting system may be extended;

(24)   Whereas this Directive does not apply to leased lines one network termination point of which is located outside the Community,

HAS ADOPTED THIS DIRECTIVE:

Article 1

Scope

This Directive concerns the harmonization of conditions for open and efficient access to and use of the leased lines provided to users on public telecommunications networks, and the availability throughout the Community of a minimum set of leased lines with harmonized technical characteristics.

Article 2

Definitions

1. The definitions given in Directive 90/387/EEC shall apply, where relevant, to this Directive.

2. In addition, for the purposes of this Directive,

— *leased lines* means the telecommunications facilities provided in the context of the establishment, development and operation of the public telecommunications network, which provide for transparent transmission capacity between network termination points and which do not include on-demand switching (switching functions with the user can control as part of the leased line provision),

— *ONP Committee* means the Committee referred to in Articles 9 and 10 of Directive 90/387/ EEC,

— *users* means end users and service providers, including telecommunications organizations where the latter are engaged in providing services which are or may be provided also by others,

— *national regulatory authority* means the body or bodies in each Member State, legally distinct and functionally independent of the telecommunications organizations, entrusted by that Member State *inter alia* with the regulatory functions addressed in this Directive,

— *simple resale of capacity* means the commercial provision on leased lines for the public of data transmission as a separate service, including only such switching, processing, data storage or protocol conversion as is necessary for transmission in real time to and from the public switched network,

— *common ordering procedure* means an ordering procedure for the procurement of intra-Community leased lines which ensures that there is commonality across the telecommunications organizations in the information that has to be supplied by the user and the telecommunications organizations, and in the format in which the information is presented.

— *one-stop-ordering* is a system whereby all transactions involving a user, required for the procurement of intra-Community leased lines, supplied by more than one telecommunications organization to a single user, can be completed at one location between the user and a single telecommunications organization,

— *one-stop-billing* is a system whereby the billing and payment transaction for intra-Community leased lines supplied by more than one telecommunications organization to a single user can be completed at one location between the user and a single telecommunications organization.

Article 3

Availability of information

1. Member States shall ensure that information in respect of leased lines, offerings on technical characteristics, tariffs, supply and usage conditions, licensing and declaration requirements, and the conditions for the attachment of terminal equipment is published in accordance with the presentation given in Annex I. Changes in existing offerings shall be published as soon as possible and, unless the national regulatory authority agrees otherwise, no later than two months before the implementation.

2. The information referred to in paragraph 1 shall be published in an appropriate manner so as to provide easy access for users to that information. Reference shall be made in the national Official Journal of the Member State concerned to the publication of this information.

Member States shall notify to the Commission before 1 January 1993, and thereafter in case of any change, the manner in which the information is made available. The Commission will regularly publish reference to such notifications.

3. Member States shall ensure that information concerning new types of leased line offerings will be published as soon as possible, and no later than two months before the implementation of the offering.

Article 4

Information on supply conditions

The supply conditions to be published pursuant to Article 3 shall include at least:

— information concerning the ordering procedure
— the typical delivery period, which is the period, counted from the date when the user has made a firm request for a leased line, in which 80% of all leased lines of the same type have been put through to the customers.

This period will be established on the basis of the actual delivery periods of leased lines during a recent time interval of reasonable duration. The calculation must not include cases where late delivery periods were requested by users. For new types of leased lines a target delivery period shall be published instead of the typical delivery period.

— the contractual period, which includes the period which is in general foreseen for the contract and the minimum contractual period which the user is obliged to accept,
— the typical repair time, which is the period, counted from the time when a failure message has been given to the responsible unit within the telecommunications organization up to the moment in which 80% of all leased lines of the same type have been re-established and in appropriate cases notified back in operation to the users. For new types of leased lines a target repair time period shall be published instead of the typical repair time. Where different classes of quality of repair are offered for the same type of leased lines, the different typical repair times shall be published,
— any refund procedure.

Article 5

Conditions for the termination of offerings

Member States shall ensure that existing offerings continue for a reasonable period of time, and that termination of an offering can be done only after consultation with users affected. Without prejudice to other rights of appeal provided for by national laws, Member States shall ensure that users can bring the case before the national regulatory authority where the users do not agree with the termination date as envisaged by the telecommunications organization.

Article 6

Access conditions, usage conditions and essential requirements

1. Without prejudice to Articles 2 and 3 of Directive 90/388/EEC, Member States shall ensure that when access to and usage of leased lines is restricted, these restrictions are aimed only at ensuring compliance with the essential requirements, compatible with Community law, and are imposed by the national regulatory authorities through regulatory means.

No technical restrictions shall be introduced or maintained for the intercommunication of leased lines and public telecommunications networks.

2. Where access to and use of leased lines are restricted on the basis of essential requirements, Member States shall ensure that the relevant national provisions identify which of the essential requirements listed in paragraph 3 are the basis of such restrictions.

3. The essential requirements specified in Article 3 (2) of Directive 90/387/EEC shall apply to leased lines in the following manner:

(a) *Security of network operations*

A telecommunication organization may take the following measures in order to safeguard the security of network organizations during the period when an emergency situation prevails:

— the interruption of the service,
— the limitation of service features,
— the denial of access to the service.

An emergency situation in this context means an exceptional case of *force majeure*, such as extreme weather, flood, lightning or fire, industrial action or lockouts, war, military operations, or civil disorder.

In an emergency situation the telecommunications organization shall make every endeavour to ensure that service is maintained to all users. The Member States shall ensure that the telecommunications organization immediately notifies to the users and to the national regulatory authority the beginning and the end of the emergency as well as the nature and extent of temporary service restrictions;

(b) *Maintenance of network integrity*

The user has the right to be provided with a fully transparent service, in conformity with the specifications of the network termination point, which he can use in an unstructured manner as he wants, e.g. where no channel allocations are forbidden or prescribed. There shall be no restrictions on the use of leased lines on the ground of the maintenance of network integrity, as long as the access conditions related to terminal equipment are fulfilled;

(c) *Interoperability of services*

Without prejudice to the application of Article 3 (5) and Article 5 (3) of Directive 90/387/EEC, the use of a leased line shall not be restricted on the grounds of the interoperability of services, when the access conditions related to terminal equipment are fulfilled;

(d) *Protection of data*

In respect of data protection, Member States may restrict the use of leased lines only to the extent necessary to ensure compliance with relevant regulatory provisions on the protection of data including protection of personal data, the confidentiality of information transmitted or stored, as well as the protection of privacy compatible with Community law.

4. Access conditions related to terminal equipment

Access conditions related to terminal equipment are considered to be fulfilled when the terminal equipment complies with the approval conditions set out for its connection to the network termination point of the type of leased line concerned, in accordance with Directive 91/263/EEC[6].

In the case where a user's terminal equipment does not comply or no longer complies with these conditions, the provision of the leased line may be interrupted until the terminal is disconnected from the network termination point.

Member States shall ensure that the telecommunications organization immediately informs the user about the interruption, giving the reasons for the interruption. As soon as the user has ensured that the non-complying terminal equipment is disconnected from the network termination point, the provision of the leased line shall be restored.

Article 7

Provision of a minimum set of leased lines in accordance with harmonized technical characteristics

1. Member States shall ensure that the respective telecommunications organizations separately or jointly provide a minimum set of leased lines in accordance with Annex II, in order to guarantee a harmonized offering throughout the Community.

2. Where leased lines which implement the standards listed in Annex II are not yet available, Member States shall take the necessary measures to ensure that these types of leased lines will be implemented by the date resulting from the application of Article 15.

---

[6] Council Directive 91/263/EEC of 29 April 1991 on the approximation of the laws of the Member States concerning telecommunications terminal equipment, including the mutual recognition of their conformity (OJ No L 128, 23. 5. 1991, p. 1).

3. The modifications necessary to adapt Annex II to new technical developments and to changes in market demand, including the possible deletion of certain types of leased lines from the Annex, shall be adopted by the Commission under the procedure provided for in Article 10 of Directive 90/387/EEC, taking into account the state of development of national networks.

4. The provision of other leased lines beyond the minimum set of leased lines which must be provided by Member States shall not impede the provision of this minimum set of leased lines.

Article 8

Control by the national regulatory authority

1. Member States shall ensure that the national regulatory authority lays down the procedures whereby it decides, on a case-by-case basis and in the shortest time period, to allow or not telecommunications organizations to take measures such as the refusal to provide a leased line, the interruption of the provision of leased lines or the reduction of the availability of leased line features for reasons of alleged failure to comply with the usage conditions by users of leased lines. These procedures may also foresee the possibility for the national regulatory authority to authorize, a priori, specified measures in the case of defined infringements of usage conditions.

Member States shall ensure that these procedures provide for a transparent decision-making process in which due respect is given to the rights of the parties. The decision shall be taken after having given the opportunity to both parties to state their case. The decision shall be motivated and notified to the parties within one week of its adoption: it shall not be enforced before its notification.

This provision shall not prejudice the right of the parties concerned to apply to the courts.

2. The national regulatory authority shall ensure that telecommunications organizations adhere to the principle of non-discrimination when they make use of the public telecommunications network for providing services which are or may be provided also by other service providers. When telecommunications organizations use leased lines for the provision of services not covered by special and/or exclusive rights, the same type of leased lines must be provided to other users on request and under equal conditions.

3. Where, in response to a particular request, a telecommunications organization considers it unreasonable to provide a leased line under its published tariffs and supply conditions, it must seek the agreement of the national regulatory authority to vary those conditions in that case.

Article 9

Common ordering and billing procedures

1. Member States shall encourage the establishment, by 31 December 1992 at the latest, in conformity with the procedural and substantive rules of competition of the Treaty and in consultation with users, of:

— a common ordering procedure for leased lines throughout the Community,
— a one-stop-ordering procedure for leased lines, to be applied where requested by the user,
— a one-stop-billing procedure for leased lines, to be applied where requested by the user. The procedure shall foresee that all price elements resulting from the national leased lines and the respective parts of international leased lines provided by the telecommunications organizations involved are identified separately in the bill for the user.

2. Member States shall report to the Commission one year after this Directive is brought into effect on the results achieved with respect to the procedures provided for in paragraph 1. These results shall be examined by the ONP Committee.

Article 10

Tariffing principles and cost accounting

1. Member States shall ensure that tariffs for leased lines follow the basic principles of cost orientation and transparency in accordance with the following rules:

(a) tariffs for leased lines shall be independent of the type of application which the users of the leased lines implement;

(b) tariffs for leased lines shall normally contain the following elements:

— an initial connection charge,
— a periodic rental charge, i.e. a flat-rate element.

When other tariff elements are applied, these must be transparent and based on objective criteria;

(c) tariffs for leased lines apply to the facilities provided between network termination points at which the user has access to the leased lines.

For leased lines provided by more than one telecommunications organization, half-circuit tariffs, i.e. from one network termination point to a hypothetical mid-circuit point, can be applied.

2. Member States shall ensure that their telecommunications organizations formulate and put in practice, by 31 December 1993 at the latest, a cost accounting system suitable for the implementation of paragraph 1.

Without prejudice to the last subparagraph, the system referred to in the first paragraph shall include the following elements:

(a) the costs of leased lines shall in particular include the direct costs incurred by the telecommunications organizations for setting up, operating and maintaining leased lines, and for marketing and billing of leased lines;

(b) common costs, that is costs which can neither be directly assigned to leased lines nor to other activities, are allocated as follows:

(i) whenever possible, common cost categories shall be allocated based upon direct analysis of the origin of the costs themselves;

(ii) when direct analysis is not possible, common cost categories shall be allocated based upon an indirect linkage to another cost category or group of cost categories for which a direct assignment or allocation is possible. The indirect linkage shall be based on comparable cost structures;

(iii) when neither direct nor indirect measures of cost allocation can be found, the cost category shall be allocated based upon a general allocator computed by using the ratio of all expenses directly assigned or allocated to, on the one hand, services which are provided under special or exclusive rights and, on the other hand, to other services.

After 31 December 1993, other cost accounting systems may be applied only if they are suitable for the implementation of paragraph 1 and have as such been approved by the national regulatory authority for application by the telecommunications organization, subject to the Commission being informed prior to their application.

3. The national regulatory authority shall keep available, with an adequate level of detail, information on the cost accounting systems applied by the telecommunications organizations pursuant to paragraph 2. It shall submit this information to the Commission on request.

Article 11

Notification and reporting

1. Member States shall notify before 1 January 1993 to the Commission their national regulatory authority as defined in Article 2, fourth indent.

2. The national regulatory authority shall make available statistical reports showing the performance in relation to the supply conditions, in particular with respect to delivery time and repair time, published in accordance with Article 3 at least for each calender year. The reports shall be sent to the Commission no later than five months after the end of the annual reporting period.

The national regulatory authority shall keep available and submit to the Commission on request the data on cases where the access to or use of leased lines has been restricted, in particular because of alleged infringements of special or exclusive rights or the prohibition of simple resale of capacity, as well as details of the measures taken, including their motivation.

Article 12

Conciliation procedure

Without prejudice to:

(a) any action that the Commission or any Member State might take pursuant to the Treaty, and in particular Articles 169 or 170 thereof;

(b) the rights of the person invoking the procedure in paragraphs 1 to 5 of this Article of the telecommunications organizations concerned or any other person under applicable national law, except in so far as they enter into an agreement for the resolution of issues between them;

the following conciliation procedure shall be available to the user:

1. Any user complaining that he has been or may be injured by the infringement of the provisions of this Directive, particularly regarding intra-Community leased lines, shall have the right to appeal to the national regulatory authority or authorities.

2. Where agreement cannot be reached at a national level, the aggrieved party may invoke the procedure provided for in paragraphs 3 and 4, by way of a written notification to the national regulatory authority and the Commission.

3. Where the national regulatory authority or the Commission finds that there is a case for further examination, following a notification based on paragraph 2, it can refer it to the Chairman of the ONP Committee.

4. In the case referred to in paragraph 3, the Chairman of the ONP Committee shall initiate the procedure described below if he is satisfied that all reasonable steps have been taken at a national level:

(a) the Chairman of the ONP Committee shall convene as soon as possible a working group including at least two members of the ONP Committee and one representative of the national regulatory authorities concerned and the Chairman of the ONP Committee or another official of the Commission appointed by him. The working group shall normally meet within 10 days of the meeting being convened. The Chairman may decide, upon proposal of any of the members of the working group, to invite a maximum of two other persons as experts to advise it.

(b) the working group shall give the party invoking this procedure, the national regulatory authorities of the Member States, and the telecommunications organizations involved the opportunity to present their opinion in oral or written form;

(c) the working group shall endeavour to reach agreement between the parties involved. The Chairman shall inform the ONP Commission of the results of this procedure.

5. The party invoking the procedure referred to in this Article shall bear its own costs of participating in this procedure.

Article 13

Deferment of certain obligations

1. When a Member State is not able to or can foresee that it will not be able to fulfil the requirements of Article 7 (1) or (2) or Article 10 (1) or (2), it shall notify the Commission of the reasons.

2. Deferment of the obligations under Article 7 (1) or (2) can be accepted only in cases where the Member State concerned can prove that the actual state of development of its public telecommunications network or the conditions of demand are such that the obligations under Article 7 would impose an excessive burden on the telecommunications organization in that Member State.

3. Deferment of the obligations under Article 10 (1) or (2) can be accepted only in cases where the Member State concerned can prove that the fulfilment of the requirements would impose an excessive burden on the telecommunications organization in that Member State.

4. The Member State shall inform the Commission of the date by which the requirements can be met and of the measures envisaged in order to meet this deadline.

5. When the Commission receives a notification in accordance with paragraph 1, it shall inform the Member State whether it deems that the particular situation of the Member State concerned justifies, on the basis of criteria set out in paragraphs 2 and 3, a deferment for this Member State of the application of Article 7 (1) or (2) of Article 10 (1) or (2) and until which date such deferment is justified.

6. No deferment can be granted in application of paragraph 2 where the non-compliance with Article 7 results from activities of telecommunications organizations of the Member State concerned in competitive areas within the meaning of Community law.

Article 14

The Commission shall examine and report to the European Parliament and to the Council on the functioning of this Directive, on the first occasion not later than three years after this Directive is brought into effect. The report shall be based *inter alia* on the information provided by the Member States to the Commission and to the ONP Committee. Where necessary, further measures can be proposed in the report for the full implementation of the aims of the Directive.

Article 15

1. Member States shall take the measures necessary to comply with this Directive before 5 June 1993. They shall forthwith inform the Commission thereof.

When Member States adopt these measures, they shall contain a reference to this Directive or shall be accompanied by such reference on the occasion of their official publication. The methods of making such a reference shall be laid down by the Member States.

2. Member States shall inform the Commission of the main provisions of national law which they adopt in the field governed by this Directive.

Article 16

This Directive is addressed to the Member States.

Done at Luxembourg, 5 June 1992.

For the Council
The President
Joaquim FERREIRA DO AMARAL

ANNEX I

PRESENTATION OF THE INFORMATION TO BE PROVIDED IN RESPECT OF LEASED LINES IN ACCORDANCE WITH ARTICLE 3 (1)

The information referred to in Article 3 (1) of this Directive shall follow the presentation given below:

A. **Technical characteristics**

The technical characteristics include the physical and electrical characteristics as well as the detailed technical and performance specifications which apply at the network termination point, without prejudice to Council Directive 83/189/EEC of 28 March 1983 laying down a procedure for the provision of information in the field of technical standards and regulations[7]. Clear reference shall be made to the standards implemented.

B. **Tariffs**

The tariffs include the initial connection charges, the periodic rental charges, and other charges. Where tariffs are differentiated, e.g. for reasons of different levels of quality of service or the number of leased lines provided to a user (bulk provision), this must be indicated.

C. **Supply conditions**

The supply conditions include at least the elements defined in Article 4 (1).

D. **Licensing requirements**

The information on licensing requirements, licensing procedures and/or licensing conditions provides a complete overview of all factors which have an impact on the usage conditions set out for leased lines. It shall include the following information, where applicable:

1. a clear description of the service categories for which the licensing procedures have to be followed and for which the licensing conditions have to be met by the user of the leased line or by his customers;
2. information on the character of the licensing conditions, in particular whether such licence is of a general nature which does not require individual registration and/or authorization, or whether the licensing conditions require registration and/or authorization on an individual basis;
3. a clear indication of the validity in time of the licence, including a review date, where applicable;
4. the conditions resulting from the application of the essential requirements in conformity with Article 6;
5. other obligations which the Member States may impose on the users of leased lines in accordance with Directive 90/388/EEC as regards packet- or circuit-switched data services, requiring the adherence to conditions of permanence, availability, or quality of service;
6. a clear reference to conditions aiming at the enforcement of the prohibition to provide services for which exclusive and/or special rights have been maintained by the Member State concerned in conformity with Community law;
7. a list referring to all documents containing licensing conditions which the Member State imposes on the users of leased lines when these are using leased lines for the provision of services to others.

E. **Conditions for the attachment of terminal equipment**

The information on the attachment conditions includes a complete overview of the requirements which terminal equipment to be attached to the relevant leased line has to fulfil in accordance with Directive 91/263/EEC.

---

[7] OJ No L 109, 26. 4. 1983, p. 8. Directive last amended by Commission Decision 90/230/EEC (OJ No L 128, 18. 5. 1990, p. 15).

ANNEX II

DEFINITION OF A MINIMUM SET OF LEASED LINES WITH HARMONIZED TECHNICAL CHARACTERISTICS, IN ACCORDANCE WITH ARTICLE 7, TO BE PROVIDED AS SOON AS POSSIBLE AND NOT LATER THAN THE DATE ON WHICH THIS DIRECTIVE IS BROUGHT INTO EFFECT

Leased line type	Technical characteristics[1]	
	Interface specifications	Performance specifications
Ordinary quality voice bandwidth	2 or 4 wire analogue	CCITT M. 1040
Special quality voice bandwidth	2 or 4 wire analogue	CCITT M. 1020/M. 1025
64 kbit/s digital	CCITT G. 703[2]	Relevant CCITT G.800 series recommendations
2 048 kbit/s digital unstructured	CCITT G. 703	Relevant CCITT G. 800 series recommendations
2 048 kbit/s digital structured	CCITT G. 703 and G. 704 (excluding section 5)[3]	Relevant CCITT G. 800 series recommendations In-service monitoring[4]

[1] The CCITT recommendations references refer to the 1988 version. ETSI has been requested to carry out further work on standards for leased lines.
[2] The majority of applications are converging towards the G. 703 specification. For an interim period, leased lines may be provided using other interfaces, based on X.21 or X.21 (a), instead of G. 703.
[3] With cyclic redundancy checking in accordance with CCITT G. 706.
[4] In-service monitoring can facilitate improved maintenance by the telecommunications organization.

For the types of leased lines listed above, the specifications referred to also define the network termination points (NTPs), in accordance with the definition given in Article 2 of Directive 90/387/EEC.

APPENDIX 29

Council Resolution of 5 June 1992 on the development of the integrated services digital network (ISDN) in the Community as a European-wide telecommunications infrastructure for 1993 and beyond

(92/C 158/01)

THE COUNCIL OF THE EUROPEAN COMMUNITIES,

Having regard to the Treaty establishing the European Economic Community,

Whereas Council recommendation 86/659/EEC[1] calls for the coordinated introduction of the integrated services digital network (ISDN) in the European Community;

Whereas Council resolution 89/196/04[2] calls for the availability of a set of European-wide compatible ISDN offerings to be implemented in the context of a Memorandum of Understanding (MoU) between the public telecommunication network operators;

Whereas Council Directive 90/387/EEC of 28 June 1990 on the establishment of the internal market for telecommunications services through the implementation of open network provision[3] calls upon the Council to adopt a specific recommendation on ISDN; whereas Council recommendation 92/. . ./EEC[4] invites Member States to implement on their territory harmonized access arrangements and a minimum set of offerings, which will therefore have a significant impact on the development of ISDN;

Whereas the European Council agreed at Maastricht on the importance of trans-European networks, including in the field of telecommunications, where ISDN may play an important role as an advanced network;

Whereas the Commission's 'Third Annual Progress Report on the coordinated introduction of ISDN in the European Community's establishes the status of the implementation of ISDN in the Member States;

Whereas the same report proposes to focus the efforts for the coordinated introduction of ISDN in the Community on the implementation of the Euro-ISDN[5],

RECOGNIZES:

1. the role which the availability of a coherent set of harmonized ISDN standards plays as an important prerequisite for the implementation of the Euro-ISDN and the significant progress which the European Telecommunications Standards Institute (ETSI) has made in this area;

2. the efforts already undertaken by the public telecommunications network operators within the framework of the Memorandum of Understanding on ISDN;

3. the importance of developing ISDN in the context of trans-European networks;

CONSIDERS THE FOLLOWING MEASURES AS NECESSARY:

4. to finalize and adopt the Euro-ISDN standards as a highest priority for ETSI, taking into account the subsequent adoption by the Community of appropriate common technical regulations in this area;

---

[1] OJ No L 382, 31. 12. 1989, p. 36.
[2] OJ No C 196, 1. 8. 1989, p. 4.
[3] OJ no L 192, 24. 7. 1990, p. 1.
[4] Not yet published in the Official Journal.
[5] The term Euro-ISDN is used to address an ISDN implementation fully based on harmonized European standards and in accordance with the Memorandum of Understanding on ISDN.

5. to continue with the coordination of the introduction of ISDN within the Community and to focus these efforts on the rapid introduction of the Euro-ISDN;

6. to promote Euro-ISDN at a world-wide level;

INVITES THE PUBLIC TELECOMMUNICATIONS NETWORK OPERATORS TO:

7. develop, harmonize to the extent suitable and publish migration plans from currently existing ISDN offerings to the Euro-ISDN, taking into account technical and commercial issues;

8. examine further harmonization in respect of the introduction and integration of packet-switched services in the context of ISDN;

9. study the feasibility of an alignment of the national ISDN signalling systems;

10. contribute, in cooperation with the other interested parties, to the identification of cross border-communication requirements arising from the completion of the internal market and the specific role which ISDN can play in that area;

11. collaborate with third countries network operators on interconnection experiments;

INVITES THE COMMISSION AND THE PUBLIC TELECOMMUNICATIONS NETWORK OPERATORS TO:

12. proceed, with appropriate consultations with users and manufacturers, to review the progress on implementing Euro-ISDN;

INVITES THE MEMBER STATES TO:

13. encourage the rapid introduction of Euro-ISDN, taking into account the application of the open network provision (ONP) principles in this area;

INVITES THE COMMISSION TO:

14. intensify consultations and develop appropriate initiatives concerning the implementation of ISDN, taking into account the general framework of trans-European networks;

15. continue to promote the identification of user requirements in the context of the European ISDN User Forum (EIUF);

16. identify and promote the application of ISDN communication means for small and medium-sized enterprises, in particular for transnational applications, in the context of the internal market;

17. promote a European-wide ISDN terminal market, in particular by the development of appropriate standards ensuring interoperability and interchangeability;

18. analyse the possibilities for a specific support to the introduction of Euro-ISDN in the less-favoured regions.

APPENDIX 30

Council Recommendation of 5 June 1992 on the harmonized provision of a minimum set of packet-switched data services (PSDS) in accordance with open network provision (ONP) principles

(92/382/EEC)

THE COUNCIL OF THE EUROPEAN COMMUNITIES,

Having regard to Council Directive 90/387/EEC of 28 June 1990 on the establishment of the internal market for telecommunications services through the implementation of open network provision[1],

Having regard to the proposal from the Commission,

Whereas Council Directive 90/387/EEC considers, *inter alia*, the principles for the application of open network provision (ONP) to the areas of packet and circuit-switched data services;

Whereas Directive 90/387/EEC provides in point 3 of Annex III for the adoption of a recommendation on the supply of technical interfaces, conditions of usage and tariff principles applying to the provision of packet-switched data services (PSDS) complying with open network principles;

Whereas packet-switched public data networks are the most common networks through which packet-switched data services (PSDS) are made available in all Member States;

Whereas packet-switched public data networks have developed on a national basis and the availability in each Member State of packet-switched public data networks with equivalent capabilities and providing full interconnectivity is important to meet the requirements of pan-European data networking for value-added services provision;

Whereas PSDSs are important in supporting value added services at a European-wide level;

Whereas Directive 90/387/EEC calls for the availability in each Member State of a harmonized PSDS;

Whereas Member States should notify to the Commission those organizations whose provision of PSDSs enables Member States to comply with the provisions of point 3 of Annex III to Council Directive 90/387/EEC; whereas other organizations may offer PSDSs in accordance with this recommendation;

Whereas, pursuant to the principle of non-discrimination, PSDSs shall be available and provided on request without discrimination to all users; whereas, therefore, the terms and conditions which apply to telecommunication organizations when using PSDSs for the provision of services for which no special or exclusive rights may be maintained should be equivalent to the terms and conditions which apply to other users;

Whereas, in accordance with Directive 90/387/EEC, the conditions of ONP may not restrict access to and use of PSDSs except in the application of essential requirements as defined in the said Directive; whereas these restrictions must be objectively justified, follow the principle of proportionality and not be excessive in relation to the aim pursued;

Whereas, in accordance with Article 3 (5) of Directive 90/387/EEC, the Commission will determine the rules for uniform application of the essential requirements in accordance with the procedure laid down in Article 10 of that Directive;

---

[1] OJ No L 192, 24. 7. 1990, p. 1.

Whereas usage conditions for PSDSs must be derived from essential requirements compatible with Community law and are to be imposed through regulatory means and not through technical restrictions;

Whereas, in accordance with Commission Directive 90/388/EEC[2], Member States may make the supply of packet- or circuit-switched data services subject to licensing or declaration procedures which are aimed at compliance with essential requirements, or trade regulations relating to conditions of permanence, availability and quality of service, or measures to safeguard the task of general economic interest which they have entrusted to a telecommunications organization for the provision of switched data services, if the performance of that task is likely to be obstructed by the activities of private service providers;

Whereas, in accordance with Directive 90/387/EEC, the Commission has published in the *Official Journal of the European Communities*[3] the list of packet-switched public data networks standards suitable for ONP; this list may be amended by further publication;

Whereas common ordering procedures, one-stop-ordering and one-stop billing and maintenance are desirable in order to encourage the use of PSDSs and the development of competition in the provision of value added services throughout the Community and have been requested by users; whereas any cooperation between organizations in that area is subject to compliance with Community competition law; whereas, in particular, such procedures should not result in price fixing or market sharing; whereas, these procedures are to be established through commercial arrangements, e.g. through memoranda of understanding;

Whereas the implementation of one-stop ordering and one-stop billing procedures by telecommunications organizations must not prevent offers by service providers other than telecommunications organizations;

Whereas, in order to promote European-wide operation by service providers using PSDSs, it is desirable to allow for a system where the called party pays for the calls on the basis of the number called, allowing the offering of free-of-charge calls to the subscriber accessing the service offered by the provider (green number type arrangements);

Whereas, in order to promote the use of PSDSs by small- and medium-size providers of value-added services, it is desirable that billing arrangements which facilitate such operations across the Community are established; whereas such billing arrangements should allow for a system where the cost of the value-added service and the cost of the call are combined in a single bill collected by the organization supplying PSDSs ('kiosk type arrangement');

Whereas it is important in this context that appropriate allocation of harmonized numbering capacity is made to allow the establishment of such service arrangements across the Community; whereas such allocation should be made in accordance with the principles of transparency and equal treatment;

Whereas quality of service as perceived by the users is an essential aspect of packet-switching; whereas information for users should allow for a comparison between achieved performance and typical or target values;

Whereas, in accordance with Directive 90/387/EEC, tariffs must be based on objective criteria, taking into account that, in a competitive environment, tariffs will align with cost; whereas they must be transparent and properly published and sufficiently unbundled in accordance with the competition rules of the Treaty; whereas they must be non-discriminatory and must guarantee equal treatment;

Whereas Member States may restrict use and provision of PSDS to the extent necessary to ensure compliance with the regulations on the protection of data, including protection of personal data,

---

[2] OJ No L 192, 24, 7. 1990, p. 10.
[3] OJ No C 327, 29. 12. 1990, p. 19. List of standards reference – Packet-switched public data networks.

the confidentiality of information transmitted or stored and the protection of privacy compatible with Community law;

Whereas other offerings provided by organizations supplying PSDSs in addition to those provided in accordance with the provisions of this recommendation shall not impede the provision of the minimum set;

Whereas, in accordance with the principle of separation of regulatory and operational functions and pursuant to the principle of subsidiarity, the national regulatory authority of each Member State should play an important role in the application of this recommendation;

Whereas, to enable the Commission to monitor effectively the application of this recommendation, it is necessary that Member States provide the relevant information requested by the Commission;

Whereas the Committee referred to in Articles 9 and 10 of Directive 90/387/EEC should play an important role in the application of this recommendation,

HEREBY RECOMMENDS:

1. That Member States ensure that on their territory a minimum set of packet-switched data services (PSDSs) with harmonized technical characteristics in accordance with Annex I is provided, taking into account market demand.

2. That modifications necessary to adapt Annex I to new technical developments and to changes in market demand be determined by the Commission in accordance with the procedure laid down in Article 10 of Directive 90/387/EEC, taking into account the state of development of the national networks.

3. That Member States take the necessary steps so that, in respect of the PSDSs provided in accordance with point 1, information is published on technical characteristics, supply and usage conditions, tariffs, licensing and/or declaration conditions and the conditions for the attachment of terminal equipment, in accordance with the presentation given in Annex II.

4. That the supply conditions referred to in point 3 include at least:

   — information concerning the ordering procedure,
   — the typical delivery periods, which are the periods counted from the date when the user has made a firm request for the service in question and in which 80% of the requests for each type of PSDSs have been put through to the users.

   Each period will be established on the basis of the actual delivery periods for each type of PSDSs during a recent time interval of reasonable duration. The calculation must not include cases where late delivery periods were requested by users. For new types of PSDSs, a target delivery period shall be published in place of the typical delivery period,

   — contractual periods, which include periods generally prescribed for contracts and the minimum contractual periods which the user is obliged to accept for each type of PSDSs,
   — typical repair times, which are the periods, counted from the time when a failure message has been given to the responsible unit within the organization supplying PSDSs up to the moment in which 80% of all PSDSs of the same type have been re-established and, in appropriate cases, notified as back in operation to the users. For new types of PSDSs a target repair time period shall be published in place of the typical repair time. Where different classes of quality of repair are offered for the same type of PSDSs, the different repair times shall be published,
   — any refund procedure,
   — target values for the indicators of quality of service established in accordance with point 6.

5. That Member States, taking into account the work of the European Conference on Postal and Telecommunications Administrations (CEPT)[4], encourage the establishment, in accordance

---

[4] One-stop shopping service Specific Schedule for PSPDN, CAC October 1990.

with the procedural and substantive rules of competition of the Treaty and in consultation with users, of harmonized procedures for user access to PSDSs, provided in accordance with the provisions of this recommendation, in particular via the establishment of the following procedures:

— a common ordering procedure for PSDSs throughout the Community, i.e. an ordering procedure for the procurement of intra-Community PSDSs which ensures that there is commonality, across the organizations supplying PSDSs, in the information which has to be supplied by the user and the organization supplying PSDSs and the format in which the information is presented,

— a one-stop ordering procedure for PSDSs, to be applied where requested by the user, i.e. a system whereby all transactions involving a user which are required for the procurement of intra-Community PSDSs supplied by more than one organization to a single user can be completed at one location between the user and a single organization supplying PSDSs,

— a one-stop-billing procedure for PSDSs, to be applied where requested by the user, i.e. a system whereby the billing and payment transaction for intra-Community PSDSs supplied by more than one organization to a single user can be completed at one location between the user and a single organization supplying PSDSs, and

— a one-stop-maintenance procedure of PSDSs, to be applied where requested by the users, i.e. a system whereby the reporting of faults for intra-Community PSDSs supplied by more than one organization to a single user can be done at one location between the user and a single organization supplying PSDSs, which will coordinate the restoration of services.

The inclusion of the provision of Community-wide charging and billing procedures, allowing notably facilities which enable the called party to pay for the calls[5] or the combination in a single bill for the charge for the calls and the charge for the value-added service used[6], is to be envisaged, taking into account its technical and administrative feasibility and commercial viability.

These harmonized procedures are to be established through commercial arrangements, e.g. through memoranda of understanding.

6. That common indicators and common measurement methods be adopted for the network performance aspects of the quality of service by organizations supplying PSDSs in accordance with this recommendation, notably for those indicators in Annex III, in order to allow for the determination of a representative sample of the performance of the PSDSs as well as the statistical end-to-end performance achieved by the network as a whole.

7. That national regulatory authorities take the necessary steps so that annual statistical information showing achieved performance in relation to the quality of service indicators identified in Annex III is made publicly available.

The first annual period should run from 1 January to 31 December 1993.

8. That tariffs be transparent, based on objective criteria and independent of the type of application implemented by the users of the PSDSs, where the same type of offerings is used.

9. That tariffs for PSDSs normally contain the following elements:

— an initial connection charge,
— a periodic rental charge,
— a usage charge,

Where other tariff elements are applied, these must be in accordance with point 8.

10. That Member States inform the Commission before 31 December 1992 of those organizations whose provision of PSDSs enables Member States to comply with the provisions of point 3 of

---

[5] Green number type arrangements.
[6] Kiosk type arrangements.

Annex III to Council Directive 90/387/EEC and, thereafter, of any changes to this information.

11. That national regulatory authorities prepare annual summary reports in particular with regard to the availability of PSDSs provided in accordance with point 1 of this recommendation. These summary reports should be sent to the Commission no later than five months after the end of each calendar year, this requirement being reviewed by the Commission in consultation with the ONP Committee in accordance with Article 9 of Directive 90/387/EEC during 1995. The Commission will transmit these summary reports to the ONP Committee.

12. That national regulatory authorities keep available and submit to the Commission on request data on the application of the supply conditions under points 3 and 4 and the statistical information under point 7.

13. That national regulatory authorities establish simple procedures for users of PSDSs which may be invoked in the event of any difficulties encountered in relation to the application of this recommendation.

14. That the Commission, in consultation with the ONP Committee, examine the results of the application of this recommendation, with a view to the fulfilment of the objectives of Directive 90/387/EEC, on the basis of the summary reports provided under point 11.

Done at Luxembourg, 5 June 1992.

For the Council
The President
Joaquim FERREIRA DO AMARAL

ANNEX I

DEFINITION OF A COMMUNITY-WIDE MINIMUM SET OF PACKET-SWITCHED DATA SERVICES WITH HARMONIZED TECHNICAL CHARACTERISTICS IN ACCORDANCE WITH POINT 1 AND RECOMMENDED TIMETABLE FOR THEIR AVAILABILITY

A. GENERAL CONSIDERATIONS

The recommendation aims at the harmonized provision by the organizations notified in accordance with point 10 of a minimum set of PSDSs in accordance with open network provision principles to users in order to facilitate the development of European-wide services.

These services should:

(i)   be made available on an adequately unbundled basis in order to give users maximum flexibility;
(ii) be structured in the following way (on a service basis):

ONP core offering:

— access/feature set(s) which must be offered by all the networks,
— user selects (one) set in order to have the basic service,
— set to be tariffed as a bundle.

ONP user options:

— feature offered by all networks on an individual basis,
— feature which may be selected by user,
— may in specific cases substitute core offerings features;
(iii) take into account technological development and the growth in availability of features not considered in the proposed service.

B. STANDARDS TO BE UTILIZED

The standards applicable for this minimum set of PSDSs with harmonized technical characteristics are in particular those in the indicative list of packet-switched public data networks standards suitable for ONP published in the *Official Journal of the European Communities*, in accordance with the procedure in Article 5 (1) of Directive 90/387/EEC. The initial indicative list of PSDS standards suitable for ONP already published in the *Official Journal of the European Communities* will be amended/updated by further publications in the *Official Journal of the European Communities*.

C. TECHNICAL CHARACTERIZATION OF EACH SERVICE AND RECOMMENDED TIMETABLE FOR IMPLEMENTATION

C.1. Offerings to be provided at the latest by 31 December 1992

SERVICE	OFFERING
X.25	**CORE OFFERING** access link data rates: 2 400, 4 800, 9 600 bit/s layer 3 for VC (one logical channel) **USER OPTIONS** additional logical channels at least to a total of 32 for 9 600 bit/s options indicated[1] in CEPT T/TE 08-02[2] as E or EA
X.28[3] dial-in only	**CORE OFFERING** access link data rate 300 bit/s (V.21 modem), 1 200 bit/s (V.22 modem) X.28 standard terminal profits **USER OPTIONS** NUI additional standardized profiles selection[4] reverse charging[4]
X.32 Unidentified service	**CORE OFFERING** for national use at least one of the two sets: 1. 2 400 bit/s (V.22 *bis* or V.32 modem) 2. 4 800, 9 600 bit/s (V.32 modem) one or more logical channels reverse charging VC operation

	X.32	CORE OFFERING

                    X.32   CORE OFFERING
              Identified service
                 dial-in only   data rates and modems as per unidentified case

                                                        identification by NUI or XID

                                                 support of DTEs as per unidentified case

                                                 one or more logical channels, VC operation

---

[1] Except: Call redirection within a network with the same DNIC
    International use of CUG facilities
    International use of reverse charging facilities
    Hunt group
    Called line address modified notification
    Extended interrupt
    CCITT specified DTE facilities

[2] Interworking aspects of packet-switched public data networks.

[3] The X.28 messages are not intended for automatic DTE operation and as a consequence
    may be nationally dependent. The progressive implementation of X.3 (1988) and X.28
    (1988) will allow to set an X.3 parameter to determine whether CCITT standardized or
    national messages shall be used at the interface.

[4] For national use.

C.2. **Offerings to be provided in addition to those in C.1 at the latest by 30 June 1993**

SERVICE	OFFERING
X.25	CORE OFFERING

                                                 access link data rate
                                               48 000 bit/s or 64 000 bit/s

                                                      USER OPTIONS

                                    additional logical channels at least to a total of 128 for
                                                  48 000 or 64 000 bit/s

                                                        Hunt group

                                    call redirection within a network with the same DNIC

                                                     extended interrupt

                                             CCITT specified DTE facilities

                                          intra-community use of CUG facilities

                                        called line address modified notifications

C.3. **Offerings to be provided in addition to those in C.1 and C.2 at the latest by 31 December 1993**

SERVICE	OFFERING
X.25	USER OPTIONS intra-community use of reverse charging facilities
X.28 dial-in only	CORE OFFERING access link data rate: 2 400 bit/s (V.22 *bis* modem) USER OPTIONS intra-community use of reverse charging facilities
X.32 Unidentified service	CORE OFFERING intra-community use of the service

ANNEX II

PUBLICATION PRESENTATION FOR THE INFORMATION TO BE PROVIDED IN RESPECT OF PACKET-SWITCHED DATA SERVICES IN ACCORDANCE WITH POINT 3

The information referred to in point 3 of the recommendation should follow the presentation given below.

A. TECHNICAL CHARACTERISTICS

The technical characteristics include the physical and electrical characteristics as well as the detailed technical and performance specifications which apply at the network termination point, without prejudice to Council Directive 83/189/EEC of 28 March 1983 laying down a procedure for the provision of information in the field of technical standards and regulations[7]. Clear reference shall be made to the standards implemented.

B. SUPPLY CONDITIONS

The supply conditions include at least the elements identified in point 4.

C. USAGE CONDITIONS

The conditions resulting from the application of essential requirements.

D. TARIFFS

In accordance with point 9, tariffs will normally include an initial connection charge, a periodic rental charge and a usage charge. Usage charge will normally include:

(a) a fixed per-call charge, based either on a minimum time and/or volume charge or on a call set-up charge;
(b) a volume related charge based on the use of an integral number of segments[8],
(c) a duration charge based on time intervals sufficiently short to avoid discrimination against short-type transactions.

[7] OJ No L 109, 26. 4. 1983, p. 8.
[8] A segment is up to 64 octets (or bytes) of user data where the octet is 8 bits.

Clear indication of other charges, e.g. charges related to quality of service, or bulk provision, should be available.

E. LICENSING AND/OR DECLARATION CONDITIONS FOR USE OF PSDSs, WHERE APPLICABLE

This should include information on any licensing conditions which have to be met by the user or by its customers.

F. CONDITIONS FOR THE ATTACHMENT OF TERMINAL EQUIPMENT

Conditions approved by the national regulatory authority, in accordance with the provision of Directive 91/263/EEC[9].

ANNEX III

INDICATORS FOR THE NETWORK PERFORMANCE ASPECTS OF THE QUALITY OF SERVICE OF PSDSs

Indicators for the network performance aspects of the quality of service of PSDSs and measurement methods should be based on the ongoing work in CEPT, and notably on recommendations T/CAC 2[10], T/CAC 3[11], T/CAC 4[12].

For each of the above performance criteria, indicators should be chosen which are representative of the service:

Availability	Unsuccessful network congestion (NC) calls ratio (UNCR),
	Service availability,
Dependability	Mean time between NC disconnections (MTNC),
Speed of service	Transmitted throughput (TTP),
	Received throughput (RTP),
	Round trip delay (RTD),
	Call set-up delay (CSD).

---

[9] OJ No L 128, 23. 5. 1991, p. 1.

[10] Indicators for the network performance aspects of the quality of service of international packet-switched services.

[11] Monitoring of network performance aspects of quality of international packet-switched service using internally derived indicators.

[12] Monitoring of network performance aspects of quality of international packet-switched service using externally derived indicators.

APPENDIX 31

Council Recommendation of 5 June 1992 on the provision of harmonized integrated services digital network (ISDN) access arrangements and a minimum set of ISDN offerings in accordance with open network provision (ONP) principles

(92/383/EEC)

THE COUNCIL OF THE EUROPEAN COMMUNITIES,

Having regard to Council Directive 90/387/EEC of 28 June 1990 on the establishment of the internal market for telecommunications services through the implementation of open network provision[1],

Having regard to the proposal from the Commission,

Whereas Council Directive 90/387/EEC considers, *inter alia*, the application of the principles of open network provision (ONP) to the integrated services digital network (ISDN);;

Whereas the full establishment of a Community-wide market in telecommunications services will be promoted by the rapid introduction of ONP principles to ISDN, as provided for in Directive 90/387/EEC; whereas ONP conditions should ensure transparency and equal access and be based on objective criteria; whereas applying ONP principles to ISDN means harmonizing the conditions for open and efficient access to and use of ISDN;

Whereas recommendation 86/659/EEC[2] calls for the coordinated introduction of the ISDN in the European Community;

Whereas resolution 89/C 196/04[3] calls for strengthening of the further coordination of the ISDN in the European Community up to 1992;

Whereas in 1989 several telecommunications organizations signed a memorandum of understanding (MoU) for the phased and harmonized implementation of European ISDN services; whereas within the framework of this MoU, a range of services has been recognized as commercially valid for ISDN and agreement has been reached on a minimum ISDN service offering to be introduced by 31 December 1993 at the latest; whereas other services will be introduced on the basis of harmonized standards according to market need;

Whereas ISDN can be considered a natural development of the telephone network; whereas it will allow, via a single access, using the existing subscriber line, the transmission of voice telephony, text, data and images in the form of a multitude of more efficient or new services;

Whereas Member States should notify to the Commission those organizations whose provision of ISDN offerings enables Member States to comply with the provisions of point 4 of Annex III to Directive 90/387/EEC; whereas other organizations may offer certain ISDN services in accordance with the recommendation;

Whereas, in accordance with Directive 90/387/EEC, voice telephony means the commercial provision for the public of the direct transport of real time speech via the public switched network or networks such that any user can use equipment connected to a network termination point to communicate with another user of equipment connected to another termination point;

Whereas Commission Directive 90/388/EEC[4] applies;

---

[1] OJ No L 192, 24. 7. 1990, p. 1.
[2] OJ No L 382, 31. 12. 1986, p. 36.
[3] OJ No C 196, 1. 8. 1989, p. 4.
[4] OJ No L 192, 24. 7. 1990, p. 10.

Whereas, in accordance with Directive 90/388/EEC, Member States may make the supply of certain services subject to a licensing or declaration procedure aimed at compliance with the essential requirements and in that case they shall ensure that the conditions for the granting of licenses are objective, non-discriminatory and transparent, that reasons are given for any refusal and that there is a procedure for appealing against any such refusal; whereas the Commission will carry out an overall assessment of the situation in the telecommunications sector, in connection with the aims of this Directive in 1992;

Whereas ISDN is a means to support both services provided under special or exclusive rights and services for which no such rights may be maintained;

Whereas, pursuant to the principle of non-discrimination, access to ISDN should be available and provided on request without discrimination to all users; whereas therefore, the terms and conditions which apply to telecommunication organizations using ISDN for the provision of services for which no special or exclusive rights may be maintained should be equivalent to the terms and conditions which apply to other users;

Whereas cross-subsidization between services provided by telecommunications organizations (TOs) under special and exclusive rights and services for which no such rights may be maintained, provided by TOs, may be incompatible with Community competition rules;

Whereas Article 4 (4) (b) of Directive 90/387/EEC provides for a period for public comment on the reports on the detailed analysis on the application of ONP to specific areas; whereas public comments on the analysis report of the application of ONP to ISDN were invited by notice in the *Official Journal of the European Communities*[5];

Whereas it became evident from public comments that users are requiring a high degree of transparency in the provision of ISDN offerings; whereas users are requiring further access arrangements to be considered, such as M- and U-type interfaces;

Whereas the European Telecommunications Standards Institute (ETSI) is developing standards for ISDN; whereas the Commission has given a special study and investigation mandate to ETSI to study the technical implications of the specification of M- and U-type interfaces in ISDN; whereas the Commission will also carry out studies on the economic and market impact related to the provision of these interfaces;

Whereas Community policy in relation to the coordinated introduction of ISDN is given in recommendation 86/659/EEC and resolution 89/C 196/04; whereas a broad range of services to be provided are defined in the abovementioned documents;

Whereas ISDN networks have developed on a national basis and the availability in each Member State of an ISDN with equivalent capabilities and providing full interconnectivity is important to meet the requirements of pan-European provision of telecommunications services;

Whereas users have stressed the value of the availability in all Member States of a minimum set of harmonized offerings;

Whereas Member States should encourage their telecommunications organizations to provide ISDN offerings in addition to the minimum set, both in response to market demand;

Whereas, however, such additional offerings should in no way impede the provision of the minimum set;

Whereas interoperability between ISDN and existing public network services should be ensured, in particular with the public voice telephony service and the public packet switched data service?

Whereas adequate and efficient interoperability between ISDN networks is essential for the provision of Community-wide services;

---

[5] OJ No C 38, 14. 2. 1991, p. 12. (Notice No 91/C 38/21).

Whereas Directive 90/387/EEC provides, in point 1 of Annex III, for the adoption of a specific directive on voice telephony;

Whereas ISDN provides for the opportunity to offer voice telephony in an efficient way; whereas, therefore, the provision of voice telephony service by means of ISDN should meet the relevant requirements of ONP applied to voice telephony;

Whereas Directive 90/387/EEC provides, in point 3 of Annex III, for the adoption of a recommendation on the supply of technical interfaces, conditions of usage and tariff principles applying to the provision of packet-switched data services (PSDSs) complying with open network principles; whereas the Council has adopted a recommendation on the harmonized provision of a minimum set of PSDSs in accordance with ONP principles[6];

Whereas ISDN may be used to provide packet-switched data services (PSDSs); whereas, therefore, the provision of data services by means of ISDN should in principle meet the relevant requirements of ONP applied to PSDSs;

Whereas, in accordance with Directive 90/387/EEC, the Commission has published in the *Official Journal of the European Communities*[7] the list of ISDN standards suitable for ONP; whereas this list may be amended by further publication;

Whereas common ordering procedures, one-stop-ordering and one-stop billing and maintenance are desirable in order to encourage the use of ISDN and the development of competition in the provision of value-added services throughout the Community and have been requested by users; whereas any cooperation between organizations in that respect is subject to compliance with Community competition law; whereas, in particular, such procedures should not result in any price fixing or market sharing; whereas these procedures are to be established through commercial arrangements, e.g. through memoranda of understanding;

Whereas the implementation of one-stop-ordering and one-stop-billing procedures by telecommunications organizations must not prevent offers by service providers other than telecommunications organizations;

Whereas, in order to promote European-wide operation by service providers using ISDN, it is desirable to allow for a system where the called party pays for the calls on the basis of the number called, allowing the offering of free of charge calls to the subscriber accessing the service offered by the provider ('green number/freephone');

Whereas, in order to promote the use of ISDN by small- and medium-size providers of value-added services, it is desirable that billing arrangements which facilitate such operations across the Community are established; whereas such billing arrangements should allow for a system where the cost of the value-added service and the cost of the call are combined in a single bill ('kiosk type arrangement');

Whereas it is important in this context that appropriate allocation of harmonized numbering capacity is made to allow the establishment of such service arrangements across the Community; whereas such allocation should be made in accordance with the principles of transparency and equal treatment; whereas numbering issues at a national and European level, including the area of ISDN, will play a major role in the future worldwide telecommunications environment;

Whereas quality of service – including delivery time and repair time – as perceived by the users is an essential aspect of the service provided; whereas information for users should allow for a comparison between achieved performance and typical or target values;

Whereas the quality of service indicators, as identified in other ONP measures, will apply where appropriate to services provided by means of ISDN;

---

[6] See page 1 of this Official Journal.
[7] OJ No C 327, 29. 12. 1990, p. 19. List of standards reference – ISDN.

Whereas, in accordance with Community law and in particular Directive 90/387/EEC, usage conditions for ISDN should be compatible with Community law and should be imposed through regulatory means and not through technical restrictions;

Whereas, without prejudice to Article 3 of Directive 90/388/EEC, restrictions on the use of ISDN may be based only on infringement of special or exclusive rights compatible with Community law, or on the conditions generally applicable to the connection of terminal equipment as laid down in Directive 91/263/EEC[8], or on essential requirements, in particular on the basis of data protection; whereas Member States may restrict use of ISDN to the extent necessary to ensure compliance with regulations on the protection of data, including protection of personal data, the confidentiality of information transmitted or stored, as well as the protection of privacy compatible with Community law; whereas those restrictions should be objectively justified, follow the principle of proportionality and not be excessive in relation to the aim pursued; whereas open access to ISDN via the proposed access arrangements should not jeopardize ISDN network integrity and security requirements;

Whereas, in accordance with Directive 90/387/EEC, tariffs must be based on objective criteria and, especially in the case of services and areas subject to special or exclusive rights, must in principle be cost-oriented; whereas they must be transparent and properly published, sufficiently unbundled in accordance with the competition rules of the Treaty and non-discriminatory and must guarantee equal treatment;

Whereas the availability of itemized billing will enable ISDN users to check their bills;

Whereas, in accordance with the principle of separation of regulatory and operational functions and pursuant to the principle of subsidiarity, the national regulatory authority of each Member State should play an important role in the application of this recommendation;

Whereas, to enable the Commission to monitor effectively the application of this recommendation, it is necessary that Member States provide the relevant information requested by the Commission;

Whereas implementation of harmonized ONP conditions for access to and use of ISDN are dependent on the state of network development and market demand in Member States;

Whereas the Committee referred to in Articles 9 and 10 of Directive 90/387/EEC should play an important role in the application of this recommendation.

HEREBY RECOMMENDS:

1. That, in line with previous Council measures on integrated services digital network (ISDN), and taking into account market demand, Member States:

   (a) ensure that, on their territory, the telecommunications organizations notified in accordance with point 15 provide an ISDN with harmonized access arrangements and a minimum set of offerings in accordance with Annex I, together with adequate and efficient interoperability between ISDNs in order to allow for Community-wide operation. Where no dates are indicated in Annex I, Member States should encourage telecommunications organizations to publish target dates for the availability of these features;

   (b) encourage the harmonized provision by the same organizations of additional offerings as identified in Annex II. This additional provision should be in accordance with international standardization and in response to market demand but should not endanger or delay the provision of the minimum set referred to in subparagraph (a).

2. That modifications necessary to adapt Annex I to new technical developments and to changes in market demand be determined by the Commission in accordance with the procedure laid down in Article 10 of Directive 90/387/EEC, taking into account the state of development of the national networks.

---

[8] OJ No L 128, 23. 5. 1991, p. 1.

3. That Member States take the necessary steps so that, in respect of the ISDN offerings provided in accordance with point 1, information is published on technical characteristics, supply conditions, contractual conditions, usage conditions, tariffs, licensing and/or declaration conditions and conditions for the attachment of terminal equipment, in accordance with the presentation given in Annex III.

Information on changes in existing offerings should be published as soon as possible and not later than two months before the implementation, unless the national regulatory authority agrees otherwise.

4. That the supply conditions referred to in point 3 include at least:
   — information concerning the ordering procedure,
   — typical delivery periods, which are the periods, counted from the date when the user has made a firm request for an ISDN offering, in which 80% of all requests for each type of ISDN offerings have been put through to the users. Each period will be established on the basis of the actual delivery periods of ISDN offerings during a recent time interval of reasonable duration. The calculation must not include cases where late delivery periods were requested by users.

Until actual data are available, a target delivery period shall be published in place of the typical delivery period,
   — typical repair times, which are the periods, counted from the time when a failure message has been given to the responsible unit within the organization supplying ISDN up to the moment in which 80% of all ISDN offerings of the same type have been re-established and, in appropriate cases, notified as back in operation to the users.

Until actual data are available, a target repair time shall be published instead of the typical repair time.

Where different classes of quality of repair are offered for the same type of ISDN offerings, the different typical repair times shall be published:
   — contractual periods, which include the periods generally provided for in the case of contracts and the minimum contractual periods which the user is obliged to accept for each type of ISDN offering,
   — any refund procedure,
   — target values for the indicators of quality of service identified in point 6.
5. That the supply of ISDN offerings be based on a contract specifying the elements of the ISDN offerings to be provided.
6. That, by 1 January 1995, at least for the bearer services identified in Annex I, common indicators and common measurement methods be adopted for the network performance aspects of the quality of service, by organizations supplying ISDN offerings in accordance with this recommendation, notably for those indicators in Annex IV.
7. That the common indicators and measurement methods referred to in point 6 be based on appropriate standards adopted by ETSI allowing for the determination of a representative sample of the performance of the ISDN offerings as well as the statistical end-to-end performance achieved by the network as a whole.
8. That national regulatory authorities take the necessary steps so that annual statistical information showing achieved performance in the following areas is made publicly available:

   — delivery periods,
   — repair times,
   — quality of service indicators, where possible those identified in Annex IV.

The first annual period should run from 1 January to 31 December 1994.
9. That Member States encourage the establishment, in accordance with the procedural and substantive rules of competition of the Treaty and in consultation with users, of harmonized procedures for user access to ISDN, in particular via the establishment of the following procedures:

— a common ordering procedure for ISDN throughout the Community, i.e. an ordering procedure for the procurement of intra-Community ISDN offerings which ensures that there is commonality across the organizations supplying ISDN offerings, in both the information which has to be supplied by the user and the organization supplying ISDN offerings and the format in which the information is presented,

— a one-stop-ordering procedure for ISDN, to be applied where requested by the user, i.e. a system whereby all transactions involving a user, required for the procurement of intra-Community ISDN offerings supplied by more than one organization to a single user, can be completed at one location between the user and a single organization supplying ISDN offerings,

— a one-stop-billing procedure for ISDN, to be applied where requested by the user, i.e. a system whereby the billing and payment transaction for intra-Community ISDN offerings supplied by more than one organization to a single user can be completed at one location between the user and a single organization supplying ISDN offerings, and

— a one-stop-maintenance procedure for ISDN, to be applied where requested by the user, i.e. a system whereby the reporting of faults for intra-Community ISDN offerings supplied by more than one organization to a single user can be done at one location between the user and a single organization supplying ISDN offerings, which will coordinate the restoration of services.

It is envisaged that, taking into account technical feasibility and commercial viability, these procedures should include Community-wide charging and billing procedures, allowing for the capability where:

— the called party pays for the calls (green number/freephone),

— the cost of the value-added service and the cost of the call are combined in a single bill collected by the organization supplying ISDN offerings, or other arrangements equally effective for users ('kiosk type arrangements').

These harmonized procedures are to be established through commercial arrangements, e.g. through memoranda of understanding.

10. That ISDN numbering plans be controlled by the national regulatory authority, in order to provide for fair competition. In particular, procedures for the allocation of individual numbers for specific services should be transparent, equitable and timely.

11. That Member States take the necessary steps so that usage conditions for ISDN are subject to scrutiny by the national regulatory authority.

12. That tariffs be transparent, based on objective criteria, independent of the type of application implemented by users where the same type of offerings is used and in principle oriented towards cost. Each ISDN offering should in principle be tariffed on an individual basis. Offerings should be sufficiently unbundled, in accordance with Community law. In addition, the tariff principles of recommendation 86/659/EEC should be taken into due account.

13. That tariffs for ISDN offerings normally contain the following elements:

— an initial connection charge,
— a periodic rental charge,
— a usage charge.

Where other tariff elements are applied, these should be approved by the national regulatory authority and must be in accordance with point 12.

14. That under the control of national regulatory authorities targets are set and published for the provision of itemized billings as a facility available on users' request, subject to technical feasibility. The level of detail given in itemized bills may be subject to relevant law relating to the protection of personal data and privacy.

15. That Member States notify to the Commission before 31 December 1992 those organizations whose provisions of ISDN enables Member States to comply with the provisions of Annex III, point 4, of Directive 90/387/EEC and thereafter any changes to this information.

16. That national regulatory authorities prepare annual summary reports covering the availability of ISDN offerings, including level of penetration, provided in accordance with point 1. These summary reports should be sent to the Commission no later than five months after the end of the calendar year, this requirement being reviewed by the Commission in consultation with the ONP Committee in accordance with Article 9 of Directive 90/387/EEC during 1995. The Commission will transmit these summary reports to the ONP Committee.

    The execution of this requirement fulfils corresponding requirements of recommendation 86/659/EEC.

17. That national regulatory authorities keep available, and submit to the Commission on request, data on the application of the supply conditions under points 3 and 4 and the statistical information under point 8.

18. That national regulatory authorities establish simple procedures for users of the ISDN offerings to invoke with regard to any difficulties encountered in relation to the application of this recommendation.

19. That the Commission, in consultation with the ONP Committee, examine the results of the application of this recommendation, in view of the fulfilment of the objectives of Directive 90/387/EEC, on the basis of the summary reports provided under point 16.

Done at Luxembourg, 5 June 1992.

For the Council
The President
Joaquim FERREIRA DO AMARAL

ANNEX I

DEFINITION OF THE HARMONIZED ISDN ACCESS ARRANGEMENTS AND THE MINIMUM SET OF ISDN OFFERINGS IN ACCORDANCE WITH POINT 1, AND RECOMMENDED TIMETABLE FOR THEIR AVAILABILITY

GENERAL CONSIDERATIONS

This Annex describes the harmonized ISDN access arrangements and the minimum set of ISDN offerings which are to be made available in all Member States.

The ISDN offerings are structured in two parts: Part A contains the minimum set of offerings which are to be made available in all Member States by 1 January 1994; Part B contains those offerings which are to be made available in all Member States according to published target dates.

The CCITT distinctions of bearer services, supplementary services and teleservices[9] are used. The bearer services and supplementary services in Part A are those indicated as the minimum service offering in the ISDN memorandum of understanding (MoU) of June 1991, and the date for implementation is in accordance with the commitment given by the signatories of the MoU.

Implementation of these offerings should take account of relevant legislation concerning data protection and privacy.

STANDARDS TO BE UTILIZED

In accordance with the procedure in Article 5 (1) of Directive 90/387/EEC, reference to relevant ISDN standards will be published in the *Official Journal of the European Communities*.

---

[9] Appropriate associations between access arrangements, bearer services and supplementary services are given in CCITT Recommendation I.250.

The initial indicative list of ISDN standards suitable for ONP already published in the *Official Journal of the European Communities* will be amended/updated by further publication in the *Official Journal of the European Communities*.

PART A.

Offerings to be made available in all Member States by 1 January 1994

A.1. Access arrangements

Access arrangements concerning the interfaces at CCITT defined reference points.

Basic rate access (2B + D) at the S/T reference point

Primary rate access (30B + D) at the S/T reference point

A.2. *Bearer service*

Circuit mode 64 kbit/s unrestricted bearer service

Circuit mode 3.1 kHz audio bearer service

A.3. *Supplementary services*

Calling line identification presentation (CLIP)

Calling line identification restriction (CLIR)

Direct dialling in (DDI)

Multiple subscriber number (MSN)

Terminal portability (TP)

A.4. *Teleservices*

Telephony (3.1 kHz bandwidth).

PART B.

Offerings to be provided in all Member States, according to published target dates and the availability of international standards

Dates for the implementation of these offerings will depend on market demand in each Member States. In accordance with point 1 (a), telecommunications organizations are to be encouraged to publish targets for the availability of each of these offerings.

B.1. *Access arrangements*

Future access arrangements to be included in the minimum set are subject to further study by ETSI and the Commission.

The situation will be reviewed at the latest by 31 December 1992, after completion of a study and investigation mandate given to ETSI on the technical implications of the M- and U-type interfaces, and completion of an economic and market assessment. Consideration should be given to the inclusion of these access arrangements into the minimum set in accordance with the procedure given in point 2 of this recommendation.

B.2. *Bearer services*

Circuit mode 64 kbit/s unrestricted bearer service on reserved or permanent mode

Packet mode bearer service provided over the B and/or D channels (see Note 1)

B.3. *Other services*

Call transfer services

Call forwarding services

Closed user group

User to user signalling

Malicious call identification

Reverse charging

Green number (freephone) for voice and non-voice applications

Kiosk billing or equivalent features, for voice and non-voice applications.

Note 1

When ISDN is used for the provision of packet-switched data services, users should, where feasible, have equivalent functionality to users of the dedicated packet network, as defined in Council recommendation 92/382/EEC[10] on the harmonized provisions of a minimum set of packet switched data services in accordance with ONP principles.

ANNEX II

ADDITIONAL OFFERINGS WHICH MAY BE IMPLEMENTED, IN ACCORDANCE WITH PROGRESS IN INTERNATIONAL STANDARDIZATION

I. Supplementary services

Advice of charge (AOC) services

Number identification services (COLP, COLR)

Call waiting (CW)

Completion of calls to busy subscribers (CCBS)

Conference services

Sub-addressing (SUB)

Three party service (3PTY)

II. Network management services[11]

Note: These supplementary services are covered by the ISDN MoU.

ANNEX III

PUBLICATION PRESENTATION FOR THE INFORMATION TO BE PROVIDED IN RESPECT OF ISDN OFFERINGS IN ACCORDANCE WITH POINT 3

The information referred to in point 3 should follow the presentation given below.

A. Technical characteristics

The technical characteristics include the physical and electrical characteristics as well as the detailed technical and performance specifications which apply at the network termination point, without prejudice to Council Directive 83/189/EEC of 28 March 1983 laying down a procedure for the provision of information in the field of technical standards and regulations[12]. Clear reference shall be made to the standards implemented.

---

[10] See page 1 of this Official Journal.

[11] The Commission has given ETSI a mandate to study network management standards.

[12] OJ No L 109, 26. 4. 1983, p. 8.

B. **Supply conditions**

The supply conditions include at least the elements identified in point 4.

C. **Contractual conditions or terms of subscription**

D. **Usage conditions**

The conditions resulting from the application of essential requirements and from the exercise of exclusive or special rights.

E. **Tariffs**

In accordance with point 13, tariffs will normally include an initial connection charge, a periodic rental charge and a usage charge.

(a) The initial charge for connection to the ISDN network may depend on the type of access and offerings.

(b) The periodic subscription charge will vary according to the type of access and range of ISDN capabilities provided.

(c) The usage charges will normally include a call duration charge and supplementary services usage charges and may also include a call-set-up charge and, in the case of packet mode bearer services, there may also be a volume related usage charge. These charges may depend on time and/or day.

Clear indication of other charges, e.g. charges related to different levels of quality of service, or bulk provision, should be available.

F. **Licensing and/or declaration conditions for use of ISDN service, where applicable**

This should include information on any licensing conditions which have to be met by the user or by its customer.

G. **Conditions for the attachment of terminal equipment**

Conditions approved by the national regulatory authority, in accordance with the provisions of Directive 91/264/EEC.

ANNEX IV

INDICATORS FOR THE NETWORK PERFORMANCE ASPECTS OF THE QUALITY OF SERVICE OF ISDN BEARER SERVICES[13]

IV.1. Indicators for all bearer services

Availability of access, defined as the average, for all connections of a given type, of the number of hours in a reasonable period for which service was available to a user, divided by the total number of hours in the period.

Mean time between interruptions, defined as the average time duration between the end of one interruption and the beginning of the next. An interruption is defined as the temporary inability of a service to be provided persisting for more than a given time duration characterized by a change beyond given limits in at least one parameter essential for the service.

Bit error ratio, defined as the ratio of the number of bit errors to the total number of bits transmitted in a given time interval (for non-speech bearer service).

IV.2. **Indicators for circuit mode switched bearer services**

---

[13] The Commission has given ETSI a mandate to develop standards covering definitions for the above quality of service indicators and appropriate measurement methods.

Connection processing delay, as defined in CCITT recommendation I.352.

Network transit delay, defined as the time which elapses between the initial offering of a unit of user data to an ISDN network by a transmitting terminal equipment and the complete delivery of that unit to the receiving terminal equipment (a unit of user data may be a bit, byte, packet, etc.).

Average figures for national calls and for intra-Community calls should be considered.

Unsuccessful calls ratio, defined as the ratio of unsuccessful calls to the total number of calls in a specified time period.

IV.3. Indicators for packet-mode bearer services

The indicators for packet-mode bearer services should in principle be the same as those featuring in the proposal for a recommendation 92/382/EEC on the harmonized provision of a minimum set of packet-switched data services in accordance with ONP principles.

Index

Norfolk Library
9 Greenwoods Road East
Box 605
Norfolk, CT 06058

FAREWELL, DOROTHY PARKER